PEACE OFFICER'S GUIDE TO CRIMINAL LAW

By:

Dr. George T. Payton

Emeritus, Administration of Justice Program

Evergreen Valley College

Formerly: Sergeant

San Jose Police Department

and

Dr. James E. Guffey

Professor, School of Professional Studies

National University, Stockton, CA Campus

Formerly: Investigator

Oakland Police Department

Illustrated by:

Tom F. Macris

Published By:

CRIMINAL JUSTICE PUBLICATIONS

(408) 274-3317

drpayton@att.net

4848 San Felipe Road

P.O. Box 150-513

San Jose, CA 95135

Twenty-seventh Edition

Other Books by the Author:

Patrol Operations
(with Sergeant Michel Amaral)

Concepts of California Criminal Law
(with James Guffey)

Peace Officer's Promotional Manual

Typesetting and Technical Assistance:

Lynn M. Snyder, Nosy Rosy Designs
nosyrosydesigns@gmail.com

The authors have made considerable efforts to ensure the accuracy and timeliness of the laws contained in this book. However, no implied or express guarantees are made. The law and court decisions that affect the law often change rapidly. It is therefore important for the reader, when applying the law, to check for its timeliness and accuracy in case the law has been revised.

ABOUT THE AUTHORS

Dr. George Payton was a former Patrol Sergeant with the San Jose Police Department for 30 years. He earned his Bachelor of Arts and Master of Arts Degrees from San Jose State University, and a Doctorate in Criminal Justice Education from the University of Southern California in Los Angeles. When he left the police department to become Department Chair at a local college, Dr. Payton transferred to the San Jose Police Reserves in order to keep abreast of new developments in the field; he was a Lieutenant to that organization. He also organized the first Regional Criminal Justice Training Academy in Santa Clara County, as well as the first supervision academy. He also established the first Campus Police at San Jose City College.

Dr. Payton served first in the U.S. Navy and was later commissioned in the U.S. Military Police. He has written books in the area of California Criminal Law, Criminal Investigation, and Police Supervision. He has also written articles for several law enforcement journals. His biographies are listed in *Leaders in Law Enforcement, Who's Who in Law Enforcement,* and *Outstanding Educators.* Dr. Payton has also received the Outstanding Criminal Justice Educator's Award.

Dr. James E. Guffey is a former police officer, investigator and evidence technician for the City of Oakland Police Department (13 years). He has a B.S. Degree in Industrial Relations, a M.A. in Police Science from Sam Houston State University, and a Ph.D. in Public Administration from Golden Gate University.

He was previously a Professor of Criminal Justice Administration at the California State University Hayward (renamed California State University, East Bay). Dr. Guffey is currently Professor of Professional Studies at National University, Stockton Campus, and is Lead Faculty for the BSCJA and the ASCJA at National University.

Dr. Guffey is a retired Lieutenant Colonel (U.S.A.R.) with 29 years of service to his country. During his U.S. Army career, he taught military science at the University of California at Davis, Fort Leavenworth, Kansas, and was an adjunct instructor at the US. Military Academy at West Point, N.Y. Dr. Guffey has had numerous articles published in various law enforcement journals. He has written one book titled *Report Writing Fundamentals for Police and Correctional Officers,* published by Prentice-Hall.

Contents at a Glance

Table of Contents

CHAPTER XII – Forgery and Checks

CHAPTER XIII – Miscellaneous Offenses

CHAPTER XIV – Control of Deadly Weapons

APPENDICES

INDICES

POST Criminal Law Learning Domains and Their Location in the Textbook

I. Property Crimes — Learning Domain #6

II. Crimes Against Persons — Learning Domain #7

III. General Criminal Statutes — Learning Domain #8

VII. Weapons Violations — Learning Domain #40

Peace Officer's Guide to Criminal Law

CHAPTER I

GENERAL ASPECTS OF CALIFORNIA CRIMINAL LAW

Rules Controlling the Enactment of Law

(A) All California Law is Statutory

This means that all of the laws in California have been proposed by an elected representative of the people. They have been voted on and passed by a body of persons elected by the people, and then printed in a book of law as a statute.

There is no common law in California. All law here is statutory. If it is not written in a book of law, there can be no violation of the law.

Many times we are confused by what we might feel is wrong, and by what is actually listed in the statutes of the state as a criminal act. For example, moral law states that sex outside of marriage is wrong. Many states have statutes against fornication. Fornication is sexual intercourse between two unmarried persons over the age of 18.

In California there is no law or statute against fornication. Therefore, if a police officer were to catch two 18-year-old people engaged in an act of sexual intercourse in the back seat of a parked car, he could legally do nothing. He might feel that it is wrong, but California law is wholly statutory. If it is not on the books, there is no violation.

(B) The Statute Must Be in English

Section 24 of Article IV of the Constitution states that all official writings and judicial proceedings shall be conducted in the English *language*. Exceptions would be terms in other languages *such as* Latin or Spanish that are understood and accepted.

(C) No Statute Will Be Too Vague, Broad or Uncertain

Laws that are vague or uncertain in their wording have long been illegal under statutory law. If it is difficult to determine exactly what act is meant by the law, or if a great number of acts could fit the description, then either the whole statute or the part that is vague can be declared unconstitutional.

An example would be part of old Penal Code Section 650.5. It states that it is illegal to "openly outrage public decency." The California Supreme Court ruled that this section was too vague and broad, and therefore unconstitutional. It is like saying that a person is bad. What does that mean?

Does it mean that he murders people, or that he picks his nose? Some people would call both acts bad, but there is quite a difference in the two.

(D) Laws Are Enforceable Only When They are in Effect During the Act

Ex Post Facto Laws

An ex post factor law is one that is enacted as a statute after the act has been committed. (U.S. Constitution, Article I, Section 9 & 10) An example of the illegality of an ex post facto law would be as follows:

Arvin Aardvark picks his nose in public. This is so offensive that his fellow citizens have a law passed against it. If Arvin stops picking his nose in public after the law is passed, he cannot be convicted for any of the acts that he committed before the law went into effect.

Repeal of Laws

By the same rule, if a law is repealed, but someone violates that law before it is repealed, he may be charged and convicted for that offense. This can be done even if the conviction is after the law was repealed. (Government Code 9608) For example, Darrel Doper is arrested for possession and use of marijuana. The next day the law is repealed. Darrel is still liable for prosecution because it was a violation when he committed the act.

Rules Controlling the Conviction of Criminal Acts

(A) Burden of Proof

In many countries, all persons are assumed to be guilty until proven innocent. In the United States the opposite is true; the burden of proving guilt initially lies with the state. The prosecution must prove two major things. First, it must prove that a crime was in fact committed; then it must prove that the defendant was the one who committed it. However, if the defendant admits the act, then uses a legal defense such as insanity, he must assume the burden of proof for that defense. He must prove that he was insane. The state does not have to prove that he was sane.

If the jury in a case was undecided as to whether he was insane or not, they must assume that he was sane. This is because the defendant has the burden of proving to the jury beyond a reasonable doubt that he was insane at the time of the act.

(B) Reasonable Doubt

The prosecution must not only convince the jury of the defendant's guilt, but must do so beyond a reasonable doubt. Reasonable doubt is not absolute proof. It is simply a reasonable and honest doubt in the mind of an unbiased, average person. It is doubt beyond amoral certainty, not absolute fact. Conclusive proof is not required. Reasonable doubt must be based on some evidence. It is a doubt for which some reason can be given, arising from the evidence presented. Reasonable doubt does not mean a mere possible or speculative doubt.

(C) Presumption of Guilt

There are certain statutes in the Penal Code that include presumptions of guilt. In cases of this type, the burden of proof is on the defendant to counter the presumption.

For example, in 23920 of the Penal Code, it states that is a person has in his possession a gun when the serial number has been removed, it is presumed that he was the one who removed it. In court he carries the burden of proof to show that he did not remove the serial number.

In Section 484 of the Penal Code, it states that employers who owe wages to other employees must tell this to any new employee they hire. If they fail to tell any new employee, and then do not pay the new employee his or her wages, the code presumes that the employer intended to defraud the new employee. In a case of this nature, the state would not have to prove that the employer had the intent to defraud. Because it is actually written in the law, the burden of proof would be on the employer to show that he or she had no intent to defraud.

(D) Questions of Fact and Questions of Law

The jury is concerned only with Questions of Fact. The judge deals with Questions of Law If the jury believes that the defendant killed his wife, that is a Question of Fact. If they believe that he killed her by the use of poison, that is a Question of Fact. (Who did what?) The judge can then rule that the law is clear that all murders by poison are murders of the first degree. That is a Question of Law. Only the judge is qualified to pass on Questions of Law. Once the judge has established this Question of Law, the jury can only find the defendant guilty of first degree murder, if they accept the fact that he murdered her by means of poison.

(E) Convictions Can Only Result From Unanimous Verdicts

All members of the jury must vote for conviction, or there can be no conviction. If one member of the jury votes for acquittal, and won't change his or her mind, it becomes a "hung jury," and the trial is ended. However, the defendant may be tried repeatedly if each trial results in a hung jury. A hung jury is not an acquittal. In most cases, however, it amounts to the same thing. This is because a trial is expensive. The District Attorney (D.A.) must not waste public money on a trial in which a conviction cannot be obtained. If it is a very important case, it may be tried several times, especially if mistakes made in earlier trials are realized and it is likely that a conviction will be obtained in the next trial.

(F) All Crimes are Crimes Against the State

A fundamental principle in criminal law is that a criminal action is prosecuted by the People. It is not prosecuted by the injured party as would be the case in civil law.

This is a greatly misunderstood concept. Often a victim of a crime will call the police or the D.A. and tell them that he has decided not to prosecute. D.A.s will often drop the case because they have a very heavy backlog of cases, and are glad to get rid of one. Another reason is that the victim is usually the main witness for prosecution, and if the victim is not willing to go to court, the case will not be very strong. Because of this, many citizens have come to believe (wrongly) that the power of prosecution rests with the victim.

Let us take the case of a woman who calls the police department every weekend and has her husband arrested for drunkenness and battery. Monday morning she always drops the charges. After a while the police get tired of being used as bouncers and would like the wife to take some positive action to stop these occurrences. They go to the D.A., relate the circumstances and ask for prosecution. The D.A. then decides to take some action to stop the woman from playing games with the administration of justice and issues a criminal complaint against the husband, then obtains a subpoena (a court order to appear) for the wife.

In the trial, the D.A. cross examines the wife under oath, and has the officers who responded to the calls testify under oath.

What can the judge do if the evidence is obvious? Find the defendant guilty. This can occur even when the victim wants the charges dropped. A wife can be asked to testify against her husband when the crime is one against her, her property, or her children.

Interpretation of the Law

(A) Letter of the Law

As previously stated, all California Law is statutory. In order to obtain a conviction in court, the officers must show that the defendant violated the Letter of the Law. This means the exact way in which the law is written. It is also described as what the statute actually says. Therefore, the exact wording in the statute itself is quite important.

Officers will find themselves in a lot of trouble if they arrest someone for an act which they think is in violation of the law, when the act mentioned in the statute is slightly different. Officers cannot tell the judge, "well, it was close." They must know the exact wording or the Letter of the Law. This will be covered under *corpus delicti.*

(B) The Spirit of the Law

The Spirit of the Law is also called "legislative intent." This means why the law was written. This is most important when enforcing the law. Every California peace officer should keep in mind the Spirit of the Law when dealing with the public.

Penal Code Section 4 states: "The rule of common law that penal statutes are to be strictly construed, has no application to this code. All its provisions are to be construed according to a fair import of their terms, with a view to effect its objects and to promote justice." This section simply means that in California laws should be enforced according to their original intent.

To illustrate, Section 22900 of the Penal

Code states that it is illegal for anyone other than a peace officer, Reserve, or special authorized private patrol officer to possess tear gas. (Except Mace) Yet Police Science Instructors in many colleges throughout the state are required to teach in-service police courses to officers on the use of tear gas. They purchase and possess tear gas in violation of the Letter of the Law.

The question is, do they violate the Spirit of the Law? The answer is obviously no. When the legislators wrote the law, they did not anticipate all the situations that would arise where persons other than peace officers would need to possess tear gas.

If a police officer were to arrest a Police Science Instructor for the possession of tear gas at a college training course, he would be following the Letter of the Law, but not the Spirit of the Law. The D.A. would never issue a complaint in a case of this type. In fact the officer would probably be chewed out by his sergeant for not using common sense. The key to applying the Spirit of the Law could be the two words "common sense."

Now let us change the situation a little. Suppose the Police Science Instructor was drunk in a bar downtown. He starts an argument with the bartender and then squirts him in the face with a Mace container. Would this possession of tear gas be in violation of the Spirit of the Law? Of course. And he should be arrested for the offense.

(C) *Stare Decisis (Precedent)*

Stare decisis is a Latin term meaning precedent. It is a common law doctrine in which precedent is binding. That is, once a single case has been decided, all cases with the same circumstances must, in the future, be decided in the same way. In 1761, Blackstone, the famous English jurist who helped interpret English common law, stated that *stare decisis* meant "rigidly finding precedent."

In California we still adhere to precedent, but not as strictly as under common law. Occasionally, judges reverse the rulings of their predecessors.

An example would be the People *v.* Hernandez (1965) in which the higher court changed the old rule pertaining to "Statutory Rape." Before this, if the girl in the case was under 18, the law was violated. After Hernandez, the high court stated that the jury should be allowed to view the girl and judge for themselves whether a reasonable person would think she was over 18 years of age. If they felt that she did appear to be over 18, they could find the defendant not guilty since there would be a lack of intent.

(D) Case Law and Citations

Criminal cases may be appealed to higher courts if there are questions of constitutional violations or improper trial procedures which would deny the defendant a fair trial. Normally constitutional violations go to the Supreme Court, and procedural problems to the Appellate Courts. When these higher courts make a decision, it becomes part of what we call case law. It provides the lower court judges with guidelines by which they can rule on new cases before them.

If a defendant or his attorney believe there is error in a lower court's decision, they may appeal to the State Supreme Court. If they are not satisfied with that decision, they can appeal to the U.S. Supreme Court. That is the Court of last resort.

Case law provides courts with interpretations of words or phrases found in criminal statutes. For example, in the law on burglary (459 PC) the term "building" is used. What is a building? Is a garage, a carport, or a cave a building? It is important to know. It can make the difference between a charge of petty theft and a charge of burglary. There is a great difference in punishment between the two. By using case law, we can look up the definition used in a higher court decision.

Both the prosecuting and defense attorneys will cite case law in trying to convince the judge to decide in their favor. Case citations weigh heavily with the judge. If he clearly goes against prior high court decisions, it is possible that the present case will be appealed. Then the higher court might reverse the judge's decision. This acts as a reprimand. It tells the judge that his decision was a bad one. No one likes to be in this position, so judges pay more attention when an attorney cites case law. The judge's real problem is to decide if the case before him is very similar to the case being cited by the attorney.

Locating Cases from Case Citations

In police journals and books on criminal law, there will often be a case citation listed after a statement or paragraph. The purpose of this is to allow the reader to look up the case. This will give better insight into the reason for the decision. It will also provide the legal theory behind that ruling. Another advantage to reading the whole decision is to find out why certain justices disagreed with the majority.

In a Supreme Court decision, a simple majority of votes will decide the outcome of a ruling and make it law. Because of this, it is important in a four to five decision to find out why the four justices disagreed. Some of the most important Supreme Court rulings in our history have been four to five decisions. Case citations usually have three parts. If there is an opposing opinion in the reports, there will be a fourth part.

Let us say we are reading a law book and come across the topic of burglary. It mentions that in some cases a shoplifter can be charged with burglary. It gives the case citation "People *v*. Carrol, 60 CA 2d 66." First, we know that the last name of the defendant in this case was Carrol. The first part of the reference gives the volume. The second part is the court symbol, or the name of the court that handed down the decision.

Examples of Court Symbols That Make Up the Second Part of the Citation

The second part of the case citation can be a Court or a Reporter (set of books that reports on several courts). Table I–1 (below) gives examples that California officers most often need.

Courts
(a) U.S. — United States Supreme Court
(b) USCA — United States Court of Appeals
(c) USCC — United States Circuit Court
(d) USDC — United States District Court
(e) Cal. (or C.) — California Supreme Court
(f) Cal. App. (or C.A.) — California District Court of Appeals

Reporters
(a) F (and the district) — *Federal Reporter*
(b) Pac. (or P.) — *Pacific Reporter* (Pacific States)
(c) Cal. Rptr. — *California Reporter* (Including C & C.A.)
(d) ALR — American Law Reports
(e) AC — Advance Reports (A paperback advance report that has not yet been assigned a regular case citation.)

Table I–1: Court or Reporter Symbols

Even the smallest California Law libraries will have the *California Reporter* which contains both the California Supreme Court and the California District Court of Appeals cases. There is a directory called the *Blue and White Book* which will give the *California Reporter* case citations that contain the California Supreme and Appellate court cases.

Sometimes the second part is described as the set of volumes that we are to look for. If there is a 2d after the court symbol, it means that there is a second edition to the set of books and that this case is located in that edition. The last part gives the page where the case begins. The interpretation of the case citation 60 CA 2d 66 would be:

60 — Volume number 60
CA — California District Court of Appeals
2d — Second series or edition
66 — The case starts on page 66

If we wanted to research the case, People *v*. Jones 12 Cal. 2d 420, we would go to the law library and look for the set of volumes covering the California Supreme Court decisions. Then we would look for the second series or edition, and find volume 12. Next we would turn to page 420 and find the case of the People *v*. Jones.

Components Needed for a Criminal Offense

Definition of Crime

According to Section 15 of the California Penal Code, a crime is:

"...an act committed or omitted in violation of a law forbidding or commanding it, and to which is annexed, upon conviction, any of the following punishments:
(a) death
(b) imprisonment
(c) fine
(d) removal from office
(e) disqualification to hold and enjoy any office of honor, trust or profit in this state."

This can be simplified into two parts:
(1) An act
 (a) committed in violation of a law forbidding it, or
 (b) committed in violation of a law commanding it
(2) for which there is an assigned punishment upon conviction.

(A) What is Needed to Constitute a Crime?

Penal Code Section 20 tells us what is needed to constitute a crime: "In every crime or public offense there must exist a union or joint operation of act and intent, or criminal negligence." We can see that in order to have a crime we must have two things. First we must have an act, and secondly, we must have intent to commit the act. It also states that criminal negligence can be substituted for the intent. Now we are going to look more closely at the three underlined terms. It is obvious that they are important, but what do they really mean?

The Criminal Act (Conduct)—*Actus Reus*

There are different ways in which the legal term act can be described. It is difficult to give one simple definition. For example, it can be some physical action, such as punching another person in the nose, or it can be the failure to act, such as the failure to feed your legal children. It can also be an act of possession where all the person does is possess some illegal item on his or her person. Here there is not necessarily any physical action involved. There is also passive participation, where the person participates in a criminal act but the participation involves no actual movement. An example would be the case of a minor who allows another to commit sodomy with him. He just lies there and allows the other person to make sexual penetration of his anus. He could be guilty of Section 286 of the Penal Code even though the "act" needed for a crime would, in this case, not involve any physical movement.

Criminal Intent

The Latin term for intent is *mens rea*. The translation means "guilty mind." It is intent that distinguishes a crime from a tort. A tort is a civil wrong. If Freddie Farkle accidentally knocks Pete Paranoid's glasses off his desk and breaks them, he is not guilty of a crime because there was no intent to do the act. It was an accident. However, Freddie is guilty of a tort or civil offense. If he refused to pay for Pete's glasses, Pete could take Freddie to a civil court and obtain a judgment against him.

There are some other differences between a crime and a tort as far as court procedures are concerned. A list of the differences follows:

CRIME

(1) There is criminal intent.
(2) The state is the prosecutor.
(3) Few settlements out of court.
(4) Damages (fines) go to the public treasury.
(5) Contributory negligence cannot be used as a defense.
(6) The purpose of prosecution is punishment.
(7) There is a statutory limit to the fines for a crime.

TORT

(1) There is no criminal intent (unless a part of a crime).
(2) The victim is the prosecutor.
(3) Most settlements are made out of court.
(4) Damages go to the victim.
(5) Contributory negligence is a defense or mitigating circumstance.
(6) The purpose of court is to restore (if possible) the original condition.
(7) There is no limit to the amount of damages that can be asked in a civil court.

Types of Criminal Intent

General Intent

General intent is sometimes called presumed intent. This is because the general conditions of the situation would indicate to an ordinary, reasonable person that the act was intentional.

Let us assume you are out on patrol and you get a call regarding a case of vandalism. When you respond, the complainant (the person who called the police) tells you that he wants his neighbor arrested because he threw a ball through his window. The neighbor states that it was an accident. He states that he was playing ball with his son and when he threw the ball, it accidentally hit the side of his house and bounced across the fence hitting his neighbor's window. He states that he offered to pay for the window, but the neighbor told him "going to jail will be your payment."

What do you do? Do you have a crime or a tort? It is obvious by the circumstances that you have a tort.

Now let us change things a bit. Suppose Herbert Honebone was playing catch in his front yard with his son, Hector. Sam Slipshod, his neighbor, came out to his front yard and caught the Honebone dog defecating on his lawn. He yelled at Herbert to come over and clean up his dog's mess. Herbert told Sam to "stick it in your ear." Sam then got a shovel and threw the excrement over the fence into the Honebone yard. Herbert Honebone got mad. He cursed out Sam and then threw the ball through Sam's front window.

Do you have a crime or a tort? It is obvious from the circumstances that there was criminal intent. It would be general intent because it is obvious that Herbert did the act intentionally.

Specific Intent

There are some crimes that involve a special intent that we call Specific Intent. In order to have this type of intent, the law states that the act must be done with this specific intent.

For example, let us take Section 220 of the Penal Code, Assault with Intent to Commit Rape. Exactly the same physical action could be two entirely different crimes depending upon the ability of the prosecution to prove specific intent.

If Larry Lacksey knocked Betsey Bloominheimer to the ground, we would have a particular physical action. If he was mad at her for standing him up on a date, it would be obvious that the intent in knocking her to the ground was anger.

If Larry did not know Betsey, and he knocked her to the ground in exactly the same way as before, but then told her "If you don't submit to me, that is just a sample of what you're going to get," we have a new purpose or intent. From what he said, we now know that this same physical act is not because of anger but for the purpose of rape.

Specific intent can be difficult to prove because the intent is in the person's mind. We have no means to expose thought in the courtroom. Sometimes motive will help prove specific intent.

Transferred Intent

Transferred Intent is sometimes called Constructive Intent. When a person has a criminal intent toward some particular person or place, and by accident or misfortune someone else or some other place becomes the victim of this criminal intent, the original intent is transferred.

For example, Huey Hardhat is going with Kitty Krump. He hears that she has been secretly seeing Homer Hashbrown. He becomes insanely jealous and buys a gun with which to shoot Homer. He goes to Kitty's apartment and finds both Kitty and Homer there. He aims the gun at Homer and fires. He misses Homer and by accident kills Kitty.

Here we have a criminal act, but no intent. Huey had absolutely no intent to kill Kitty Krump, whom he loved. In criminal law, however, this would be a case of transferred intent. Huey is just as guilty of murder as if he had originally intended to shoot Kitty.

Motive

Sometimes people get motive and intent confused. Motive is why the person committed the crime. In California law, motive is not required to obtain a conviction. It is nice to know, and juries, being human beings, want to know the motive. Still it is not essential. You can legally obtain a conviction without the motive ever being known.

For example, Professor Thadwick Humpastump is lecturing to his class of 70 students, and all of a sudden turns to Flossie Furd in the front row and states "I have thought about this for a week, and it's the only way," then pulls out a gun and shoots her. His statement shows premeditation, and there are 69 witnesses. (Flossie can't talk)

If Thadwick refuses to give a motive for his act when questioned, he can still be convicted of murder. Everyone would naturally like to know, but he could carry the secret to his grave and still be convicted.

From the standpoint of the prosecution, it is much easier to obtain a conviction if some motive can be shown. Because of this, the officer who is investigating the case should make every effort to gather evidence that will show motive.

Criminal Negligence

As stated before, Criminal Negligence can be substituted for intent. If it were not for this, there would be very few convictions for traffic offenses. Well over half of all traffic offenses are committed without intent on the part of the driver. Police officers need not be on the department very long before they realize this fact. Sometimes the sergeant will tell them that there have been too many accidents at a particular intersection, and there have also been too few citations issued there.

It is a proven fact that the issuing of traffic citations at a particular spot will result in a reduction of accidents there. This can save lives. Because of this, most departments keep statistics on the number of accidents that occur in any particular area.

When officers park near an accident-prone intersection, they readily see from their side view that most of the drivers going through the stop sign or red light do so because they simply do not have their mind on what they are doing. Maybe their kids are screaming in the back seat, or their wives are talking to them, or it might be that their heads are "in the clouds."

The Vehicle Code states that when persons drive vehicles, they will give their full attention to driving and the road ahead. This is the key to criminal negligence. It applies when there is a lawful obligation.

If the law places a legal responsibility upon a person such as in the case of someone driving a vehicle, then failure to uphold that responsibility can amount to criminal negligence.

As we will see later under the topic of involuntary manslaughter, persons may be guilty when they perform lawful acts, but without due caution and circumspection. The Appellate Court in People *v.* Hurley, (13 C.A. 2d 208) stated that acting without due caution and circumspection was the same as criminal negligence.

Corpus Delicti

Corpus delicti is a Latin term meaning "body of the crime." This can be confusing if you take the term literally. It really means "parts of the crime." A term used more often is "elements of the crime."

Just as a human body has many parts, so does the legal description of a crime have many parts. Each crime is made up of at least two parts. These are important because each one must be proved in court in order to obtain a conviction. It is like a three-legged milking stool. If one of the legs is missing, and you try to sit on it, you will fall on your posterior. If one of the elements of a crime is missing, the same thing will happen to you in court. The law requires that the prosecution establish the *corpus delicti* of a crime being charged. Failure to prove or establish any part of this is a bar to further prosecution. In other words, no conviction.

Since the first officers responding to a call are in the best position to gather evidence, they MUST KNOW THE ELEMENTS OF THAT CRIME so that they can gather evidence or obtain

statements that can later be used in court to prove the elements.

Since all law in California is statutory, all of the elements of a crime required in order for the law to be violated will be in the code. Sharp police officers will always carry a Penal Code in their patrol cars. Failure to consider one element of a crime can cause a false arrest or result in the case being lost in court.

For example, let us consider the offense of carrying a concealed revolver on one's person. There are four elements:

(1) The weapon is designed as a gun — 16520 PC
(2) It fires a projectile by force of an explosion — 16520 PC
(3) The barrel length must be less than 16 inches — 16520 PC
(4) The weapon is concealed on the person — 25400 PC

If Officer Jones stops Percy Pester at night under suspicious circumstances, and has reason to believe he might be armed and dangerous, he may "pat down" the suspect in an effort to locate weapons. If he finds that Percy is carrying a concealed (but unloaded) .38 caliber Colt revolver, and it has a special barrel that is 17-inches long, he had better not arrest him for Section 25400 of the Penal Code (Carrying a Concealed Weapon), because one of the elements states that the barrel must be under 16 inches. The third element of that crime is missing. Any arrest for that section would be a false arrest.

(A) Breaking Down A Crime By Its Elements

The elements of crimes are found in the Penal Code. It is sometimes difficult to separate them because they are lumped together in a sentence or two and are often subtle. Law books are available that break down the elements in a 1-2-3 fashion.

In this book, most of the crimes will be broken down into the elements for you. Still it is a good idea for you to learn how to do it yourself. The key to separating the elements in a crime is to determine which parts would have to be proved in a separate manner. The thing that will help you is to look for the small but important words "and" and "or." Sometimes they are implied. You can tell this by reading the section. "And" means that there is an additional element following. "Or" means that there is an optional element following. Read the following section from the Penal Code and try to break it down without looking at the explanation.

Abduction (265 PC)

Every person who takes any woman unlawfully, against her will, and by force, menace or duress, compels her to marry him, or to marry any other person, or to be defiled, is punishable by imprisonment in the state prison.

Elements of the crime broken down

(1) The unlawful taking of a woman
(2) Against her will
(3) By means of
  (a) force or
  (b) menace or
  (c) duress
(4) And compels her to
  (a) marry him or
  (b) marry another or
  (c) be defiled (sexual violation)
(5) Is guilty of a felony.

(B) How are the Elements of the *Corpus Delicti* Proved?

The elements can be proved by circumstantial evidence, which is evidence that tends to prove; it need not be absolutely conclusive proof; it can be proved through photographs. It can also be proved by any one of the five senses, NOT just the sense of sight. Thieves have been convicted on the testimony of blind persons. In one California case, a blind person was able to positively identify the suspect by his footsteps. Several experiments were conducted in court where the suspect came into the courtroom with other persons, each time he was in a different position within the group. Each time the blind witness was able to pick him out of the group.

Proof of the *corpus delicti* only has to be "beyond a reasonable doubt." Many times it appears that a case is lost because the defense is able to find a good loophole. When this happens, it is the fault of the prosecution. They were really not able to prove the elements of the *corpus delicti.*

Corpus delicti is very important to the police officer in knowing exactly what charge to use in "booking" the suspect. If he is "booked" for an offense for which the elements cannot all be proved, the officer is at fault.

For example, in a case of "purse snatch," the crime can be either robbery or grand theft. To be robbery, there must be some force or fear. The force must be more force than is needed to just carry off the goods. If the suspect approached the victim so quietly she didn't see or hear him, and if he grabbed the purse off her arm before she had a chance to resist or give it up voluntarily because of fear, it would be grand theft (theft from the person of another). Knowing the elements of the *corpus delicti* can be very important.

(C) Confessions and Admissions

The difference between a confession and an admission is that a confession is an admission of guilt, whereas an admission is simply an admission of a particular fact. For example, if a person admitted that he murdered his ex-wife, that would be a confession. If he admitted that he was at her apartment on the night she was killed, that would be an admission.

Confessions and admissions cannot be used to prove the elements of the *corpus delicti.* The elements must be proved FIRST. Once the elements of the crime are proved, then the confession or admission can be accepted.

The reason for this is that many mentally ill persons come to the police department and confess to crimes that they did not actually commit. Sometimes the crimes are real, sometimes they are not. It would be a miscarriage of justice to convict such persons when the only proof that a crime existed was their confession. We must be able to prove in court that a crime was actually committed.

Prima facie proof is all that is needed to make a confession admissible. *Prima facie* is a Latin term meaning on "first face." It means the way that things would be judged on first appearance, or on the first examination.

An officer hears a woman scream and then a shot. He runs up an alleyway and finds a woman lying dead. A man is standing next to her with a gun in his hand. It would be natural for the officer to assume, on *prima facie* evidence, that the man was the one who shot her. In reality, the man might have heard the woman scream and ran out to find her lying in the alleyway, and then picked up the gun next to her without thinking. The police officer does not have a crystal ball. Therefore, he or she must go on *prima facie* evidence until such time as other evidence changes the situation.

Classification of Offenses

In California there are three classifications of public offenses (16 PC). They are:

(1) Felonies;
(2) Misdemeanors; and
(3) Infractions.

A felony is a crime which is punishable with death or by imprisonment in the state prison. All other crimes or public offenses are misdemeanors except those offenses that are classed as infractions. (17 PC)

There is also a borderline classification called an ordinance. There is some debate from a legal standpoint as to whether violation of a city or county ordinance is really a "crime" when considering the legal definition of that word.

(A) City or County Ordinances

Based on the premise that a crime is a public wrong, the definition of which is enacted by the state legislature (this power is given to the states by the Tenth Amendment), and that it is prosecuted in the name of the state, some writers in criminal law feel that violation of an ordinance is not really a crime, but a quasi-civil offense due to the fact that it applies only in local jurisdictions and is not statewide in its application. There is also doubt as to whether or not the state can delegate such authority. Since each city and county is really a public corporation given a charter by the state, their jurisdiction is limited by that charter.

How do we know which crimes are felonies or misdemeanors?

After each crime listed in the Penal Code, there will be found a punishment. The punishment determines whether the crime is classed as a felony or a misdemeanor.

Sometimes the punishment for both a felony and a misdemeanor will be found listed at the end of the crime description. This is called a "wobbler." When this happens, the judge has a choice of punishment, and it will usually be determined by the circumstances in the case.

(B) Importance of Crime Classifications for Officers in the Field

When an officer is on duty in the field, there are two considerations when determining the classification of a crime:

Crimes Under Investigation

The rule here is simply to consider the maximum punishment. This can be very important to the officer in knowing how much force to use in handling a case. Officers cannot use their guns in handling misdemeanors; they can in felonies. The laws of arrest are also affected by the classification of a crime. **Officers cannot arrest for misdemeanors not committed in their presence; they can arrest for felonies.**

Let us consider a practical situation. You are on patrol duty and you get a call of a family fight. You have been there many times before, and you know that the husband is very mean when he has been drinking and will beat up his wife. When you arrive, you find that the husband is drunk. By California law, this is not a violation, as drunkenness is only illegal in public. None of the complaining neighbors would give their name over the phone, and the wife, who has a fresh black eye, refuses to place her husband under arrest because she is very much afraid of him. If this were a misdemeanor, there would be little that you could do. However, Section 273.5 of the Penal Code states that causing "traumatic injury upon spouse" can be either a felony or a misdemeanor. This being the case, you could arrest the husband for a felony, at least getting him out of the house overnight, and maybe prevent a serious injury to his wife later.

Crimes for Which Sentence Has Already Been Passed

The key to classification of crimes where the sentence has already been passed is WHERE SENTENCED NOT WHERE SENT.

It is very common for a criminal to be sentenced to state prison, and then given probation. The judge feels the criminal should not escape imprisonment altogether, so as a condition of probation, he or she sends (not sentences) the criminal to county jail for a month.

This person is now an ex-felon. If you were to simply ask him where the judge sent him, or check the record of imprisonment, you could very likely come to the conclusion that since he was sent to a county jail he was convicted of a misdemeanor.

Why is this important to the officer in the field? Sometimes there are restrictions on ex-felons that are not placed on ex-misdemeanants. For example: Section 29800 of the Dangerous Weapons Control Law states that an ex-felon cannot possess a firearm capable of being concealed (this means a pistol or revolver). If, during patrol duty, you stop an ex-felon and find that he has an unloaded revolver in the car, it is very important to know that he is an ex-felon and not an ex-misdemeanant. Remember that his original sentence was to state prison. If he goofs up while on probation, the judge could make him serve the original state prison sentence.

Juvenile Law Sentences

Where under prior law, a judge sentencing a youth to a CYA facility had to declare it to be a misdemeanor, he may under the new law, declare it to be a felony.

(C) Infractions

Infractions are new to criminal law. They are technically offenses and not crimes. It is a fine technicality. Because of this, an infraction is not punishable by imprisonment. (19.6 PC)

The Purpose of Infractions

Infractions were instituted in an effort to make the administration of justice run more smoothly. Parking violations, for example, are classed as infractions. Previously, they were crimes. When they were crimes, the defendant was entitled to his "day in court" with full privileges. This included a jury trial and the services of a public defender. It is impractical to have a jury trial and also provide a public defender for a $10 dollar parking ticket. Yet that was what the defendant was entitled to under the old system.

Under the rules on infractions, a legal trade-off has resulted. A person cannot be sent to jail for an infraction. To compensate for this, he is not entitled to a jury trial or the services of a public defender. He can only go before a trial judge to plead his case. However, if he is arrested on a traffic warrant that has resulted from his failure to properly take care of the original ticket, then the rules on infraction do not apply. For all other practical purposes, the provisions of law relating to misdemeanors shall apply to infractions. (19.7 PC)

Parties to Criminal Acts

(A) Principals

In California, the classification of persons involved with a criminal act is very simple. If a person was involved in any way with the crime, in the preparation or carrying out of that crime, he would be classed as a principal. The basic acts involved in making one a principal are as follows: (31 PC)

(1) Commits a crime.
(2) Aids and abets the commission of a crime (with intent).
(3) Advises and encourages commission of crime.
(4) Gets another drunk by fraud or force for the purpose of causing him to commit a crime.
(5) Compels another to commit a crime by threats, command, or coercion.

There is another part that concerns advising and encouraging children and the mentally disabled to commit a crime, but it would be adequately covered under (3).

In some states as in common law, there are degrees of principals as well as accessories before the fact. In California there is just one simple classification if the person is in any way involved with the criminal act itself or its preparation. In California, all principals are equally guilty. This might seem harsh at times. It means that the person who drives the "getaway car" is just as guilty as his co-principal who holds up the liquor store and kills the clerk. In law they are both equally guilty. In practice, they may be both found guilty, but the amount of time that they serve in prison will be quite different. Even when the death penalty was enforced, the driver of the "getaway car" was also convicted of first degree murder, but was given the lesser prison term for first degree rather than the death penalty.

The purpose of the rule on all principals being equally guilty is to prevent one person trying to shift the blame for the crime onto someone else. It is also to discourage persons from becoming involved in any way with a criminal act.

(B) Accessories

In California there are only accessories after the fact. There are no accessories before the fact. Because of this, the term accessories is often used by itself when referring to accessories after the fact.

According to Section 32 of the California Penal Code, an accessory is defined as: "Every person who, after a felony has been committed, harbors, conceals, or aids a principal in such felony, with the intent that said principal may avoid or escape from arrest, trial, conviction or punishment, having knowledge that said principal has committed such felony or has been charged with such felony or convicted thereof, is an accessory to such felony." The basic elements of this offense might be briefed as follows:

(1) Who assists a felon to escape criminal justice,
(2) After the felony has been committed,
(3) Knowing that he has committed or is charged with or has been convicted of a felony,
(4) Is an accessory.

The most difficult element to prove in this offense is that regarding the fact that the accessory knew that the person whom he assisted has either committed a felony or is wanted for a felony.

A mother who assists her son would technically be classed as an accessory, yet the D.A. would be hesitant to prosecute her for that charge because a jury, or some members of that jury, would be reluctant to find her guilty. After all, she is doing what all mothers should do.

In the investigation of such an offense, the details are important. Did the accessory do any particular act or acts that could be used as circumstantial evidence to prove awareness of the person's involvement? Was the felon wounded? Were there newspapers in the house with headlines of the crime or the escape? Did the Accessory take special precautions to prevent anyone knowing the felon was in his home? Did he keep the blinds drawn or closed? Did he refuse to accept visitors? Did he make arrangements for the felon to leave town and use fictitious names on reservations?

The punishment for an accessory is much less than that for a principal. It can be either a felony or a misdemeanor. The type of offense would be the determining factor.

Attempts to Commit Crime

The attempt to commit a crime is a crime in itself. As a crime, it must have both act and intent. Some crimes in the Penal Code are actually listed as attempts and have specific punishments. Apart from those cases, attempts are generally punishable by not more than half of the maximum punishment if the crime had actually been completed.

What is an Attempt? (21aPC)

The law on attempts has only two elements:

(1) A direct, but ineffectual act done toward the commission of a crime which would have resulted in the completion of that crime,
(2) With intent that the crime be committed.

(A) Abandonment of an Attempt

Abandonment of an attempt is a defense, but only before the attempt itself is started. "Abandonment is a defense if the attempt to commit a crime is freely and voluntarily abandoned before the act is put in process of final execution, and when there is no outside cause prompting such abandonment." (People *v.* Von Hecht, 133 Cal., App. 2d, 25)

(B) Attempts that are also Assaults

Some of the difficulties of understanding attempts can be made easier if it is understood that when an attempt is also an assault there is an added element to prove. For example, in Assault with a Deadly Weapon (245 PC) or Assault with Intent to Commit Murder, when a gun is used, the elements of assault and attempt must be combined. The elements of assault are: "An unlawful attempt, coupled with a present ability to commit a violent injury on the person of another."

This means that when an attempt is also an assault, it must be an act that is capable of being committed. This is not so for an ordinary attempt. In the crime of Attempted Auto Theft (an ordinary attempt), if the thief notices that someone left the key in the ignition then jumps in and turns the key to start the car, the crime of attempt is complete. This is true despite the fact that the battery had been removed making it impossible to start the car.

Now let us look at an attempt that is also an assault. Marvin Mudgeskippy keeps a loaded revolver in his desk drawer. One night, his mother removes the bullets because she knows that her son has a bad temper. The next week, Marvin has an argument and a fight with his brother, Morton. He reaches into the drawer, grabs the gun, aims it at Morton and pulls the trigger twice. This is not an attempted murder because it does not have the "present ability" for completion and it is an assault type of crime. A type of attempt that requires the "ability" element. It is impossible to kill a person by "firing" an unloaded gun.

However, if the impossibility of completion is due to chance, the act qualifies as an attempt. For example: Fred Finklestork normally sleeps in the north bedroom of his house in a bed next to a large window. Wally Widdlewhomp, who has a grudge against Fred, goes to the bedroom window, which is open, and shoots five times into the bed. By chance, Fred slept on the couch that night. It is impossible to shoot someone who is not there. The key, however, is that Fred was not there by chance. He normally sleeps in that bed. The act is, therefore, an attempted murder.

(C) The Overt Act Necessary for an Attempt

Probably the best way to understand just what type of overt act is needed for an attempt is to give some examples.

(1) Trying to steal a car by getting in and turning the ignition key although the battery is dead.
(2) Cutting a lock on the door with bolt cutters, attempting burglary.
(3) Reaching into a person's pocket to steal, even though the pocket is empty.
(4) Lighting the fuse connected to an explosive.
(5) Firing a gun at where the burglar thought the officer was standing even though he had moved and was not there.

Some attempts are crimes even if they are not capable of being completed, if the crime cannot be completed due to chance (such as the victim moving), mechanical error (bullet was faulty), or human intervention (someone stopped the criminal from proceeding further); it is still an attempt.

It can be difficult to determine whether an attempt is legally possible. Determining whether a crime appears possible to commit and when it is absolutely impossible to commit is not easy. It is best to study the decisions of the high courts.

Conspiracy 182 PC

The crime of conspiracy is uncommon on the local level. It is more often prosecuted in federal courts. Conspiracies come to the attention of the police usually because one member of that conspiracy decides to notify the authorities.

The purpose of the law on conspiracy is to prevent serious crimes from occurring, and to punish those planning such crimes. Technically the crime does not have to be serious, but those are the ones that end up in court. The law on conspiracy (182 PC) takes up half a page in the Penal Code, but can be explained in a few words. This section wastes much space in order to give examples.

The elements of conspiracy are as follows:

(1) Two or more persons
(2) Conspire (or agree)
(3) To commit a crime (other situations are rare), and
(4) One member commits an overt act, beyond the mere agreement, towards the completion of the crime.

One person cannot commit conspiracy. There must be two or more involved in the agreement, or there is no conspiracy.

(A) The Overt Act Necessary for Conspiracy

The overt act needed for a conspiracy to be in operation need not be significant; it can be a small act such as buying postage stamps with which to mail a bomb. Conspiracy to commit a crime outside of California is not punishable in this state.

(B) The Scope of a Conspiracy

The scope of a conspiracy lasts longer than the crime that is the object of the conspiracy. For example the crime of robbery is over when the perpetrators have escaped from the scene. The conspiracy is not over until its common purpose or objective has been completed. In the case of robbery, it is the obtaining of money. Until all members of the conspiracy to commit the robbery have received their intended share of the money, the conspiracy is not technically over. The whole scope of the criminal act is called the *res gestae.*

(C) Merging

The crime of conspiracy does not merge with the crime once it is completed. They become two separate offenses and the persons who are involved can be charged with both conspiracy and the crime which they conspired to commit.

Conspiracy by Members of Criminal Street Gang 182.5 PC

(1) Any person who actively participates in any criminal street gang (186.22 PC)
(2) Knowing it's members engage in or have engaged in a pattern of criminal activity (186.22 PC)
(3) And who willfully promotes, furthers, assists or benefits from that criminal conduct
(4) Is guilty of conspiracy.

Conspiracy to Commit Identity Theft 182 (6) PC

Conspiracy to commit Identity Theft as defined in Section 530.5 can be punished by an extra fine of up to $25,000.

Chapter I Case Citations

Study Questions for Chapter I

(1) California law is statutory only when it covers laws in the Penal Code. T or F

(2) Statutory law is that type of law that is written in a code. T or F

(3) Some California cities have some common laws. T or F

(4) Fornication is sexual intercourse between two unmarried persons over 18. T or F

(5) Fornication is a misdemeanor in the State of California. T or F

(6) Former Penal Code section 650.5, which stated that it is illegal to "openly outrage public decency" was a good catchall law backed by the California Supreme Court. T or F

(7) An *"ex post facto"* law is one that is passed after the offense has been committed. T or F

(8) *Ex post facto* laws are only acceptable in Federal Courts. T or F

(9) When a private citizen sees a crime being committed, he is legally obligated to take some preventive action to stop the crime. T or F

(10) In the United States, all defendants are considered innocent until proven guilty. T or F

(11) If a person pleads "not guilty by reason of insanity," the burden of proof rests with him to convince the jury that he was insane at the time of the crime. T or F

(12) Reasonable doubt is a doubt beyond a moral certainty. T or F

(13) Reasonable doubt is a doubt for which some reason can be given, arising from evidence presented in the trial. T or F

(14) If a statutory law includes a presumption, then the defendant has the burden of proof to show that the presumption is false. T or F

(15) In some cases, juries rule on "Questions of Law." T or F

(16) When the jury has to decide the punishment for first degree murder when it is committed by poison, this would be a "Question of Law" and not a "Question of Fact." T or F

(17) If the jury believes that the defendant committed the act, crime or offense, this would be an example of "Question of Fact." T or F

(18) In California, all members of the jury must agree on a verdict, or it is a "hung jury." T or F

(19) A hung jury is by law the same as an acquittal. T or F

(20) If the victim of an assault tells the prosecutor that he does not want to press charges, the D.A. cannot take the case to court. T or F

(21) A subpoena is an order of the court demanding that a person appear in court. T or F

(22) A wife cannot be forced to testify against her husband if the crime is one of hitting her. T or F

(23) Another way of describing the "Letter of the Law" is WHAT THE LAW STATES. T or F

(24) The "Spirit of the Law" is the same thing as "legislative intent." T or F

(25) The "Spirit of the Law" is a good enforcement policy, but has no basis in written law. T or F

(26) The term *"stare decisis"* is a Latin term meaning that a ruling of a prior or preceding case is binding upon the present case. T or F

(27) The U.S. Supreme Court is the "Court of Last Resort." T or F

(28) Case law provides courts with interpretations of words or phases not found in criminal statutes. T or F

(29) In a Supreme Court decision, a simple majority of one vote makes the ruling legal. T or F

(30) The letter symbol for the California Supreme Court is ____________________

(31) The letter symbol for the District Court of Appeals is ____________________

(32) The letter symbol for the U.S. Supreme Court is ____________________

(33) In the case citation "60 C.A. 2d 66," the "60" stands for ____________________

(34) In the above case citation, the "2d" stands for ____________________

(35) In the above case citation, the "66" stands for ____________________

(36) All laws in California must be in English except for terms. T or F

(37) Section 15 of the Penal Code states that failure to perform a required act is classed as a crime. T or F

(38) In order for there to be a crime or public offense, there must exist both ____________ and ____________________

(39) Give an example of an offense involving "criminal negligence." ____________________

____

(40) Illegal possession of contraband, forbidden by law, is classed as an "act," even though there is often no physical overt act involved. T or F

(41) "Passive participation" is an example of an "act" necessary for a crime. T or F

(42) The Latin term *"Mens Rea"* means ____________________

(43) A tort is a ____________________ wrong.

(44) In a tort, the prosecutor of the case is the victim. T or F

(45) General intent is sometimes called "presumed" intent. T or F

(46) Specific intent is the easiest type of intent to prove in court. T or F

(47) Arnold Aardvark gets mad at Bernie Badbetter and throws a rock at him. He misses Bernie and hits Claude Clump by mistake. This type of intent is called ____________ intent.

(48) The above intent is also called ____________________ intent.

(49) In California law, motive is a required part of the *corpus delicti.* T or F

(50) Acting without due caution and circumspection is the same as criminal negligence. T or F

(51) The term *"corpus delicti,"* when translated literally means ____________________
____

(52) The above term, when translated into a practical meaning, means ________________
____

(53) In California courts, every one of the elements of the *corpus delicti* must be proved in order for a conviction to be obtained. T or F

(54) The crimes mentioned in the Penal Code will have all of the elements included in the description of those crimes. T or F

(55) The elements of the *corpus delicti* can be proved by circumstantial evidence. T or F

(56) The term "circumstantial" means:

(A) ____goes around things (B) ____tends to prove

(C) ____absolute proof (D) ____legally acceptable

(57) A witness can only help prove the elements of the *corpus delicti* when he has actually seen them. He cannot use his other senses. T or F

(58) Proof of the *corpus delicti* of a crime need only be that which proves beyond a reasonable doubt. T or F

(59) In some cases the elements of the *corpus delicti* can be proved by just the confession of the defendant. T or F

(60) Proof that is accepted on first appearance or "first face" is called________________

(61) A crime that is punished by imprisonment in state prison is called a ______________

(62) A crime that is punished by imprisonment in county jail is called a _______________

(63) A "wobbler" is the term for:

(A) ____a drunk (B) ____a crime that has just been put into the Penal Code

(C) ____a child molester (D) ____a crime that can be either a felony or a misdemeanor

(64) When working in the field, an officer should consider the maximum sentence that is listed in the Penal Code for a particular crime, for crime classification. T or F

(65) The key to the final classification of a crime is where the person is sent. T or F

(66) A person convicted of a felony but given probation and never sent to jail or prison would still technically be classed as a felon. T or F

(67) Infractions are offenses and not crimes. T or F

(68) In an infraction, the defendant is entitled to a trial by jury. T or F

(69) A person can be sent to jail as punishment for an infraction. T or F

(70) Percy Pester lends Harry Hardrock a revolver, knowing that he is going to use it in a holdup. Percy would be:

(A) ____an accessory before the fact. (B) ____guilty of no legal offense.

(C) ____legally not as guilty as Harry. (D) ____just as guilty as Harry.

(71) In California a person who "advises and encourages" the commission of a crime is classified as a/an ____

(72) Nelly Nefarious gets her friend, Sally Simpleton, drunk so that she will have the courage to let the air out of her landlord's tires because he has been mean to her. Nelly would be just as guilty of the crime of vandalism as would Sally. T or F

(73) A person cannot be an accessory after the fact if the crime was a misdemeanor. T or F

(74) An employee who gives a burglar a map of the building where he works, showing the location of the alarm terminals and the safes, would be classed as an accessory. T or F

(75) A person cannot be an "accessory after the fact" if the person he assisted was only "charged" with a felony, and not convicted of one. T or F

(76) A mother who gives her son medical care after he has been shot in a holdup would not be legally classed as an accessory after the fact. T or F

(77) Accessories and principals are both equally guilty in California. T or F

(78) The word "corroborated" means:

(A) ____discredited (B) ____supported by evidence

(C) ____legally accepted (D) ____recorded

(79) An attempt to commit a crime is itself a crime in California. T or F

(80) Attempts to commit crimes are generally punishable by about one half of the maximum punishment for the crime if it were actually committed. T or F

(81) Larry Lump gets a gun and goes into a liquor store to hold it up. He enters the store and looks around, waiting for a lone customer to leave. Just then a uniformed officer comes into the store for a pack of cigarettes. Larry gets scared and leaves the store. Since Larry voluntarily gave up the robbery, he would not be guilty of an attempt. T or F

(82) Kevin Krump reaches his hand into Mervin Mushmuscle's coat pocket, hoping to find some money there. There is none, so he is not guilty of attempted theft. T or F

(83) Arvin Aardvark gets mad at Flossie Furd and takes a gun from his glove compartment with the intent to shoot her. Forgetting that the gun was unloaded he aimed it at Flossie and pulled the trigger. He is guilty of attempted murder. T or F

(84) A person could not be charged with attempting to commit a crime if the crime he attempts is not legally possible of being committed due to one or more of the elements of the *corpus delicti* being missing. T or F

(85) Officer Lackmore, a young rookie policeman, is asked by the Chief to dress up like a woman and walk around in the local park where there have been several recent rapes. On the first night, Officer Lackmore is attacked by Harry Hack who tries to rape what he thought was a woman. Harry cannot be charged with attempted rape. T or F

(86) The word "perpetrator" means:

(A) ____the victim (B) ____the accessory

(C) ____the person who committed the crime (D) ____the person who called the police

(87) If the jury feels that just one of the conspirators is guilty, they may find just one guilty and the others innocent. T or F

(88) The overt act needed for a conspiracy to be legally started can be very slight. T or F

(89) It takes two or more persons to commit the overt act needed to legally begin a conspiracy. T or F

(90) Three men conspire to kidnap a millionaire's son for one half million dollars. When they seize the boy, the conspiracy to kidnap is complete. T or F

(91) A conspiracy occurred in California to cheat the slot machines in Las Vegas, Nevada. Even though the conspiracy was to commit a crime outside of the state, it would be tried in the state of California just as though the crime were to be committed here. T or F

ESSAY QUESTIONS

(1) Describe the difference between a crime and a tort.

(2) Explain the differences between the Spirit of the Law and the Letter of the Law.

CHAPTER II

LAWS OF ARREST

The Miranda Decision

When a suspect has been "taken into custody or otherwise deprived of his freedom of action in any significant way," he must be advised of his rights and "knowingly and intelligently" waive them before any statement can be used against him in a court of law. (Miranda *v.* Arizona, 384 United States 436) Before discussing the laws of arrest, we will cover the Miranda decision, because statements made after an arrest are protected by this decision.

Miranda is based on the Fifth and Sixth Amendments to the U.S. Constitution. It was a five to four decision. This means that four justices of the U.S. Supreme Court felt that the decision was not a good one. The Miranda decision is an interpretation of the purpose of the Fifth and Sixth Amendments. The restrictions set forth by this decision are not found in the Amendments verbatim. The Amendments are listed as follows:

Fifth Amendment: "No person shall... be compelled, in any criminal case, to be a witness against himself;"

Sixth Amendment: "In all criminal prosecutions, the accused shall enjoy the right to... have the assistance of counsel for his defense."

The Amendments cover other things as well; only those pertaining to self-incrimination and the right to an attorney have been listed.

In this decision, the court majority felt that in order for these rights to be fully extended to citizens, the police have a legal obligation not only to notify suspects of their rights under these Amendments, but if the suspects so desire, provide an attorney for them. If they cannot afford an attorney, the court felt that the local jurisdiction is obliged to provide attorneys for them. The court further ruled that if suspects do not wish to talk to the police, all further questioning will stop immediately. The court also condemned certain interrogative techniques, not on the basis that they would or even could cause an innocent person to admit guilt, but because they involved "tricks." Miranda does not apply to the investigative stage of the process.

(A) When should suspects be read their rights?

This is a difficult question which depends on the circumstances, but for the purpose of this chapter it is not important since all persons who have been arrested would be covered under Miranda.

In the People *v.* Fioritto (68 Cal 2d 714) the Supreme Court stated that if the defendant refused to answer when questioned by the patrol officer at the time of arrest, but a short while later confessed to a detective, the confession was not admissible. However, in the case of People *v.* Miller (40 CA 3d 228), the defendant confessed two days after first refusing to talk. The court upheld the confession on the basis that he had proper time to reconsider, and that the confession was truly voluntary.

If a suspect has been notified of his rights under Miranda and refuses to talk, any statement made thereafter cannot be used in court to show his guilt. However, if he makes a statement to the police a short time after refusal, then later, when he testifies in court, denies the statement or tells a different story, the original statement may be admitted into evidence for the purpose of impeaching him. (Jarros *v.* New York, 401 United States 222) (Oregon *v.* Hass, 421 United States) (People *v.* Nudd, 12 Cal 3d 204).

(B) What are suspects› rights under Miranda?

The U.S. Supreme Court has held under Miranda that suspects must be notified of four basic rights. When they have been so notified, they must be questioned to determine whether they understand the rights, then asked if they wish to make a statement, or to waive their rights. The rights are:

(1) You have the right to remain silent.
(2) If you do say anything, it can and will be used against you in a court of law.
(3) You are entitled to an attorney during all stages of the proceedings.
(4) If you cannot afford an attorney, one will be provided.

Once suspects have been notified of these basic rights, they must be asked two questions:

(1) Do you understand these rights? (If the answer is yes, the next question is asked.)
(2) Do you wish to waive these rights?

(C) How do suspects waive their rights?

In Miranda, it clearly states that the waiver must be "articulated." If it is not verbal, there is in effect no waiver. Nodding of the head will not be accepted. Rights must also be waived intelligently.

The only exception is if a person is mute and either writes a confession, or makes the confession to another person who understands sign language. In this case it is better to have the suspect sign the waiver, although the fact that a non-police interpreter is taking the statement should remove any implication of police coercion from the confession.

(D) Private Persons' Arrests

Private persons including private police personnel are not covered under Miranda, or for that matter, any of the restrictive rules applied to police such as search and seizure regulations. (Stapleton *v.* Superior Court, 70 Cal. 2d 97) (U.S. District Courts also support this concept) Therefore, any statements made by a suspect during a private person's arrest will be admitted in court.

The courts are hesitant about accepting statements made to private persons or private police when regular police officers are present. They feel that it is probably a matter of subterfuge, and that the private persons or private police are acting under the suggestions or influence of the police in an effort to avoid the restrictions of Miranda.

The Laws of Arrest

(A) Who may make an arrest? (834 PC)

An arrest may be made by a peace officer or by a private person. The definition of a peace officer is found under Section 830 PC and its various subsections. Peace officers' authority extends to any place in the state under the following three conditions:

(1) They are making the arrest in the jurisdiction where they work.

(2) They have prior consent from the law enforcement head in the jurisdiction where they are about to make the arrest.
(3) When there is immediate danger to person or property, or of escape, from the perpetrator about to be arrested.

(B) What is an arrest? (834 PC)

An arrest is taking a person into custody, in a case and in a manner authorized by law. An arrest may be made by peace officers or private persons.

Notice that the term "private persons" is used. Too often in police work we use the term "citizens' arrest." That term is not correct. Any human being may make an arrest in California, foreign citizens as well as American citizens, so don't get confused by this common terminology.

(C) If a person feels that the arrest is false, can he resist?

Section 834a PC states "If a person has knowledge, or by the exercise of reasonable care, should have knowledge, that he is being arrested by a peace officer, it is the duty of such person to refrain from using force or any weapon to resist such arrest." If the arrest is truly false, the person being arrested should go along with the arrest after explaining the circumstances that make it false. If the officer still follows through with the arrest, the person arrested could initiate a civil suit.

(D) How is an arrest made? (835 PC)

(1) An actual physical restraint of the person or
(2) Submission to the custody of an officer.

(E) How much physical restraint may be used?

(1) "The person arrested may be subjected to such restraint as is reasonable for his arrest and detention." (835 PC)
(2) The arresting person may use reasonable force to
    (a) effect the arrest or
    (b) to prevent escape or
    (c) overcome resistance. (835a PC)

(F) What must a person making an arrest say?

To make an arrest, the person making the arrest must notify the person being arrested that:

(1) He or she is under arrest
(2) For what specific offense
(3) By what authority. (841 PC)

Peace officers in uniform need not cite the authority since their badges and uniforms show this. Officers in plain clothes must show their badges. If they catch the suspect actually engaged in committing or attempting to commit the offense, they need not notify him of the offense. If the officers are in immediate pursuit of the offender after he has committed the crime, they need not notify him of the offense as part of the arrest. If, after the arrest, the suspect requests to know the offense for which he is being arrested, the person making the arrest must inform him. (841 PC)

(G) When can forced entry be made for arrest?

Under 844 PC, to make an arrest:

(1) A private person, if the offense is a felony;
(2) Peace officers, in a felony or a misdemeanor;
(3) May break open a door or window of a house in which there is a person to be arrested, or in which they have reasonable grounds for believing him to be,
(4) **After** they have demanded admittance, AND
(5) Identified themselves, AND
(6) Explained the reason for desiring admittance.

In the People *v.* Ramey, the California Supreme Court held that the "knock and notice" provisions of 844 PC are not "carte blanche" grounds for entry, and that some condition must exist where the obtaining of a warrant would not be practical. They felt that such an intrusion into the privacy of the home is "one of the most awesome incursions of police power into the life of an individual." This does not apply to chasing the suspect into a home during the course of a "hot pursuit." (People *v.* Lloyd, 216 CA 3d 1425)

(H) When can an arrest be made? (836 & 837 PC)

(1) <u>By a Peace Officer (836 PC)</u> A peace officer may arrest a person in obedience to a warrant. Without a warrant, the officer may arrest under the following circumstances:
    (a) When the officer has reasonable cause to *<u>believe</u>* that the person has committed a public offense in the officer's presence.
    (b) The person arrested has committed a felony, even if not in the officer's presence.
    (c) When the officer has reasonable cause to *<u>believe</u>* that the person has committed a felony, whether or not one has in fact been committed.
(2) <u>By a Private Person (837 PC)</u> Any person may make a private person's arrest when:
    (a) a crime has been committed or attempted in his or her presence.

(b) the suspect has committed a felony, even if not in his or her presence.
(c) a felony has actually been committed, and the person has reasonable cause to believe the suspect committed it.

Other Arrests Without Warrant (836(d) PC)

A peace officer may arrest without warrant if the suspect commits assault or battery (or the officer has probable cause to believe it occurred) on:

(1) A current or former spouse, fiance or fiancee, a current or former cohabitant, or
(2) A person with whom the suspect is or has been having an engagement relationship, or has (or is presumed to have) parented a child, a child of the suspect (or whose parentage is challenged), or a child who is the child of one of the above persons, or
(3) A person who is related to the suspect by consanguinity or affinity (close relationship other than by blood) within the second degree.

Officer's Duty to Inform Domestic Violence Victims of Right to Arrest

When a peace officer is handling a domestic violence call, it shall be mandatory that the officer make a good faith effort to inform the victim of the right to make a "private person's arrest," and how it can be performed. (836b PC)

Arrests Under Protective Orders (836(c) PC)

(1) When a peace officer is responding to a call alleging a violation of a protective order,
(2) And the officer has reasonable cause to believe that the person listed in the order has committed an act in violation of the order,
(3) And has received notice of that order,*
(4) The officer may arrest without the violation occurring in his or her presence.
* If the victim shows the officer a copy of proof of service of the order, it shall be *prima facie* evidence that the suspect was served.

Proof Protective Order was Issued (836(2) PC)

The person to whom the protective order has been issued will have been assumed to have notice of the order when:

(1) The victim shows the officer proof of service, or
(2) The officer finds that the order is on file at headquarters, or
(3) The suspect was present at the protective order hearing, or
(4) The suspect was notified by a peace officer that order was issued.

The Primary Aggressor (836(3) PC)

(1) Where mutual protective orders are issued
(2) Liability for arrest applies to the person reasonably believed to be the primary aggressor.
(3) In identifying the primary aggressor, the officer shall consider:
    (a) The intent of the law to protect victims of domestic violence.
    (b) The threats creating fear of physical injury.
    (c) The history of domestic violence between the persons involved.
    (d) Whether either person involved acted in self defense.

(I) Arrest for Misdemeanors Not Committed in the Officer's Presence

Although it is not stated, examining the above conditions for making a legal arrest will show that an arrest cannot be made for a misdemeanor not committed in the person's presence. The exceptions when peace officers can arrest for misdemeanors not committed in their presence are:

(1) When the officers have a warrant of arrest. (836 PC)
(2) When the officers arrest a juvenile whom they have reasonable cause to believe has committed a misdemeanor. (625 W & I)
(3) When the suspect has committed assault or battery on school property. (241.2 PC)
(4) When the officer has reasonable cause to believe that the suspect has committed assault or battery on a firefighter, EMT, or MIC paramedic, while on duty. (241 PC)
(5) An officer can arrest without a warrant when there is a traffic accident and driving under the influence is suspected for any of the following reasons (40300.5 CVC):
    (a) The suspect is observed in or about a vehicle that is obstructing a highway.
    (b) The suspect will not be apprehended unless arrested immediately.
    (c) The suspect may cause injury to himself or herself unless immediately arrested.
    (d) The suspect may destroy or conceal evidence of the crime unless immediately arrested.
(6) When the person arrested has violated 25850 PC (CCW), although not in the officer's presence; whenever the officer has reasonable cause to believe that the person to be arrested

has violated this section, whether or not this section has, in fact, been violated:
(7) CCW at airport
(8) Misdemeanor escape.

626 & 631 W & J

Juveniles must be delivered to a probation officer within 24 hours. A petition must be filed within 48 hours.

836(d) PC

(1) When an officer has reasonable cause to believe that the suspect has committed assault or battery
(2) Upon
   (a) a spouse
   (b) a cohabitant, or
   (c) the parent of his or her child,
(3) The officer may immediately (not hours later) arrest the suspect without a warrant,
(4) Whether or not the offense was in fact committed.

(J) Summoning Assistance

Section 839 PC states that "any person making an arrest may orally summon as many persons as he deems necessary to aid him therein."

Posse Comitatus

Posse comitatus is a Latin term meaning the "power of the state to summon assistance in carrying out the law." The word *"posse"* that we hear in westerns comes from this term. In the movies, the sheriff "gets a *posse* together." In legal terms, he summons assistance to make an arrest. Any person summoned under *posse comitatus* has all the authority of a formally deputized officer. (Monterey County *v.* Industrial Acc. Comm., 199 Cal. 221)

Refusing to Assist a Peace Officer (150 PC)

Repealed in 2019.

(K) Laws Regarding the Unlawful Use of Force (147 PC - 149 PC)

Every officer who is guilty of willful inhumanity or oppression toward any prisoner under his care or in his custody is punishable by a fine not exceeding four thousand dollars ($4,000) and by removal from office. (147 PC) Every public officer who, under color of authority without lawful necessity, assaults or beats any person, is guilty of a felony. (149 PC)

These are criminal offenses, and in order for a conviction to be had, it must be shown that there was both act and criminal intent. Some officers are afraid that if they need to use force in order to make a legal arrest, they will be liable under this law.

The phrase "without lawful necessity" is an element of this offense. This is a debatable subject. How much force is really necessary? Because of this, many arrested persons will sue police officers and the police department on the grounds that the officer used too much force. Again, in order to obtain a criminal conviction, all members of the jury must be convinced beyond a reasonable doubt that the officer did willfully and with criminal intent, use excessive force. In Section 147 the terms "willful inhumanity" and "oppression" also indicate an intentional and criminal act.

(L) Protection from Civil Liability as a Result of a Legal Arrest (836.5b PC)

There will be no civil liability on the part of any public officers acting within the scope of their authority for false arrest or false imprisonment because of an arrest which is lawful or which the officers had reasonable cause to believe was lawful.

(M) Releasing or Delivering of Prisoners

(1) A private person who has arrested another for the commission of a public offense must, without unnecessary delay, take the person arrested before a magistrate (judge), or deliver him to a peace officer. (847 PC)
(2) A peace officer, when arresting without a warrant, shall take the prisoner before the nearest or most accessible magistrate in the county in which the offense is triable. (849 PC)
(3) A peace officer may release from custody, instead of taking before a magistrate, any person under the following circumstances:
   (a) The officer is satisfied that there are insufficient grounds for making a criminal complaint against the person arrested.
   (b) The person is arrested only for intoxication and no further proceedings are desirable.

(c) The person is arrested for being under the influence of a drug and is delivered to a hospital or facility for treatment, and no further proceedings are desirable.
(d) The person is arrested for driving under the influence and is delivered to a hospital for medical treatment that prohibits immediate delivery before a magistrate.
(e) The person is arrested only for being under the influence of a controlled substance or drug, and such person is delivered to a facility or hospital for treatment, and no further proceedings are desirable.

(4) The record of arrest of a person released pursuant to paragraph 3(a), 3(c), or 3(e) listed above shall include a record of release. Thereafter, the arrest shall not be deemed an arrest, but a detention only. In these cases the person shall be issued a certificate signed by the detaining officer describing the action as a detention (851.6 PC).

The Misdemeanor Citation (853.6 PC)

When the arrest is for either a misdemeanor or an infraction, a misdemeanor citation may be issued rather than making a physical arrest. The citation is signed by the suspect as a promise to appear in court at the time and date on the citation. A copy is given to the arrestee. Unless waived by that person, the time specified in the notice to appear must be at least 10 days after the arrest.

Duties When Misdemeanor Citation is Issued (853.5 & 853.6 PC) (Briefed)

A suspect arrested for a misdemeanor who does not demand to be taken before a magistrate, may be released on a misdemeanor citation.

Officers shall then, as soon as practicable, file the duplicate copy of the citation with the specified magistrate, who will in turn, then fix the amount of bail according to Section 1275 PC (based on the seriousness of the offense, the suspect's prior arrests, and the probability of his appearing in court).

Prior to the court date, the defendant may post such bail. If at the arraignment, the defendant or his counsel does not appear, the magistrate may declare the bail forfeited, and may, at his discretion, order that further proceedings cease.

At the time of the arrest, the officer may:

(1) Book the person prior to being released.
(2) Indicate on the citation that the person shall appear at the arresting agency to be either:
(a) booked or
(b) fingerprinted
prior to the assigned court appearance.

The arresting agency shall provide the cited person with verification, either on the copy of the citation or on a separate form, that the process was completed. If the citation has such a notation, the judge shall verify that the person complied with the demand before the court process starts. If there is no verification, the judge shall order that it be done before further proceedings begin. However, if both sides stipulate before the judge that the process is not necessary, the proceedings may begin.

If the suspect has violated a Protective Court Order involving domestic violence, that person shall be booked rather than being released on a citation. However, if the officer feels that the interest of justice may be better served by using a citation and can qualify this in the report, the suspect may be cited. This law does not affect bail or the release on "O.R."

If the arrestee does not have satisfactory evidence of identity, he or she will be required to place a fingerprint or thumbprint on the notice to appear.

Discretion in Domestic Violence Arrests (853.6 PC)

(1) When there is a written department policy on domestic violence arrests
(2) This amendment allows more leeway in determining whether or not the officer will cite the suspect or take him before a judge.

Duties When the Misdemeanor Citation is Not Issued

If the arrested person is not released on a misdemeanor citation, then at the time of booking, the arresting officer, the booking officer or a superior, or other such person so designated, shall make an investigation to determine whether the suspect should be released. Whenever the arrested person is not released on a written notice to appear, the arresting officer shall, on a special form indicate the reason for not releasing the prisoner (only one need be listed). Reasons that may be listed are:

(a) Arrestee was so intoxicated he was a danger to self or others, or appeared he could have been.
(b) Arrestee was in need of medical care or examination, or could not care for his own safety.

(c) The person was arrested for one or more of the offenses listed in Section 40302 CVC.
(d) Arrestee had one or more outstanding warrants.
(e) Arrestee did not have satisfactory identification.
(f) Arrestee's release would jeopardize the prosecution of some offense.
(g) There was a reasonable likelihood that the offense or offenses would continue or resume.
(h) The safety of persons or property would be imminently endangered by arrestee's release.
(i) Arrestee demanded to be taken before a magistrate as soon as possible, or refused to sign the citation.
(j) Any other good reason.

(N) Lawful Detention

There are two stages, short of an arrest, in the process of stopping a suspect in public.

Consensual Encounters

In a consensual encounter, the officer "asks" and does not "demand" the suspect to stop. Questions may be directed to the suspect such as "do you live near here?" If the answer is no, the suspect may then be asked for some identification. The suspect may even be asked to remove his hands from his pockets. The key is that the suspect is not "ordered" to do anything, and is free to leave at any time. (People *v.* Ross, 217 CA 3d 879)

If during the encounter, the officer develops reasonable suspicion, the stop can become a detention, or if reasonable cause develops, the officer can proceed to an arrest.

Detention Short of Arrest

There are two qualifications for a detention:

(a) Reasonable suspicion that a crime has been committed. This must be based on facts that can be explained in the officer's reports or on the stand in court. (People *v.* Raybourn 218 CA 3d 308)
(b) Reasonable suspicion that the suspect might have committed the crime.

The courts are not generally satisfied by a police officer's "hunches" or statements that "the guy just didn't look right," or "he looked like a bum or a no-good." If an officer cannot present a reasonable basis for suspicion in the form of facts, then the best approach would be based on a consensual encounter. In People *v.* Jones, (96 Cal. App. 3d 820), the Appellate court stated "A detention occurs if the suspect is not free to leave at will. If he is kept in the officer's presence by physical restraint, threat or force, or assertion of authority."

There is nothing in the Penal Code regarding lawful detention. We must rely on case law for information. Lawful detention is the stopping of a person by the police based on reasonable cause, yet without enough cause to justify an arrest. The acts of the suspect or the circumstances surrounding the situation are such that a peace officer could justify the fact that public safety demands such stopping.

In People *v.* Mickelson, (59 Cal. 2d 448), the California Supreme Court stated: "We do not believe that our rule permitting temporary detention for questioning conflicts with the Fourth Amendment. It strikes a balance between a person's interest in immunity from police interference and the community interest in law enforcement. It wards off pressure to equate reasonable cause to investigate with reasonable cause to arrest, thus protecting the innocent from the risk of arrest when no more than reasonable investigation is justified."

(O) Warrants of Arrest

To obtain a warrant of arrest, an officer must first obtain a criminal complaint and present it, with an affidavit listing the probable cause for making an arrest, before a magistrate. If the magistrate feels that the probable cause is sufficient, he will make out a warrant of arrest and will fix the amount of bail for that offense. (806, 815a PC)

Who are Magistrates?

A magistrate is an officer having power to issue a warrant for the arrest of a person charged with a public offense. (807 PC) The following persons are magistrates:

(a) The judges of the Supreme Court
(b) The judges of the Courts of Appeal
(c) The judges of the Superior Courts

Only a magistrate can issue a warrant of arrest.

Who Can Serve a Warrant of Arrest? (816 PC)

Only a peace officer or an authorized public officer can serve a warrant of arrest. A private person cannot serve a warrant of arrest. A magistrate may, however, orally order a peace officer or private person to arrest someone committing an offense in his presence. (838 PC)

When Can a Warrant of Arrest Be Served?

Felony Warrant:

An arrest for a felony can be made on any day and at any time of the day or night. (840 PC)

Misdemeanor Warrant (or infraction):

An arrest for a misdemeanor or infraction cannot be made between the hours of 10:00 PM of any day, and 6:00 AM of the succeeding day unless:

(a) The arrest is made in public.
(b) The arrest is made when the person is in custody for another lawful arrest.
(c) The warrant has been endorsed for night service (upon good cause).

If the warrant is a traffic warrant, the officer may issue a citation instead of arresting. (818 PC)

Can a Warrant Be Served When it is Not in the Possession of the Officer?

842 PC states that an arrest by a peace officer acting under a warrant is lawful even if the warrant is not in the officer's possession at the time of the arrest. If requested, the warrant must be shown to the officer as soon as possible. If the warrant is being held by an out-of-town agency, a telegraphic copy of the warrant, or an abstract of the warrant may be sent by teletype or other electronic devices (e.g., fax, computer). It must contain on its face all information that is on the original warrant.

When officers stop suspects in the field and find there are warrants for them at headquarters, they should make sure to get the badge number of the clerk who searched for the warrant. This is because the warrant may have been served at an earlier time, but the "want" card was not removed from the files. If this is the case, and the officers make the arrest and bring the suspect to headquarters where the warrant cannot be found, they have a case of false arrest on their hands.

Sometimes the clerk who searched for and found the warrant holds on to it, waiting for the officers to arrive at headquarters. If they take a long time in getting there, the clerk may step out for a break and take the warrant. When the officers arrive, no one can find the warrant. If the officers mention the badge number that dispatch gave them, the other clerks would know immediately who it was, and the fact that he or she had gone on a break.

Duties of Officers Serving Out-of-Town Warrants (821 PC)

Officers making an arrest on a warrant issued in another county must, without unnecessary delay, inform the defendant in writing of his right to be taken before a magistrate in the county of arrest. They must also note on the warrant or abstract of that warrant that the defendant has been so informed. He can then be admitted to bail in the amount listed on the warrant, provided that he appears before the court issuing the warrant within 25 days.

If the defendant does not avail himself of the opportunity for bail, the agency issuing the warrant must be notified and he must be picked up by that agency within five days of the arrest and taken before the court issuing the warrant. If the requesting agency is more than 400 miles away, the time is five court days.

Civil Liability from Serving a Warrant (Civil Code 43.5a)

If an officer arrests on a warrant, and the warrant is regular on its face, and the peace officer acts without malice and in reasonable belief that the person arrested is the one referred to in the warrant, there shall be no civil liability, and no cause for action against the officer.

(a) Regular on its face: This means that it has been signed by the judge and all the basic information is there. An officer should ALWAYS check a warrant on its face.
(b) Reasonable belief: The officer is not expected to be psychic, but if the warrant describes a person as 5-feet tall and born on June 4, 1949, and the person arrested is 6-feet tall and looks 20 years old, even if he has the same name, it is not reasonable to believe he is the one listed on the warrant. In this, as well as most other cases, the term "reasonable" means what would seem reasonable to members a the jury.

The Felony Summons — Summons in Lieu of Warrant or Arrest (813 PC)

(1) When a felony complaint has been filed
(2) And the magistrate is satisfied that a felony has been committed and that it is reasonable to believe that the suspect committed it,
(3) And the D.A. requests it,

In the Superior Court of Santa Cruz County Judicial District

COUNTY OF SANTA CRUZ, STATE OF CALIFORNIA

DOB ______________ Ht. ______________ Wt. ______________ **WARRANT** CASE NO. __________

Hair ______________ Eyes ______________

CITATION NO.	LICENSE NUMBER	TIME ISSUED	DATE ISSUED
SECTION VIOLATED			

DATE: ______________________

BAIL: ______________________

The people of the State of California, to any Sheriff, Constable, Marshal or Police Officer in this State:

Complaint upon oath having been this day laid before me, Judge of the Superior Court of Santa Cruz Judicial District, County of Santa Cruz, State of California, by __________________________ that the offense described was committed by ____, and accusing the person named.

You are therefore commanded forthwith to arrest the above named defendant.

Witness my hand and seal, on the date shown above.

____

JUDGE OF THE SUPERIOR COURT

COUNTY OF SANTA CLARA **SHERIFF'S DEPARTMENT**

NOTIFICATION: SECTIONS 821 & 822 P.C.

You,____, are hereby notified, pursuant to Sections 821 & 822 of the California Penal Code, that you have the right, if you desire, to be taken before a Magistrate of Santa Clara County on the Warrant(s) of Arrest listed below.

CHARGE(S)	CO. ISSUING WARRANT	BAIL

I, the undersigned, hereby acknowledge having read the above notification.

1. ____ do — do not
2. ____ do — do not
3. ____ do — do not
4. ____ do — do not

Dated:______________________ Signed: ______________________
(Defendant's Signature)

Pkg. #:______________________ ______________________
(Arresting or Booking Officer)

(4) A summons shall be issued instead of a warrant of arrest.

A summons shall not be issued under the following conditions:
(1) The offense charged involves violence.
(2) The offense charged involves a firearm.
(3) The offense charged involves resisting arrest.
(4) The suspect has one or more outstanding warrants.
(5) The prosecution of any offense would be jeopardized.
(6) There is a reasonable likelihood that the offense would continue.
(7) The safety of persons and property would be jeopardized.
(8) There is reasonable belief that the suspect would not appear at the time and place specified.

When appearing for an arraignment, the suspect will show the arraigning judge proof that the booking procedure has been completed.

The felony summons is like the misdemeanor citation, but for non-violent felonies. The suspect is not arrested on the spot, but is allowed to go through the booking process to fit his or her own schedule. This must be done prior to the first court appearance.

The summons can only be served by a peace officer or a public officer with special authority. A copy of the summons will be given to the defendant and to the magistrate handling the case.

(P) The Rights of a Person After Arrest

Right to Phone Calls (851.5 PC)
(a) Immediately upon being booked (or as soon as practicable).
(b) No later than three hours after arrest (except when physically impossible).
(c) An arrested person has the right to make at least three complete phone calls. These calls can be to three of the following: (1) An attorney; (2) A bail bondsman; (3) A relative.
(d) At no expense to him, (unless long distance).
(e) Signage regarding right to phone calls must be posted at detainment facilities in English, and in the predominant non-English language spoken in the area.
(f) Arresting officer must inquire as to whether the arrested person is a custodial parent of a minor child, and if this is the case, inform the arrested person that they are entitled to up to two additional phone calls to arrange for child care.
(g) It is a misdemeanor for a public officer or employee to deprive an arrestee of these rights.

Time Restrictions in Appearing Before a Magistrate (825 PC)

The defendant must, in all cases, be taken before a magistrate without unnecessary delay, and, in any event, within 48 hours after arrest, excluding Sundays and holidays, provided. However, when the 48 hours expires at a time when the court in which the magistrate is sitting is not in session, such time shall be extended to include the duration of the next regular court session on the judicial day immediately following. If the court is in session, the arraignment shall take place during that session, holidays excepted.

Right of Attorney to Visit Prisoner (825 PC)

After such arrest, an attorney, at the request of the prisoner or any relative of his, may visit the person so arrested.

Right of Physician, Surgeon or Psychiatrist to Visit Prisoner (825.5 PC)

Any physician and surgeon, including a psychiatrist, licensed to practice in this state, who is employed by the prisoner or his attorney to assist in the preparation of the defense, shall be permitted to visit the prisoner while he is in custody.

6159 Government Code

Allows jails to accept credit cards for bail.

Arrests of Mentally Ill Persons (5325 W & I and 5150 W & I)

When a mentally ill person is taken into custody, he must be orally notified of the officer's name and department, the reason for the detention, where he will be taken, his right to leave a note or make a phone call, and the fact that all his rights will be given to him by the mental health staff.

(Q) Immunity From Arrest

The purpose of immunity from arrest is to prevent a person from being arrested in order to prevent his performing an important function. This has been interpreted as being immunity from civil arrest or arrest by warrant. An example would be the arrest of a citizen while he is on his way to vote in a legal election or the arrest of a legislator en route to the legislature in order to vote on the passage of a bill. A criminal offense such as a breach of the peace would not come under this immunity.

(R) Diplomatic Immunity

This type of immunity has caused much debate. It has been held to be immunity from prosecution more than immunity from arrest. The problem in dealing with this immunity is knowing whether or not the person is actually entitled to it. From the standpoint of the police officer in the field, the person should be taken into custody and turned over to a superior at headquarters. There have been numerous cases of foreigners who have claimed diplomatic immunity when they were not technically entitled to it. Not all members of a diplomatic staff have this immunity and it is difficult for the officer to know all the conditions that might be involved. Temporary detention may be best.

(S) Duties When Arresting a Foreign National (834c PC)

Based upon the 1963 Vienna Convention on Consular Relations Treaty:

(1) When an officer arrests and books or detains for more than two hours,
(2) A foreign national (a non-U.S. citizen),
(3) The officer shall advise the person that he or she has the right to communicate with an official from the consulate of his or her country.
(4) If that person declares his or her wish to consult that official, the officer must immediately notify the person in the department or agency assigned to that duty.
(5) The person so assigned will then contact the consulate of the proper country and make notification that a national of that country is in custody, and wishes to be contacted.

There are 140 countries that have signed this treaty. By 1999, 56 of them required mandatory notification. Rather than officers memorizing these countries, it would be sensible to make an immediate notification for any foreign national that requests this right.

(T) Juvenile Arrests

At first Miranda did not apply to juveniles. In 1968, however, the Gault decision declared that juveniles as well as adults were entitled to the protection of the Constitution. In California, the Welfare and Institutions Code (625 W & I) makes it mandatory that juveniles be warned of their rights under Miranda when they are arrested. It is only mandatory for adults when you wish to use their statements in court.

<u>Temporary Custody of a Minor (625 W & I)</u>

(1) A peace officer may, without a warrant, take into temporary custody a minor
(2) (a) who is under 18 and described in 601 W & I (uncontrollable) or 602 W & I (criminal offender); or
   (b) Who is a ward of the court; or
   (c) For whom a court order has been issued and the officer has reasonable cause to believe that the juvenile has violated that order; or
   (d) Who has escaped from a court ordered commitment; or
   (e) When the minor is found in any street or public place and is suffering from any illness or injury requiring care or treatment.

When a minor is taken into temporary custody, the officer shall advise the minor of his or her Miranda rights. (Juveniles are not, however, entitled to bail or a jury trial. (In re Gault)

<u>Notification of Parents & Right to Phone Calls (627 W & I)</u>

(a) When an officer takes a minor to juvenile hall, that officer shall take steps to notify the minor's parents, guardian or responsible relative that the minor is in custody and where he is being held.
(b) No later than one hour after the arrest, the minor shall be advised of his or her right to at least two phone calls.
   (1) One phone call completed to a parent, guardian or responsible relative.
   (2) Another call completed to an attorney. There is no charge for the calls if they are local and in the presence of a public officer.

(U) Juveniles Arrest for Status Offenses (207 W & I)

In 1979, the law was amended regarding the type of detention allowed for juvenile arrests if the arrest was for a status offense only. (e.g. 601 W & I). Prior to this, 507 & 654 W & I required that status offenders be placed only in a non-secure facility or a special "Crisis Resolution" home. This allowed a runaway to walk out the back door of a facility as soon as he was left there by the police. The law states that:

(1) Juveniles arrested for 601 W & I offenses (runaway uncontrollable) or 213.3 W & I (willful disobedience of a lawful order of juvenile court)
(2) Can be held in a secure facility
(3) For up to:
    (a) 12 hours in order to check for warrants when there is reasonable cause to believe outstanding warrants for the minor exist;
    (b) 24 hours in order to locate the minor's parents, if they are not easily contacted;
    (c) 72 hours if the parents are very difficult to locate.
(4) Such juveniles may be placed in a "Juvenile Hall" containing criminal violators provided there is no contact with such violators.

(V) Arrests for Infractions (853.5 PC)

(1) When officers attempt to issue a citation
(2) For an infraction
(3) They may ask the person for identification.
(4) If the person refuses to
    (a) show identification, or
    (b) sign the citation,
(5) He may then be taken into custody.

(W) Peace Officer Arrest of Probationer

When a peace officer has reasonable cause to believe that a person on probation is violating any term or condition of probation or conditional sentence, the officer may, without warrant or other process, re-arrest the person and bring him or her before the court.

(X) Duties at Domestic Violence Calls When Arrest is Made (13701 PC)

When an arrest is made at a domestic violence call, the officer must give the victim a department-developed form stating the victim's legal options, and stating that the attacker, despite arrest, may be released on bail.

Quotas

Quotas in Arrests or Citations (41602 CVC)

No department shall establish quotas for issuance of citations or number of arrests to be made.

Quotas and Promotion (41603 CVC)

No department shall base promotion, dismissal or demotion in any part on a "quota system" for arrests or citations.

Chapter II Case Citations

Study Questions for Chapter II

(1) The famous U.S. Supreme Court decision regarding the rights of arrested persons pertaining to confessions is the ______________________________ decision.

(2) The famous U.S. Supreme Court decision regarding the rights of arrested persons pertaining to confessions was based on the________and ________ Amendments to the Constitution.

(3) The above court decision regarding confessions was unanimous. T or F

(4) An arrested person who wishes to waive his rights against self incrimination and the right to legal counsel must:

(A) ____sign a statement to that effect (B) ____nod his head in agreement

(C) ____agree verbally (D) ____have two witnesses

(5) A person who makes a private persons' arrest must notify the arrested person of this right to protection against self incrimination. T or F

(6) Only a citizen of the United States can make a "Citizen's Arrest." T or F

(7) A person who has good reason to believe that an arrest is false may resist the arrest. T or F

(8) In making a legal arrest, the arrestee must be notified of all but one of the following:

(A) ____the fact that he is under arrest (B) ____where he will be jailed

(C) ____the offense for which arrested (D) ____the authority for the arrest

(9) All arrested persons must by law be notified of their rights in order for the arrest to be legal. T or F

(10) A peace officer who is in uniform and wearing a badge need not notify an arrestee of the authority for the arrest. T or F

(11) A peace officer can never forcibly enter a home to make an arrest for a misdemeanor. T or F

(12) A private person cannot forcibly enter a home for an arrest under any circumstances. T or F

(13) A private person can arrest for a misdemeanor not committed in his presence if the suspect admits his guilt. T or F

(14) A peace officer can arrest a person for misdemeanor drunken driving even though it was not committed in his presence if an accident has occurred. T or F

(15) When a person has committed a felony, although not in his presence, a private person can arrest him. T or F

(16) Arvin Aardvark commits a felony. There is reasonable evidence to indicate to a reasonable person that he did commit it. Which of the following is true?

(A) ____A peace officer cannot arrest. (B) ____Neither of them can arrest.

(C) ____A private person can arrest. (D) ____A warrant is needed for an arrest.

(17) A private person may legally summon as many persons as he deems necessary to assist him in making an arrest. T or F

(18) The Latin term that refers to the "power of the state to summon assistance in carrying out the law" is called ____

(19) It is a felony to unnecessarily beat a prisoner. T or F

(20) If an officer makes a felony arrest based on the identification of a crime victim, and it later turns out to be a case of mistaken identity, the officer can be successfully sued in civil court for false arrest. T or F

(21) Peace officers may legally release from custody a person arrested only for being drunk, if they release him to a responsible adult. T or F

(22) A person who is under the influence of drugs may be taken to a hospital and it may be classed as not being an arrest. T or F

(23) When officers make an arrest and later find evidence that the suspect is not guilty, they shall release him and shall issue him a certificate stating that the detention was a______ ____ and not an arrest.

(24) Case law provides our major guidelines for temporarily detaining a suspect for questioning or investigation. T or F

(25) There are no specific statutory provisions for temporarily detaining a person who has done nothing, but is stopped for questioning or for investigation. T or F

(26) A criminal complaint must normally be obtained first before a warrant of arrest can be issued. T or F

(27) All felony arrest warrants list the amount or conditions of bail. T or F

(28) The D.A. can issue a warrant of arrest. T or F

(29) A private person can serve a misdemeanor warrant. T or F

(30) A felony warrant can be served day or night. T or F

(31) A misdemeanor warrant can not be served between the hours of ______________ and ____ unless endorsed.

(32) A misdemeanor warrant cannot be served at night, even in public. T or F

(33) A judge can endorse a misdemeanor traffic warrant so that it can be served at night. T or F

(34) Officers must have warrants in their possession in order to make arrests under those warrants.

T or F

(35) What may be substituted for an out-of-town warrant? ______________________

(36) Officer Smith arrests Larry Lacker on an out-of-town warrant for rape. He can be taken only before the judge issuing the warrant. T or F

(37) A person arrested on an out-of-town warrant must appear before the issuing judge ______________________ days after posting bail.

(38) If an arrestee on an out-of-town warrant does not post bail, he must be picked up by the agency where the warrant originated within ______________________ days.

(39) A warrant of arrest that was complete except for the judge's signature, would still be "regular on its face." T or F

(40) An arrested person is entitled to at least______________ phone call(s) after booking.

(41) An arrested person is entitled to make a phone call no later than ______________ hours after arrest.

(42) Local phone calls made at "booking" are at the arrestee's expense. T or F

(43) A defendant must in all cases be taken before the magistrate within__________ hours, excluding Sundays and holidays.

(44) General immunity applies only to civil arrest. T or F

(45) Miranda does not apply to juveniles. T or F

(46) In California, peace officers must Mirandize all juveniles when making an arrest. T or F

CHAPTER III

HOMICIDE

Elements

The four elements of homicide are:

(A) the killing
(B) of a human being, or a fetus
(C) by a human act or agency
(D) when death occurs within 3 years and 1 day.

Any one of the elements can be proved by circumstantial evidence, and no body need be produced in order for a conviction to be obtained. There need be no direct evidence of death produced, nor is a confession essential to a conviction. (People *v*. Scott, 176 Cal. App. 2d 458)

(A) The Killing

There need not be an intent to kill. The death, however, must be the proximate result of some human act, not necessarily a direct result, and can also be caused by omitting an act required by law.

Definition of Death

According to 7180 of the Health and Safety Code, a person shall be considered dead if he has suffered "Total and irreversible cessation of brain function." Determination will require the opinion of two independent physicians.

Transplanting Body Parts (7182 H & S)

When a part of the deceased is used for direct transplantation, neither the physician making the determination of death nor the physician making the confirmation shall participate in removing or transplanting of a part from the deceased's body.

Officer's Right to Search Bodies of Accident Victims (27491.3 Gov. Code)

This law allows officers to search deceased accident victims to see if there is a card on their person that indicates a wish to donate vital organs.

(B) A Human Being, or a Fetus

A fetus becomes a "human being" when it has been born and has established its own independent circulation, not relying on the circulation of the mother. The umbilical cord need not be severed.

The definition of the term "fetus" has changed considerably over the years. In 1976, the California Appellate Court, in People *v*. Smith (59 CA 3d 751) declared that a fetus must be viable (it moves) and must have reached the stage where it would be capable of living by itself if it were separated from the mother's womb.

(C) By a Human Act or Agency

The death cannot be brought about by an "act of God," such as a lightning bolt or a flood. It must be the result of some human act. To better understand this element, we should cover the doctrine of Proximate Cause.

Proximate Cause

Proximate cause means that whenever a death results from the natural and probable consequences of a particular act, that act is the proximate cause of the death. The key question here is: If the original act had not occurred, would the victim have been in a position where he would have died?

If a stack of dominoes were stood on end, spaced about an inch apart, and someone knocked one over, it would in turn knock the next one over and so on until the last one fell. The proximate cause of the last domino falling was the fact that someone knocked over the first one even though it was remote from the last domino.

Examples:

(a) If a non-fatal wound were opened up by movement on the part of the victim, and he bled to death, the person causing the wound would be guilty of unlawful homicide. (People *v*. Cord, 157 Ca. 562)

(b) If the victim were quite ill, and suffered a wound that in itself was not fatal, but the wound accelerated his death, the perpetrator would be guilty of unlawful homicide. (People *v*. Moan, 65 Cal. 532)

(c) If the victim were to receive a non-fatal wound from a bullet, but the victim were to die on the operating table due to the shock of the operation, the assailant would be guilty of unlawful homicide. (People *v*. Freudenberg, 121 Cal. App. 2d 564)

(d) The perpetrator hits the victim over the head and leaves him lying on a dark road at night. A short time later an automobile runs over the victim and kills him. The original assailant is guilty of unlawful homicide. If he had not left him unconscious in the road, he would not have been run over by the automobile. (People *v*. Fowler, 178 Cal. 657)

(e) The perpetrator shot the victim in the abdomen. The pain was so severe that the victim committed suicide. The person who shot him would be guilty of unlawful homicide. (People *v*. Dallen, 21 CA 770) (People *v*. Lewis, 124 Cal. 551)

(f) Two men grabbed the victim and demanded his money. In an effort to get away from them, he broke loose and fell into the path of an oncoming cable car, causing his death. The two men were guilty of unlawful homicide.

(g) A man cut his wife with a knife. In fear she ran to the bathroom and locked herself in. The wound, if treated, would not have been fatal, but the woman lost consciousness from loss of blood and then bled to death. The husband is guilty of unlawful homicide.

(h) In People *v*. Studern, 59 Cal. App. 547, the District Court of Appeals stated that if a person creates a breach of the peace and through the excitement thus induced the death of a bystander by a brain hemorrhage, that death is the natural and probable consequence of such disturbance of the peace, and such person may be convicted of manslaughter.

(D) When Death Occurs Within Three Years and a Day After the Initial Stroke or Cause of Death Administered

In the computation of such time, the whole of the day on which the act was done shall be considered the first day. (194 PC) Originally, the time was one year and one day, but due to the advances of medical science and the ability of doctors to keep a person technically alive for years, the law was changed. If the victim does not die within three years and one day, the charge would be assault with a deadly weapon, or assault with intent to commit murder.

If death occurs after that time, it is a rebuttable presumption that the killing was not criminal. This means that the D.A. can charge a defendant with unlawful homicide, but the burden of overcoming the presumption rests with the prosecution.

Mitigating Circumstances

If the prosecution proves the elements of homicide, excluding manslaughter and lawful homicide, and the defendant claims mitigating circumstances, the burden of proof for the mitigating circumstances is on the defendant. (189.5 PC)

Breakdown of Homicide in California

(A) Unlawful Homicide (Felonious)
- (1) Murder
  - (a) First Degree
  - (b) Second Degree

(2) Manslaughter
- (a) Voluntary
- (b) Involuntary
- (c) Vehicular

(B) Lawful Homicide
- (1) Excusable
- (2) Justifiable
  - (a) Peace Officers
  - (b) In General

(A) Unlawful Homicide

(1) Murder (187 PC)

Murder is the unlawful killing of a human being, or a fetus, with malice aforethought.

Malice (188 PC)

Since malice may be expressed or implied, it is expressed when there is manifested a deliberate intention unlawfully to take away the life of a fellow creature; it is implied when no considerable provocation appears, or when the circumstances attending the killing show an abandoned and malignant heart. It could be assumed from the action.

Malice is shown when an act is done in an unlawful and felonious way, intentionally and with no legal reason. When a person intentionally commits an unlawful act, and knows or should know that the act endangers the life of another, and it does result in someone's death without there being extenuating circumstances, provocation, or sudden passion, malice is presumed. (People *v.* Semone, 140 Cal. App. 318) In order for there to be malice, there need not be hatred or personal ill-will toward the victim. It does not imply deliberation. It does, however, denote a purpose and design as contrasted with accident and misfortune.

Malice in first degree murder is expressed. In second degree murder it is implied. It is sometimes difficult for juries to determine from the facts in a case whether the malice was expressed or implied.

What types of acts are necessary for murder?

(1) Willful, deliberate, and premeditated killing,
(2) Statutory violations where the intent to kill is not required,
(3) Wanton and irresponsible acts.

Penal Code Section 188 was amended to make the crime of murder applicable only to accomplices who act with malice aforethought or who were major participants in a felony that resulted in a death and who acted with reckless indifference to human life. Prior law allowed a non-killer who knowingly participated in a crime or felony that resulted in death to be convicted of the crime of

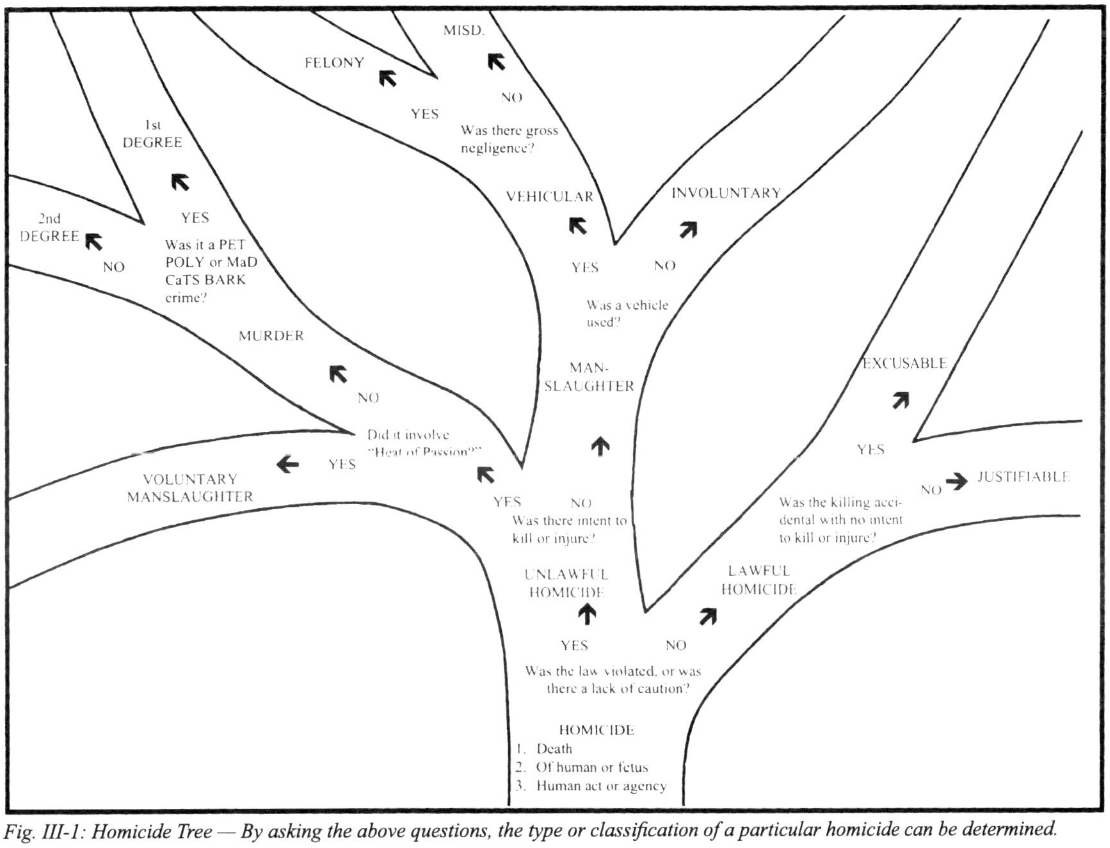

Fig. III-1: Homicide Tree — By asking the above questions, the type or classification of a particular homicide can be determined.

murder. The new law also allows persons previously convicted under the "natural and probable consequences" or "felony murder" principles to apply to have their convictions reduced or dismissed.

DEGREES OF MURDER

(1) First Degree Murder

Special Circumstances (189 PC)

There are 15 conditions that make murder first degree murder. Fourteen of them are statutory; one of them is conditional and debatable in court. Murder is first degree when the killing is perpetrated during, or by means of:

(1) Willful deliberation and premeditation;
(2) Explosives, a destructive device, (16460 PC) armor penetrating ammunition or a weapon of mass destruction (11418 PC)
(3) Torture;
(4) Poison;
(5) Lying in wait.
(This is one of the oldest known conditions for first degree murder. The Old Testament, (Exodus 21:14) states "If a man kill his neighbor on set purpose, and by lying in wait for him; thou shalt take him away from my altar that he may die.")

Felony Murder Rule

Murder is also first degree when the death results during the commission or attempt to commit one of the following crimes:

(1) mayhem
(2) drive-by shooting
(3) carjacking
(4) train wrecking
(5) torture
(6) selected sex offenses
(7) burglary
(8) arson
(9) robbery
(10) kidnapping

When the killing results from one of the statutory offenses, there need not be an intent to kill. It can be an accident.

A crime such as robbery is not over when the victim is held up. Fleeing the scene is also part of the crime; if the perpetrators hit and kill someone in a crosswalk while fleeing the scene, it still comes within the scope of the crime, and would be first degree murder. (People *v.* Chavez, 37 Cal. 2d 656)

There are two memory keys that will assist in remembering these 14 points:

MaD CaTS BARK		**PET POLY**	
Ma–	Mayhem	**P–**	Premeditated
D–	Drive-by shooting	**E–**	Explosives
		T–	Torture
Ca–	Carjacking		
T–	Train Wrecking	**Po–**	Poison
S–	Selected sex offenses (261, 286, 288, etc.)	**Ly–**	Lying in wait
B–	Burglary		
A–	Arson		
R–	Robbery		
K–	Kidnapping		

Definitions:

(1) **Willful:** means a purpose or willingness to commit the act or to omit the required act. It does not mean that the person intended to violate any law or to injure another.
(2) **Deliberate:** means that the thought was formed or arrived at, as a result of careful thought and the weighing of the various considerations. It is sometimes considered synonymous with premeditation.
(3) **Premeditation:** To think about and resolve in one's mind before doing. The length of time is not as important as the intent.

Changes went into effect on PC 189 on January 1, 2019. This law restricts the felony murder rule to apply only to people who:

(1) Actually commited the act of killing a person
(2) Aided the killing with an intent to kill
(3) Acted with reckless disregard to human life during the commission of a felony, or
(4) Participated in the commission of a felony where a law enforcement officer was the victim of homicide

This law allows those who are serving sentences for felony murder to be resentenced, and some have already been released from custody. But one judge recently sided with an Orange County prosecutor seeking felony murder charges, according to reports.

Torture With Intent to Kill

If a person tortures another with intent to kill, and that person dies, and a death penalty law is not in effect, the sentence shall be life imprisonment without possibility of parole.

Murder Because of Victim's Status (190.03 PC)

(1) When a person commits first degree murder
(2) And the killing is because of the victim's disability, gender, or sexual orientation, or
(3) Because of the defendant's perception of that status,
(4) The sentence shall be life without the possibility of parole.

Conviction By Judge Without Jury (190.05(f) PC)

If the defendant was convicted by a judge, sitting without a jury, the penalty hearing shall be by a jury unless waived by the defendant and the prosecutor. This also applies if the defendant pled guilty or *nolo contendre.*

The Death Penalty

In 1967, the California Supreme Court, in Rockwell *v.* Superior Court, declared the death penalty unconstitutional because it was mandatory and did not allow for mitigating circumstances.

In 1972, in the Furman Decision, the U.S. Supreme Court stated that the death penalty, as it was then being administered in certain states, could be a possible violation of the Eighth Amendment (Cruel and Unusual Punishment) and the Fourteenth Amendment (Equal Protection Under the Law). As a result, more than 30 states enacted new capital punishment laws.

In 1976, the U.S. Supreme Court decided that capital punishment was permissible in certain cases. The high court upheld the laws of Florida, Texas and Georgia. These states required a separate stage in the trial in which the "trier of fact" can consider mitigating circumstances. (Those which tend to reduce the seriousness of the act), and aggravating circumstances (Those which appear to make the action more serious).

As a result, a new capital punishment bill was presented to the legislature by Senator Deukmejian (SB 155). It was passed by the legislature and vetoed by Governor Brown. On August 11, 1977, the veto was overridden by the legislature, and the new death penalty became law.

The Death Penalty Bill (190.1 PC)

This bill creates a three phase process that determines whether a defendant will actually be sentenced to death.

PHASE I:

Innocence or guilt is determined by the "trier of fact."

PHASE II: (PC 190.2)

Special circumstances are determined. This can be from the same trial in which the defendant is found guilty. The Special Circumstances are:

(1) Victim killed for financial gain (contract).
(2) Defendant has prior murder conviction.
(3) Defendant guilty of multiple murders.
(4) Murder committed by explosives.
(5) Committed while avoiding arrest or escaping from authorities.
(6) Committed by explosives that were delivered or mailed.
(7) Victim was a peace officer on duty or a former peace officer and was killed intentionally in retaliation because of past duties.
(8) Victim was a federal peace officer on duty or off duty and killing was for purpose of retaliation.
(9) Victim was a firefighter on duty.
(10) Victim was a witness killed to prevent testimony and killing was not part of original crime.
(11) Victim was prosecutor killed for retaliation.
(12) Victim was a judge or former judge killed in retaliation.
(13) Victim was a government official killed in retaliation.
(14) Killing was heinous, atrocious or cruel.
(15) Killed by lying in wait.
(16) Victim killed because of race, color, religion or nationality.
(17) Committed during commission of or while fleeing the scene of the following crimes:
    (a) Robbery (211 or 212.5 PC)
    (b) Kidnapping (207, 209, or 209.5 PC)
    (c) Rape (261 PC)
    (d) Sodomy (286 PC)
    (e) Child Molesting (288 PC)
    (f) Oral Copulation (287 or former 288a PC)
    (g) Burglary (460 PC)
    (h) Arson (451 PC)
    (i) Train Wrecking (219 PC)

(j) Mayhem (203 PC)
(k) Rape by Instrument (289 PC)
(l) Carjacking (215 PC)

Note: To prove the special circumstances of kidnapping or arson if there is specific intent to kill, it is only required that there be proof of the elements of those felonies. If so established, those two special circumstances are proven even if the felony of kidnapping or arson is committed primarily or solely for the purpose of facilitating the murder.

(18) Murder involved torture.
(19) Victim killed by poison.
(20) Retaliation against juror.
(21) Drive-by shooting.
(22) With intent to kill, but was a principal and not the actual killer.
(23) With reckless indifference to human life and as a major participant aids, abets, counsels, etc. one of the above crimes.

PHASE III: (190.3 PC)

In this phase, the prosecution can introduce evidence that shows "aggravating circumstances," and the defense can introduce evidence to show "mitigating circumstances." There are limits to what the prosecution can introduce. Only evidence of prior violent convictions can be admitted. The defense must be made aware of this evidence beforehand so they may prepare a rebuttal. Types of "mitigating circumstances" that may be presented in this phase are the defendant's mental state, his age and the actual extent of participation in the murder. If the jury is unable to reach a unanimous verdict on the "special circumstances," there is an automatic sentence of life imprisonment without possibility of parole.

This bill "allows the Trier of Fact to focus on the individual, to examine what kind of person he or she is, and what punishment is appropriate to the crime committed."

Finding Special Circumstances (190.4 PC)

If more than one special circumstances is charged, the trier of fact must rule on each special circumstance based on evidence presented at the trial. Reasonable doubt about any special circumstance will negate a finding on that special circumstance. The trier of fact must find the special circumstance either true or untrue.

If the defendant was convicted by a court trial (before a judge only) or plead guilty, the special circumstances shall be determined by a jury. If both sides agree, the defendant can waive the jury and the special circumstances will be determined by a judge.

If, in phase II, the trier of fact determines that one or more special circumstances is true, the next step is phase III where a special hearing will determine the final punishment.

If the jury trier of fact cannot decide by a unanimous verdict, the court will dismiss the jury and impanel a new one. If the second jury is unable to reach a unanimous verdict, the judge can either impanel another jury, or sentence the defendant to 25 years in prison.

When a jury returns a verdict imposing the death penalty, the judge must automatically review that verdict and state on the court record the legal basis for his or her reasoning. Section 1181 PC lists the reasons for a retrial.

All death verdicts receive an automatic appeal. (1239 PC)

In the penalty phase, if the jury cannot reach a unanimous verdict on the punishment the judge will impanel a new jury. If the new jury cannot reach a verdict, the judge can either impanel another jury or sentence the defendant to life imprisonment, without possibility of parole.

Death Penalty Not Imposed on Minors (190.5 PC)

The death penalty shall not be imposed upon any person who is under the age of 18 at the time of the commission of a crime.

Killing Operator of Paid Transportation (190.25 PC)

When someone kills the driver of paid transportation for hire, or a ticket or station agent for the organization when he should reasonably know that the victim worked in such capacity, the punishment is life without parole.

"End of Life Option Act" (443 HSC)

An adult with the capacity to make medical decisions may opt for an aid-in-dying drug if they have a physician-confirmed terminal disease. They must be able to self-administer the drug. There are several steps/requirements that must be satisfied to make this a legal procedure. The terminally ill person must request the aid-in-dying drug in writing using the form listed in HSC 443.11.

Knowingly altering or forging a request for an aid-in-dying drug to end an individual's life without his or her authorization, or concealing or destroying a withdrawal or rescission of a request for an aid-in-dying drug is punishable as a felony if the act is done with the intent or effect of causing the individual's death (443.17 HSC).

Knowingly coercing or exerting undue influence on an individual to request or ingest an aid-in-dying drug for the purpose of ending his or her life, or to destroy a withdrawal or rescission of a request, or to administer an aid-in-dying drug to an individual without his or her knowledge or consent, is punishable as a felony (443.17 HSC).

Death Penalty Method (3604 PC)

(1) When a defendant is sentenced to death, he or she may choose either lethal gas or injection.
(2) If the prisoner refuses to choose, death shall be by lethal injection.

(b) Second Degree Murder

Second degree murder is distinguishable from first degree murder in that, while the element of malice aforethought is present in both, the killing is not premeditated and is without considerable provocation. Malice in first degree murder is expressed while the malice in second degree murder is implied. *(See malice.)*

If the killing is committed during a felony not listed under first degree, it is at least second degree murder. If it is an act involving natural consequences dangerous to life, and the person performing the act knows this, the act need not be unlawful for any resulting death to be classed as second degree murder. (People *v*. Phillips, 64 A.C. 629). An example would be dropping coins from a tall building onto a sidewalk where people are passing, not intending to hit anyone, but by accident hitting and killing a pedestrian.

Although most deaths resulting from drunken driving are classed as vehicular manslaughter, they can be classed as second degree murder. In People *v*. Wallace, 2 Cal. App. 2d 238, the courts affirmed that the death of a pedestrian as the result of the defendant driving an automobile while intoxicated could be classed as second degree murder. This also applies to deaths that result from the irresponsible driving of a stolen vehicle. (People *v*. Pulley, 225 Cal. App. 2d 366).

The malice required for second degree murder may be shown by the severity and extent of injuries inflicted upon the victim, or by the condition in which the victim is left by the perpetrator. (People *v*. Taylor, 189 Cal. App. 2d 490)

When an adult administers narcotics to a minor, and the minor dies from the injection, it is classed as second degree murder since it involves a felony. (People *v*. Poindexter, 51 Cal. 2d 142)

Inherently Dangerous Misdemeanors

If a wanton act is intentionally performed, and the natural consequences of that act are dangerous to human life, any death resulting from such act is murder of the second degree, even though the unlawful act may only amount to a misdemeanor. (People *v*. Copley, 32 Cal. App. 2d 74) In order for the misdemeanor to qualify, it must be one that is inherently dangerous to human life.

Example: If a parent abandoned a young child on a busy freeway at night it would be a violation of 271 PC or 273a PC, both misdemeanors. If, in panic, the child were to run out into traffic and be killed, the parent would then be guilty of murder in the second degree because the misdemeanor was inherently dangerous.

(2) Manslaughter (there are three types) (192 PC)

192(a) Voluntary manslaughter

In voluntary manslaughter, there is the intent to kill, but it is brought on by sufficient provocation. This provocation is called "Heat of Passion."

Voluntary manslaughter is a willful act, engendered by sufficient provocation, and characterized by the presence of an intent to kill and the absence of premeditation, deliberation, and malice aforethought... To be sufficient to reduce a homicide to manslaughter, the heat of passion must be such as would naturally be aroused in the mind of an ordinary, reasonable person (a person of ordinary self-control) under the same facts and circumstances. (People *v*. Bridgehouse, 47 Cal. 2d 406)

The heat of passion which will reduce a killing to manslaughter may be created by words of abuse or reproach. (People *v*. Valentine, 28 Cal. 2d 121)

The classic "textbook" example of voluntary manslaughter: A husband goes on a hunting trip. Because the hunting is bad, he returns home two days early. When he enters the house, gun in hand, he finds his wife in bed with a neighbor. He loses his temper and shoots his wife or the neighbor.

This is a "textbook" example because the jury will nearly always find the defendant guilty of voluntary manslaughter, even in cases where it appears that the shooting may not have involved heat of passion. The jury feel they are upholding the moral standards of the community. If they find the defendant guilty of second or first degree murder, they are in effect saying that finding your spouse in bed with another is really not that serious, and that one should not lose one's temper in such a situation.

As of January 2015, a California defendant charged with first degree murder will no longer be able to argue that, because he killed while in the throes of "gay panic," his act constituted the lesser offense of voluntary manslaughter. (California Assembly Bill 2501; Penal Code section 192(a) and (f).)

California's new law represents the Legislature and Governor's finding that no reasonable person, upon discovering the true sex of a potential or actual sexual partner, would fly into a rage or panic and kill the partner. (The law says it's "objectively unreasonable" for someone to react this way.)

The new law is intended to prevent the legal consequences of the following scenarios: The defendant and the victim are engaged in romantic activities when the defendant discovers that the victim is not of the gender that the defendant thought he or she was; or the victim attempts to initiate unwanted sexual conduct with the defendant. The defendant reacts by killing the victim, and is charged with murder.

Those who argue against the death penalty often use the argument that most murders are done in the heat of passion when the person does not think about the penalty. Whether a person is for or against the death penalty, any student of law should know that a killing under these circumstances is classed as voluntary manslaughter. There is no state that has death as punishment for voluntary manslaughter, only first degree murder.

(b) Involuntary Manslaughter (192(b) PC)

There are three conditions that could cause a death to come under the classification of involuntary manslaughter. They are:

(1) In the commission of a misdemeanor.
Example: Clyde Crashcup gets mad at Homer Hashbrown and punches him in the nose while they are working at a construction site. Homer loses his balance and falls onto a piece of reinforcing rod. It punctures a vital organ and Homer dies. There is no intent to kill, but the proximate cause of the death is the misdemeanor that Clyde committed by punching Homer in the nose.

(2) In the commission of a lawful act that might produce death in an unlawful manner, or without due caution and circumspection.
Example: Bernard Boozer goes hunting with his new high-powered rifle. He stays up late the first night playing cards and "hitting the bottle." The next morning he goes out hunting for a deer. After an hour of seeing nothing, he notices some movement in a clump of bushes. He aims his rifle and fires. Out rolls another hunter, shot through the head. Bernard was performing a legal act. He had a license from the state of California authorizing him to hunt deer. However, he did this act without due caution and circumspection.

(3) Failure to perform a legal duty. (This is not listed in the code, but is listed in case law; it is the "omission" side of #1).
Example: Millie Munchkin has an illegitimate son. She finds his presence painful, so she locks him up in the attic. Because she finds him psychologically unpleasant, she often forgets to feed him. As a result, he finally dies from malnutrition. Section 270 of the Penal Code makes it a legal duty for parents to feed their children.

A more recent well-publicized example of involuntary manslaughter was the case of People *vs.* Conrad Murray who was hired by Pop Star Michael Jackson as a personal physician. Dr. Murray administered a sedative to Mr. Jackson that is normally used only in a surgical environment, and Mr. Jackson subsequently died. The prosecution was able to prove gross negligence, and the jury found Dr. Murray guilty of involuntary manslaughter with the maximum sentence of 4 years.

In involuntary manslaughter there is no intent to kill. The law also states that none of these subdivisions apply to acts committed in driving a vehicle.

(c) Vehicular Manslaughter (192(c) PC)

In Vehicular Manslaughter, there is no intent to kill. It is similar to Involuntary Manslaughter except it involves a vehicle or vessel. If the act involves Gross Negligence, the punishment is greater. The following acts do not involve driving or operating while under the influence.

(1) Commission of a misdemeanor, with gross negligence.
Example: Arvin drives 60 miles an hour in a residential area, skids around a corner on two wheels, hits a child in the street and kills her.

(2) Commission of a misdemeanor with no gross negligence.
Example: Sam is driving 35 MPH in a 25 MPH zone, and hits a young child who runs into the street.

(3) Commission of a lawful act which might produce death in an unlawful manner, with gross negligence.
Example: Fred has a driver's license and is driving under the speed limit. A car full of girls comes alongside Fred's car. They invite his passenger, Larry, to join them. Fred tells Larry to lean out the window and he will drive close to the other car so Larry can climb over. As Fred moves his car closer, Larry slips and falls half out of the car. Fred drives too close and Larry is crushed between the two cars.

(4) Commission of a lawful act which might produce death in an unlawful manner, with no gross negligence.
Example: Henry has a driver's license and always drives under the speed limit. He is giving some friends a lift home from high school, and the car is full. Mike, another friend, asks for a lift also, but since the car is full, Henry tells Mike he will have to ride on the hood of the car. Mike hops on the hood and Henry takes off driving about 20 MPH. As Henry drives down the street, a car pulls out of a driveway and Henry slams on the brakes. Mike flies off the hood into the path of the other car and is killed.

The following acts involve killing another while driving under the influence, but without gross negligence.

(5) Driving under the influence and while committing a misdemeanor.
Example: Tom is driving while under the influence. He is doing 30 MPH in a 25 MPH zone. He hits and kills a woman in a crosswalk.

(6) Driving under the influence and driving lawfully, but in a way which might produce death (e.g., without due caution).
Example: Al is driving while under the influence. He has a driver's license and is driving just under the speed limit. He hits and kills a woman crossing the street.

Proximate Cause:

Section 191.5(f) PC states that in Vehicular Manslaughter the death must be a proximate result of committing the unlawful act, or the lawful act which might produce death.

Death Resulting From Fraudulent Accident (192(c)(3) PC)

Driving a vehicle in connection with a violation of Making Fraudulent Claims (550 PC), where the vehicular collision or vehicular accident was knowingly caused for financial gain and proximately resulted in the death of any person. This provision shall not be construed to prevent prosecution of a defendant for the crime of murder. (People *v.* Watson, 30 Cal 3d 290)

Gross Vehicular Manslaughter While Intoxicated (191.5 PC)

The unlawful killing of a human being without malice aforethought while driving a vehicle in violation of 23140, 23152, or 23153 CVC, or operating a vessel in violation of 655 H & N Code (DUI), when the killing is the proximate result of:

(1) Commission of misdemeanor (apart from driving while intoxicated) with gross negligence.
Example: Tom has been drinking and is intoxicated. As he is driving home he stops at a red light next to a friend. He challenges the friend to race him to the next light. When the light turns green Tom accelerates quickly to a very high speed. Near the end of the block an elderly man steps out from behind a parked car and is hit by Tom's car. He dies.

(2) Commission of a lawful act (apart from driving while intoxicated) which might produce death in an unlawful manner (e.g., driving without due caution), and with gross negligence.
Example: Al is driving while under the influence of alcohol. He has a license and is driving just under the speed limit. He is so drunk that he drives onto the curb, hits a

group of people standing at a bus stop, and kills two of them.

Gross Negligence:

The term "Gross Negligence" is a question of fact for the jury to decide. Some courts have called it "throwing all caution to the wind," "a complete lack of diligence," or "a complete indifference to safety." The term shall not prohibit a charge of murder when facts show wantonness and a conscious disregard for life to support a finding of implied malice, or of other evidence showing malice. (People *v*. Watson, 30 Cal 3d 290) (1981)

Examples of Gross Negligence:

- Driving 80 miles an hour on a city street (People *v*. Markham, 153 Cal. App. 2d 260);
- Drag racing on a city street (People *v*. Kemp, 150 Cal. App. 2d 654);
- Hitting a person in a marked safety zone when it was clearly marked and visibility was good (People *v*. Flores, 83 CA 2d 11).

(3) Lawful Homicide

(A) Excusable Homicide (195 PC)

There are three things to look for in classifying a death under the heading of excusable homicide:

(a) There is no intent to kill.
(b) No law is violated (lawful homicide).
(c) There is no lack of due caution.

The key words to excusable homicide are accident and misfortune. The two sets of conditions that make a death excusable homicide are:

(1) Committed by accident and misfortune when doing any lawful act by lawful means with usual and ordinary caution, without unlawful intent.
(2) When committed:
   (a) by accident and misfortune in the heat of passion upon any sudden or sufficient provocation, OR
   (b) by accident and misfortune upon a sudden combat when no undue advantage is taken nor any dangerous weapon used when the killing is not done in a cruel or unusual manner.

Examples:

(1a) A father has told his son not to shoot his BB gun in the back yard when other kids are present. He looks out the kitchen window and sees him doing just that. He calls him in and tells him that he did not obey and he is going to get a spanking. The father gives his son one good swat, and the boy feels that he has had enough. He wiggles loose from his father's grip and falls against the stove, hitting his head. It causes a bad concussion that kills him.

(1b) Officer Smith is cleaning his gun in the kitchen. When he is finished, he reloads it and starts to put it back into his holster. It slips out of his hands, falls to the floor and fires. The bullet goes through the wall into the next room and kills Officer Smith's sleeping baby.

(2a) You are walking down the main street in town with your wife. There are a bunch of "scumbags" loitering around the front of one store. As you and your wife pass, one of them lifts up the back of your wife's dress with a long bamboo cane and makes an obscene remark. You blow your top and punch him in the nose. He falls back and his head hits the bumper of a parked car. The blow to his head kills him. Explanation: The death was not intentional; it was by accident and misfortune. The proximate cause was the punch in the nose. This was brought about by heat of passion, by an act that would be both sudden and sufficient provocation. No undue advantage was taken. No dangerous weapons were used, and the killing was not done in a cruel or unusual manner.

(2b) You are sitting in a bar when a big fight starts, and everyone joins in. Someone comes up to you and takes a swing. You jump up and punch him in the nose. He falls and hits his head against the brass rail at the bar. This causes a concussion which kills him.

(4) Justifiable Homicide

(There is the intent to kill or injure)

Two classifications: justifiable homicide by peace officers, and justifiable homicide in general. Justifiable homicide is lawful homicide for which there is no criminal punishment. (199 PC)

(a) Justifiable Homicide by Peace Officers (196 PC)

(1) In obedience to any judgment of a competent court. (execution)
This section was enacted in 1872, and there were no changes until January 1, 2020. Prior to this update, police could use lethal force under reasonable circumstances. Under the new law, an officer can use lethal force only when necessary.

(2) When the homicide results from a peace officer's use of force that is in compliance with Section 835a.

(3) **835a PC - Police Officer Use of Deadly Force - Definitions**

A peace officer is justified in using deadly force upoon another person only when the officer believes, based on the totality of the circumstances, that such force is necessary for either of the following reasons:

(a) To defend against an imminent threat of death or serious bodily injury to the officer or another person,

(b) To apprehend a fleeing person for any felony that threatened or resulted in death or serious bodily injury, if the offier reasonably believes that the person will cause death or serious bodily injury to another unless immediately apprehended.

(i) A peace officer shall make reasonable efforts prior to the use of force to identify themselves as a peace officer and warn that deadly force may be used unless the officer has grounds to believe the person is aware of those facts.

A peace officer shall not use deadly force against a person based on the danger that person poses to themselves.

In addition to narrowing the circumstances under which a police officer can use lethal force, the legislation also means that after a deadly shooting, the actions of police officers that led up to the violent encounter will be considered in the decision of whether or not the shooting was in fact "necessary." Since the law is new, it remains to be seen how it will affect court cases where police officers have historically been successful in defending their decision to kill a suspect.

Peterson *v.* City of Long Beach

The California Appellate Court in Peterson *v.* City of Long Beach et. al., ruled the shooting of a fleeing burglary suspect was not justified because he was running away from the officer, was apparently not armed, and presented no threat of great bodily harm. This decision seems to give burglars a license to run. Most important, it overrules the statutory law (fleeing felons).

(b) Justifiable Homicide Generally (Including Peace Officers) (197 PC)

(1) When resisting any attempt at murder or a felony, or to do great bodily injury on any person. Since murder is a felony, it need not have been included in this section. It was put there as an example. The part on an "attempt to do great bodily injury on any person" is a debatable matter. What action would amount to an attempt at great bodily injury?

The other party in this situation is dead and cannot testify. Usually this section applies when a person comes to the aid of another who is being victimized. The victim's testimony is also important.

(2) Defense of habitation, or property or person, against one who:

(a) manifestly intends by

(i) violence or

(ii) surprise

(b) to enter the habitation of another

(c) to commit a felony or do some great bodily injury upon any person

OR:

(a) manifestly intends in a violent, riotous, or tumultuous manner

(b) to enter the habitation of another

(c) for the purpose of offering violence to any person inside.

The second part needs little explanation. If a person tries to violently enter a house, his actions in themselves justify both fear and self-defense. There are some key words in the first part. They are "manifestly," "surprise," and "to commit a felony." (Violence is covered in part 2.)

Manifestly means that the perpetrator does some particular act that leaves no doubt as to his intent. Examples might be cutting the screen outside a bedroom window so the person could then jimmy the window open, using some device such as a jimmy on an outside door, or turning the doorknob on a door and entering the house.

Although there is not a great deal of case law in this matter, the California Supreme Court in People *v.* Flanagan, 50 Cal. 2, stated that "the killing must be actually or apparently necessary." The term "apparently" leaves much room for interpretation, and since the other party is dead, we have only the word of the person doing the killing.

Example:

A woman shoots her husband coming in the house late at night. She tells the police that she thought it was a burglar, and that her husband told her he was not coming home for another day or two. Even if she murdered him, it would be almost impossible to obtain a conviction in court, especially if she was a good actor and shed lots of tears for her "dear, beloved husband."

The term "surprise" means that the perpetrator, or "victim" in the killing, performed his manifest act in such a way as to avoid detection. The term "to commit a felony" is more difficult. The courts allow a certain amount of conjecture. Why did the person try to enter the house in a surreptitious manner if not for the purpose of a felony? Even if it was to steal some small item, it would still be burglary and that is a felony.

Occasionally a householder will kill someone entering the house at night by accident and misfortune. A woman who lived alone heard a noise like someone opening a window in the middle of the night. She got a gun and went to the bedroom that belonged to her son, opened the door and saw a figure coming through the window. She shot and killed the intruder, who turned out to be her son who was in the Navy. His ship had come in for repairs and he was given a last minute leave. He arrived home very late and did not want to wake his mother, so he tried to get into his own bedroom through the window. Why wouldn't this be classed as excusable homicide? It was by misfortune. The answer is that the woman did intend to either kill or injure the person she shot. In excusable homicide, there is no intent to kill or injure.

(1) Killing of Trespassers

There seems to be a common misunderstanding among the general public regarding the killing of trespassers. Trespassing is a misdemeanor. Unless the trespasser makes some manifest act that would indicate an intent to enter the habitation, he is just a misdemeanor trespasser. He may be arrested, and that force used that is necessary to effect the arrest, but no deadly force may be used based solely on the fact that he is trespassing. (People *v.* Corlett, 67 Cal. App. 2d 33) Any person killing another for trespassing alone is guilty of felonious homicide. (People *v.* Doyell, 48 Cal. 85)

(2) Warning to Intruder: Defense of Habitation

When a person feels that the intruders might be armed and dangerous, he is under no obligation to give warnings before shooting. (Nakashima *v.* Takara, 8 Cal. App. 2d 35)

(c) Self Defense (and defense of certain others) Limitations (198 PC)

Section 197 PC states that self defense is lawful when there are reasonable grounds to apprehend a design to do some great bodily injury, and imminent danger of such design being accomplished. In order for self defense to be legal, it must appear to the person who is fearful of attack, as a reasonable person, not only that there is reason to believe he or she is in danger of receiving great bodily harm, but that he or she actually does believe this (People *v.* Head, 105 Cal. App. 331). In other words, there needs to be evidence that the danger exists, and the person must believe it.

(1) Bare Fear

Section 198 PC states that bare fear alone cannot justify a killing. There has to be some circumstance or overt act apart from this fear. Otherwise, every little old lady on the street at night could be shooting every man that came near her because she was sincerely fearful that they would attack her. The fear, along with some overt act, must not be based on subjective feelings. It must be fear that would be aroused in the average person in like circumstances.

(2) Previous Threats

Previous threats by themselves, when not accompanied by some hostile act, would not justify a homicide. (People *v.* Lynch, 101 Cal. 229)

Sam Slipshod tells Freddie Farkle in front of 100 witnesses that the next time he sees him he is going to kill him. The next day Sam comes to Freddie's house and knocks on the front door. Freddie could not shoot Sam when he opens the door. Sam would first have to commit some overt act that would cause a reasonable person to feel he was about to commit great bodily harm. It could be very slight. Reaching into his coat would be an example. The law does not require that the person wait until the assailant actually pulls out a gun and points it at him and starts to pull the trigger before he can act. (People *v.* Hatchett, 63 Cal. App. 2d 144)

(3) Overt Acts Cannot be Created by Slayer

The law does not allow the slayer to create a situation where the person slain is challenged to fight or goaded into losing his temper and during the altercation makes some overt act that might justify self defense. (People *v.* Finall, 31 C.A. 479)

(4) Amount of Force Limited by Circumstances

The defense must be against great bodily harm and not just a simple battery. Again, the justification must be based on that of a reasonable man and not just the slayer. The force used must be reasonable. (People *v.* Morine, 61 Cal. 371)

(5) There is No Duty to Retreat in California

In some states and in many countries, it is required that a person who is attacked take one step back to show he does not wish to become involved in combat. In California, a person may not only stand his ground and defend himself, but he may pursue his assailant until he has secured himself from danger. (People *v.* Zuckerman, 56 C.A. 2d 366). It is to the slayer's advantage, how-ever, if it can be shown that he did retreat, and that the attacker continued his assault. It would help remove any suspicion that the slayer acted hastily.

(6) When the Danger Has Passed, So Has the Justification

Once the danger from great bodily injury has passed, so has the justification for using deadly force against the attacker. The right to self defense exists only as long as the danger itself exists. (People *v.* Keys, 62 C.A. 2d 903). An exception would be if the assailant is running off to better arm himself. In this situation, the danger has not ceased but threatens to become greater.

If Horace Hickle attacks Lester Lump with a club which Lester is able to dodge, and Horace runs off stating "I'm going into the house to get a shotgun to finish you off," the danger has not ceased. It has increased. Lester will have a difficult time dodging a shotgun. At this point, although Horace appears to be retreating, Lester can use deadly force in self defense.

(7) The Instigator in a Fight Loses the Right to Self Defense

The person who starts the fight cannot use the excuse of self defense. It is too difficult to determine whether a fight was started to create a situation where the instigator can kill the other person. Percy Pester comes into a bar looking for a fight. He sees Arnold Aardvark having a beer. Arnold is smaller than he is, so he knocks his beer over. Arnold objects and Percy tells him to come outside or he will "deck" him right there. They go outside to fight. Arnold is a better fighter than Percy thought. Percy becomes fearful that Arnold will cause him great bodily injury, so he pulls out a knife and stabs Arnold, who dies. Percy claims self defense and uses the doctor's report to show how badly Arnold had beaten him. Percy has no defense since he was the instigator of the fight.

Exceptions:

(1) A peace officer never loses the right to self defense using objectively reasonable force (835a PC)
(2) If the instigator of a fight gives up, and the fight continues, he can regain the right to self defense. (People *v.* Hoover, 107 C.A. 635)
(3) Private persons making legal arrests.

The reason that a peace officer never loses the right to self defense even though he may be the instigator, is because when he is the instigator he is acting in behalf of the state and law and order. There are times when he must instigate the action. He places a person under arrest, and that person refuses to go. He first tries to talk the prisoner into going along peacefully, but there comes a time when he must lay hands on him and forcibly restrain him. (Also private person's arrest.)

When a private person is the instigator of a fight, and then gives up, he is in effect ending the first fight. Percy is getting the worst of the fight that he started, so he tells Arnold "you're a better man than I thought; I give up." Technically the first fight is now ended. Arnold replies "You might have given up, but I just got started," and continues to fight. Percy can now legally use self defense.

(8) Mutual Combat (197 PC)

There is a difference between a duel and mutual combat. A duel is any combat with deadly weapons, fought between two or more persons, by previous agreement, or upon previous quarrel. Mutual combat is simply physical combat with or without weapons that has been agreed upon by all parties involved. In mutual combat, both parties are considered instigators so both parties lose the right to self-defense, unless one of them gives up. Killing another in mutual combat is murder. (People *v.* Bush, 65 Cal. 129)

(d) When Apprehending a Felon, Lawfully Suppressing Any Riot, or Lawfully Keeping and Preserving the Peace, When Done by Lawful Ways & Means

The legislative intent of this section is to encourage citizens to assist in the preservation of the peace. This does not allow citizens to grab a shotgun and go to a riot and start shooting people. There must be an apparent or real imminent danger involved. (People *v.* Roe, 189 Cal. 548) At many riots, however, there is this danger. Today it is very doubtful that the police would welcome a group of irate, trigger-happy citizens at the scene of a riot. They have enough trouble on their hands as it is.

Mandatory Duty to Report Murder Etc. (152.3 PC)

(1) Those persons who reasonably believe that they observed the commission of
 (a) Murder (187 PC)
 (b) Rape (261 PC)
 (c) Child Molesting (288 PC)
(2) And the victim is under 14 years of age
(3) Shall report the crime to a peace officer
(4) By any means of communication.
(5) Failure to do so is a misdemeanor.
 Exceptions:
 (a) Those related to any of the parties by blood or marriage.
 (b) Those covered by privileged communications. (e.g. Attorney)
 (c) Those whose failure is based on mistake of fact.
 (d) Those whose failure is based on reasonable fear for their safety or that of their family.

SUICIDE

Aiding and Abetting Suicide (401 PC)

(1) Every person who deliberately aids, advises or encourages,
(2) Another to commit suicide,
(3) Is guilty of a felony,
(4) Except when their actions are compliant with the provisions of the End of Life Option Act H & S Code, Div. 1, Part 1.85, Section 443.

ACCIDENTAL DEATH

Concealment of Accidental Death (152 PC)

(1) Every person who, having knowledge of an accidental death,
(2) Actively conceals or attempts to conceal that death
(3) By either:
 (a) concealing the body, or
 (b) impeding the discovery of the body, or
 (c) destroying evidence or instrumentalities of death
(4) Is guilty of a misdemeanor.

Chapter III Case Citations

Study Questions for Chapter III

(1) In a trial for homicide, a conviction cannot be had unless the body of the victim has been found. T or F

(2) Whenever a death results from the natural and probably consequences of a particular human act, it is said that the person responsible for that act is guilty of homicide under the Doctrine of ______________________

(3) Ronella Rimp shoots her boyfriend Herbert Hickup with a .22 pistol after she loses her temper in an argument. It is a minor wound, but Herbert is taken to the hospital to have the bullet removed. The hospital is crowded and Herbert is left on a gurney in the cold hallway of the hospital. He dies from shock. Ronella is guilty of unlawful homicide. T or F

(4) Three men stop Lester Lump and try to rob him. He tries to get away from them, and in doing so, he runs in front of a bus in a fit of panic. The bus hits and kills him. The three men are guilty of unlawful homicide. T or F

(5) In order for a death to be classed as a homicide, the victim must die within what time? ______________________ and ______________________

(6) If the defendant in a homicide trial presents mitigating circumstances, the burden of proof for those mitigating circumstances rests with the defendant. T or F

(7) The Penal Code section for Murder is ______________________ PC.

(8) The malice aforethought in First Degree murder is expressed. In Second Degree murder it is ______________________

(9) In order for there to be malice in murder, there must be a feeling of personal ill will toward the victim. T or F

(10) Percy Pester poisons his wife Priscilla. Percy is guilty of what class of homicide? ____ ______________________ and ______________________

(11) Pete Paranoid is mad at the Post Office for firing him. He plants a bomb in the entrance of the Post Office so that it will go off late at night and not injure anyone. At the time that it goes off, a custodian is sweeping up and is killed. Pete is guilty of what class of homicide? ______________________

(12) The "Ca" in MaD CaTTS BARK stands for ______________________

(13) Perry Pyro sets fire to his abandoned building at night so that he can collect insurance on it. Unknown to Perry, there is a vagrant sleeping under the house. He is burned to death. Perry is guilty of arson and ______________________

(14) In legal terminology, the term "willful" means that the person willfully intended to violate the law or injure another. T or F

(15) All deaths that result from the commission of a felony are classed as at least ________ ______________________

(16) If a person committed a wanton misdemeanor that resulted in a death, he could be guilty of murder. T or F

(17) A death from driving while intoxicated could be classed as second degree murder. T or F

(18) The severity and extent of injuries can be used to show the malice in second degree murder. T or F

(19) In voluntary manslaughter, there is the intent to kill. T or F

(20) In voluntary manslaughter, the term "heat of passion" is judged by the subjective feelings of the slayers and not how others might feel in that situation. T or F

(21) Many persons who commit murder do so in the "heat of passion." T or F

(22) While committing a misdemeanor, Arvin Aardvark accidentally kills someone. The death would be classed as ______________________________

(23) Because Betsey Bloominheimer neglects her child, the child starves to death. The death would be classed as ______________________________

(24) Herbert Honbone goes rabbit hunting. While hunting, he comes across an abandoned shed. Just for the fun of it, he fires several shots into the shed. Unknown to him there were two boys playing in the shed, and a bullet killed one of them. What classification of homicide is this? ______________________________

(25) Clyde Crashcup kills Fred Farkle in an auto accident after Clyde went through a stop sign. Clyde is guilty of what type of homicide? ____________________

(26) Harvey Hinkle is driving under the speed limit and kills a young child who jumps out in front of his car from behind a parked car. This is classed as what type of homicide?

____

(27) Vehicular Manslaughter is classed as a felony when it can be shown that there was ___ ______________________________ on the part of the driver.

(28) Hector Honk spanks his son for stealing something. Unknown to Hector, his son had a bad heart, and a valve ruptures during the spanking. His son dies. Hector is guilty of what type of homicide? ______________________________

(29) Harry Hucklebump is working on the roof of his house, repairing shingles. His hammer slips from his hands and slides off the roof and falls on his baby son who is laying on a blanket on the lawn. It hits the baby in the head and kills him. Harry has committed what type of homicide? ______________________________

(30) An execution is an example of what type of homicide? ____________________

(31) Officer Jones receives a call on the radio regarding a bank robbery in progress. He arrives just as the robber runs out the front door of the bank with a bag of money. Officer Jones sees the robber has a gun. After two more warnings, Officer Jones shoots at the robber and kills him. This is classed as what type of homicide according to the Penal Code? ______________________________

(32) One night Buster Badbetter, a private person, hears a woman scream. He looks out the window and sees Harry Hotsocks trying to forcibly rape a woman in the lot next door. He grabs his deer rifle and shoots Harry while he is attempting this felony. If he kills Harry, it would be classed as ______________________________

(33) Franny Farkle hears a noise at night. Her husband is away on business. She grabs a gun and goes to the kitchen where she sees someone starting to climb in the window. If she shoots and kills the intruder, it would be classed as______________________

(34) Fanny is very upset at killing the intruder and after the police leave, she tries to go back to sleep but finds it very difficult. After an hour she hears another noise. She grabs her gun again and looks out the window. She sees a prowler sneaking around the yard. Because she is afraid that he might break in, she shoots and kills him in the backyard. This would be classed as ______________________________

(35) In order to kill an intruder under "Defense of Habitation," the householder or slayer must give a warning before shooting the intruder who is entering his house. T or F

(36) In claiming "Self Defense," a slayer has a legal defense based on a combination of bare fear and previous threats. T or F

(37) To claim "Self Defense" in California, the person doing the killing has the duty to first retreat a step or two before defending himself. T or F

(38) A person is never allowed to kill in self defense if the attacker runs off. T or F

(39) The instigator of a fight can never under any circumstances use self defense as a legal excuse. T or F

(40) A private person who is the first to use force in making a legal arrest, does not lose the right to self defense. T or F

(41) Killing another in mutual combat is considered to be murder. T or F

(42) In mutual combat, neither party can gain the right to self defense. T or F

(43) A peace officer on duty never loses the right to self defense. T or F

(44) A defendant who has been convicted of murder can be sentenced to death if he has a prior conviction of ______________________________

(45) Name two of the crimes listed under 190.2 PC that carry the death penalty if someone is intentionally killed while committing one of them ____________________ and ______________________________

CHAPTER IV

CRIMES OF RESTRAINT, ROBBERY AND EXTORTION

Kidnapping

In California there are two types of kidnapping: regular kidnapping and ransom kidnapping.

(A) Regular Kidnapping (207 PC)
(Also called Simple Kidnapping)

The description of kidnapping in the penal code takes half a page. This is because the code is trying to be descriptive and give examples. In 1990 a major change was made in that "holding or detaining" was added to the offense. The elements of regular kidnapping are:

(1) The unlawful moving, holding or detaining of a person (asportation or detention)
(2) Against his or her will
(3) By force or any other means of instilling fear.

<u>Exceptions</u>:

(1) Victim under 14 is taken to protect him or her from danger of imminent harm.
(2) Victim taken under 834, 837 PC (legal arrest).

This law now applies to victims kidnapped in another state and brought to California.

<u>Movement (Asportation)</u>

At one time the courts allowed any movement to comply with this element. Recent courts, however, have required that the movement be "substantial" not "trivial." There is no simple mathematical formula for "substantial" distance. The courts judge this based on the total circumstances. If the distance moved places the victim in a more dangerous situation regarding personal safety or chances of rescue, the distance would be "substantial." If the movement was incidental to some other purpose, it would be "trivial."

<u>Detention:</u> Restricting one's free movement.

<u>Against his or her will:</u>

This term is all inclusive. It denotes a lack of free will on the part of the person being moved. A child or a mentally ill or mentally deficient person is not capable of giving consent. However, in cases of this sort, it must be shown that there was an illegal purpose or illegal intent. (People *v*. Oliver, 55 Cal. 2d 761) This illegal intent or purpose need not be shown in other kidnappings.

(a) Consent by fraud: (there is no consent)

If a person got into an automobile voluntarily, but later the driver took this person against his will to a place he did not want to go, it is kidnapping. (People *v*. Trawick, 78 Cal. App. 2d 604)

Obtaining the permission of the victim through threats or coercion is the same as having no permission. There is really no free will permission. (People *v*. Dagampat, 167 Cal. App. 2d 492)

(b) Kidnapping as Part of Another Crime

When the kidnapping is incidental to, and a means of accomplishing another crime, only the more serious crime can be charged. (People *v*. Nelson, 233 Cal. App. 2d 440) Also see Penal Code Section 654. The movement must be above and beyond that necessary to complete the crime.

The problem in multiple offenses is to determine when the kidnapping is a separate offense. For example, if someone held up a gas station and then took the attendant hostage so that he could better effect his escape, this would still be part of the robbery. There would, however, be a distance at which the escape would have been accomplished and the taking of the attendant any further would be a separate crime of kidnapping. The California Supreme Court stated that in cases of this sort, they would have to judge each case on its own merits.

Moving a person under 14 from one place to another for the purpose of Lewd and Lascivious acts is also kidnapping. (207 PC)

Exceptions:

Kidnapping can also be a violation of false imprisonment.

Punishment for Kidnapping (208 PC)

The crime is a felony punishable by 3, 5, or 8 years.

(B) Kidnapping for Special Purposes (209 PC)

Ransom kidnapping involves two separate offenses. In 1951 the California legislature changed the wording of 209 PC, and separated kidnapping for ransom from kidnapping for robbery. In the part on kidnapping for ransom, they make the word "kidnapping" optional. In the part of kidnapping for robbery, they did use the word kidnapping only. This is important as we will see later.

In 1998, the legislature added other purposes after Robbery and legislated that the movement for those other purposes must be substantial.

The basic elements are as follows:

Subsection (a):

(1) The seizing, enticing or kidnapping of another (not necessarily moving)
(2) For the purpose of
 (a) ransom, or
 (b) extortion.

Punishment:

(a) Victim suffers no bodily harm — Life Imprisonment (Possible parole)
(b) Victim suffers bodily harm or death — Life Imprisonment (No parole)
(c) Victim confined in very dangerous manner — Life Imprisonment (no parole)
(d) If given probation, minimum 12 months in county jail

Subsection (b):

(1) Kidnapping another
(2) For the purpose of
 (a) robbery
 (b) rape
 (c) spousal rape
 (d) oral copulation
 (e) sodomy, or
 (f) rape by instrument (289 PC)

Punishment:

Life imprisonment with possibility of parole.

Substantial Movement Required (209(2) PC)

(1) Subsection (b) shall not apply
(2) Unless the movement is beyond that needed for the commission of the underlying offense, AND
(3) It increases the risk of harm to the victim over that normally present in the underlying offense.

Definition of the Term "Bodily Harm"

In the famous case of People *v*. Chessman, 38 Cal. 2d 166, the high court stated that the term means "any touching of the person of another against his will and with physical force in an intentional, hostile and aggravated manner of the projection of such force against his person." In this definition the word "intentional" is used. In the law itself, it does not state that. It merely states that the victim "suffer bodily harm."

Examples of Bodily Harm:

- Forcing victim to commit an act of oral copulation. (People *v*. Chessman, 38 Cal. 2d 166)
- Forcible rape. (People *v*. Brown, 29 Cal. 555)

Self inflicted injuries suffered when trying to escape are NOT examples of bodily harm. (People *v*. Gilbert, 63 Cal. 2d 690). However, when the injuries occurred as a result of the victim jumping out of a moving car after the kidnapper threatened to rape her, the court held that the threats were the proximate cause of the injuries and the law applied. (People *v*. Monk, 56 Cal. 2d 288)

In 1969 the California Supreme Court handed down a landmark decision regarding the "kidnapping for purposes of robbery" part of 209 PC. (People *v*. Daniels, 202 C.A. 3d 671) In this particular case Daniels and his co-principal, Simmons, committed a series of robberies in the vicinity of the University of Southern California. In each of these robberies, the victims were women; the perpetrators not only robbed the victims, but also either raped them or forced them to engage in abnormal sex acts.

In Daniels, the court felt that the distance involved in each robbery and rape or sex offense was not greater than that necessary to commit the robbery. As a result, they reversed the kidnapping charges thus eliminating the punishment of death which a jury could and did recommend at that time if the victim suffered bodily harm. Had this decision been handed down during the Chessman appeals, he would not have been executed.

When robbery occurs during a kidnapping, the crime becomes "kidnapping for robbery," whether or not the kidnapper originally intended to rob the victim. (People *v*. Brown 29 Cal. 555) Because in 1990 the legislature changed the law on 207 PC to include "holding or detaining," the rules for 209 PC have also changed—movement above and beyond that needed for the robbery no longer need be proved. Today the Daniels case would have not been overturned. However, the death penalty is no longer a punishment for 209 PC with harm to the victim. (Unless victim is killed.)

(C) Kidnapping as Part of Carjacking (209.5 PC)

When a person is kidnapped as part of a carjacking, punishment is life with possible parole.

(D) Extortion by Posing as Kidnapper (210 PC)

This covers the person who did not commit the kidnapping, but tries to "cash in" on the offense by posing as the kidnapper and demanding ransom.

(E) Taking Hostages (210.5 PC)

(1) Who falsely imprisons another (236 PC)
(2) For the purpose of:
  (a) Protection from arrest, or
  (b) Using victim as a shield
(3) And this substantially increases the risk of harm to the victim
(4) Is guilty of a felony.

(F) Abduction (265 PC)

(1) The unlawful taking of a woman
(2) Against her will
(3) By means of
  (a) force or
  (b) menace or
  (c) duress
(4) And compels her to
  (a) marry him or
  (b) marry another or
  (c) be defiled (sexual violation).

(G) Abduction of Person Under 18 for Purposes of Prostitution (267 PC)

(1) Every person who takes away any person under the age of 18
(2) From his or her parent, guardian or person having legal charge
(3) Without their consent
(4) For the purpose of prostitution.

(H) Enticing of Unmarried Female (266 PC)

(1) A person who inveigles or entices any unmarried female
(2) Of previously chaste character (virgin)
(3) Under 18 years of age
(4) To any place for the purpose of prostitution or illicit carnal acts

OR:

(1) A person who by fraudulent means
(2) Procures any female
(3) To have illicit carnal connection (sexual relations) with another person.

These previous sections are for the purpose of controlling general organized prostitution.

(I) False Imprisonment (236 PC)

False imprisonment is the unlawful violation of the personal liberty of another. This section is very broad, and may border on unconstitutionality because it is vague. This is a criminal offense, so criminal intent must be proved. False arrest is also false imprisonment.

Police departments can have insurance for false arrest, but not for false imprisonment. It is illegal to have insurance against criminal acts. It in effect encourages the act if a person is insured against its penalty. Also, you cannot have insurance against serving a sentence.

(J) Human Trafficking (236.1 PC)

(1) A person who deprives or violates the personal liberty of another

(2) With the intent to obtain forced labor or services,

(3) Is guilty of human trafficking.

When the victim of human trafficking is a minor child or when a victim of any age is forced into prostitution or other sex crimes, prison sentences are more severe. All human trafficking crimes are felonies.

<u>Punishment for False Imprisonment (237 PC)</u>

The crime of False Imprisonment is a "wobbler."

(K) Locked Occupied Vehicles (22516 CVC)

No person shall leave standing a locked vehicle in which there is any person who cannot readily escape therefrom. Although this section uses the term "any person," it is used mostly when parents lock young children in the car. The legislative intent is to prevent injury or death should the car catch fire, or in some way be in danger of severe damage, and the persons inside cannot escape.

Child Abduction

(A) Child Concealment (277 PC)

(1) In the absence of a court order determining custody rights

(2) Every person having a right of custody of a child

(3) Who maliciously takes, detains, conceals or entices away that child

(4) Without good cause

(5) And with the intent to deprive another of their custody rights.

(B) Child Abduction (278 PC)

(1) Every person not having custody right of a child

(2) Who maliciously takes, detains, conceals or entices away that minor child

(3) With the intent to detain or conceal that child from a person or agency having lawful custody.

Child stealing is a specific intent crime, and as long as the perpetrator has that intent and commits some overt act, the crime is complete despite the final objective not being completed (People *v.* Bormman, 85 *Cal. Rptr.* 638)

Child stealing does not necessarily involve the use of force (People *v.* Casagranda, 43 CA 2d 818). Neither does the word "take" require force (People *v.* Bormman, 85 *Cal. Rptr.* 638).

The fact that the victim was able to break free and run away when the perpetrator tried to force her into his car did not affect the elements of Child Stealing (People *v.* Palmer, 50 CA 2d 697).

The fact that the child goes with the perpetrator willingly has no bearing on the crime of Child Stealing (People *v.* Moore, 67 CA 2d 789).

(C) Concealment of Child With Intent to Deprive Custody (278.5 PC)

(1) Every person having a legal right of custody or visitation of a child

(2) Who detains, conceals, takes or entices away that child

(3) With the intent to deprive another of their right of custody or visitation.

Where the defendant told his ex-wife that she could visit their daughter but would not tell her where the daughter was located violated this law (People *v.* Lortz, 187 *Cal. Rptr.* 89)

(D) Protective Custody (279.6 PC)

(1) A peace officer who is investigating a violation of 277, 278, or 278.5 PC

(2) May take into protective custody any child

(3) When it appears to the officer that someone is about to flee the jurisdiction with that minor child.

<u>Definition</u>:

<u>Good Cause</u>: A good faith and reasonable belief that the taking (etc.) is necessary to protect the child from bodily injury or emotional harm. These are difficult cases to handle. To begin with, they are borderline civil in nature, and if possible, should be handled through the D.A.'s office. An

irate parent will often call the police because the other parent, who has temporary legal custody, is 10 minutes late in returning the child. They are more interested in being vindictive than in the welfare of the child.

Since these cases are listed in the Penal Code, police officers do have a legal responsibility, but they often need the wisdom of Solomon to properly handle them. With divorce rates continuing as they are, this problem will certainly not decrease. Sometimes these problems can be better handled through the attorney of the complainant.

The officer's main concern here should be the safety of the child, and if there is some indication that there is a danger to the child, immediate action should be taken. An example would be where the parent having legal custody has had mental problems or drinking problems, and has indicated that he would rather kill the child than send him back to his ex-wife. If the mother reports that the father took the child, as he was legally entitled to do, but that he was so drunk he could barely walk, and that he drove off with the child, then some action should be taken to try and apprehend the father before he is involved in an accident and harm comes to the child.

Robbery and Extortion

Although robbery and extortion are found a considerable distance apart in the Penal Code, they are so similar in many respects that it is best to cover them both at the same time so that they can be compared. The slightest change in one element can require that a suspect be charged with extortion rather than with robbery. The student of criminal law should know these differences.

Robbery (211 PC)

The term "robbery" is often misused by the general public. They will too often say that they were robbed when they really mean that they were the victim of theft. They will often call the police department and state that they have been robbed when in reality they are reporting that their house was burglarized. The newspapers are no help in this matter, since they constantly misuse the word. Will the real "robbery" please stand up?

The Elements of Robbery

(A) The felonious taking (asportation)
(B) Of the personal property of another
(C) From their person or immediate presence
(D) Against their will
(E) Accomplished by means of force or fear

(A) The Felonious Taking or Asportation

The key to asportation is the fact that there is movement, not how far the property was moved.

In one case the victim was ordered by the armed robber to throw his wallet on the ground. The robber was arrested before he could pick up the wallet and convicted in court of armed robbery. He contested the conviction on the grounds that the first element of asportation was not completed, as he did not move the wallet one inch. The Appellate Court held that the movement of the money from the victim's pocket to the floor was at the robber's command, and was therefore asportation. (People *v*. Quinn, 77 Cal. App. 2d 734)

In a similar case, an armed robber entered a bar and ordered the bartender to place the money on the bar. When the bartender put the money on top of the bar, a patron hit the robber over the head and captured him. A conviction of robbery was upheld even though the perpetrator did not touch the money. As in the first case mentioned, there was a movement of money at the robber's command, and that satisfied the element of asportation. (People *v*. Wellman, 141 Cal. App. 2d 101)

(B) The Personal Property of Another

The property taken does need not belong to the victim. In the case of a gas station robbery, the money taken does not belong to the attendant; the important fact is that it does not belong to the robber. (People *v*. Downs, 114 Cal. App. 2d 758)

If the person taking the property happens to own or have legal title to it, his taking the property cannot be classed as robbery. If a certain piece of property is owned by one person, but in the possession of another, and the possessor refuses to give it to the person owning it, and the owner retrieves the property by means of force or fear, it will not be classed as robbery because the second element of robbery "Of the personal property of another" is missing. (People *v*. Vice, 21 Cal. 334)

Even if the property did not belong to the person taking it, if he had a reasonable faith that it did belong to him, he could avoid a charge of robbery by using the defense of Mistake of Fact. (People *v*. Sheasby, 83 Cal. App 459)

(C) From Their Person or Immediate Presence

Normally this element would not need much interpretation. "From their person" is from their body. "From their immediate presence" is from an area where they have access to the property. There have been situations, however, where the courts have held that the term "immediate presence" can be wider in definition. If the robber were to force the victim into another room, tie him up and then return to where the money was kept and take it without the victim being present, it would still be considered to be from his immediate presence. (People *v*. Dean, 66 Cal. App. 602)

This also applies where the perpetrator scares the victim into running off and leaving his property. (People *v*. Sylvis, 72 Cal. App 632) It would not be theft if the perpetrator pointed a gun at the cashier of a movie who ran out the back door of the booth in fear, and the perpetrator then entered the booth and took the money. It would be robbery. (People *v*. Davis, 100 Cal. App. 179)

(D) Against Their Will

This is the major difference between robbery and extortion. Sometimes it might appear that the victim is going along with the robbery, but this is due to force or fear. He may have been given a choice of "your money or your life." Showing that the taking was not against the victim's will is a good defense because this is an essential element.

An unusual conviction of robbery occurred after the defendant forced the victim at gun point to participate in a dice game in which he lost all of his money. (People *v*. Unipeg, 118 Cal. App. 485) It was held to have been against his will.

(E) Accomplished by Means of Force or Fear

The small word "or" here is very important. It means that there is a choice of the two. Both of them are not necessary for this element to be completed. (People *v*. Ferrara, 31 Cal. App. 1)

Force

In order for force to be a valid element, it must be more force than is needed to carry off the property. This rule is important, especially in the common crime of "Purse Snatch." The mere fact that the perpetrator took the purse from the victim does not necessarily mean that force was used.

If a person were to sneak up on the victim, and slip the purse from her arm so quickly that she did not have time to grab and hold on to it, or for that matter, give it up voluntarily out of fear, the element of force would not apply. The only force used in this case is that needed to carry off the purse.

Now let's change the situation a bit. Harry Hashbrown sneaks up on Tilly Tiddlywink with the intent of grabbing her purse. She hears him coming and guesses that he is after her purse. When he grabs for the purse, she holds on for dear life. He pulls harder and she holds on tighter. A tug-of-war ensues. Finally Harry gives a strong pull and gets the purse loose and runs off with it. This is robbery because the force used was more than that needed just to carry off the purse. In police work, the term "Strong Arm Robbery" is used for a robbery where the property is taken from the victim by force.

Fear

Section 212 of the Penal Code states that "the fear mentioned in section 211 may be either:

(a) the fear of an unlawful injury to the person or property of the person robbed, or of any relative of his or member of his family. OR
(b) the fear of an immediate and unlawful injury to the person or property of any one in the company of the person robbed at the time of the robbery."

At times the defense attorney will try to shame the victim into stating that he really wasn't afraid of the robber. If he is able to accomplish this neat little trick, it would be of no avail. In the People *v*. Borra, 123 Cal. App. 482, the Appellate Court noted that the circumstances can supply the proof of fear even though the victim might state that he wasn't afraid.

In the case of People *v*. Callihan, 81 Cal. App. 2d 928, the court stated that "intimidation" is the same as "fear" in the crime of robbery.

Back to Harry and Tilly... If Harry told Tilly that she had better give him her purse, or he would smash her dentures, and she did give him the purse, the element of fear would prevail.

Robbery can be proved by circumstantial evidence, as can degree of robbery. Where a person is assaulted and because of the assault is rendered unconscious, and he or she finds that some property is missing upon regaining consciousness, it is enough evidence for the jury to convict for robbery. (People *v*. Hubler, 102 Cal. App. 2d 689)

<u>Degrees of Robbery</u>

(A) First Degree Robbery (212.5 PC)
(1) Robbery of an inhabited
  (a) dwelling etc.,
  (b) vessel (21 H & N Code)
  (c) trailer coach
  (d) floating home, or
(2) Robbery of an operator of paid transportation
(3) Person using ATM, or person in the vicinity after having used ATM,
(4) Is first degree robbery. (penalty 3, 4 or 6 yrs.)

(B) Second Degree Robbery
All other robberies are second degree.

<u>Robbery of a Pharmacy</u>

Whenever the robbery is of a pharmacy or a pharmacist, or other person in control of narcotics (controlled substances) and the purpose of the robbery is to obtain narcotics, the judge must give the longer of the three optional sentences.

<u>Carjacking (215 PC)</u>
(1) The felonious taking (asportation)
(2) Of the automobile of another
(3) From their person or immediate presence
(4) Against their will
(5) Accomplished by means of force or fear. (3–5 or 9 years in state prison)

Extortion (518 PC)

Extortion is often referred to as "blackmail." The key difference between robbery and extortion is that in extortion the victim willingly parts with the property or other consideration (e.g., gives consent to the operation). This is a very broad crime, and can be used when robbery does not apply. For example, look at page 82 and compare the conditions of "fear."

<u>Example</u>: Harrison Dunkenheimer and his girlfriend, Kitty Krump, are walking down the street. Mervin Messup approaches them and tells Harrison that if he does not give Mervin $10 tomorrow he is going to cut off one of Kitty's ears. Harrison believes Mervin is telling the truth and gives him the $10. Is it robbery or extortion? It is extortion for two reasons:
(1) for robbery a girl friend does not come under the term "any relative."
(2) for robbery, "anyone in his company" must be subjected to an immediate possibility of injury, not tomorrow, as was the case here.

In the crime of extortion, "third persons" can be objects of the threat to be carried out any time.

"Other consideration" means anything of value including sexual conduct or an image of an intimate body part.

518 PC expressly excludes from the definition of extortion consideration consisting of sexual conduct or an intimate image obtained by anyone under 18 years of age.

<u>Other Differences</u>
(1) There need be no asportation or taking on the part of the perpetrator. The money could be sent in the mail. It could be sent to a third party or deposited in a bank account.
(2) What is obtained can be the official act of a public officer rather than just personal property of another as in robbery.
  <u>Example</u>:
  On the day that the city council is voting on a raise in police salaries, an officer in the vice detail calls Councilman Larry Lillywaiver and tells him that if he does not vote for the raise, he will tell everyone that Larry was arrested in Kansas City for indecent exposure.
(3) The fear can be fear of secrets being exposed.

Organized crime groups use the "shakedown" or "payoff" type of extortion where a person pays the organization a certain amount of money to stay in business, or his place will "accidentally" burn down. Some protest organizations today are using a borderline type of extortion, where businesses are boycotted, or pickets will drive customers away.

If you attend a football game, and park your car on the street, and are then approached by a tough looking juvenile who states that he will watch your car for ten dollars and see that the air is not let out of your tires, what is the offense if you give him the money? It would most likely be extortion because you are in effect going along with the scheme.

Written Threats and Ransomware (523 PC)

Extortion threats by letter are the same as threats by force or fear except:

(1) Threats must be placed into the letter or other writing;
(2) The victim does not need to hand over the money or property, or even commit to handing over the money or property.

Likewise, introducing ransomware into any computer system or network with the intent to extort money or other consideration from another person is considered extortion whether or not any money or property was actually received from the victim. Ransomware is a computer contaminant or malicious software that can block access to data and programs with the intent to extort money from the victim in exchange for restoring access.

Extortion – Penalty (520 PC)

(1) Every person who extorts property or other consideration from another,
(2) Under circumstances not amounting to robbery or carjacking,
(3) By means of force or any threat,
(4) Shall be punished by imprisonment in the state prison for two, three, or four years.

Comparison of the *Corpus Delicti* of Robbery (211 PC) and Extortion (518 PC)

Robbery

(1) The felonious taking (asportation)
(2) Of the personal property of another
(3) From the victim's person or immediate presence
(4) **Against his or her will,**
(5) By means of force or fear

Fear in Robbery Can Be

(1) Threat of unlawful injury (at any time) to
  (a) the victim, or
  (b) the victim's property, or
  (c) any relative of the victim
  OR:
(2) The fear of immediate & unlawful injury to:
  (a) the victim, or
  (b) the victim's property, or
  (c) anyone in the victim's company

Extortion

(1) The obtaining (not necessarily taking)
(2) Of
  (a) the property or other consideration of another or
  (b) an official act of a public officer
(3) **With his or her consent**
(4) Induced by wrongful use of force or fear
(5) Or under color of official right.

Fear in Extortion Can Be

(1) Threat of unlawful injury (at any time) to:
  (a) the victim, or
  (b) the victim's property, or
  (c) any relative of the victim, or
  (d) any other person
  OR:
(2) Fear of being accused of a crime (victim or relative) OR
(3) Fear of deformity, disgrace or crime being exposed
  OR
(4) Fear of any secret being exposed

Chapter IV Case Citations

Study Questions for Chapter IV

(1) The Penal Code section for simple kidnapping is ________________________ PC.

(2) Asportation means

(A) ____criminal intent (B) ____guilt

(C) ____movement or taking (D) ____without permission

(3) In a case of simple kidnapping, a child or mentally deficient person is not considered mentally capable of giving consent to movement. T or F

(4) In simple kidnapping, if permission to move the victim is obtained through coercion, it is not considered to be a case of legal consent or permission. T or F

(5) Betty Binkle voluntarily agrees to accept a ride from Harry Hotsocks but later when he wants to drive to the local "lover's lane," she objects. Harry drives there anyway. Because she voluntarily agreed to ride with him at first, this would not be a case of illegal kidnapping. T or F

(6) Gary Gat holds up a liquor store and moves the clerk to a back room against his will. He ties him up and leaves with the money. Gary is guilty of both robbery and kidnapping. T or F

(7) The Penal Codes section for Ransom Kidnapping is______________________ PC.

(8) In Ransom Kidnapping, there must be some movement in order for the crime to be complete. T or F

(9) In Kidnapping for Robbery, there has to be some movement. T or F

(10) Larry Lacksey stops Linda Lackmore at gun point as she is walking to her car. He forces her to go to her car, and while there, he takes money from her purse and then rapes her. He is guilty of kidnapping for purposes of robbery. T or F

(11) Rape is considered "bodily harm" as used in the section on Ransom Kidnapping. T or F

(12) A kidnapping victim tries to escape when the kidnappers have temporarily left, and while trying to escape, she injures herself. This would be an example of "bodily harm" under the section on Ransom Kidnapping. T or F

(13) Huston Hardrock hears on the radio that Benny Boop's 5-year-old daughter Betty Boop is missing. He calls up Mr. Boop and tells him that he has kidnapped Betty, and that if Benny wants to see her again, he had better put $10,000 in a bag and leave it at a special place. Since Huston did not actually kidnap Betty, he would only be guilty of Fraud. T or F

(14) Abduction means:

(A) ____the same as rape (B) ____taking a woman against her will

(C) ____seduction (D) ____ fornication

(15) In the crime of "Enticing of an Unmarried Female" (266 PC), the victim must be a virgin. T or F

(16) A person who is guilty of false arrest is also guilty of false imprisonment. T or F

(17) In the crime of "Child Stealing," the child must be under the age of ______________.

(18) In the crime of "Child Stealing," the child must be taken against his or her will. T or F

(19) Kitty and Fred Frump decide to separate. They have one child, Franny Frump. They agree between themselves that Fred can take Franny on Sundays until 7 P.M. One Sunday Fred keeps Franny all night. He is therefore guilty of section 279.6 PC, "Concealing a child by those having limited custody." T or F

(20) The Penal Code section for Robbery is ________________________________ PC.

(21) In the crime of Robbery, there must be some asportation. T or F

(22) In Robbery, the robber must gain physical possession of the money or goods. T or F

(23) A person who takes from another, at gun point, what is legally his (belonging to the person with the gun) can be charged with robbery. T or F

(24) If a person forcibly takes property from another, when that property was stolen from a third party by the possessor, the action would not be robbery. T or F

(25) Horace Hickle lends Hector Honk a fishing rod. Hector refuses to give it back. Horace goes to Hector's house and at knife point takes a fishing pole that he believes is his. Later Horace finds that the pole is not his, but one that looks like his. Horace is guilty of robbery. T or F

(26) If Horace was charged criminally on the above action, his defense would be based on one of the defenses listed in 26 PC. It is called_____________of _______________

(27) For robbery to be a crime, the money or property must be taken from the person of the victim, and not near him. T or F

(28) Harvey Hump goes to a grocery store and pulls out a gun. The owner runs out the back of the store in fear. Harvey then helps himself to the money in the cash register. This is a case of theft rather than robbery.____ T or F

(29) The major difference between Robbery and Extortion is that in Extortion, the victim consents or goes along with the act. T or F

(30) In Robbery, both force and fear are necessary. T or F

(31) Sam Sneak comes up behind an elderly woman and slips her purse off her arm before she realizes what happened. This act amounts to "force" as listed in the crime of Robbery. T or F

(32) In police work, the term used for robbery where the perpetrator robs the victim by force rather than by fear, is called ____________________________________robbery.

(33) Sam Slipshod tells Lester Lump that if he doesn't give him $10 tomorrow he will cause bodily harm to Lester's girl friend Millie. As a result, Lester gives Sam $10. What crime do we have? ____

(34) The circumstances are what determine fear in robbery rather than the victim's statement that he really wasn't afraid. T or F

(35) Harry Hashbrown knocks Sam Slipshod unconscious. When Sam comes to, he finds that his wallet is missing. Under these circumstances, this evidence is enough for the jury to convict Harry of robbery. T or F

(36) The crime of Extortion requires some "Asportation." T or F

(37) Officer Smith calls City Councilman Joey Pop and tells him that if he doesn't vote for the police pay raise tonight, the newspapers will be given a copy of an arrest record showing that Joey Pop was arrested for possession of heroin as a juvenile. Joey complies with the demand. Officer Smith is guilty of ________________________

CHAPTER V

TYPES OF ASSAULT AND MAYHEM

Assault Type Offenses

Assault (240 PC)

Simply an attempt to commit battery. The three elements to the crime of assault are:

(1) An unlawful attempt (to commit battery)
(2) Coupled with the present ability
(3) To commit a violent injury upon the person of another.

The term "simple assault" is often used interchangeably with the term "assault," and has been given recognition by the Appellate Court in the People *v*. Egan, (91 Cal. App. 44)

The words used in the elements of assault are very important. The way the high courts have interpreted these words has a great bearing on what actually comes under the classification of assault. The four most important terms are:

Unlawful

There are certain assaults that are lawful. They would be athletic events such as boxing or football, medical operations, self defense, and the force used in making lawful arrests.

Attempt

It must be remembered that this offense is an attempt and not the completion of the attempted offense. There need be no contact with the victim. The victim need suffer no injury.

Present Ability

Present ability means the act attempted can be carried out, or is capable of being completed by the assailant. The key is the ability of the person attempting the unlawful act, and not the fact that some condition not controlled by the assailant prevents the intended injury from being inflicted.

If a person fired at a police officer through a roof at a point where he believed the officer to be, but the officer was not hit because he or she had moved, that assailant would be guilty of unlawful assault. (People *v*. Lee Kong, 95 Cal. 666)

On the other hand, if the assailant were to point an empty revolver at another person who was a short distance away, it would not be classed as an assault because it is physically impossible for that gun to fire. In other words, there is no present ability. (People *v*. Bennett, 37 Cal. App. 324)

If there was ammunition in the clip, but no shell in the chamber of the gun, and the gun was pointed at another person, there would still be an assault because the present ability was there. The assailant had only to work the mechanism quickly, and a shell would have been in the chamber ready to fire. (People *v*. Simpson, 134 Cal. App. 646)

If the assailant throws a rock or other heavy object at the victim, the distance can be very important. If the distance is such that the object thrown can come close to the victim, yet not close enough to hit him, it would be "impossible" for a person to throw such an object and there would be no present ability, and thus, no assault. This would be so even though there was both an act and intent. (People *v*. Yslas, 27 Cal. 630)

Violent Injury

The words "violent injury" are misleading. It sounds like something very severe. From a legal standpoint, it can be something quite simple and minor in nature.

In the People *v*. Bradbury, 151 Cal. 675, the court stated that "The kind of physical force is immaterial; it may consist in the taking of indecent liberties with a woman or laying hold of her and kissing her against her will." The term "violent injury" as used in the section on assault merely means the unlawful application of physical force upon the person of another.

If Herbert Hickup took a swing at Clyde Crashcup and missed him, it would be classed as an assault. Threatening to kill persons, then pointing a loaded gun at them is assault. (People *v*. Montgomery, 15 Cal. App. 315) Spitting at a person and missing would be the attempt to make an unlawful application of force upon the person of another, and would be classed as an assault.

Actions That Do Not Justify Assault

Words of abuse do not justify an assault. As long as there is no threat of injury, the assailant cannot legally assault another just because he has used words of abuse, insult or reproach. In this case, the assailant should remember the childhood saying, "Sticks and stones may break my bones, but names will never hurt me."

Assaulting a Peace Officer or Firefighter (241 PC)

The elements of the offense are as follows:

(1) Assault on:
 (a) a peace officer,
 (b) a firefighter,
 (c) an emergency medical technician or paramedic, doctor or nurse,
 (d) custodial officer (241.1 PC),
 (e) against ANY person on
  (i) the property or
  (ii) vehicle, of a public or private transit company (241.3 PC),
 (f) uniformed lifeguard (with citation power issued by local government),
 (g) uniformed peace officer working for school district (241.4 PC),
 (h) traffic officer (non-sworn),
 (i) animal control officer,
 (j) school employee (241.6 PC),
 (k) process server (22350 B & P),
 (l) juror (for revenge) (241.7 PC),
(2) When that person knows or should know that the victim is one of the above, or
(3) When the above victim is performing his or her duties.

Other Special Assaults (241.2 PC)

(1) Upon any person when on school grounds (Kindergarten – Community College).
(2) Upon any person in a publicly maintained or operated park (not when used for professional sports or commercial events).

Assault With Electrical Charge Weapons (244.5 PC)

Assault with a Taser or Stun Gun is a wobbler when the victim is a peace officer or firefighter.

Definition: A Stun Gun or Taser is a weapon capable of temporarily immobilizing a person by the infliction of an electrical charge.

Assault With a Deadly Weapon (ADW) (245 PC)

Assault with a deadly weapon is more often referred to as "ADW" when used in the field by police officers. The elements are:

(1) Every person who commits an assault upon the person of another
(2) With
 (a) a deadly weapon (other than a firearm)
 (b) deadly instrument, or
 (c) by any means of force likely to produce great bodily injury.

Definition of Deadly Weapon

A deadly weapon is any object, instrument, or weapon which, from the manner in which it is used, is capable and likely to produce death or great bodily injury. (People *v.* Franklin, 70 Cal. 641) For this particular section, the definition depends not upon the purpose for which the instrument was made, but the manner in which it was used. (People *v.* Robertson, 217 Cal. 671)

Examples of Items Classed as Deadly Weapons

(a) sock filled with salt
—(People *v.* Valliere, 123 Cal. 576)
(b) iron pipe or bar
—(People *v.* Car, 131 Cal. App. 644)
(c) broken bottle
—(People *v.* Sampson, 75 Cal. App. 2d 521)
(d) nail file
—(People *v.* Russell, 59 Cal. App. 2d 660)
(e) automobile
—(People *v.* Claborn, 224 Cal. App. 2d 38)

Circumstantial Evidence

Many times, an ADW occurs but when the police arrive at the scene, the weapon has disappeared. Can ADW be proved without the weapon being produced? Yes, through testimony of witnesses and through the wound itself. If the wound is severe, and such that it could only have been made with a sharp deadly instrument, the courts have held that this circumstantial evidence will suffice. (People *v.* Stevens, 15 Cal. App. 294)

Cases Where ADW Has Not Occurred

A person who fires a gun into the air in order to frighten another person, without any intent of injuring or killing him, would be guilty of 417 PC, but not ADW. (People *v.* McGee, 31 Cal. 2d 229)

If, during an argument, a person pulled out a gun and stated "Don't come any closer; your life is in danger," the person's purpose in this display is not to commit an assault, but to protect himself. (People *v.* Diamond, 33 Cal. App. 2d 518)

ADW Includes Battery With a Deadly Weapon

It was the feeling of legislators that assaulting a person with a deadly weapon was such a serious offense, that they did not legislate a more serious offense of Battery with a Deadly Weapon.

Hands as Deadly Weapons

Hands may be classed as deadly weapons if it can be shown that a person was trained in such a way that his hands were truly dangerous (e.g. karate expert). Burden of proof is on the state.

Patrol officers usually receive ADW calls when an actual battery has occurred. They must be careful not to associate the term ADW with "Battery" with a deadly weapon. If they do, they may handle a case that only involves an assault and no battery, and "kiss off" the case on the grounds that no battery had occurred.

ADW Cases Where Assailant Has No Weapon

We usually think of ADW as an assault where the assailant possesses a deadly weapon. There can be cases of ADW where the victim receives great bodily injury but not from an assailant's weapon. (People *v.* Tallman, 27 Cal. 2d 209)

For example: where the assailant pushed another person out of a window, the bodily injury would occur from the sidewalk, not from a weapon. (People *v.* Emmons, 61 Cal. 487) Banging another's head against a parking meter (People *v.* Conley, 110 Cal. App. 2d 731), would be another example.

<u>ADW on a Peace Officer, Firefighter, Transportation Worker, Custodial Officer, (245(d), 245.2 & 245.3 PC)</u>

(1) Committing ADW on one of the following:
   (a) peace officer
   (b) firefighter
   (c) transportation worker, or passenger (245.2 PC)
   (d) custodial officer (245.3 PC)
(2) When the person knows or should reasonably know that the victim is one of the above,
(3) And the victim is actually engaged in the performance of his or her duty.

<u>ADW With Machine Gun or Assault Weapon (245(a)(3) PC)</u>

ADW with either a machine gun (16880 PC) or an assault weapon (30510 PC) is punishable by 4, 8, or 12 years in prison.

<u>ADW With an Assault Weapon Against a Peace Officer (245(d)(3) PC)</u>

ADW against a peace officer or firefighter by use of either a machine gun or an assault weapon is a felony is punishable by 6, 9, or 12 years in prison.

<u>Assault With a Deadly Weapon on a School Employee (245.5 PC)</u>

(1) Assaulting school employee/board member
(2) With a weapon other than a firearm

(3) When the perpetrator knows or should know that the employee or board member is performing his or her duties.
  (a) If weapon is a firearm. (4-6-8 yrs.)
  (b) If weapon is taser or stun gun. (2-3-4 yrs.)

Types of Assaults

There are many special types of assaults in the Penal Code that involve specific intent (the assault is for a particular set purpose). Examples would be:

(A) Throwing Missiles at Vehicle (219.1 PC)
(1) Unlawfully projects any missile
(2) At a vehicle operated by a common carrier
(3) Or any other unlawful act
(4) With intent to wreck such vehicle, and does,
(5) Or with intent to cause bodily harm, and does.
Common carrier: a vehicle used for commercial purposes such as a truck and trailer or a bus.

(B) Throwing or Shooting at Trains (219.2 PC)
(1) Every person who throws or shoots a missile
(2) At a
  (a) train (cable car) (street car)
  (b) bus or
  (c) water craft
(3) Used for carrying passengers or freight in this state.

(C) Assault or Attempted Murder Upon Government Officials (217.1 PC)
(1) Assault or Attempted Murder upon Executive or Judicial Official
(2) For the purpose of:
  (a) retaliation for an official act or
  (b) preventing official performance.

(D) Assault With Intent to Commit Rape, etc. (220 PC)
(1) Every person who assaults another
(2) With intent to commit:
  (a) rape
  (b) sodomy
  (c) mayhem
  (d) oral copulation
  (e) assisting in rape or penetration with foreign object
  (f) child molestation.

(E) Assault With Caustic Chemicals (244 PC)
(1) Every person who willfully and maliciously
(2) Throws or causes to be thrown on the person of another (this actually makes it battery),
(3) Any
  (a) vitriol (sulfuric acid), or
  (b) corrosive acid, or
  (c) flammable substance, or
  (d) caustic chemical of any nature
(4) With the intent to:
  (a) injure the flesh of such person, or
  (b) disfigure the body.

(F) Assault With Firearms on Inhabited Dwelling or Occupied Building, Vehicle, etc. (246 PC) (Felony)
(1) Maliciously and willfully discharges a firearm
(2) At an inhabited or occupied
  (a) dwelling house
  (b) building
  (c) motor vehicle
  (d) house car (as in 362 CVC)
  (e) camper (as in 243 CVC) or
  (f) aircraft.
Inhabited: means someone normally lives there. They need not be there at the time.

(G) Negligent Discharge of Firearm (246.3 PC)
(1) The willful discharge of a firearm
(2) In a grossly negligent manner
(3) When it could reasonably result in either injury or death to another human being,
(4) Is guilty of a wobbler.

Previous laws required that criminal intent be proven for conviction. This law requires only proof of negligence; it is not simple negligence, however, but "gross negligence," and thus more difficult to prove. The law gives no clear definition of "gross negligence" so courts usually rely on appellate court definitions used in vehicular manslaughter such as "complete disregard for safety of others," or "complete throwing to the wind of all caution."

(H) Shooting at Aircraft or Building (247 PC)
(1) Any person who willfully and maliciously discharges a firearm
(2) At
  (a) an unoccupied aircraft (Felony) or
  (b) an inhabited building or house (Wobbler)
(3) Unless with the owner's permission.

(I) Assaulting Occupied Aircraft With Laser (247.5 PC) (Wobbler)
(1) Willfully and maliciously discharging a laser
(2) At an aircraft
(3) Whether in motion or in flight
(4) While occupied.

(J) Assault or Battery on School Property (243.5 PC)

In addition to any other punishment, a person who commits assault or battery on school property during school hours, may at the discretion of the judge, be ordered to pay restitution to the victim or perform community service.

(K) Assault or Battery on Police Horse or Dog (600 PC)
(1) Willfully and maliciously without legal justification
(2) Does any of the following:
 (a) Commits assault or battery or
 (b) Administers poison or a stupefying substance, or
 (c) frightens, teases, agitates, hinders, or harasses
(3) Any police horse or dog
(4) Supervised by a peace officer on duty or a volunteer acting under direct supervision of a peace officer.

It is a felony to cause death or serious injury to such animal.

(L) Firing a Gun from or at an Occupied Vehicle (246.1 PC)
(1) Who, upon conviction of murder, attempted murder, or manslaughter
(2) Perpetrated from or at an occupied vehicle
(3) On a public street or highway
(4) Apart from other punishment, the court shall have the vehicle used in the offense declared a nuisance and sold at public auction.

(M) Drawing or Exhibiting Firearm or Other Deadly Weapon (417 PC)

Section A:
(1) Every person who, except in self-defense, in the presence of another person
(2) Draws or exhibits any deadly weapon other than a firearm
(3) In a rude, angry or threatening manner, or
(4) Who unlawfully uses such weapon in any fight or quarrel,
(5) Is guilty of a misdemeanor (min. 30 days).

Section B:

Who does the above with a firearm (loaded or unloaded) is guilty of a misdemeanor. (min. 9 mos.)

Section C:

Who does the above in the immediate presence of a peace officer, and knows or should reasonably know that the victim is a peace officer engaged in the performance of his or her duties is guilty of a Wobbler. (min. 9 mos.)

Section D:
(1) Who does the above
(2) With a firearm
(3) On the grounds of: either
 (a) a day care center or
 (b) a facility where recreation programs for those under 18 are conducted.

Section E:
(1) Who does the above
(2) With a deadly weapon or firearm
(3) As a threat to a person in the process of cleaning up graffiti or vandalism.

(N) Displaying Firearm at Motor Vehicle (417.3 PC)
(1) Drawing or exhibiting any firearm (loaded or unloaded) in a threatening manner,
(2) Except in self defense,
(3) In the presence of a person in a motor vehicle
(4) Proceeding on a public street or highway
(5) When it would cause a reasonable person to fear bodily harm. (felony)

(O) Displaying Imitation Firearm (417.4 PC)
(1) Who, except in self-defense,
(2) Draws or exhibits an imitation firearm
(3) In a threatening manner against another
(4) As to cause a reasonable person apprehension or fear of bodily harm. (misdemeanor)

Imitation Firearm:

A replica of a firearm that is so substantially similar as to lead a reasonable person to conclude that the replica is real.

(P) Drawing or Exhibiting Firearm With Intent to Resist Arrest (417.8 PC)
(1) Every person who draws or exhibits any firearm or other deadly weapon, whether or not loaded,
(2) With the intent to resist or prevent the arrest or detention of himself or another person,
(3) By a peace officer,
(4) Is guilty of a felony.

(Q) Seizure of Firearms at Family Violence Incident (18250, 18265 PC)

(1) Any peace officer at the scene of a family violence incident involving a threat to human life or physical assault
(2) Shall take temporary custody of firearm or deadly weapon
(3) That is in plain sight or discovered through consensual or lawful search.
(4) It shall be kept for a minimum of 48 hours, but no longer than five business days.
(5) The officer shall give the owner or possessor a mandated receipt.

(R) Misuse of Laser Scope or Pointer (Misd.) (417.25 PC)

(1) Who aims or points a laser scope or laser pointer
(2) In a threatening manner
(3) With the intent to cause a reasonable person fear of bodily harm.

Definitions:

Laser Pointer: A hand-held laser beam device or demonstration laser product that emits a single point of light amplified by the stimulated emission of radiation that is visible to the human eye.

Laser Scope: A portable battery-powered device capable of being attached to a firearm and of projecting a laser light onto objects from a distance.

(S) Aiming Laser Scope or Pointer at Peace Officer (Misd.) (417.26 PC)

(1) Who aims or points a laser scope or laser pointer
(2) At a peace officer
(3) With intent to cause the officer apprehension or fear of bodily harm
(4) And knows or should reasonably know that the targeted person is a peace officer.

(T) Other Offenses Involving Laser Scope or Pointer (Infr.) (417.27 PC)

The following acts with lasers are illegal:

(1) Selling to a minor, 17 years or younger, unless accompanied by an adult.
(2) Possession of a laser pointer on school premises unless it is for valid school-related purposes.
(3) Directing the beam of a laser pointer
    (a) at the eye of another person, or
    (b) into a moving vehicle with the intent to annoy the recipient.
(4) Pointing the beam directly or indirectly into the eye of
    (a) a guide dog,
    (b) a signal or service dog, or
    (c) a police dog.

Battery Type Offenses

(A) Battery (242 PC)

Battery is any willful and unlawful use of force upon the person of another. It is often called a completed assault. If Harvey Hinkle swings at Mervin Mushmuscle and misses, it is assault. If he connects with Mervin's nose, it is battery.

Since battery is a completed assault, and since assault can be a very minor thing, battery can be very minor. Examples are:

(1) Grabbing a person's coat sleeve.
(2) Pushing another person out of the way.
(3) Pouring water on a person.
(4) Spitting at a person and hitting him.
(5) Setting a dog on another when the dog bites or touches him.
(6) Forcing another car off of the road.
(7) Turning a water hose on someone.

There can be no battery without also having an assault. Assault is a lesser offense of battery. If a jury believes that Harvey Hinkle did in fact take a swing at Mervin Mushmuscle, but that he really didn't touch him, they can find him guilty of the lesser offense of assault rather than the original charge of battery. There need be no injury nor infliction of pain in order for there to be a battery.

(B) Battery With Special Circumstances (243 PC) (Wobbler)

(1) Committing a battery upon the person of:
    (a) a peace officer
    (b) a custodial officer (243.1 PC)
    (c) a firefighter
    (d) emergency medical personnel (nurse, physician, EMT)
    (e) a lifeguard
    (f) a process server
    (g) a traffic officer
    (h) an animal control officer
    (i) a school employee (243.6 PC)
    (j) a juror involved in the defendant's case (243.7 PC)
    (k) a sports official (243.8 PC)
    (l) ANY person on
        (i) the property (incl. parking lots), or
        (ii) any vehicle

of either a private or public transit provider. (243.3 PC)

(2) When the person knows or should reasonably know the victim is one of the above persons

(3) And the victim is actually engaged in the performance of his or her duties. (Note: To counter the Cory Decision, this law now covers peace officers in uniform performing duties in a private capacity as part-time or casual private security.) (People *v.* Cory, 21 Cal 3d 738)

(4) Other victims under this law:
   (a) any person, when they suffer "serious bodily injury" as a result of the battery
   (b) a spouse
   (c) a person with whom the defendant is cohabiting
   (d) a person who is the parent of the defendant's child
   (e) former spouse
   (f) a fiancé or fiancee
   (g) a person with whom there is or was a "dating or engagement relationship."

Dating Relationship:

When there are frequent, intimate associations, primarily characterized by the expectation of affectionate or sexual involvement independent of financial considerations.

For b, c, and d, punishment includes completion of a Batterer's Treatment Program. For a second conviction of this section—a minimum of 48 hours in jail. Serious bodily injury is defined as a serious impairment of physical condition, including, but not limited to, the following conditions:

(1) Loss of consciousness.
(2) Bone fracture.
(3) Protracted loss or impairment of function of any bodily member or organ.
(4) A wound requiring extensive suturing.
(5) Serious disfigurement.
(6) A concussion.

(C) Battery on Certain Properties (243.2 PC)

(1) When battery is committed on any person
(2) On
   (a) school property
   (b) park property
   (c) grounds of a public or private hospital.

(D) Felony Battery by Inmates (243.15 PC)

Battery by an inmate is a felony (wobbler) when the victim is not another inmate. (Example: guards, nurses, doctors and visitors)

(E) Sexual Battery (243.4 PC)

(a) While Victim is Restrained
   (a) touching an intimate part of another
   (b) while victim is unlawfully restrained
   (c) by the accused or an accomplice
   (d) against the will of the person touched
   (e) for the purpose of sexual arousal, sexual gratification, or sexual abuse.

(b) When Victim is Institutionalized
   (a) touching intimate part of another
   (b) when victim is institutionalized for medical treatment
   (c) and is seriously disabled, or medically incapacitated
   (d) and it is against the will of the victim
   (e) for the purpose of sexual arousal, sexual gratification or sexual abuse.

(c) Victim Unconscious of Nature of Act
   (a) Who commits sexual battery
   (b) When the victim is unconscious of the nature of the act
   (c) Because the perpetrator fraudulently represented the act as serving a professional purpose
   (d) When no such purpose was served.

(d) Punishment

The above offenses are punishable as "wobblers."

(e) Employer/Employee Sexual Harassment

If the victim was an employee of the defendant, the punishment shall be increased.

(f) Definitions:

Touches: physical contact with the skin of another person, whether accomplished directly or through the clothing of the perpetrator.

Intimate part: the sexual organ, anus, groin, or buttocks of any person, and the breast of a female.

Institutionalized: in a hospital, medical treatment facility, nursing home or mental hospital.

Seriously Disabled: person with a severe physical or sensory impairment.

Medically Incapacitated: incapacitated as a result of prescribed sedatives, anesthesia or other medication.

Sexual Battery does not include 261 or 289 PC.

(F) Mayhem (203 PC)

(1) Every person who unlawfully and maliciously
(2) Deprives a human being of a part of his body
(3) OR

(a) disables a part of his body
(b) disfigures a part of his body
(c) renders a part of his body useless
(d) cuts or disables the tongue
(e) puts out an eye
(f) slits the nose, ear, or lip.

According to 7 PC, subsection 4, "Maliciously" means "to vex, annoy, or injure another person, or an intent to do a wrongful act, established either by proof or presumption of law."

The crime of mayhem requires no malice aforethought, deliberation or premeditation. (People *v*. Wright, 93 Cal. 564) Nor is it required that the assailant intended the particular injury suffered by the victim, as long as the attack is unlawful and malicious. (People *v*. Nunes, 47 Cal. App. 346).

Although the wording of the statute states "slits the ear, etc.," in People *v*. Goldern, 62 Cal. 542, it was held that biting off part of the victim's ear amounted to mayhem.

In the Nunes case mentioned above, the phrase "puts out the eye" was held to mean any injury to such an extent that the victim could not use it for practical purposes of life.

Mayhem was made a crime in the Middle Ages in an effort to stop a great number of potential soldiers from becoming unfit for military duty through duels. Another reason was to add another felony to the list of crimes for which the Crown could seize a person's estate or property. Today most charges of mayhem are reduced the next morning to battery, or changed to ADW. It is only in serious cases that the charge will stick. Lacerating another's lip or nose by blows to the face, not with a sharp instrument, are not examples of mayhem. (People *v*. Sears, 62 A.C.A. 783)

(G) Aggravated Mayhem (205 PC)

When mayhem is committed with an extreme indifference to physical or psychological well being of another, the punishment will be life imprisonment (with possibility of parole).

(H) <u>Torture (206 PC)</u>

(1) Who with the intent to cause cruel or extreme pain and suffering
(2) For the purpose of revenge, extortion, persuasion or sadistic motivation
(3) Inflicts great bodily injury upon the person of another
(4) Shall be imprisoned for life.

<u>Note</u>: Torture does not require any proof that the victim suffered pain.

(I) Corporal Injury to Child (273d PC)

(1) Any person who willfully inflicts upon any child (under 18)
(2) Any
   (a) cruel corporal punishment
   (b) inhuman corporal punishment, or
   (c) injury resulting in traumatic condition, is guilty of a "wobbler."

Upon conviction for a second offense of this section within a 10-year period, a four-year enhancement is added to the original sentence.

(J) Battery Against Cohabiting Person (273.5 PC)

(1) Any person who willfully inflicts corporal injury resulting in a traumatic condition,
(2) Upon any spouse, former spouse, cohabitant, former cohabitant, fiancé, someone with whom the offender has, or previously had, an engagement or dating relationship, or the father or mother of his or her child,
(3) Is guilty of a "Wobbler."

<u>Cohabiting</u>: Living together in a husband and wife relationship

Because the second element uses the term "opposite sex," two individuals of the same sex who are living together in a state of cohabitation do not come under this section when one commits battery upon the other.

<u>Traumatic Condition</u>: A minor or serious injury of the body, external or internal, caused by physical force. The term "traumatic condition" seems to imply something very serious. Yet the Appellate Court in People *v*. Burns, (88 Cal. App. 2d 867) stated that the term meant "a bodily injury caused by the application of force." This is a very broad interpretation and could include such things as a slap or punch to the face or body where a visible mark is left. If there is a mark on the body, it indicates that some blood vessels have broken from the blow, and although this can be done very easily on some people, it would amount to a "bodily injury caused by the application of force."

This section can be used as an "Ace-in-the-Hole," but only in the interest of justice. When an officer responds to a family fight and the husband is drunk and has punched his wife and she is afraid to have him arrested, the officer can use 273d as a means of making an arrest; he would not otherwise be able to do so. The purpose of this arrest would be to protect the wife from possible serious injury.

Because it would, in effect, be making a felony out of what would normally be a misdemeanor (battery); the next morning the D.A.'s office would probably drop the charge to battery.

Prosecution for Section 273.5 may be commenced within 5 years of the crime (for crimes that are committed on or after January 1, 2020), and to crimes for which the statute of limitations that was in effect prior to January 1, 2020, has not run out as of January 1, 2020.

Confidential Status of 273.5 Victims

Victims of 273.5 PC can have their names and addresses declared confidential. (Gov. Code 6254)

Violation of Temporary Restraining Order (273.6 PC)

(1) Willfully and knowingly violates a temporary restraining order.
(2) By molesting, attacking, striking, threatening, sexually assaulting, battering, harassing, telephoning, destroying personal property, contacting, either directly or indirectly, by mail or otherwise, coming within a specified dis-distance of, or disturbing that person's (or other member of that person's household) peace, or repeated contact by mail with the intent to harass.
(3) Applies to out-of-state TROs.

Disclosing the Location of a Domestic Violence Shelter (273.7 PC)

(1) Malicious disclosure, without authorized permission,
(2) Of the location of a domestic violence shelter
(3) Is a misdemeanor.

Victims of Domestic Violence Card (13701 PC)

(1) When there is an alleged violation of 243, 261, 261.5, 262, 273.5, 286, 287, former 288a, or 289 PC
(2) The responding officer shall give the victim a "Victims of Domestic Violence" card that includes the following information:
    a. emergency hotlines for local battered women shelters and centers for rape victim counseling. It will also list the proper procedures for the victim to follow, and give the general toll-free phone number for the California Victims' Compensation Program (1-800-777-9229).
    b. A simple statement on the proper procedures for victims to follow after a sexual assault;
    c. A statement that sexual assault by a person who is known to the victim or is a spouse is a crime;
    d. A statement that domestic violence or assault by a person who is known to the victim or is a spouse is a crime;
    e. A statement informing the victim that strangulation may cause internal injuries and encourages the victim to seek medical help.

Chapter V Case Citations

Study Questions for Chapter V

(1) Some assaults are lawful. T or F

(2) In order to have an assault, a person who "swings" at another must actually hit him. T or F

(3) Hector Honk points an unloaded gun at Clyde Crashcup. This would be an example of Assault. T or F

(4) The term "Violent Injury" as used in the crime of assault, indicates that an injury be severe or at least visible. T or F

(5) Taking "indecent liberties" with a woman is an example of battery. T or F

(6) Kissing a woman against her will is battery. T or F

(7) Pointing a loaded gun at a person and threatening to kill him would be an assault. T or F

(8) Battery is a completed assault. T or F

(9) Spitting at a person and missing is an assault. T or F

(10) Pouring a glass of water onto a person is an example of battery. T or F

(11) In order for there to be a battery, there must also be some injury or infliction of pain on the victim. T or F

(12) The Penal Code section for Assault is ________________________________ PC.

(13) The Penal Code section for Battery is ________________________________ PC.

(14) The Penal Code section for ADW is ________________________________ PC.

(15) In ADW, the person assaulting the victim must use a weapon of some sort. T or F

(16) In order to obtain a conviction in court for ADW, the weapon must be produced. T or F

(17) In order to scare his neighbor, Larry Lurch fires a gun into the air. This would be an example of ADW. T or F

(18) The offense "Assault with Caustic Chemicals" (244 PC) is really "battery" with caustic chemicals. T or F

(19) The term "Vitriol" as used in 244 PC, means:

(A) ____sulfuric acid (B) ____ invisible
(C) ____blinding (D) ____ liquid

(20) In section 246 PC, "Assault with Firearms on Inhabited Dwelling," the building must be occupied by some human being at the time of the shooting. T or F

(21) In section 247 PC, pertaining to firing at an airplane, the airplane must be in the air for this section to be in effect. T or F

(22) 417 PC "Drawing or Exhibiting a Firearm in a Threatening Manner" applies only if the firearm is loaded. T or F

(23) 417 PC "Drawing or Exhibiting a Firearm in a Threatening Manner" applies only to the exhibiting of firearms. T or F

(24) In Mayhem, the term "slits the ear" also includes biting off part of the ear. T or F

(25) In Mayhem, "puts out the eye" includes any act that injures the eye so that sight is lost. T or F

(26) Punching another in the lip and causing it to split is an example of mayhem. T or F

(27) What is the Penal Code section for "Corporal Injury To Child?" ________________PC

(28) In "Corporal Injury to Child," the child must be the child of the person who is causing harm to the child. T or F

(29) In "Battery of Cohabitant," 273.5 PC, the victim must be the spouse of the perpetrator. T or F

(30) Words of abuse can, in some cases, justify an assault. T or F

(31) Under 273.5 PC, "Battery of Cohabitant," a black eye is classed as a "traumatic condition." T or F

CHAPTER VI

SEX OFFENSES

Sexual Conduct

Sexual conduct in California is permissive. This means that if there is no law prohibiting a specific sexual act, then that act is permissible. Remember that California law is "statutory," and must be written in order for it to be law.

Fornication

The concept of fornication is often misunderstood, especially by non-native Californians. Fornication is sexual intercourse between an unmarried male and female who are both over 18 years of age. Since there is no statute declaring this act illegal, it is permissible as long as both parties to the act are over 18 years of age, and have agreed. If the agreement is somehow obtained by fraud, it is legally not a valid agreement. Such acts are often observed by patrol officers while checking out their beat, especially if the beat contains a "lover's lane."

Rape and Related Offenses

(A) Rape (261 PC)

The crime of rape has four elements. Three are constant; the fourth varies according to how the rape was accomplished.

The elements of rape are:

(a) An act of sexual intercourse
(b) Accomplished with a person
(c) Not the spouse of the perpetrator
(d) Under any of the following circumstances:
   (1) The victim is incapable because of mental disease, defect, or disorder, or because of physical disability, of giving legal consent, and this condition is known or should reasonably be known to the perpetrator.
   (2) It is accomplished against the victim's will by means of force, violence, duress, menace, or fear of immediate and unlawful bodily injury to the victim or another.
   (3) The victim is prevented from resistance by any intoxicating narcotic or anesthetic substance and this is known or should be known by the accused.
   (4) The victim is unconscious of the nature of the act, and this is known to the accused. "Unconscious of the nature of the act" means one of the following:
      (i) Was unconscious or asleep.
      (ii) Was not aware, knowing, perceiving or cognizant that the act occurred.
      (iii) Due to the perpetrator's fraud, the victim was not aware, knowing, perceiving or cognizant that the act occurred.

(iv) Due to the perpetrator's fraudulent representation that the sexual penetration served a professional purpose when no professional purpose was in fact served, the victim was not aware, knowing, perceiving or cognizant of the true nature of the act.

(5) The victim submits under the belief that the person committing the act is someone known to the victim other than the accused, and this belief is induced by artifice, pretense, or concealment by the accused, with intent to induce the belief.

(6) The act is accomplished against the victim's will by threatening to retaliate in the future against the victim or any other person, and there is a reasonable possibility the perpetrator will execute the threat. As used in this paragraph "threatening to retaliate" means a threat to kidnap or falsely imprison, or to inflict extreme pain, serious bodily injury, or death.

(7) The act is accomplished by threat to use authority of a public official to
- (i) incarcerate,
- (ii) arrest, or
- (iii) deport,

the victim or another, and the victim has reasonable belief that the perpetrator is a public official.

Penetration (263 PC)

The essential guilt of rape consists in the outrage to the person and feelings of the victim of the rape. Any sexual penetration, however slight, is sufficient to complete the crime. The element of penetration can be proved by both circumstantial evidence and direct evidence. (People *v*. Vicencio, 71 CA 2d 361).

Probation & Suspended Sentences Prohibited

Because studies in 1977 showed that less than 50% of all persons convicted of rape were actually sentenced to state prison, this law prohibits a convicted rapist from receiving either probation or a suspended sentence if he has violated sections 261(2) Forcible Rape, 261(3) Rape by Threat of Great Bodily Harm, or 264.1 Rape Acting in Concert (Gang Rape).

A conviction for rape may be had solely on the testimony of the victim; there need be no corroboration. (People *v*. Frye, 117 C.A. 2d 101). This is unusual in criminal law. Legislators feel that rape is a severe crime, and there is often little evidence that can be used as corroboration. However, the jury must be convinced beyond a reasonable doubt that the victim is telling the truth. The defense attorney will certainly put the victim through a very difficult cross examination.

Rape is an unusual crime in that it is often falsely reported, yet studies show that it is reported only about half of the time that it occurs. It seems that many rape victims are so embarrassed at having been so personally violated, they refuse to report it. Since the crime is so often falsely reported, investigating officers must be careful in questioning the victim to obtain vital information. The sooner the rape is reported, the more likely will the testimony of the victim be accepted in court. There was one case where the complaint was received three weeks after the rape occurred. The courts stated that it was not made within a reasonable time, and held the complaint as inadmissible. (People *v*. Corey, 8 C.A. 720)

Element (a), Proof of Penetration

The first step by investigating officers should be to take the victim to a hospital where a doctor may perform an examination to determine if there is evidence of sexual penetration. If the doctor can find evidence of sperm or semen, it is good prima facie evidence of penetration, but not proof positive. It could have been put there by the husband or boyfriend. When investigating a case of this nature, and the doctor finds such evidence, officers should confidentially ask victims if they have recently had sexual intercourse with anyone else. If yes, the blood type or DNA of that person should be obtained. Then a special request should be sent to the crime lab to obtain the blood type or DNA from the semen. If it is different, it would block the defense in court that the semen belonged, not to the de- fendant, but to the victim's boyfriend or husband.

Other ways in which penetration can be corroborated is when the victim has become pregnant or contracted a venereal disease. In some cases the fact that the victim has received physical injury such as scrapes and bruises is corroboration.

Element (b), Accomplished With a Person

This means that the victim must be a human being and not an animal. It also means that a woman can now legally commit rape on a male.

Element (c), Not the Spouse of Perpetrator

Under section 261 of the Penal Code, a spouse cannot rape another spouse. Rape of a Spouse is covered under section 262 PC.

The "Principal" Concept of Rape

Under the California classifications of "Principals," a person, male or female, who assists another to commit rape is just as guilty as the person who physically commits the rape. This could create an exception to 261 PC in that a husband could be guilty of the rape of his wife if he assisted another man to rape her.

Element (d), Subsections of

(a) Where the Victim is of Unsound Mind

Legal consent requires that the victim have an intelligence capable of understanding the act, its nature and its possible consequences (People *v.* Griffin, 117 C 583). This can be difficult to determine in some cases. Technically this subsection would cover a person who is under the mental age of 18, just as the crime of "Unlawful Intercourse" (Old Statutory Rape) covers a person under the chronological age of 18. However, the measuring of mental age is not a precise science, and any defense attorney could bring experts to show that tests can vary by as much as five years.

To play it safe, the D.A. will want the victim to have a very observable lack of mental age, one that all the members of the jury will easily be able to detect by observing her on the stand. Because of this, the prosecutor will often want to personally talk to the victim in cases of this nature.

(b) By Means of Force, Duress, Menace or Threat of Unlawful Injury to Another

The resistance of the victim, to support a charge of rape, need only be such as to make non-consent and actual resistance reasonably manifest. (People *v.* Cook, 10 CA 2d 54) Consent is a positive cooperation in the act—an attitude pursuant to an exercise of free will. The person must act freely and voluntarily and have knowledge of the nature of the act or transaction involved.

The victim need resist only until physical penetration occurs, at which time the crime is complete. Failure to resist after that time is immaterial. (People *v.* Cook)

Definitions:

Duress:

(1) A direct or implied threat of force, violence, danger, hardship, or retribution.
(2) To coerce a reasonable person of ordinary susceptibilities to perform an act which otherwise would not have been performed.
(3) Agrees to an act to which one would not normally submit.

Further Corroboration:

Total circumstances of the situation, including victim's age and relationship to defendant must be considered in determining existence of duress.

Menace:

Any threat, declaration or act which shows an intention to inflict injury upon another.

Consent:

For sections 261, 286, 287, 289 or former 288a PC, consent means a positive cooperation in an act or attitude involving the use of free will. The victim must not only act freely and voluntarily, but know the nature of the act. A current or previous dating relationship shall not be sufficient to prove consent.

Neither admissibility of evidence or burden of proof is affected by this definition. (261.6 PC).

The Mistaken Belief Rule on Consent

In 1975, the high court allowed a defense based on an honest belief that the victim was consenting to the act even if no consent was given.

In 1992, the California Supreme Court narrowed this rule by requiring that the defendant offer "substantial evidence of equivocal conduct" when using this defense. He must show that the victim did something that would cause a reasonable person to believe that he or she had consented, based on conduct or words.

Consent in Sex Offenses (261.7 PC)

(1) In prosecutions under sections 261, 286, 287, 289 or former 288a PC,
(2) In which consent is an issue of defense,
(3) Evidence that the victim suggested, requested or otherwise communicated to the defendant that he use a condom or birth control device,
(4) Without additional evidence of consent,
(5) Is not sufficient to constitute consent.

(c) Where the Victim is Prevented from Resistance by Threats or Drugs

This now includes threats to do future harm, not only to the victim, but to another person.

Where the rapist held a knife against the victim's throat and told her he would cut her throat if she cried out, the court held that she was in no way required to resist under such circumstances. (People *v*. Trapps, 152 CA 2d 413)

Where the rapist had a knife and threatened to kill her child, and where she was allowed to use a contraceptive device to avoid pregnancy, the court held that she was not required to resist. (People *v*. Blandership, 171 CA 2d 66)

Threats as used in this subsection need not be expressed in words or through exhibition of a weapon, but may be expressed by other acts and conduct. (People *v*. Flores, 62 CA 2d 700)

Rape through the use of drugs may be proved by circumstantial evidence. (People *v*. Crosby, 17 CA 518)

Where the victim and the defendant had consumed intoxicants, and she was seen lying unconscious with the defendant nearby, and she later discovered physical evidence that someone had sexual intercourse with her, the courts held that this circumstantial evidence along with other evidence was enough for conviction. (People *v*. O'Brien, 130 C 1)

(d) Where Victim is Unconscious of the Nature of the Act

There is little in California case law in this area. There have been a number of convictions, but none have been contested to higher courts where they could have interpretive rulings. One of the earliest cases occurred in England in 1887 in Regina *v*. Flattery. The victim was under the impression that she was submitting to a surgical operation. Instead the doctor took advantage of the situation and sexually penetrated her vagina.

Consent Obtained by Fraud

An even earlier case occurred in the United States in 1872. In Don Moran *v*. People of Michigan, a doctor fraudulently induced a female patient to believe that sexual intercourse was essential to her medical treatment. She believed and submitted. Later the court held that her consent was obtained by fraud. A conviction was sustained.

(e) Where the Victim Believed that the Perpetrator Was Her Spouse

There are two common types of cases where this can occur. One is where the perpetrator sneaks into the bedroom of a sleeping woman whose husband is away. She senses that someone is in the room getting undressed. He then gets into bed, and the woman, assuming that it is her husband, allows the act of penetration to take place. When she discovers that it is not her husband, the penetration has been made and the act of rape is complete.

The other type of case is where the perpetrator goes through a fraudulent or sham marriage with the victim, and she, believing it legitimate allows the perpetrator to have sexual intercourse with her. (People *v*. McCoy, 58 CA 534) This type of offense could also be a violation of 266 PC.

(f) Threats to Victim or Other Person of Harm in Future

This is similar to subsections (2) and (3) except that it involves a threat of harm in the future, and, unlike (3), it can be harm to another person and not just the victim of the rape. It can also involve a threat to kidnap or falsely imprison the victim or another person.

(g) Threat to Use Authority Against the Victim

Because there are so many illegal aliens in California, some women have become victims of rape and sexual abuse through threats of arrest, imprisonment or deportation. The perpetrators are not necessarily immigration or governmental authorities. They do, however, claim to be persons of authority who have the power to arrest, imprison or initiate deportation proceedings.

(B) Rape of a Person Who is Spouse of Perpetrator (262 PC)

Rape of a person who is the spouse of the perpetrator is an act of sexual intercourse accomplished under any of the following circumstances:

By means of:

1. (262(1) PC) Where it is accomplished against a person's will by means of force, violence, duress, menace, or fear of immediate and unlawful bodily injury on the person of another;
2. (262(2) PC) Resistance prevented by intoxicating, anesthetic or controlled substance;
3. (262(3) PC) Where a person is at the time unconscious of the nature of the act, and this is known to the accused; Incapable of resisting because the victim:
   a) was unconscious or asleep;
   b) was not aware, knowing, perceiving, or cognizant that the act occurred;
   c) was not aware, knowing perceiving, or cognizant of the essential characteristics of the act due to the perpetrator's fraud in fact;
4. (262(4) PC) Where an act is accomplished against the victim with threat to retaliate against the victim;
5. (262(5) PC) Where the act is accomplished against the victim by threatening to use authority of public official to incarcerate, arrest or deport.

(C) Gang Rape Etc. (264.1 PC)

(1) Who commits 261, 262 or 289 PC
(2) By force or violence
(3) Against the will of the victim
(4) And voluntarily acts in concert with another person
(5) Is guilty of a felony. (5, 7, or 9 years)

(D) Rape Victim Treatment

The Health & Safety and Penal Codes contain laws pertaining to the treatment of rape victims.

(a) 13823.9 PC:

Counties with populations of over 100,000 shall have, at all times present or on call at the county hospital, clinic or other emergency medical facility, specially trained professional personnel to examine victims of rape and other sexual assaults and abuse. This shall be at no cost to the victim or agency bringing the victim to the hospital.

(b) 1491 H & S:

These personnel shall also provide free testing for venereal disease and pregnancy for the victims of rape and other sexual assaults.

(c) 1492 H & S:

A county hospital shall provide victims treated in connection with sexual assault, with information regarding assistance to which they may be entitled, together with claim forms issued by the California Victim Compensation Board.

(d) 13823.5 PC:

The Office of Emergency Services shall adopt and provide county hospitals with a standard form (or electronic version) to be filled out by the examining doctor or qualified healthcare professional. It shall be confidential and copies provided only to the victim, defendant, prosecuting agencies and the Department of Justice. There are some exceptions upon court order with the victim's notification.

(e) 13823.7 PC:

A protocol for the medical treatment of sexual assault and abuse victims shall be adopted pursuant to section 13823.5 PC.

(f) 13516 PC:

The Commission on Peace Officer Standards and Training (POST) will establish standard procedures which may be used in the investigation of alleged sexual assaults, and will be included in the basic POST course. This section encourages the establishment of Sex Crime Investigation Units.

(g) 11116.10 PC:

Rape victims shall be notified by the prosecuting attorney of the final outcome of the case and its disposition. This must be requested by the victim.

(h) Protection of Rape Victim's Address and Phone Number (Ev. Code 352.1):

Upon request of the D.A., a rape victim's address and phone number will be restricted and not revealed in court. It also includes victims of 264.1, 286(c) or (d), 287 (c) or (d), or former 288a PC.

(i) Evidence of Prior Sexual Conduct (Ev. Code 1103):

Evidence of prior sexual conduct on the part of a rape victim will be prohibited unless it was with the defendant.

(j) Jury Instruction in Rape Code (1127d PC):

In a rape case, the jury will NOT be instructed by the judge to the effect that the victim's past sexual activities could affect her testimony.

(k) Use of term "Unchaste Character" (1127e PC):

The term "unchaste character" is NOT to be used in criminal cases involving rape (261 PC) or Unlawful Intercourse (261.5 PC).

(l) Moral Support for Victims Who Provide Testimony During Trials (868.5 PC):

(1) Victims of
  (a) rape
  (b) illegal oral copulation or illegal sodomy
  (c) human trafficking
  (d) certain obscene matter violations, particularly involving children
  (e) child abuse
  (f) elder or dependent adult abuse

And prosecuting witnesses for cases involving
  (a) prostitution, pimping and pandering

(2) May have present at both the preliminary hearing and trial
(3) A person of their choosing
(4) To remain in court for moral support.

(m) Witness Testimony – Therapy Dogs (868.4 PC):

If requested by either party in a criminal or juvenile hearing, if a therapy dog is available and the court approves, a child witness or victim who is entitled to a support person per 868.5 PC has the opportunity to have a therapy dog accompany him or her while testifying in court.

(n) Rape Victims' Consent to Medical Examination (6927 FC):

A minor, 12 years or older, who reports that she has been raped, can give consent for a medical examination without parental permission.

(o) Confidentiality of Victim's Name and Address (6254 Gov. Code):

Although police records are considered public records, and available to the public, the names and addresses of sex crime victims can be restricted when requested by the victim or a guardian. This applies only to the following offenses: 220, 236.1, 261, 261.5, 262, 264, 264.1, 265, 266, 267, 269, 273a, 273d, 273.5, 285, 286, 288, 288a, 288.3, 288.5, 288.7, 289, 422.6, 422.7, 422.75, 646.9, and 647.6 PC.

(p) Duty of Police to Notify Sexual Offense Victims of Name Confidentiality (293 PC):

(1) A peace officer who receives a report of a sexual offense
(2) Must notify victims that their names and addresses can become a matter of public record
(3) Unless they request to be exempt under 6254 Govt. Code.
(4) The notification shall be indicated in the officer's report.

(q) Requiring Victim of Sex Crime to Take Polygraph (637.4 PC & 782 & 1103 Ev. Code):

It is illegal to demand that a victim of a sex offense by force or threat take a polygraph test as a prerequisite to filing an accusatory pleading (criminal complaint). A court may not order a victim or witness in a case involving sexual assault, to submit to a psychiatric exam to assess credibility. The victim's prior sex acts are not admissible.

(r) Victim Advocates (679.04 PC):

(1) A victim of sexual assault involving sections 261, 261.5, 262, 273.5, 286, 287 and 289 PC
(2) Has the right to have
  (a) victim advocates, and
  (b) a support person of his or her choosing present at any interview by law enforcement authorities, district attorneys, or defense attorneys. However, the support person may be excluded from an interview by law enforcement or the district attorney if they determine that the presence of that person would be detrimental to the purpose of the interview. They must also notify the victim that the victim advocates and support person have the right to be present when the defense attorney or investigators conduct an interview.

(s) Exclusion From Medical Evidentiary Exam (264.2 PC):

A support person may be excluded from a medical evidentiary or physical examination if the law enforcement officer or medical advisor determines that the presence of that individual would be detrimental to the purpose of the examination.

(t) Sexual Assault DNA Bill of Rights (680 PC):

Law enforcement agencies have an obligation to victims of sexual assaults in the proper handling, retention, and timely DNA testing of rape kit evidence or other crime scene evidence and to be responsive to victims concerning the developments of forensic testing and the investigation of their cases.

A law enforcement agency shall not destroy or dispose of rape kit evidence or other crime scene evidence from an unsolved sexual assault case before at least 20 years, or if the victim was under 18 years of age at the time of the alleged offense, before the victim's 40th birthday.

Officers' Duties When Handling Victim of Specified Sex Offenses (264.2 PC) or Domestic Violence

(1) Whenever there is an alleged violation of 261, 261.5, 262, 273.5, 286, 287 or 289 PC
(2) The assigned officer shall:
  (a) provide the victim with a "Victims of Domestic Violence" card, and
  (b) notify the local Rape Victim Counseling Center that the victim is being transported to a hospital for examination.
(3) If there is to be a medical, evidentiary or physical exam, the victim shall have the right to have a Sexual Assault Victim counselor AND at least one other support person of the victim's choosing to be present during the exam.
(4) If a sexual assault has been claimed, the medical provider shall notify the victim (orally or in writing) of the victim's legal right to have the designated persons present during the exam.
(5) The hospital may verify with the assigned officer that the counseling center has been notified.

(E) Inducing Illegal Sex by Fraud or Fear (266c PC)

In 1986 this section was added to existing case law to make it clear that inducing sex by fraud was illegal. It also covers cases where consent is obtained by fear.

(1) Every person who induces another,
(2) Other than the spouse of the perpetrator,
(3) To engage in
  (a) sexual intercourse,
  (b) oral copulation, or
  (c) sodomy,
(4) When the consent is obtained by fraud or with the intent to create fear (in a reasonable person) of physical injury or death to the victim or a relative,
(5) And which does in fact induce that fear,
(6) And causes the victim to act contrary to his or her free will,
(7) Is guilty of a wobbler.

(F) Unlawful Intercourse (261.5 PC)

Unlawful intercourse is the same as the old "Statutory Rape." It has been given a new name to remove it from the rape category since it never was really rape. It still has the same elements as "Statutory Rape." They are:

(1) An act of sexual intercourse
(2) Accomplished with a person
(3) Not the spouse of the perpetrator
(4) When the victim is under the age of 18 years.

Under the old law, if a victim was under 18, the defendant was guilty. There were no extenuating circumstances. Today there is one. If the "victim" appears to be over 18, the jury or judge, as a "Question of Fact" can determine whether the victim appears to be over 18. If they find he/she does, it removes the element of criminal intent, and the defendant may be found not guilty. (People *v.* Hernandez, 61 Cal. 2d 537)

A person may be guilty of unlawful intercourse even if the victim is married. (People *v.* Derbert, 138 Cal. 467) It is no defense if the perpetrator is younger than the victim and the victim was really the aggressor. (People *v.* Derbert, supra) The victim could even have children. If she were under the age of 18, the law would still apply.

Different Subsections and Former Jeopardy

If the defendant is charged with one subsection of 261 PC, and the jury finds that he is really guilty of another subsection, they may still find him guilty of rape under 261 of the Penal Code. (People *v.* Craig, 17 Cal. 2d 453)

Example:

The defendant is charged with rape by force and violence, but it is later found in court that it was accomplished by fraud. The conviction will be sustained. Rape is not divided into degrees, and all rapes come under the same penal code section. (People *v.* Snyder, 75 Cal. 323)

Defenses for the Charge of Rape

By knowing the two major defenses used in rape cases, an officer can better assist the prosecution by providing evidence to counter them.

(1) Identity

Where the suspect is not known to the victim, it is common for the defendant to simply deny that he is the one who committed the crime. He claims that he is a victim of improper identification.

An accumulation of circumstantial evidence such as clothing fibers, hair, blood, footprints, semen or such evidence which might not be good enough as positive evidence, could still add to the weight of the victim's testimony. Fingerprints on beer cans or weapons found at the scene will prove identity.

(2) Consent

One of the most common defenses in a charge of forcible rape is that it was not forcible, but with consent of the victim, especially if the victim knows the suspect. The best way to counter this defense is to show evidence of marks, scratches, bruises, contusions or torn clothing. It is important that such evidence be photographed in color. A search for witnesses might turn up someone who heard a cry for help, or saw a struggle but was afraid to call the police. (See also 261.7 PC, Consent in Sex Offenses, on page 104.)

Sex With Confined Consenting Adults (289.6 PC)

(1) Any employee of a public or private detention facility or law enforcement agency,
(2) Who engages in sexual activity with any consenting adult,
(3) Who is confined in a detention or correctional facility, jail, transporting vehicle or holding room.

Exception: Legal conjugal visits
(2nd offense is a felony).

Molesting Sections

(A) Lewd and Lascivious Acts With Children Under 14 (288 PC)

(1) Any person who willfully and lewdly commits any lewd or lascivious act,
(2) Upon
  (a) the body or
  (b) any part or member thereof
(3) Of a child under the age of 14 years of age,
(4) With the intent of arousing, appealing to, or gratifying the lust, passions, or sexual desires
(5) Of either
  (a) the perpetrator or
  (b) the child.

The sex of the child is not mentioned and can be male or female (People *v*. Curtis, 1 Cal. App. 1); it does not matter if the child participated voluntarily in the act. (People *v*. Piccionelli, 175 Cal. App. 2d 391) The act need not be obscene, or for that matter of a sexual character; it just has to be done with the intent mentioned. (People *v*. Hobbs, 109 Cal. App. 2d 189)

Examples of acts under 288

(a) Rubbing a clothed part of the body (People *v*. Dabner, 25 Cal. App. 630)
(b) Feeling the breast of a female child (People *v*. McCurdy, 60 Cal. App. 449)
(c) Feeling the child's legs (People *v*. Halistic, 69 Cal. App. 174)
(d) Placing the child's hands on his private parts (People *v*. Anthony, 20 Cal. App. 2d 586)
(e) "French kissing" the child (People *v*. Ash, 70 Cal. App. 2d 583)
(f) Removing the child's underwear (People *v*. Lanham, 137 Cal. App. 737)

As in the crimes of rape and sodomy, the testimony of the child need not be corroborated. (People *v*. Wilder, 151 Cal. App. 2d 698) In fact, the child need not be called as a witness. (People *v*. Ewing, 71 Cal. App. 138)

(B) Annoying or Molesting Children Under 18 (647.6 PC)

(1) Every person who
  (a) annoys or
  (b) molests
(2) Any child under the age of 18.

Although it doesn't specifically state it in the letter of the law, there is a connotation of abnormal sex motivation on the part of the offender. (People *v*. Pallares, 112 Cal. App. 2d 895)

The words "annoy" and "molest" are often used synonymously. They have been interpreted as meaning: to disturb, to inconvenience, to irritate, to trouble, to hurt, or to vex.

Other Sex Offenses

(A) Annoying or Molesting Adults (Disorderly Conduct) (647 PC)

(1) An individual who engages in,
(2) Or solicits anyone to engage in,
(3) Lewd or dissolute conduct
(4) In any
  (a) public place

(b) place open to the public
(c) place exposed to public view.

(B) Sexual Offenses Permissible Between Consenting Adults, But Illegal Under Certain Conditions (incl. 286, 287, former 288a, & 289 PC)

Sodomy (286 PC)

(1) Sexual conduct consisting of contact between the penis of one person,
(2) And the anus of another person,
(3) Where penetration, however slight, occurs. This act is legal between consenting adults with the following exceptions:
  (a) Victim was under age of 18.
  (b) Against the victim's will and by means of force, violence, duress, menace, or fear of immediate and unlawful injury on either the victim or another person; or by threats to retaliate in the future against the victim or any other person.
  (c) When the parties are in jail or a correctional facility (prison).
  (d) The victim was incapable of giving consent because of a mental disorder or developmental disability, and accused knew or should have reasonably known this.
  (e) The same as above, but both persons are confined to a state mental hospital.
  (f) The victim is unconscious of the nature of the act, and the accused knew or should have reasonably known this. (E.g., the victim was unconscious or asleep or unable to perceive the nature of the act.)
  (g) Resistance was prevented by any intoxicating, anesthetic or controlled substance, and this was known or reasonably should have been known by the accused.
  (h) The victim believed that the suspect was victim's spouse, or someone known to the victim other than the accused (induced by any artifice or pretense by the accused.)
  (i) Resistance is overcome by threatening to use the authority of a public official to arrest, jail or deport the victim, and the victim reasonably believed this.

Conditions (j) and (k) do not necessarily involve being against the victim's will. They are listed because they affect the degree of punishment.

  (j) Accused is over 21 years of age and victim is under 16 years of age.
  (k) Victim is under 14 years of age and is 10 years younger than accused.

"Unconscious of the Nature of the Act" means incapable of resisting because of one of the following conditions:

(a) Victim is unconscious or asleep.
(b) Was not aware, knowing, perceiving or cognizant of the act.
(c) Was not aware, knowing, perceiving or cognizant due to perpetrator's fraud.
(d) Was not aware, knowing, perceiving or cognizant because of perpetrator's fraudulent representation that sexual penetration served a professional purpose, when it did not.

Oral Copulation (287 PC)

(1) The act of copulating the mouth of one person
(2) With the sexual organ or anus of another.

This act is legal between consenting adults, but with the same exceptions as listed under 286 PC. Touching the mouth to the sexual organ of another completes the offense. There need be no penetration. (People *v.* Bennet 119 CA 2d 224)

Except for acts listed in Section 288, oral copulation with a child under age 18 is a wobbler, depending on the circumstances, such as age of the victim. Oral copulation with a child under 14, or an individual over the age of 21 who performs this act with a child under 16, is a felony.

Sexual Penetration With Foreign Object (289 PC)

(I) Definitions

"Sexual Penetration"

(1) The act of causing the penetration, however slight,
(2) Of the genital or anal opening of the victim
(3) Or causing another to commit the act
(4) For the purpose of sexual arousal, gratification or abuse
(5) By any foreign object, substance or device or an unknown object.

The conditions are the same as sections 286 and 287 PC, except it does not have the condition "(c)" of while being incarcerated in a jail or prison.

Foreign Object:

Any instrument, substance or device including any part of the body, but not the penis.

Unknown Object:

(1) Any foreign object, substance, device, instrument or part of the body including a penis
(2) When the victim did not know the nature of the device.

(II) Types of Offenses Under 289 PC

(a)

(1) Any person who commits an act of sexual penetration
(2) Against the victim's will
(3) By means of force, violence, duress, menace or fear of immediate and unlawful injury to
(4) The victim or another person.

(b)

(1) Who commits the above act by means of threat to retaliate against the victim or another person
(2) In the future
(3) And such threat is reasonably possible.

(c)

(1) Who commits the above act
(2) When the victim is incapable of giving consent
(3) Because of a mental disorder or developmental or physical disability
(4) And this is or should be reasonably known to the perpetrator.

(d)

(1) Who commits the above act
(2) Against a person incapable of giving consent
(3) Because of mental disorder or developmental or physical disability
(4) When both parties are confined to a private or public mental facility.

(e)

(1) Where victim's resistance is overcome by an intoxicating, anesthetic or controlled substance
(2) And victim's condition was known or reasonably should have been known by the accused.

(f)

(1) Where penetration is allowed because of a belief that the perpetrator is the victim's spouse
(2) and this belief is induced by artifice, pretense or concealment practiced by the accused.

(g)

(1) Where sexual penetration is made
(2) Against the victim's will
(3) Because of threats by the accused to use the authority of a public official,
(4) To either arrest, incarcerate or deport the victim or another person
(5) And the victim had reasonable cause to believe it was so.

(h)

(1) Who violates 289 PC
(2) When the victim is unconscious of the nature of the act
(3) And this is known to the perpetrator
(4) Or the person causing the act to be committed.

(C) Incest (285 PC)

(1) Persons within the degrees of consanguinity
(2) Who either
 (a) Intermarry with each other, or
 (b) Who commit fornication or adultery.

Consanguinity: means "within blood relationship," and covers the relationships mentioned in Family Code 2200. If the act is performed with the consent or agreement of both parties, both parties are guilty. (People *v.* Stratton, 141 Cal. 604)

2200 FC: Marriages between parents and children, ancestors and descendants of every degree, brothers and sisters of the half as well as the whole blood, and between uncles and nieces or aunts and nephews, are incestuous and void from the beginning, whether the relationship is legitimate or illegitimate.

If a party to incest is not aware of the blood relationship, then criminal intent is missing, and that party would not be guilty. If one of the persons involved is aware of the blood relationship, and the other is not, only the person who is aware would be guilty. (People *v.* Patterson, 102 Cal. 239)

Any relative of the half blood is covered under incest. If a man had sex relations with his half sister's daughter, he would be guilty of incest. (People *v.* Womack, 167 Cal. App. 2d 130)

It is important that officers investigating incest cases search for and obtain birth certificates of the parties involved. Cases that have gone to court where the father is accused of having sexual relations with his daughter, and in court it was found to the prosecution's surprise that, unknown to anyone but the parents, the daughter was adopted at birth. If the daughter was adopted, she does not come within the degrees of consanguinity.

(D) Bestiality (286.5 PC)

(1) Any person who has sexual contact with an animal
(2) With the purpose of
 (a) sexual arousal or gratification
 (b) abuse or
 (c) or financial gain
(3) Is guilty of a misdemeanor.

This section does not apply to any lawful and accepted practice of veterinary medicine performed by a licensed veterinarian.

(E) Aggravated Sexual Assault on a Child (269 PC)

(1) Any person who commits any of the following acts upon a child under the age of 14, and 7 or more years younger than the person committing the assault
  (a) rape
  (b) sodomy
  (c) oral copulation
(2) When the act is accomplished by force, violence, menace or fear of bodily injury against the victim or others
(3) Is guilty of a felony (15 years to life - state prison).

(F) Distribution or Exhibition of Lewd Material to a Minor (288.2 PC)

(1) Every person who,
  (a) knowing a person is a minor, or
  (b) failing to exercise care in ascertaining their true age,
(2) Sends, exhibits, offers (etc.) by any means (including telephone, internet and physical delivery)
(3) Any harmful matter (313 PC) to that minor
(4) With the intent of arousing lust or passion (etc.) in either the perpetrator or the victim
(5) For the added purpose of seducing the minor
(6) Is guilty of a "wobbler." (2nd offense = felony)

(G) Sexual Exploitation of Patient by Health Professional (729 B & P)

The old requirement that the abuse or misconduct be "substantially related to the qualification for which a license was issued" has been deleted.

The law originally applied to psychotherapists. It now includes physicians and surgeons.

(1) When a physician, psychotherapist, or surgeon commits an act of
  (a) sexual intercourse
  (b) sodomy
  (c) oral copulation
  (d) sexual (lewd) contact
(2) With either
  (a) a patient, or
  (b) a former patient
  (when the doctor-patient relationship was terminated for the purpose of engaging in sexual relations)

Definition:

Sexual contact means the touching of an intimate part of the patient for the purpose of sexual arousal, gratification, or abuse.

(H) Indecent Exposure (314 PC)

(1) Every person who willfully and lewdly
(2) Exposes either his
  (a) person, or
  (b) private parts thereof
(3) In any
  (a) public place, or
  (b) place where there are present persons to be offended or annoyed thereby;
  OR:
(1) Any person who
  (a) procures,
  (b) counsels, or
  (c) assists any person to
    (i) expose himself,
    (ii) take part in any model exhibition, or
    (iii) exhibit himself in public in view of a number of persons
(2) When such is
  (a) offensive to decency, or
  (b) adapted to excite
    (i) vicious thoughts or acts, or
    (ii) lewd thoughts or acts.

If the perpetrator enters an inhabited dwelling, trailer coach or inhabited part of a building without consent, then exposes himself, it is a wobbler. This seems to be a very common offense in the State of California. It is a male-oriented offense, and usually presents no danger to the victim. It is more of a public nuisance. Most offenders are incapable of performing a normal sex act and psychologists suggest that their actions are ways of overcoming the trauma of being impotent. By exposing themselves and shocking a woman, they in effect are proving to themselves that their sex organs are important as our social mores proclaim.

Most offenders are sent to medical facilities and treated as mentally disordered sex offenders rather than criminals. However, since the recidivism rate is high, a second conviction can be a felony and the perpetrator can be sent to state prison. There has been little success in curing or correcting persons with this condition. It is difficult to obtain convictions in court because this offender is very good at picking the type of woman who will either refuse to testify in court because of embarrassment, or "falls apart" under cross examination.

This section cannot be used to convict for "topless" and "bottomless" acts because of the element that states that someone will be offended or annoyed by the act. Any person going into a topless bar knows what he or she will see there.

It is difficult to obtain convictions on the increasing number of persons bathing on the beach in the nude since one of the elements is the act be done lewdly, and these persons are not doing it for lewd purposes.

(I) Sexual Offenses Committed by Persons with AIDS (12022.85 PC)

(a) Any person who commits one or more of the offenses listed below with knowledge that he or she has Acquired Immune Deficiency Syndrome (AIDS) or that he or she carries antibodies of the Human Immunodeficiency Virus (HIV) shall receive a three-year enhancement for each violation.

(b) Subdivision (a) applies to the following crimes:
   (1) Rape (261 PC)
   (2) Unlawful Intercourse (261.5 PC)
   (3) Rape of a Spouse (262 PC)
   (4) Sodomy (286 PC)
   (5) Oral Copulation (287 PC or former section 288a PC)

Sexual Offender Registration Act (290 PC)

This section is the longest and most detailed in the Penal Code. It has been briefed to list only material important or useful to the patrol officer.

Who Must Register and When

Those convicted of the below list of offenses must register in the state of California within five days of being released from a correctional institution. Thereafter, they will register annually

(a) within five (5) days of their birthday, or
(b) when they move, or
(c) when they change their name.

The following persons must register more often:

(a) those who have no residence address (homeless, transients) must register every 30 days
(b) those declared to be a "Sexually Violent Predator" (6600 W & I) must register every 90 days.

This requirement includes offenses committed outside the state if the same elements in this state would qualify for registration. It includes those found guilty but mentally ill in the sanity phase of trial.

- 207 or 209 PC – With intent to commit 261, 286, 288, 288a, or 289 PC.
- 220 PC – Assault with intent to commit rape, sodomy, aiding or abetting rape or penetration with a foreign object, child molesting, or to cause penetration by a foreign object.
- 236.1 (b) (c) – Human trafficking.
- 243.4 PC – Sexual battery.
- 261(1) PC – Mentally incapable of giving consent.
- 261(2) PC – Forcible rape.
- 261(3) PC – Rape by threats etc.
- 261(4) PC – Victim is unconscious of the nature of the act.
- 261(6) PC – Threat of future retaliation.
- 262 PC – Rape of spouse with violence.
- 264.1 PC – Aiding another to commit rape.
- 266 PC – Seduction for prostitution.
- 266(c) PC– Inducing consent to sexual act.
- 266h(b) PC – Pimping.
- 266i(b) PC – Pandering.
- 266j PC – Procurement of a child.
- 267 PC – Abduction for prostitution.
- 269 PC – Sexual assault of child.
- 272 PC– With lewd & lascivious conduct.
- 285 PC – Incest.
- 286 PC – Sodomy.
- 287 PC or former 288a PC – Oral copulation.
- 288 PC – Child Molesting (under age of 14).
- 288.2 PC – Sexual stimulation of minor (felony).
- 288.3, 288.4 PC – Contact of minor with intent to commit sexual offense.
- 288.5 PC – Continuous child abuse.
- 288.7 PC – Sexual intercourse, sodomy, oral copulation, sexual penetration with child age 10 or under.
- 289 PC – Sexual penetration by foreign object.
- 311.1 PC – Sale or distribution of matter depicting sexual conduct by a minor.
- 311.2 PC – Producing or exhibiting obscene matter.
- 311.3 PC – Sexual exploitation of child.
- 311.4 PC – Employing minor in pornography production and distribution.
- 311.10 PC – Advertising obscenity depicting minors.
- 311.11 PC – Possession of child pornography.
- 314(1) PC – Indecent exposure.

- 314(2) PC – Assisting another to commit indecent exposure.
- 647.6 PC – Molesting or annoying children. under 18 (formerly 647a PC).
- 647a PC – Soliciting lewd and lascivious conduct (former)
- 653f(c) PC – Soliciting sex offenses
- An attempt to commit any of the above.
- Anyone subject to judicial commitment as a mentally disordered sex offender or sexually violent predator. (6250, 6300 W & I)

Definitions:

High Risk Sex Offender

(1) One who, within the last five (5) years, has been convicted of an offense under section 290.4(1)(a) PC

(2) And at least two (2) of these offenses have been tried separately

(3) And the defendant has been:

(a) adjudicated a sexually violent predator, or

(b) convicted of multiple crimes on a complicated list of offenses based on violent non-violent, sexual/non-sexual crimes.

Sexually Violent Predator (6600(a)1 W & I)

(1) A person who has been convicted of a sexually violent offense against one or more victims

(2) And for which he has served time

(3) And who has been diagnosed with a mental disorder that makes that person a danger to the health and safety of others

(4) And he is likely to engage in sexually violent criminal behavior.

Registration or Reregistration After Incarceration: Documentation and Procedures Required (290.015 PC)

(1) Statement indicating employer's contact information and location of workplace

(2) Fingerprints and current photo

(3) License plate number of vehicle owned or regularly driven by registrant

(4) List of all Internet Identifiers used by the registrant if the court determines that the registrant used the Internet in their crime (Internet Identifier means electronic mail address or user name for instant messaging or social networking). As an example, this would apply to registrants who used the internet to traffic their victims.

(5) Signed statement that registrant must provide additions or changes on Internet Identifiers within 30 days of the change,

(6) Review notice that registrant may be required to register in another state where the registrant relocated

(7) Proof of residence (i.e. California driver's license, utility bill, printed checks).

290 Registrants Shall Not Live With Other 290 Registrants (3003.5 PC)

(1) When a person is required to register under 290 PC

(2) That person may not, during the period of parole,

(3) Reside with another 290 registrant in a single family dwelling

(4) Unless they are related by blood, marriage, or adoption.

(5) The code lists numerous offenses that qualify one as a Sexually Violent Predator.

Exception: A residential facility which serves six or fewer persons.

When Registrant Lives On College Campus

Registrants who live on a campus of any two or four-year college must register with the campus Chief of Police.

Registered Sex Offender Information Via the Internet (290.46 PC)

(1) As of July 1, 2005, the Department of Justice will make available to the public via the Internet www.meganslaw.ca.gov.

(2) The Internet website will include the following information:

(a) Name, aliases and photo

(b) Physical description

(c) Gender and race

(d) Date of birth

(e) Offenses for which suspect must register (not full criminal record)

(f) Suspect's community of residence and ZIP code (in certain cases, street address)

Requirements to Access Sex Registrant Information Via the Internet

(1) Any person required to register pursuant to Section 290 shall not enter the sex registrant website.

(2) Those accessing information must not use it for purposes of discrimination (i.e. health insurance or loan) or harassment of a registrant.

(3) Information may not be used to commit a crime.

(4) No information will be given that would identify the victim(s) of offenses.
(5) Law enforcement agencies and their personnel are immune from liability for good-faith conduct involving these procedures.
(6) Information is only to be used to protect those at risk.

Notification of Release of Sexual Offenders (290.6 PC)

When a sex offender is to be released from a correctional institution, the local law enforcement department shall be notified within fifteen days of release of the name, address, description and conviction information of the person to be released.

Sexual Offender Registration Within Six Days (290.85 PC)

(1) When parolees required to register under 290 PC are released from prison or jail
(2) They must, within six days of release, show proof of registration to their parole agent.
(3) They shall also give any updates regarding a change in residence or employment to their parole agent within five working days.

290 Registrants Working With Children (290.95 PC)

(1) All persons required to register under 290 PC
(2) When applying for employment or volunteer work
(3) Must notify their prospective employer or supervisor of their 290 status
(4) When the job or volunteer work involves:
    (a) working in an unsupervised setting with minor children, or
    (b) supervisory or disciplinary power over children
    (c) if the victim of the offense under 290PC was under 16 years of age, the registrant is forbidden to work or volunteer under the conditions found in section (a) above.
(5) Failure to do so is a misdemeanor.

DNA Sampling for 290 Registrants and Other Serious Offenders (296, 296.1 PC)

(1) Whoever is convicted of
    (a) a felony offense under 290 PC, or
    (b) murder (190 or 190.05 PC), or
    (c) assault or battery or ADW under the following sections (217.1, 220, 241.1, 243, 243.1, 243.3, 243.4, 243.7, 244, 245, 245.2, 245.3, or 245.5 PC),
(2) Shall, upon discharge, provide two specimens of blood, a saliva sample, right thumb print and full palm print of each hand.
(3) These samples shall be forwarded to the Dept. of Justice for DNA and other genetic typing and filing in a computerized data bank system.
(4) As of January 1, 2009, any adult arrested or charged with any felony offense shall be required to submit blood and saliva samples.

Chemical Castration (645 PC)

(1) When a person has been convicted of 286(c) or (d), 287(c) or (d), 288(b)(1), former 288a or 289(a) or (j).
(2) And the victim is under the age of 13
(3) that person may, as a condition of parole,
(4) Undergo medroxyprogesterone acetate treatment or its equivalent (chemical castration)
(5) In addition to any other punishments or restrictions
(6) If a person undergoes a permanent surgical alternative, he shall not be subject to this section.

Habitual Sexual Offender (667.71 PC)

There are approximately 50,000 registered sex offenders in California, many of whom repeat their offenses. Because of this, the California legislature has passed special laws in the hope of more effectively controlling these persons.

A "Habitual Sexual Offender" is one who has been previously convicted of one or more of the offenses listed below and who is convicted in the present proceeding of one of that same list of offenses, and the charge as Habitual Sexual Offender is listed in the information.

Offenses:

(1) Rape, 261(a)(2) PC
(2) Rape of spouse, 262(a)(1) PC
(3) Gang rape, 264.1 PC
(4) Lewd act on child, section (a) or (b) of 288 PC
(5) Sexual penetration by foreign object, 289 PC
(6) Three or more acts of child molesting, 288.5 PC
(7) Sodomy by force or fear, 286 & 286(d) or 286(c) PC
(8) Oral copulation with minor by force or fear, subdivision (c) or (d) of 287 or former 288a

(9) Kidnapping for purposes of child molesting, 207(b) PC
(10) Kidnapping for purposes of sex, 208 PC
(11) Ransom kidnapping with forced sex offense, 209 PC
(12) Aggravated sexual assault of a child, 269 PC
(13) A sexual offense in another jurisdiction that is the same as one of the above.
Punishment:
25 years to Life.

Chapter VI Case Citations

Study Questions for Chapter VI

(1) The Penal Code Section for Rape is______________________________ PC.

(2) Any sexual penetration, however slight, is sufficient to complete the crime of rape. T or F

(3) If a woman states that she was raped and the jury believes her, the defendant may be convicted even though there was no corroboration to the testimony. T or F

(4) A woman can be convicted of rape. T or F

(5) A woman can rape a man according to California law. T or F

(6) Under 261 PC, a man can only be charged with the rape of his wife if he is a principal. T or F

(7) Millie Mashpott is a single 23-year-old woman. She has the mental age of 14. She is legally entitled to consent to an act of sexual intercourse under California law. T or F

(8) A prostitute cannot bring a charge of rape against a man who came to her as a customer. T or F

(9) Tilly Tiddlytoes has had intercourse with her boyfriend 100 times and has given him permission each time. They are living together in an apartment. She could not legally charge him with rape if she refused permission the next time, and he forced the act. T or F

(10) Kitty Krump is parked in a car with her boyfriend. He makes sexual advances toward her. She tells him no, and makes a slight token resistance. Thinking that she is playing hard to get, he goes ahead anyway and makes sexual penetration. He can be charged with rape. T or F

(11) Flossie Furd is necking with a boyfriend. He makes sexual advances toward her. She says no and resists. Because he is stronger than Flossie, he goes ahead and makes penetration. The minute he makes penetration, she decides to stop resisting and enjoy it. Under these conditions it is not legally a rape. T or F

(12) If a rape victim uses a contraceptive device, it is a bar to prosecution for rape. T or F

(13) A rape victim who consents to intercourse because of threats of bodily harm can only charge rape if the threat is to her own person and not a threat to others. T or F

(14) A doctor tells his adult female patient that her medical problems are caused by a lack of sexual intercourse, and that if she was to have sexual intercourse, her problem would go away. Because of this, she consents to let the doctor have sexual intercourse with her. The courts held this to be rape because her consent was obtained by ______________

(15) Unlawful intercourse refers to sex relations with a victim who is under the age of ____

(16) If the jury feels that a 17-year-old girl looks like she is over 18, they can legally find the defendant charged with "unlawful intercourse" not guilty. T or F

(17) A man cannot be charged with unlawful intercourse if the victim is married and has children. T or F

(18) If a 17-year-old girl seduces an 18-year-old boy, he could be charged with the offense of "unlawful intercourse." T or F

(19) Larry Lacksome is charged with 261.2, forcible rape. During the trial, evidence is presented that convinces the jury that Larry really committed the rape by using an anesthetic drug (261.3 PC). The jury can find Larry guilty of 261.3 PC in the same trial. T or F

(20) The term "consanguinity" means:

(A) ____without legal foundation (B) ____with sanction of law

(C) ____sex relations with a relative (D) ____within blood relationships

(21) If a half brother and half sister who have the same mother have sex relations with each other, this would be classed as incest. T or F

(22) A father who has sex relations with his adopted daughter is guilty of incest. T or F

(23) In illegal sodomy, the uncorroborated testimony of the victim can be enough for conviction. T or F

(24) In thc crime of bestiality, penetration must be of the animal's anus or vagina. T or F

(25) The Penal Code section for "Lewd and Lascivious Acts with children" is _______ PC.

(26) The previous listed section applies to children under the age of__________________

(27) "French kissing" a child is a violation of the law on child molesting. T or F

(28) If a young child voluntarily participates in an act that amounts to "child molesting," the perpetrator cannot be charged with the crime. T or F

(29) In child molesting, the testimony of the child need not be corroborated. T or F

(30) Name one condition under which oral copulation would be illegal. _______________

(31) Married couples are exempt from the law on oral copulation when it is done in the privacy of their own home; and they both consent. T or F

(32) In section 647.6 a PC, "annoying or molesting children under 18," the Penal Code states that the annoying must be of a sexual nature. T or F

(33) The Penal Code section for indecent exposure is__________________________ PC.

(34) Indecent exposure applies only when the perpetrator's private parts are exposed in public. T or F

(35) Topless dancers can be convicted of indecent exposure. T or F

(36) A health faddist, who is "sunbathing" on a secluded beach is liable to prosecution for the section on indecent exposure. T or F

(37) The Penal Code section for Sexual Offender Registration is____________________

(38) Under the laws on Sexual Offender Registration, convicted offenders must register with the Sheriff or the Chief of Police within ____________ days after release. If they move after that, they must re-register at the new location within _______days.

(39) A recidivist is one who:

(A) ____returns to the scene of the crime (B) ____molests young girls

(C) ____repeats his criminal actions (D) ____moves around a lot

(40) Under a recent California Supreme Court decision, the Court felt that sex registration requirements violated the ___________ Amendment (cruel and unusual punishment) if the sex offense charged would be classed as a ______________________________

CHAPTER VII

CRIMES AGAINST PUBLIC JUSTICE, HEALTH, WELFARE AND MORALS

Crimes Against Public Justice

Bribery

There are many criminal statutes in the Penal Code regarding bribery. They cover public officers, judges and jurors, legislators, trustees, city council members and supervisors, members of public boards, telegraph supervisors, witnesses, athletes, referees and umpires. Most statutes are similar since the elements of bribery are almost the same in each case. The five classifications under which laws on bribery come are where:

(1) A person outside of influence offers a bribe.
(2) A person outside of influence gives a bribe.
(3) A person of influence solicits a bribe.
(4) A person of influence agrees to accept a bribe.
(5) A person of influence actually accepts a bribe.

This chapter will list only four sections on bribery. They will deal with offenses involving "executive officers."

Peace officers come under the classification of executive officers since they are involved in the executive branch of government. (People *v.* Mathews, 124 Cal. App. 2d 67). So do district attorneys, city attorneys and police commissioners. (People *v.* Hallner, 43 Cal. 2d 715)

(A) Offering Bribes to Executive Officers (67 PC)

(1) Anyone who offers or gives any bribe
(2) To an executive officer in this state
(3) With specific intent to influence him in any act, decision or opinion,
(4) Is punishable by 2-3-4 years in prison and office disqualification.

(B) Offering Bribes to State Employees (67.5 PC)

(1) Every person giving or offering as a bribe
(2) To any
  (a) ministerial officer,
  (b) employee or
  (c) appointee
(3) Of the state, county or local government
(4) Shall be guilty of a felony or misdemeanor
(5) Based on the theft classification of the article offered according to the law on grand and petty theft.

(C) Asking For or Receiving Bribes (68 PC)

(1) Every
  (a) executive officer
  (b) ministerial officer
  (c) employee or
  (d) appointee
(2) Of the state, county or local government
(3) Who
  (a) asks for
  (b) receives or
  (c) agrees to receive
(4) Any bribe
(5) With the agreement or understanding that it will influence a vote, opinion or action in his official capacity
(6) When
  (a) such matter is pending or
  (b) may be brought before him
(7) Shall forfeit his office
(8) And shall forever be disqualified from holding office.

(D) Asking for or Accepting Gratuity or Reward (70 PC)

(1) Every
  (a) Executive officer,
  (b) Ministerial officer
  (c) Employee or
  (d) Appointee
(2) Of the state, county or local government
(3) Who knowingly
  (a) asks,
  (b) receives, or
  (c) agrees to receive
(4) Any
  (a) emolument (salary, fee)
  (b) gratuity or
  (c) reward or
  (d) a promise of any of these
(5) Except when it is authorized by law
(6) Is guilty of a misdemeanor.

<u>**The Value of a Bribe**</u>

It is not necessary to the completion of the crime of offering a bribe that the thing offered have a present existence or a definite or ascertained value. (People *v.* Vincilione, 17 Cal. App. 513) The thing offered must have some value though, or there is no incentive for the bribe.

(E) Selling or Giving Devices That Promise Immunity From the Law (146d PC)

(1) Every person who sells, or gives to another
(2) Any
  (a) membership card,
  (b) badge or
  (c) other device
(3) Where it can be reasonably inferred by the recipient that display of the device will result in less rigorous enforcement of the law
(4) Is guilty of a misdemeanor

(F) Offering Bribe to Witness or Person Having Material Information (137 PC)

(1) It is illegal to offer or promise a bribe to:
  (a) a witness or person about to be called as a witness or
  (b) a person about to give material information about a crime to a law enforcement official. (Felony)
(2) It is illegal to use
  (a) force,
  (b) threats, or
  (c) fraud

  to induce any person to give false testimony, to give false information that is material to a crime, or to withhold true material information about a crime from a law enforcement official.

<u>Exception:</u> An attorney advising a client.
<u>Law Enforcement Official:</u> Includes prosecuting attorneys, Attorney General and Deputies and any peace officer.

(G) Commercial Bribery (641.3 PC)

(1) Everyone who solicits, accepts, or agrees to accept anything of value over $250.00
(2) Other than in trust for the employer,
(3) Without the knowledge of the employer,
(4) In return for using the defendant's position to benefit the briber, or:
(5) One who either offers or gives such bribe,
(6) Is guilty of commercial bribery. (Misd.) Over $1,000 is a felony.

Perjury Type Offenses

(A) Perjury (118 PC)

Every person who, having taken an oath to testify, declare, depose or certify truly before any competent tribunal, officer or person in any of the cases in which such an oath may by law be administered, willfully and contrary to such oath, states as true any material matter which he knows to be false; every person who testifies, declares, deposes, or certifies "under penalty of perjury" in any case in which such testimony, declarations, depositions or certification is permitted by law under "penalty of perjury" and willfully states as true any material matter which he knows to be false, is guilty of perjury. The five elements of perjury are:

(1) The defendant took an oath to testify, declare, depose or certify truthfully,
(2) Before competent tribunal, officer or person.
(3) Such oath was taken in a case in which such oath may by law be administered;
(4) Willfully and contrary to such oath, he stated as true that which he knew to be false.
(5) The statement was regarding a material matter in the case.

(B) False Affidavits as to Affiant's Testimony (118a PC)

Any person who, in any affidavit taken before any person authorized to administer oaths, swears, affirms, declares, deposes or certifies that he will testify, declare, depose, or certify before any competent tribunal, officer, or person, in any particular manner, or to any particular fact, and in such affidavit willfully and contrary to such oath states as true any material matter which he knows to be false, is guilty of perjury. If, in a later action, the defendant makes a statement that is contrary to that in the affidavit, it shall be prima facie evidence that the affidavit was falsely sworn.

(C) Oath Defined (119 PC)

The term "oath," as used in the last two sections, includes an affirmation and every other mode authorized by law of attesting the truth of that which is stated. (Affirmation: An attesting to the truth without an oath.)

To convict for perjury, it must be shown that the perjury was knowingly false (People *v.* Dixon, 99 Cal. App. 2d 94). It need not be shown that the false statement was made with the intent of injuring or hurting another person. (People *v.* Darcey, 59 Cal. App. 2d 342). A statement made on the stand, by an honest mistake, cannot be classed as perjury (People *v.* Von Tiedeman, 120 Cal. 128). However, if a witness does lie on the stand, and it is brought to his attention, and he then corrects himself, this is not an automatic defense to a charge of perjury (People *v.* Baranov, 201 Cal. App. 2d 52).

If a welfare applicant falsely filled out an affidavit from the county, and that affidavit was not one that was required to be filled out under oath, there could be no conviction of perjury since an element of perjury is that the oath be one in which such an oath may by law be administered (People *v.* French, 134 Cal. App. 694).

Persons who lie on the stand about their age, because of vanity, when it is not important to the case, are not guilty of perjury. On the other hand, minors arrested for possession of alcohol who lie on the stand about their age would be guilty of perjury because their age is a material matter.

Showing that the witness stated under oath that he did not recall the matter referred to in the question, when in fact he did remember it, would be sufficient grounds for perjury (People *v.* Gusati, 220 Cal. App. 2d 456).

(D) When is perjury material?

The best test of materiality is whether the testimony would have influenced the decision of the tribunal trying the case. Even if the testimony is false, it is not perjury unless it influenced the court upon a material issue (People *v.* Sagehorn, 140 Cal. App. 2d 138).

(E) Testimony as Opinion

Witnesses presenting testimony in the form of opinion rather than straight answers, when the opinion represents a clear falsehood, may be guilty of perjury (People *v.* Dixon, 99 Cal. App. 2d 94).

(F) Affidavits

The word affidavit in 118a PC also means deposition. To be perjury, an affidavit must pass out of the possession of the perjurer (People *v.* Robles, 117 Cal. 681).

(G) Depositions

A deposition is a sworn statement taken before a trial. The person making the statement is entitled to review a typed copy of the deposition and make corrections. This deposition can later be used in court. Legal representation is present from both sides during the time questions are asked of the person from whom the deposition is taken.

(H) Corroboration

Penal Code section 1103a states: "Perjury must be proved by the testimony of two witnesses, or of one witness and corroborating circumstances." As with testimony of an accomplice, the corroborative evidence need not be very strong.

(I) Subornation of Perjury (127 PC)

Every person who willfully procures another person to commit perjury is guilty of subornation of perjury, and is punishable in the same manner as if personally guilty of the perjury so procured. Although it isn't stated in the law, it is necessary that perjury be actually committed, and that it be committed as a result of the person procuring the perjurer to commit the act.

Soliciting and Compounding of Crimes

(A) Soliciting Criminal Acts (653f PC)

California has no general solicitation law. The laws dealing with solicitations are covered in specific criminal code sections. The major law is Penal Code section 653f.

(1) Every person who, with criminal intent,
(2) Solicits another to
  (a) offer or accept a bribe,
  (b) join in offering or accepting a bribe,
  (c) join in the commission of:
    (i) murder
    (ii) robbery
    (iii) burglary
    (iv) grand theft
    (v) receiving stolen property
    (vi) extortion
    (vii) rape by force or violence
    (viii) perjury
    (ix) subornation of perjury
    (x) forgery
    (xi) kidnapping
    (xii) assault with a deadly weapon
    (xiii) arson
    (xiv) sodomy by force or violence
    (xv) oral copulation by force or violence
    (xvi) rape with foreign object
    (xvii) child molesting
    (xviii) use of force or threat to prevent witness from testifying
    (xix) carjacking
    (xx) listed narcotic violations
    (xxi) computer-related crimes/operate internet site offering to assist others in locating hacking services
(3) Is guilty of soliciting.

The crime of soliciting need not involve an overt physical act. The act necessary for this offense can be verbal. This offense covers three special areas:

(1) Soliciting bribery
(2) Soliciting certain felonies listed
(3) Special corroboration needed
  (a) two witnesses or
  (b) one witness and corroboration.

It is not necessary that the person being solicited agree to the conditions of the soliciting.

In California there is no general solicitation law. It is only statutory. It applies only to those offenses mentioned in law. Some of the more common sections found in the Penal Code are 647 (a), (b) and (c), and 266 (h) and (i).

(B) Compounding Crimes (153 PC)

There are four elements to this offense:

(1) Any person who, having knowledge of a crime
(2) Receives or agrees to receive something of value
(3) In return for
  (a) concealing that crime, or
  (b) refraining from prosecution, or
  (c) withholding evidence
(4) Except in cases provided for by law.

As with soliciting, all that is needed for the overt act here is an agreement to compound or conceal the crime. The easiest definition of the word "compounding" would be "concealing."

Reimbursement For Civil Damages Is Permissible

As long as the victim does not make an agreement to compound the crime, he may accept compensation from the perpetrator for any injuries or damage received during the commission of the crime. This is his legal right and could be obtained through a civil lawsuit if the perpetrator were not to pay for the injury or damages.

The Compromising of Misdemeanors

The fourth element of Compounding a Crime states "Except in the cases provided for by law." Penal Code Sections 1377, 1378 and 1379 list the conditions where a crime may be legally compounded or compromised. The conditions are:

(1) the crime is a misdemeanor
(2) the victim is entitled to civil reimbursement
(3) the court agrees to the compromise
(4) the perpetrator pays the court costs
(5) the action is officially recorded in the minutes.

For example: the victim of an assault suffered a broken nose and the doctor bill was $150.00. Later when his temper cooled down, he realized that he started the argument and had probably deserved the punch in the nose. He then makes an agreement with the perpetrator to forget about the whole thing if he pays for the doctor bill.

This should be the end of the matter, but if the victim later got mad at the perpetrator, he could initiate criminal proceedings. The perpetrator's only protection is to follow through on the last three elements listed above. Once it is recorded officially in the minutes, it is a bar to further prosecution, and the victim could not later reopen the case.

(C) Exceptions to a Compromise (1377 PC)

(1) Victim is a peace officer on duty.
(2) Act was done riotously.
(3) Act was done with intent to commit a felony.

If any of these conditions exist, the crime may not be legally compromised.

Crimes of Threat and Harassment

(A) Threats to Commit an Offense Against the Person or Property of Another (701-08 PC) (Use of "Peace Bond")

When someone goes before a magistrate with a complaint that a person has threatened to commit an offense against the person or property of another, the magistrate must examine the informer and any witnesses under oath, take their statements in writing and have them sign them.

If the case seems to be valid, the magistrate will make out a warrant of arrest for the party making the threats. When he is arrested, he will appear before the judge and present his side. If the judge feels there is a danger of the threats being carried out, he can make the suspect post a bond not exceeding $5,000 to ensure that he does not carry out his threats (sometimes referred to as a Peace Bond). It is good for six months. If he fails to post the bond, he can be jailed.

(B) Temporary Restraining Orders Harassment (527.6 CCP)

The legislature intended this act to protect individuals' rights to pursue safety, happiness and privacy as guaranteed by the State Constitution.

(1) When one person is subject to harassment
(2) By a knowing and willful course of conduct
(3) Which would cause a reasonable person to suffer substantial emotional distress
(4) By acts directed to a specific person
(5) And the harassment causes substantial emotional distress
(6) And serves no legitimate purpose
(7) The person harassed may seek a Temporary Restraining Order and an injunction prohibiting harassment for a period of up to 15 days by filing a petition.

Violation of Harassment Restraining Order

(1) When an officer responds to a situation involving harassment,
(2) And the victim states that a protective order has been issued,
(3) But does not have a copy of that order,
(4) The officer shall immediately make an attempt to verify the existence of that order. (This includes out-of-state orders.)

If the officer determines that a protective order has been issued, but not yet served:

(1) The officer shall immediately notify the respondent of the terms of the order (whether or not the suspect is under arrest and in custody).
(2) The notification can be done verbally or by showing the suspect a copy of the order for purposes of 273.6 and 29825 PC.

(3) If the officer determines that the protective order does exist, it shall be enforced at that time.

Definition:

Course of Conduct:

(1) A pattern of conduct composed of a series of acts over a period of time, however short

(2) Showing a continuity of purpose. (Does not include constitutionally protected activity.)

Immediate Family Member:

A spouse, parent, child, or any person related within the degrees of consanguinity, within the second degree (up to first cousins), or any other person who regularly resides in the household, or who within the prior six months, regularly resided in the household.

(C) Procedures for Temporary Restraining Order (527.6 CCP)

(1) A copy of the Temporary Restraining Order is served on the defendant.

(2) Within 21 days, a hearing shall be held so the defendant's side can be heard.

(3) If the judge feels that it is warranted, he may issue an injunction against such action.

(4) The injunction is good for a maximum of three years and is renewable.

(5) Copies of "TRO" or injunction shall be delivered to the local police agency so they can make the beat officer aware of its existence (includes out-of-state TROs).

(6) Willful disobedience of such order or injunction is a misdemeanor chargeable as 166 PC Contempt of Court.

(D) Violation of Court Order (166(a)4 PC)

(1) Willful disobedience of any process or order

(2) Lawfully issued by any court

(3) Is a misdemeanor.

Punishment for Contempt of Court (166(c) PC)

(1) A second subsequent conviction for knowingly violating any protective or "stay away" court order

(2) In a pending criminal proceeding involving domestic violence, or

(3) Issued as a condition of probation in such a case

(4) Shall constitute contempt of court

(5) And shall be punished by one year in jail and/or $1,000 fine.

(E) Intimidation of Victims and Witnesses (136 PC)

It is a wobbler to prevent, in any way, witnesses or victims from reporting crimes or proceeding with the prosecution of crimes. This can be a "Circumstance of Aggravation" for punishment. It can be an Enhancement if there is great bodily injury.

Intimidation of Victim or Witness (136.1 PC)

(1) Who knowingly and maliciously prevents or dissuades any witness or victim from attending or giving testimony in any trial, legal proceeding or hearing, or

(2) Knowingly and maliciously attempts the above

(3) Is guilty of a misdemeanor.

Under the Following Conditions This Offense is a Felony

(1) The act is accompanied by force or threat of force or violence upon the witness, victim, or another. This includes threats against property owned by any of these classes of people.

(2) The act is in furtherance of a conspiracy.

(3) The act was committed in another jurisdiction but if committed here would be a violation.

(4) The person guilty of intimidation is acting as an agent or "go between" at the request of another person, and is committing the act for financial or material gain. Under these circumstances all parties involved are equally guilty.

Other Rules Pertaining to 136.1 PC

(1) The law is violated whether or not the attempt was successful.

(2) If the use of force, involving great bodily injury, is shown, it can be used as evidence for an enhancement (increase of sentence). It can also be used in showing "aggravating circumstances" to increase the sentence.

(3) If the crime was a violent felony and the person making the threat is a member of a criminal street gang, the punishment has been increased to a "wobbler" with an additional three-year sentence.

(F) Threatening of Victims or Witnesses and Police Protection (136.2 PC)

(1) When a court of jurisdiction believes that a victim or witness has been intimidated or dissuaded, or that it will likely occur,

(2) The court may issue orders that the defendant, or other person
    (a) will not violate the provisions of 136.1 PC,
    (b) will not communicate with the victim or witness, except through an attorney and under reasonable restrictions set by the court, or
    (c) will appear before a hearing to determine the facts in the case.
(3) The court may also order the police agency of jurisdiction to provide protection for victims or witnesses and their immediate families (if they reside in the same household or in reasonable proximity).

Note: There must exist a clear and present danger of harm and the order must pertain to a limited and specific period of time, or else the court must have the consent of the law enforcement agency.

(4) A protective order may require defendant to be placed on electronic monitoring if the local government adopts the policy to do so. If a protective order is issued, the defendant may not possess any firearm.

(G) Threats Against Victims or Witnesses by Person Convicted of Violent Offense (139 PC)

(1) Every person convicted of one of the felony offenses listed under 2990 PC
(2) Who willfully and maliciously communicates to a witness or victim of the crime for which he was convicted
(3) A credible threat to use force or violence upon that person or that person's immediate family
(4) Is guilty of a "wobbler."

The punishment for threatening witnesses or victims must be a consecutive sentence, and cannot merge with other sentences.

(H) Threats Against Witnesses Who Have Cooperated With Police or Prosecutors (Wobbler) (140 PC)

(1) Willfully threatening to use force or violence against a victim, witness or third person, or
(2) Threatening to take, damage, or destroy property belonging to any of the above
(3) Because they provided assistance or information to a peace officer or prosecutor in a criminal or juvenile proceeding.

(I) Threatening Others With Criminal Activity (Generally) (422 PC)

(1) Threatening to commit a crime which may result in another's death or great bodily harm,
(2) With the intent that it be taken as a threat,
(3) Even if there is no intent to carry it out,
(4) And the threat is made in such a way as to make the victim reasonably believe the threat will be carried out immediately,
(5) And the victim has a reasonably sustained fear for his or her safety, or the safety of an immediate family member.

(J) Terrorist Threats (422 PC)

(1) Willfully threatening to commit a crime
(2) Which will result in death or great bodily injury to another
(3) With the specific intent that the statement be taken as a threat
(4) Even if there is no intent to carry it out
(5) Under conditions such that the person receiving it has a reasonable belief in the prospect of immediate execution
(6) Thus has a reasonable and sustained fear for:
    (a) his or her own safety, or
    (b) the safety of his or her immediate family.

Definition:

Terrorize:

To cause a person of ordinary emotions and sensibilities to fear for his or her personal safety.

(K) Terrorism Through Symbols (11411 PC)

Section B:

(1) Any person who places or displays a sign, mark, symbol, emblem or other physical impression (e.g. a swastika)
(2) Upon the private property of another, without permission
(3) For the purpose of terrorizing the owner or occupant (Wobbler), OR

Section C:

(1) Engages in a pattern of conduct for the purpose of terrorizing
(2) An owner or occupant of private property, OR
(3) In reckless disregard of terrorizing the owner or occupant,
(4) By placing or displaying a sign, mark, symbol, emblem or other physical impression (ex.: a swastika)

(5) On the private property of another
(6) Two or more times,
(No purpose need be shown) (Wobbler), OR

Section D:

(1) Any person who burns or desecrates a cross or other religious symbol,
(2) Knowing it to be a religious symbol,
(3) On the private property of another, or on the grounds of a primary, junior high, or high school, without authorization,
(4) For the purpose of terrorizing the owner or occupant, or
(5) In reckless disregard of the risk of terrorizing
(6) The owner or occupant of that property,
(7) Is guilty of a wobbler.

(L) Hate Crimes (422.6 PC)

Section A:

(1) No person shall by force or threat of force
(2) Willfully injure, intimidate, interfere with, oppress or threaten,
(3) Any person in the free exercise of their state or federal constitutional rights,
(4) Because of
    (a) That person's race, color, religion, ancestry, national origin, disability, gender or sexual orientation, OR
    (b) A perceived belief that the victim falls within one of these categories.

Section B:

(1) No person shall vandalize or deface the property of anyone in the above categories,
(2) For the purpose of either intimidating them or interfering with their Constitutional rights,
(3) Because they either fit, or the accused believes that they fit, one of the above categories. (People *v.* Superior Court (Aishman) 1995, 10 Cal 4th 735)

(M) Harassment Offense Committed by Use of Communication Equipment (653m PC)

Section A:

(1) Every person who with intent to annoy,
(2) Telephones another or makes contact by electronic communication device and
    (a) uses any obscene language, or
    (b) makes threats of injury
(3) To
    (a) that person, or
    (b) any member of his or her family, or
    (c) that person's property.

Section B:

(1) Every person who makes repeated contact with another by phone or electronic communication device
(2) With intent to annoy another,
(3) Whether or not there is a conversation
(4) Does not apply to calls made in good faith.

Section C:

(1) Any offense committed by use of a telephone may be deemed to have been committed when and where the telephone call or calls were made or received. Any offense committed by the use of an electronic communication device or medium, including the Internet, may be deemed to have been committed when and where the electronic communications were originally sent or first viewed by the recipient.
(2) To another's place of work
(3) With the intent to annoy another
(4) Except when made in good faith
(5) When:
    (a) there is a TRO, injunction or court order prohibiting such action, or
    (b) more than 10 calls are made in any 24-hour period
(7) Whether or not conversation occurs;
(8) Made to an adult or emancipated minor
(9) Who is either a present or former:
    (a) spouse,
    (b) cohabitant,
    (c) personinvolvedinanengagementordating relationship, or
    (d) person who has had a child by the caller.

Section D:

(1) Every person who makes contact with another by phone or electronic communication device
(2) With the intent to annoy another,
(3) And leaves a message that the party return the call at a later time
(4) And then either uses obscene language, or refuses to identify him or herself.

This section was added after obscene phone callers found "loopholes" in sections (A) and (B). They would call a number and ask that the victim return their call at a later time. When the call was returned, they would then make the obscene call, or just "breathe heavily." The D.A. could not prosecute because the perpetrator did not make the call as was required by the elements of the crime.

Examples of Electronic Communication Devices:

Includes telephones, cellular phones, computers, video recorders, fax machines, pagers, personal digital assistants, smart phones, video phones, TTY/TDD devices.

Jurisdiction:

The jurisdiction for obscene phone calls is the locality where the call was made, or where the call was received.

(N) Stalking (646.9 PC) (Misdemeanor)

(1) Any person who willfully, maliciously and repeatedly follows or torments another person,
(2) And who makes a credible threat with the intent to place that person in reasonable fear for his or her own safety, or for the safety of his or her immediate family
(3) In person or by phone, mail, or electronic communication device
(4) Is guilty of the crime of stalking.

Punishment:

If the suspect has existing a Temporary Restraining Order or injunction (or both) prohibiting the behavior described against that same party, the crime is a felony. A second offense of 646.9 PC is a felony. The court can order counseling as a condition of probation.

Definitions:

Course of Conduct:

(See definition on page 126.)

Credible Threat:

Verbal or written threat or a threat implied by a pattern of conduct or combination of verbal or written statements and conduct, made with intent and apparent ability to carry them out which would cause reasonable persons to fear for their safety or safety of members of their immediate family.

Harassment:

(1) A knowing and willful "course of conduct" directed at a specific person, which seriously alarms, annoys, torments or terrorizes the person, and which serves no legitimate purpose.
(2) The "course of conduct" must be such as would cause a reasonable person to suffer substantial emotional distress, and
(3) Must actually cause that distress to victim.

Immediate Family Member:

(See definition on page 126.)

Exception:

This law shall not apply to lawful conduct during labor picketing.

Notification of Release

Prison or jail officials must notify victims or witnesses by telephone or certified mail, 15 days before a stalking violator is released. If he escapes, victims or witnesses must be notified as soon as possible.

(O) Contempt of Court for Crime of Stalking (166 PC)

(1) Any person convicted of 646.9 PC (Stalking)
(2) Who then again contacts a victim by phone, mail, electronic communication device, or directly
(3) Will have an increased penalty of one year in jail and/or $5,000. As a condition of probation, perpetrator must:
    (a) participate in a Batterer's Treatment Program, or
    (b) make payments to the Battered Women's shelter, or
    (c) pay the victim's costs for counseling and treatment.

Restitution and child payments have priority over the above. Where the victim is a spouse, community property may not be used for restitution until all other financial resources are exhausted. Any person who, while violating a court order to avoid a particular person or victim, causes any injury to that person, must serve at least 48 hours in jail.

(P) Emergency Protective Order From Stalking (646.91 PC)

(1) When a peace officer has reasonable grounds to believe that a person is in immediate and present danger of being stalked
(2) He may ask a judge for an emergency protective order.
(3) The request must be in writing and be signed by the officer.
(4) The request must convince the judge that:
    (a) there are reasonable grounds to believe there is an immediate and present danger of stalking, and
    (b) the emergency order is necessary to prevent the stalking activity.
(5) If issued, the officer must serve it on the person so restrained.
(6) The officer shall also give a copy to the protected person.
(7) The officer shall also file a copy of the order with the court as soon as possible.

(8) A peace officer who acts in good faith is protected from civil and criminal liability.
(9) Nothing in this protective order shall deny a person's constitutional rights such as free speech.

(Q) Release of Person Arrested for Stalking (646.93 PC)
(1) When a person is arrested for stalking and is released on bail
(2) The Sheriff shall give notice to the D.A.'s Domestic Violence Unit where the victim resides.
(3) That unit shall inform the sheriff or jail of the person or persons (victim(s)) that should be notified.
(4) If there is a bail hearing, the prosecutor shall make all reasonable efforts to notify the victim(s) of the bail hearing.
(5) The victim(s) may be present at the hearing and make a statement regarding bail for the suspect.
(6) If bail is granted, the judge may impose restrictive conditions such as not contacting the victim by any means.

Family Violence and Crimes Against Adult Dependents

(A) Domestic Violence Restraining Order (527 CCP)

A temporary restraining order, good for 30 days may be granted upon evidence that a person who was living with another person was guilty of acts of violence resulting in physical injury. Law enforcement agencies in the jurisdiction where the person to be protected lives shall receive copies of such restraining orders. This is for the purpose of verifying the existence of such an order by officers in the field responding to family disturbance calls.

(B) Enforcing Restraining Order Not in Officer's Possession (13710 PC)

When officers respond to a domestic violence call and learn that there is a valid restraining order on one of the parties involved, they will call police records to confirm it. If the restraining order is confirmed, the officers may serve it at that time as if it were in their possession.

(C) Non-Support of Spouse (270a PC)
(1) Every person who is able to provide for his or her spouse's support,
(2) Who willfully abandons and leaves his or her spouse destitute, or
(3) Who refuses or neglects to provide such spouse with the basic necessities,
(4) Unless by the spouse's conduct the person was justified in abandoning such spouse,
(5) Is guilty of a misdemeanor.

(D) Neglect of Indigent Parent (270c PC)
Except as provided in Family Code 4410-4414.
(1) Every adult child, having the ability to do so,
(2) Who fails to provide the basic necessities
(3) For an indigent parent
(4) Unless covered as an exception under 206.5 of the Civil Code.
(5) Is guilty of a misdemeanor

Freeing Adult Child of Obligation to Care For or Support Adult Parent (4410-4414 PC)

An adult child may file a petition in the county where a parent of the child resides, requesting that the court make an order freeing the petitioner from the obligation otherwise imposed by law to support the parent. If the parent does not reside in this state, the petition shall be filed in the county where the adult child resides.

The court shall make the order requested pursuant to Section 4410 only if the petition alleges and the court finds all of the following (4411 FC):
(a) The child was abandoned by the parent when the child was a minor.
(b) The abandonment continued for a period of two or more years before the time the child attained the age of 18 years.
(c) During the period of abandonment, the parent was physically and mentally able to provide support for the child.

(E) Inflicting Pain on Dependent Adult (368(b)(1) PC)

It is illegal to inflict physical or mental pain on any dependent adult (Misd.). "Dependent Adults" are those who, because of age or physical or mental disorder, cannot properly care for themselves.

Felony if the harm is severe. 368 PC covers theft or embezzlement from such adults.

(F) Emergency Protective Custody of "Endangered Adults" (15700 et seq W & I Code)

As people live longer, they are more often not able to care for themselves. As a result, the number of cases of older adults being abused has greatly increased. This new law will allow peace officers the ability to intervene to protect such adults.

(1) Peace officers may take into "emergency protective custody"
(2) Dependent or older adults who are exposed to immediate risk of serious injury or death
(3) Due to suspected abuse or neglect
(4) And who are apparently unable to protect themselves from the situation or condition.
(5) If appropriate, the officer will take the victim for medical evaluation.
(6) The officer should then notify
    (a) Superior Court
    (b) next of kin
    (c) Adult Protective Services.

(G) Abuse of Elderly (368 PC)

Section (b)

(1) Who, under circumstances likely to cause great bodily harm,
(2) Willfully causes or permits any elder or dependent adult to suffer, or
(3) Inflicts upon them unjustifiable physical pain or mental suffering, or
(4) Having care or custody of an elder or dependent adult,
(5) Allows that person to be in a situation where their health is endangered
(6) Is guilty of a "wobbler."

Section (c)

The same as above, but under circumstances NOT likely to cause great bodily harm. Under these circumstances it is classed as a misdemeanor.

Section (d)

(1) Any person having care or custody of an elder or dependent adult,
(2) And steals or embezzles the property or money of that person,
(3) Is guilty of a "wobbler" if the value is over $950, or
(4) Is guilty of a misdemeanor if the value is $950 or less.

Definitions for 368 PC

Elder: Any person who is 65 years or older

Dependent Adult: Any person between the ages of 18 and 64 who has physical or mental limitations that affect their ability to protect themselves or their rights regardless of whether the person lives independently. This includes a patient in a 24-hour health facility under 1250 H & S Code.

Caretaker: A person who has the care, custody or control or who holds a position of trust with an elder or dependent adult.

Criminal Acts Against Children

(A) Failure to Provide (270 PC)

Penal Code section 270 deals with providing minor children with the basic necessities of life. The five basic necessities of this section are:

(a) Clothing
(b) Food
(c) Shelter
(d) Medical attendance
(e) Other remedial care

(1) Failure to Provide for Child, Rules

(a) Failure of parent to provide basic necessities for a legal child is a misdemeanor.
(b) When a court has officially declared a person to be the parent of a particular child, and that person fails to provide the basic necessities for that child.
(c) When one parent has the legal custody of a child; or when one parent voluntarily provides for a child; This does not relieve the other parent from criminal responsibility for providing for that child.

(2) Proof of Criminal Liability

The fact that a parent did abandon, or fail to provide for his child is prima facie evidence that such act was willful and without lawful excuse.

(3) Determining Income for Ability to Provide

In determining the ability to provide, ALL income including gifts shall be considered.

(4) Liability Provisions Regarding Marital Status

(a) These sections shall apply regardless of the fact that the parents of a child are divorced.
(b) An unborn child is considered to be a living person as far as this law is concerned.

(5) Artificial Insemination

A husband who consents in writing to artificial insemination shall be deemed to be the father of any resulting child.

(B) Desertion of Minor (271 PC)

(1) Every parent of any child under the age of 14
(2) Any person to whom any such child has been entrusted for purpose of nurture or education
(3) Who deserts such child in any place with intent to abandon child
(4) Is guilty of a wobbler.

Parental Obligation: (272(2) PC)

A parent or legal guardian to any person under the age of 18, shall have the duty to exercise reasonable care, supervision, protection and control over their minor child.

(C) Contributing to the Delinquency of a Minor (272 PC)

1(a) Every person who:

(i) commits any act, or
(ii) omits the performance of a duty

(2) Which causes, tends to cause or encourages a person under 18
(3) To come under 300, 601, or 602 W & I Code, or
(4) Induces
   (a) any person under the age of 18 or
   (b) a ward of the juvenile court
(5) To
   (a) refuse to obey a lawful order of the juvenile court or
   (b) live in such a manner as to come under section 300, 601 or 602 W & I Code
(6) Is guilty of a misdemeanor.

1(b) Influence of Adult Strangers:

(1) Any adult stranger who is 21 or above
(2) Who knowingly contacts or communicates with a minor 12 years or younger
(3) For the purpose of persuading, luring, or transporting that minor
(4) Away from the minor's home or place where parents know he is located
(5) For any purpose
(6) Without express consent of parents
(7) And with intent to avoid consent.

1(c) Exceptions to This Law. This law shall not apply to:

(1) Emergency situations where the minor is threatened with imminent bodily, emotional or psychological harm.
(2) Where contact with the minor is within the scope and course of employment.
(3) The adult is a volunteer of a recognized civic or charitable organization.

Definitions:

(1) Contact (or Communication): includes but is not limited to the use of a phone or the internet (17538 B & P)
(2) Stranger: A person of casual acquaintance with whom no substantial relationship exists, or a person with whom a relationship has been established or promoted for the primary purpose of victimization.
(3) Express Consent: Oral or written permission that is positive, direct and unequivocal, requiring no inference or implication to understand its meaning.

(D) Welfare & Institutions Code Sections 300, 601 & 602

Jurisdiction of the Court (300 W & I)

Any person under the age of 18 years who comes within any of the following descriptions is within the jurisdiction of the juvenile court which may adjudge such person to be a dependent child of the court:

(1) Who is in need of proper and effective parental care or control:
   (a) has no parent or guardian,
   (b) has no parent or guardian willing to exercise, or capable of exercising, such care or control, or
   (c) has no parent or guardian actually exercising such care or control.
(2) Who is destitute, or who is not provided with the necessities of life, or who is not provided with a home or suitable place of abode.
(3) Who is physically dangerous to the public because of a mental or physical disorder, deficiency or abnormality.

(4) Whose home is an unfit place by reason of neglect, cruelty, depravity, or physical abuse by either parent, or by guardian or other person having custody or care of said juvenile.
(5) The child has been sexually abused or has been commercially sexually exploited.
(6) The child's parent or guardian caused the death of another child through abuse or neglect.
(7) The child's parent has been incarcerated or institutionalized.
(8) The whereabouts of parents are unknown.
(9) The child has been freed for adoption by both parents.
(10) The child's sibling has been abused or neglected.

Refusal to Obey Authority (601 W & I)

Any minor between 12 and 17 years of age who persistently or habitually refuses to obey the reasonable and proper orders or directions of his parent, guardian, custodian or school authorities, or who is beyond the control of such person; or any person who is a habitual truant from school within the meaning of any law of this state, or who from any cause is in danger of leading an idle, dissolute, lewd, or immoral life, is within the jurisdiction of the juvenile court which may judge such person to be a ward of the court.

Under the Due Process clause of the U.S. Constitution, the state high court has ruled that the underlined sections of 601 are broad and vague by today's standards, and that 601 is a non-criminal "status" offense which must be handled differently than 602 offenses. Legislation has corrected some of the problems resulting from this ruling.

Violation of Law by a Minor (602 W & I)

Any person who is under the age of 18 years when he or she violates any law of this state or of the United States or any ordinance of any city or county of this state defining crime, or who, after having been found by the juvenile court to be a person described by section 601, fails to obey any lawful order of the juvenile court is within the jurisdiction of that court, which may adjudge such person to be a ward of the court.

(E) Emancipation of Minors (7001-7002 FC)

(1) Minors under the age of 18
(2) May petition the Superior Court for a "Declaration of Emancipation"
(3) When there is no parental or guardian objection and when
    (a) the minor has entered into a valid marriage, or
    (b) the minor is on active military duty, or
    (c) with consent, is willingly living apart from the parents and is properly managing his or her own financial affairs.
(4) Such emancipation will be stated on the minor's driver's license or DMV identification card upon application of the minor.

(F) Child Not to be Confined With Adults (273b PC)

(1) No child under the age of 16 years
(2) Will be placed in
    (a) any place of confinement or
    (b) in any courtroom or
    (c) in any transportation vehicle
(3) In company with adults charged with or convicted of crime
(4) Unless in the presence of a proper official.

(G) Willful Abuse or Injury to Person or Health of Child (273a PC)

Section A:
(1) Any person who, under conditions likely to produce great bodily harm or death
(2) Willfully causes or permits any child to suffer; or
(3) Inflicts unjustifiable:
    (a) physical pain or
    (b) mental suffering; or
(4) Having custody of any child,
    (a) willfully causes or permits their person or health to be injured; or
    (b) willfully causes or permits such child to be placed in such a situation that its person or health is endangered,
(5) Is guilty of a wobbler.

Section B:
(1) Any person who, under conditions or circumstances OTHER than those likely to produce great bodily harm or death,
(2) Willfully commits any of the acts in Section A above,
(3) Is guilty of a misdemeanor.

(H) Intimidating Juvenile Relatives (11414 PC) (Misdemeanor)

(1) Intentionally harassing a child or ward of another person,
(2) When that child is under the age of 16,

(3) And it is because of the adult relative's employment. (e.g., Adult relative whose child is harassed works at an abortion clinic.)

Definition:

"Harass" means a knowing and willful conduct directed at a specific child that seriously alarms, annoys, torments or terrorizes the child and serves no legitimate purpose. The conduct must be such as would cause a reasonable child to suffer that effect.

(I) Fatal Abuse of Child Under 8 Years of Age (273ab PC) (Felony, 25 to Life)

(a)

(1) Any person having the care or custody of a child under 8 years of age, who
(2) Assaults the child by means of force,
(3) That to a reasonable person would cause great bodily injury,
(4) And it results in the death of that child.

(b) Same circumstances as above but results in the child becoming comatose due to brain injury or suffering permanent paralysis (felony-life with possibility of parole).

(J) Immoral Practices in Presence of Children (273g PC)

Any person who in the presence of any child indulges in any degrading, lewd, immoral or vicious habits or practices or who is habitually drunk in the presence of any child in his care, custody or control, is guilty of a misdemeanor. (The term "habitually" is often hard to define. Most jurisdictions accept three times as being sufficient.)

11165.4 & 6 PC Peace officers using reasonable force within the scope and course of their duties shall not be liable under child a laws.

(K) Inflicting Cruel Punishment Upon Child (273d PC)

(1) Who willfully inflicts upon a child
(2) Cruel or inhuman corporal punishment
(3) Or injury resulting in a traumatic condition
(4) Is guilty of a felony.

(L) Child Abuse Reporting (11166(a) PC)

(1) Who, in his or her professional capacity or scope of employment,
    (a) has knowledge, or
    (b) observes a child and concludes, or
    (c) reasonably suspects,
(2) That a child is a victim of child abuse or neglect,
(3) Shall report by phone to a child protection agency
(4) Immediately, or as soon as possible,
(5) And shall prepare and send a written follow-up report to that agency within 36 hours of becoming aware of that situation.
(6) Persons under (1–f, g & h) must have received training before this section applies to them.

Requirements do not include mental suffering or endangerment of emotional well being.

<u>Definitions (11165.7 PC):</u>

<u>Child Care Custodian:</u> Teacher, administrator, supervisor of child welfare attendance, or certificated pupil personnel employee of any public or private school or day camp; licensed day care worker; administrator of community care facilities; headstart teacher, licensing worker or evaluator; public assistance worker; employee of a child care institution.

<u>Medical Practitioner:</u> Physician, surgeon, psychiatrist, psychologist, dentist, resident, intern, podiatrist, chiropractor, licensed nurse, dental hygienist, or anyone licensed under Div. 2 B & P Code.

<u>Non-medical Practitioner:</u> State or county health employee, coroner, paramedic, marriage and family counselor, religious practitioner who deals with children.

<u>"Neglect" Defined (11165.2 PC)</u>

As used in Article 2.5 of the Child Abuse and Neglect Reporting Act, "neglect" means negligent treatment or maltreatment of a child by a person responsible for the child's welfare under circumstances indicating harm or threatened harm to the child's health or welfare. It includes both acts and omissions on the part of the responsible person.

(M) Reporting Child Abuse (11166(h) PC)

(1) If two or more persons are required to make a report under 11166 PC,
(2) They may, by mutual agreement, assign one person to do the reporting in a single report within 36 hours by telephone.
(3) If that designated person fails to make the report and others in the group are aware of it, each person then has the individual responsibility to make the report.

(N) Agency Duties of Reporting Child Abuse (11166(j-k) PC)

County Probation and Welfare Departments

(1) The agency shall immediately, or as soon as practically possible, report by telephone
(2) To:
  (a) the law enforcement agency of jurisdiction, and
  (b) the agency handling cases under 300 W & I, and
  (c) the D.A.'s Office
(3) Known or suspected cases of child abuse (as in 11165.6 PC)
(4) With the exception of 11165.2(b) PC (Not seeking medical help for religious reasons, etc.)
(5) If the case involves newborn infants suffering as a result of the mother's substance abuse, a report will be made only to the County Welfare Department.
(6) A written report shall also follow up the telephone report within 36 hours.
(7) If a child receiving welfare services has been identified as the victim of commercial sexual exploitation, it must be reported within 24 hours.

Under 11166, a child who is believed to be a victim of commercial exploitation, is missing, or has been abducted, shall be reported to law enforcement for entry into the National Center for Missing & Exploited Children, and the Crime Information Center Database of the F.B.I.

Law Enforcement Agencies

(1) The agency shall immediately, or as soon as practically possible, report by telephone,
(2) To:
  (a) the agency handling cases under 300 W & I, and
  (b) the D.A.'s Office
(3) Known or suspected child abuse cases reported to it.
(4) If the case comes under 11165.2(b) PC (not seeking medical help for religious reasons, etc.), the report shall be made only to the County Welfare Department.
(5) When a law enforcement agency becomes aware of a known or suspected case of a person who is responsible for a child's welfare committing or knowingly allowing that child to suffer abuse, the agency shall report the case to the County Welfare Department by telephone. Within 36 hours, the agency shall follow up with a written report.

(O) Failure to Report Child Abuse (11166(c) PC) (Punishment)

(1) Any person who fails to report an instance of child abuse as required by law
(2) Which he or she knows to exist, or should reasonably know to exist
(3) Is guilty of a misdemeanor (6 months and/or $1,000 fine).

(P) Case Law Regarding Exigency Entry in Child Abuse Violations

(1) People *v.* Sutton, 134 *Cal. Rptr.* 921

In this case an officer responded to a police radio report of children being left alone. Standing at the threshold of the residence he observed small children present. He then saw the defendant exit a car in a highly intoxicated state and enter the residence. The Court of Appeals (2nd Dist.) ruled that under the Doctrine of Necessity the officer did not violate the defendant's Fourth Amendment rights by entering the residence and a bedroom to check on the children's safety.

The fact that the officer received a call on the police radio, based on a neighbor's complaint that the children were left alone, was sufficient probably cause to make the entry. The court further stated that the police dispatcher did not have to appear in court to corroborate reasonable cause.

The court also ruled the officer was justified in putting his foot in the doorway when the defendant opened the door since the officer could have broken down the door for the purpose of making an arrest, once probable cause had been established.

(2) People *v.* Roberts, 47 Cal 2D, 374

The California Supreme Court stated that "necessity" often justifies actions which would otherwise constitute trespass, especially when prompted by the motivation of preserving life or property. In this case, the officer was justified to enter based on knowledge that a sick person resided there and he heard moans coming from inside.

(3) People *v.* Roman, 64 *Cal. Rptr.* 268

An officer, on prior occasions, had responded to the defendant's apartment to investigate a felony child abuse complaint. He observed from outside the apartment a 2-year-old child on the floor in what appeared to be an unconscious state. The court stated that this observation was ample grounds to make entry under the exigency exception. It further stated that an officer investigating a complaint is not required to disregard what is apparent to any passerby. Officers investigating a suspected child abuse case should, at first, consider the injuries as serious until they have satisfied themselves to the contrary.

(4) In re Dawn O. et al. 128 *Cal. Rptr.* 852

Neighbors called police at 10 p.m. regarding a 5-year-old girl who was out on the street alone. The responding officer took her to her apartment in an effort to contact her mother. The girl said that she had a younger sibling at home. The officer knocked on the door but there was no answer and the door was locked. The girls told the officer of another door that was open in the back. Inside, the officer found two infants who had been left alone. There was also a loaded rifle on the floor of one room. The children were all taken into protective custody. The mother claimed that the officer did not have the right to enter. The officer had responded to previous calls regarding the mother's negligence. The court upheld the entry and search. It further stated that the lateness of the hour further corroborated the right to enter.

(5) Badillo *v.* Superior Court, 294 P2d 23

This case ruled that where police do not have a warrant, the burden of proof rests on the prosecution to show justification of entry and search.

(6) Vale *v.* Louisiana, Supra 399 United States 35

The court stated that "In absence of a showing of true necessity, that is, an imminent and substantial threat to life, health or property, the constitutionally guaranteed right to privacy must prevail."

(7) People *v.* Ramey, Supra 127 *Cal. Rptr.* 629

The California Supreme Court ruled that exigent circumstances are exceptions to the prohibition against warrantless entries into a home to make an arrest.

Moral Offenses

(A) Bigamy (281 PC)

(1) Every person having a spouse living
(2) Who marries or enters into a registered domestic partnership with any other person
(3) Is guilty of bigamy.

Exceptions: (282 PC)

(1) When the former marriage or former registered domestic partnership whose spouse by such marriage or registered domestic partnership has been absent for five successive years and is not known to be dead or alive; or
(2) The marriage or registered domestic partnership has been legally dissolved (e.g. divorce, annulment.)

(B) Obscene Matter (311 PC)

Based on the U.S. Supreme Court decision in Miller *v.* California (37 L. Ed. 2d 419) the California legislature changed the definition of "Obscene and Harmful Matter."

Explanation of Terms:

(1) Obscene Matter:

Taken as a whole, which to the average person, applying contemporary statewide standards, appeals to the prurient interest and which, taken as a whole, depicts or describes in an offensive way, sexual conduct; and which, taken as a whole, lacks serious, artistic, political or scientific value.

(a) When it appears from the nature of the matter or the circumstances of its dissemination, distribution or exhibition, that it is designed for clearly defined deviant sexual groups, the appeal of the matter shall be judged with reference to its intended recipient group.
(b) In prosecutions under this chapter, when circumstances of production, presentation, sale, dissemination, distribution, or publicity indicate that the matter is being commercially exploited by the defendant for the sake of its prurient appeal, such evidence is probative with respect to the nature of the matter, and can justify the conclusion that the matter lacks serious, artistic, political, or scientific value.
(c) In determining whether the matter taken as a whole lacks serious literary, artistic, political, or scientific value in description or representation of such matters, the fact that the defendant knew that the matter depicts persons under the age of 16 years engaged in sexual conduct, as defined in 311.4, subdivision (c) PC, is a factor which can be

considered in making that determination.

(2) "Matter":
(a) printed or written matter (e.g. book) or
(b) pictorial representation (e.g. book) or
(c) statue or figure or
(d) recording (record, tape, wire etc.) or
(e) reproduction.

(3) "Person":
Any individual, partnership, firm, association, corporation or other legal entity.

(4) "Distribute": To transfer possession of.

(5) "Knowingly": Being aware of the character of the matter or conduct.

(6) "Exhibit": To show.

(7) "Obscene live conduct":
Any physical human body activity, whether performed or engaged in alone or with other persons, including but not limited to singing, speaking, dancing, acting, simulating, or pantomiming, taken as a whole, which to the average person, applying contemporary statewide standards appeals to the prurient interest, is conduct which, taken as a whole, depicts or describes in a patently offensive way sexual conduct and which, taken as a whole, lacks serious literary, artistic, political or scientific value.

(8) Determining That Conduct is in Fact "Obscene Live Conduct":
The rules for determining whether or not live conduct is classed as obscene is the same as that for determining "Obscene Matter."

Definition:

Prurient: an itching; longing; of persons, having lascivious longings; of desire, curiosity, lewd.

Heller *v.* New York, and the Seizing of Films

In the past the laws on search and seizure made it very difficult to seize obscene films. In the U.S. Supreme Court decision on Heller *v.* New York, the high court ruled that if a judge views a film and then signs a warrant, the exhibitor is not entitled to a prior adversary hearing. That hearing could stall things while the exhibitor made great amounts of money. In the city of New York, a theater operator grossed $1 million over a nine month period from the showing of "Deep Throat."

(C) Penalty for Sending, Selling, Distributing, Publishing, Obscene Matter (311.2 PC)

Section A:
(1) Who knowingly sends, orders or brings into this state,
(2) For sale or distribution. or:
(a) possesses, prepares, publishes or prints
(b) with intent to distribute or exhibit to others
(c) or offers to do the above, or to exhibit
(d) any obscene matter
(3) Is guilty of a misdemeanor.

Section B:
(1) When anyone does the above for commercial consideration
(2) Knowing that it depicts a person under the age of 18
(3) Personally engaging in (or simulating) listed sex acts is guilty of a felony. (2-3-6 years) (Maximum fine of $100,000)

(D) District Attorney, Upon Conviction, Can Sue for Court & Investigative Costs (3496 CC)

Section A:
(1) This section shall not apply to a projectionist
(2) When employed by a licensed business operator
(3) When acting within the scope of his employment
(4) Unless he has a financial interest in the business.

Section B:
(1) Sections 311.2 A & B shall not apply to any employee
(2) When acting within the scope of employment
(3) When employed by a licensed business operator
(4) Unless he has a financial interest in the business
(5) And has no control over the exhibition.

(E) Obscene Live Conduct in Public Prohibited (311.6 PC)

(1) Those involved in live obscene conduct
(2) Before one or more persons
(3) In any
(a) Public place
(b) Place exposed to public view
(c) Any place open to public or a segment thereof
(4) Regardless of
(a) admission charges or
(b) membership requirements
(5) Are guilty of a misdemeanor.

Validity of Local Ordinances Regulating Exposure of Wait Persons or Entertainers (318.5 PC)

Nothing in this code shall prohibit a city or county from passing ordinances prohibiting wait persons or entertainers, or any other persons paid or not, from exposing their breasts, buttocks or genitals. This applies to establishments that serve food or beverages including alcoholic beverages. This does not apply to a theater, concert hall or similar establishment which is primarily devoted to theatrical performances.

Exceptions are as follows (312.6 PC & 312.7 PC):

(1) Materials used in legitimate scientific or educational purposes.
(2) When a person runs a computer web service and has no control over material fed into that service.
(3) In sections pertaining to minors, they do not apply to legally emancipated minors.
(4) Lawful conduct between spouses when one or both of them are under 18.
(5) Employers for actions of their employees or agents, unless that action is within the scope of their employment, and the employer has knowledge of or authorizes the employees' conduct.
(6) The person has taken reasonable and appropriate action, in good faith, to restrict or prevent transmission or access to this material.
(7) The material is unsolicited or the person receives the matter without knowledge or consent (311.3 PC).
(8) Owners or operators of web sites.

Adoption of Laws Relating to Acts and Exhibition of Nudity in Public Places (318.6 PC)

Nothing in this code shall invalidate a law or prohibit the adoption of an ordinance by a city or county if such ordinance relates to live acts, demonstrations, or exhibitions which occur in public places, places open to the public, or places open to public view involving exposure of the private parts or buttocks of any participant, and if such ordinance prohibits an act or acts which are not expressly authorized or prohibited by this code.

The provisions of this section shall not apply to a theater, concert hall, or similar establishment primarily devoted to theatrical performances.

(F) Obscene Materials Seizure (312.3 PC)

If obscene material is seized, depicting a minor under 18 engaged in, or simulating sexual conduct, the material can be forfeited even if no conviction is sought or obtained. Added examples for the definition of "Obscene Matter" in the previous sections "Any representation of information, data, or image, including, but not limited to, any film, filmstrip, photograph, negative, slide, photocopy, videotape, video laser disc, computer hardware or software, computer floppy disk, data storage media, CD-ROM, or computer generated equipment or any other computer generated image that contains or incorporates in any manner any film or filmstrip."

The legislature codified its approval of People *v.* Cantrell (7 CA 4th 523) that matter depicting persons under the age of 18 engaging in or simulating sexual conduct is limited to visual works that depict that conduct.

(G) Harmful Matter

Definition: (Briefed)

Harmful Matter has the same definition as "Obscene Material" except that it ends with the words "and which taken as a whole lacks serious literary, artistic, political or scientific value for minors." When it appears from the nature of the matter or the circumstances of its distribution or exhibition that it is designed for clearly defined deviant sexual groups, the appeal of the matter shall be judged with reference to those groups.

In prosecutions under this chapter, where circumstances of any part of its operation indicate that the matter is being commercially exploited for the sake of its prurient appeal, such evidence is probative (it proves something about the nature of the matter) and can justify the conclusion that the matter lacks serious literary, artistic, political or scientific value.

In determining whether the matter taken as a whole lacks serious literary, artistic, political or scientific value in description or representation of such matters, the fact that the defendant knew that the matter depicts persons under the age of 16 years engaged in sexual conduct, as defined in 311.4 PC, is a factor which can be considered in making that determination.

(H) Distribution of Harmful Matter (313.1(c) PC)

Pornographic phone messages have now been added to the law prohibiting coin operated pornographic machines available to minors. This applies to public places (The old law only covered places near public schools). If the distributor can show that he has taken reasonable efforts to restrict minors, it can be used as a defense.

(1) Knowingly offers, distributes, sends, causes to be sent, or exhibits harmful matter to a minor in any public place,
(2) By any means whatever, including telephone,
(3) Without exercising reasonable care in determining whether or not the recipient is a minor.

<u>**Recorded Telephone Messages:**</u>

It is not a violation of the Public Utilities Code for the phone company to transmit harmful matter over the phone. However, they must take precautionary measures to prevent minors from receiving such messages. This shall be done by requiring the recipient to use a credit card and to give a previously issued access identification code.

(I) Harmful Matter Involving Person Under the Age of 18 (311.3 PC)

It is illegal to knowingly print, develop, duplicate, or exchange any film, photograph, slide, negative or video tape in which a person under the age of 18 is engaged in an act of sexual conduct.

(J) Sending Harmful Matter to Minors (288.2 PC)

<u>Section (a):</u>
(1) Every person who
 (a) having knowledge that a person is a minor, or
 (b) failing to use reasonable care in determining a minor's true age,
(2) Knowingly distributes, sends, exhibits, etc. any harmful matter (313 PC)
(3) With the intent of arousing, appealing to, or gratifying the lust, passions, or sexual desires of that minor
(4) With the intent of seducing a minor
(5) Is guilty of a wobbler. (2nd offense is a felony)

<u>Section (b):</u>
(1) Who does any of the above
(2) By means of electronic mail, the internet, or a commercial online service
(3) Is guilty of a "wobbler." (2nd offense is a felony)

<u>Exceptions:</u>
(1) Parents or guardians in aid of legitimate sex education.
(2) Acts committed for legitimate scientific or educational purposes.
(3) Telephone and cable companies and internet or commercial online service providers when transmitting or broadcasting telephone, cable television, internet, or commercial online services.

(K) Importing Commercial Child Pornography (311.1 PC) (Wobbler)

(1) Who knowingly sends, causes to be sent, brings or causes to be brought into this state for sale or distribution, OR
(2) While in this state, possesses, prepares, publishes, produces, develops, duplicates or prints,
(3) With intent to distribute or to exhibit or to exchange with others, or
(4) Actually do or offer to do
(5) Any obscene matter,
(6) Knowing it shows a person under 18 engaging in or simulating sexual conduct (311.4 PC).

<u>Exceptions:</u>

Legally emancipated minors, peace officer investigations, legitimate medical education.

(L) Involving Minors in Pornography (311.4 PC) (Briefed)

<u>Section A:</u>
(1) Who, knowing that a person is a minor
(2) Hires him to perform in or assist in acts listed in 311.2

<u>Section B:</u>
(1) Knowingly promotes, employs, uses, persuades or coerces or
(2) Who, having guardianship, permits
(3) A minor under 18 years of age
(4) To engage in either
 (a) photography or
 (b) a live performance
(5) Involving sexual conduct with persons or animals
(6) For commercial purposes
(7) Is guilty of a felony (3-6-8 years)

<u>Section D (1):</u>

Sexual conduct is any of the following (real or simulated) between persons of any sex or with animals:
(1) Sexual intercourse
(2) Anal intercourse
(3) Masturbation
(4) Bestiality
(5) Sexual sadism/masochism
(6) Lewd and lascivious conduct
(7) Lewd and lascivious excretory functions

(M) Polanco-Ferguson Anti-Child Pornography Act (311.11 PC)

(1) Every person who possesses or controls any matter such as film, photocopies, filmstrips, slides or videos, etc., involving the use of a person under the age of 18 years,
(2) Knowing it depicts that person engaging in or simulating sexual conduct (Def: 311.4 PC)
(3) Is guilty of a "felony."
Increased sentence if the matter contains more than 600 images of persons under 18 or 10 images of persons under 12 years of age, or the matter portrays sexual sadism or machoism involving a person under 18 years of age.
<u>Note:</u> It is not necessary to prove that the matter is obscene to establish a violation.

<u>Exceptions:</u>

Drawings, figurines, statues or film rated by the MPAA or live or recorded telephone messages transmitted as part of a commercial transaction.

(N) Records Required on Porno Distribution (1309.5 & 1309.6 Labor Code)

(1) Any person knowingly involved in distribution
(2) Of material depicting a minor under 18
(3) Engaging in or simulating sexual conduct
(4) Will keep and maintain records of names and addresses of the persons from whom the material was obtained.
(5) Such records will be kept for three years.

<u>Punished as civil penalty. Maximum, $7,500.</u>

(O) Film Processors or Computer Technicians' Duty to Report Pornography (11165, 11165.7 & 11166 PC)

If a film processor or computer technician, in the course of their job duty, sees any media materials depicting a child under the age of 18, engaged in sexual conduct, he must report it to the police, along with a copy of the material, within 36 hours.

Abortions

As of 2000, Abortion sections in the Penal Code have been repealed. However, this is covered in California Health & Safety Code Section 123460 to 123468 (Reproductive Privacy Act). Section 123468 states the performance of an abortion is unauthorized if either of the following is true:

(a) the person performing the abortion is not a healthcare provider authorized to perform an abortion; or
(b) the abortion is performed on a viable fetus, and both the following are established:
  (1) in good faith medical judgment, the fetus was viable; and
  (2) the continuance of pregnancy posed no risk to the life/health of the pregnant woman.

Roe *v.* Wade (U.S. Supreme Court – 1973)

In this important decision, the Supreme Court broke abortion rights into three stages:

(1) First three months: The state cannot interfere.
(2) Second three months: The state may regulate abortions only in ways that would be reasonably related to the woman's health.
(3) Third three months: The state can either ban abortions outright, or regulate them.

Gambling Offenses

There seems to be a great misconception about gambling. Not all gambling is illegal, only those games or under the conditions listed in the statutes.

Lotteries

(A) Lottery Defined (319 PC) (Briefed)

(1) Any scheme for the disposal of property
(2) By chance or lot
(3) Among those who have paid or have promised to pay anything of value
(4) For the chance of obtaining such property, or a share thereof,
(5) Regardless of what name it is called.

The key to lotteries is the phrase "by chance." If there is skill involved, it is not a lottery. For example, pitching pennies involves skill, so it is not illegal. A football pool is a lottery because you pick a score out of a hat – chance comes into the picture.

(B) Reverse Vending Machines (319.5 PC)

The laws on lotteries or gaming are not violated by the reverse vending machine which pays money at random for empty beverage containers.

(C) Lotteries, Bingo Games – Non-Profit (326.5 PC)

Bingo is legal under the following conditions:

(1) The game is operated by:
- (a) organizations exempt from payment of bank & corporation tax,
- (b) mobile home park associations, or
- (c) senior citizen organizations,
- (d) charitable organizations affiliated with a school district.

(2) When an ordinance has been passed by the city or county
(3) Proceeds are to be used for charitable purposes only.
(4) No person shall receive or pay a wage or profit.
(5) No minors are allowed to play.
(6) It is conducted only on property owned or leased by an organization.
(7) The property is used by the organization for offices or meetings.
(8) The games shall be open to the public and not members only.
(9) Games shall be operated and staffed without pay, by the members only.
(10) Promotion and supervision shall be conducted by members only.
(11) No other legal entity except the organization shall hold a financial interest in the game.
(12) All profits shall be kept in a special account and not co-mingled with any other account or fund.
(13) Rent, overhead and administrative costs shall not exceed 20% of proceeds before cost of prizes or $2,000 per month whichever is less.
(14) The organization conducting the game must be licensed by the city or county who may impose a license fee not to exceed $50.
(15) All players must be physically present during the game.
(16) The total value of prizes shall not exceed $250 per game.
(17) The city council or county board of supervisors may specify that organizations whose gross receipts exceed $5,000 can use a minimum percentage only for charitable purposes.

Definition:

Bingo (326.5(o) PC)

Bingo is a game of chance in which prizes are awarded on the basis of designated numbers or symbols on a card which conform to numbers or symbols that are selected at random.

(E) Chain Letters and Pyramid Schemes (327 PC)

(1) Who
- (a) operates,
- (b) contrives,
- (c) prepares,
- (d) sets up, or
- (e) proposes

(2) Any endless chain scheme
(3) Is guilty of a misdemeanor.

Definition:

An "endless chain" means any scheme for disposal or distribution of property whereby participants pay a valuable consideration for the chance to receive compensation for introducing one or more additional persons into participation in the scheme or for the chance to receive compensation when a person introduced by the participant introduces a new participant.

Exception:

This does not include payment based upon sales made to persons who are not participants in the scheme and who are not purchasing in order to participate in the scheme.

Gaming

(A) Gaming (330 PC) (Briefed) (Misd.)

(1) Any person involved in any game of:
- (a) Faro
- (b) Monte
- (c) Roulette
- (d) Lansquenet
- (e) Rouge et noire
- (f) Rondo
- (g) Tan
- (h) Fan tan
- (i) Seven-and-a-half
- (j) Twenty-one
- (k) Hokey-pokey or
- (l) any banking or percentage game

(2) Played with any device (e.g. cards or dice)
(3) For anything of value.

Since this section was written in the 1800's, some of the games are now unknown and cannot even be found in any book on gambling. A "banking" or "percentage game" is one where the house or person running the game takes a percentage of each pot as a fee, or is responsible for payment of all the bets, taking all that is won, and paying out all that is lost. (Lowrie, In re, 43 Cal. App. 564)

(B) Gambling Ships (11319 PC)

(1) It is illegal for a vessel or water craft to leave from and return to a California port
(2) When, during the cruise, gambling that is illegal in California,
(3) Is knowingly permitted, even if outside of state waters.

Exception:

Cruise ships coming from or going to foreign ports or ports in other states.

(C) Larceny: Cheating (332 PC)

(1) Using any means whatever (such as cards or other implements) or
(2) Betting on sides or hands of any game
(3) And fraudulently obtains another's money or property by such means
(4) Is guilty of larceny (petty or grand by amount)

Definitions:

Fraudulently Obtains: To gain unfair advantage for any player or participant through a technique or device not sanctioned by the rules of the game.
Value: The value assigned to the chips, tokens, or markers used in the game.

(D) Mechanical Devices to Control Games of Chance (334 PC)

(1) It is illegal to own, operate, manufacture or sell
(2) Mechanical devices to control
    (a) games of chance, or
    (b) any "razzle-dazzle" game where points are accumulated in successive games toward a total number of points needed to win.

(E) Prohibited Games (337j PC)

(1) It is unlawful for any person who has not procured and maintained all required federal, state and local licenses
(2) To deal, operate, conduct any controlled game, or
(3) To receive, directly or indirectly, any compensation or reward percentage or share of the revenue for running any controlled game, or
(4) Knowingly permitting any gambling equipment to be manufactured, stored or repaired in any building or premises that the person owns or leases when that person is not licensed.
(5) Manufacturing, distributing, or repairing any gambling equipment, or
(6) Knowingly permitting a controlled game to be conducted on property over which that person has control.

No fee may be calculated as a portion of wagers or winnings. Fees charged for all wagers shall be determined and collected prior to the start of play. Flat fees on each wager may be assessed at different collection rates, but no more than five collection rates may be established at each table. Sullivan *v.* Fox (1978) 189 Cal. App. 3d 673.

Definition:

Controlled Game means any game of chance or gambling device played for anything of value that is not prohibited by statute.

A Controlled Game does not include:

(1) Bingo
(2) Parimutuel betting on horse races
(3) California state lottery
(4) Card games in private homes where there is no percentage fee

Rules for Controlled Games:

(1) The amount of fee is fixed in advance.
(2) No minimum wager in any game, round, or hand.
(3) No fee deducted from amount wagered.
(4) Same fixed fee collected from all players.
(5) Fee collection does not violate local ordinances.

Bookmaking

(A) Pool-Selling, Bookmaking, Bets and Wagers (337a PC)

(1) Who engages in pool-selling or book-making, with or without writing, at any time or place.

(2)` (a) Who keeps or occupies any room, tent, building, vessel, or enclosure of any kind
  (b) With a book, papers, apparatus, device or other paraphernalia
  (c) For purposes of recording bets, wagers or pools
  (d) On the outcome of any contest or trial of endurance of person or animal, or between persons or animals
  (e) or mechanical apparatus, or upon the result of any lot, chance, casualty, unknown or contingent event whatsoever.

(3) (a) Who receives, holds, or handles any money or consideration of value
  (b) Offered for the purpose of being pledged, bet or wagered
  (c) Upon the result of any trial or contest of skill, speed, power or endurance between persons or animals, or
  (d) On a mechanical apparatus of lot or chance.

(4) (a) Who, for any reason
  (b) At any time
  (c) Makes a bet or wager
  (d) Upon any contest of skill, speed or power of endurance
  (e) Of person or animal, or mechanical apparatus
  (f) Or upon the result of any lot, chance or unknown event.

(5) (a) Who, being the owner, lessee or occupant
  (b) Of any building, vessel, place, stand grounds or enclosure
  (c) And for any reason
  (d) Permits that space to be used in any manner prohibited by (1), (2), (3), or (4).

(6) (a) Who makes, offers, or accepts any bets
  (b) Upon the result of any contest of skill, speed or power of endurance
  (c) Of person or animal, or mechanical apparatus.

This section shall not only apply to persons who may commit any of the acts designated in subdivisions one to six inclusive of this section, as a business or occupation, but shall also apply to every person or persons who may do in a single instance any one of the acts specified.

(B) Criminal Profiteering (186 PC) (Organized Crime Bill)

When selected laws under 186.2 PC are violated for financial gain two or more times by organized crime or anyone engaged in a "pattern of criminal profiteering," apart from criminal prosecution, all assets obtained from that venture shall be seized by the local or state government and forfeited as part of the punishment. (This takes the profit out of organized crime, especially arson, gambling, narcotics, prostitution, murder, robbery and theft.)

(C) Touts (337.1 PC) (Misdemeanor)

<u>Definition:</u>

Anyone who, knowingly and decidedly, by false representation attempts to, or does persuade, procure or cause another person to wager on a horse in race to be run in this State or elsewhere, and upon which money is wagered in this State, and who asks or demands compensation as reward for information or purported information given in such case is a tout and is guilty of touting.

A common example of touting is where the tout, an expert on horses and gambling odds, picks four or five horses that are bound to win a race. He then looks for a "mark" (or sucker) and tells him that he has inside information on the race, but he is broke. He tells the mark that he will give him the name of the winning horse on the condition that, when the horse wins, the tout gets 10% of the winnings. The tout then looks for other marks, and gives them the same routine but names different horses. He tells each person to meet him at a different place after the race. Whichever horse wins, the tout has a mark who thinks he won because of the inside information given him by the tout. He gladly shares 10% of the winnings. Those who lose chalk it up to experience. If it is a close race, they may still believe in the tout since the horse he named "just missed it by a head."

<u>Other Sections on Gambling</u>

There are many other sections dealing with certain types of gambling and certain types of gambling devices that are illegal. Space does not permit a full coverage of all of these laws. When you have time, read them over in the Penal Code.

Crimes Against Public Health & Ecology

(A) Unlawful Dumping of Offensive Matter on Public or Private Property (374.3 PC)

Section A:
(1) Dumping, or causing to be dumped
(2) Any waste matter
(3) In or upon any
  (a) highway or road,
  (b) right-of-way,
  (c) private property by easement, license or trespassing
  (d) public property (not including dumps).

Section B:
(1) Placing, causing to be placed, depositing or dumping
(2) Any rocks or dirt
(3) In or upon any
(a) private property without owner's consent, or
(b) public property without consent.

Punishment:

Violators are guilty of an infraction, and each day the violation continues shall be considered a separate offense. The court may order the violator to remove or pay for the removal of the dumped material. As a condition of probation, the violator may be ordered to pick up waste matter for a specified number of hours as directed by the court.

(B) Dumping of Hazardous Waste (374.8 PC)

The unlawful dumping of hazardous waste materials and liquids is a wobbler.

(C) Offensive Substances in Place of Assemblage (375 PC) (Felony)

Section A:
(1) It is unlawful to
  (a) throw, drop, pour, deposit, release, discharge, expose, or
  (b) attempt to do any of these acts
(2) In public places, including but not limited to:
  (a) theaters,
  (b) restaurants,
  (c) places of business, or
  (d) places of amusement
(3) Any substance or matter of any kind
(4) That is injurious to person or property or is nauseous, sickening, irritating, or offensive to any of the senses.

Section B:
(1) It is illegal to manufacture, prepare, or possess
(2) Any of the above material or substance
(3) With intent to use it in a place of public assemblage

Section D:
(1) It is illegal to disperse in the air or vaporize
(2) Any substance that causes
  (a) serious illness or
  (b) permanent injury.
(3) It is illegal to use any
  (a) tear gas
  (b) mustard gas
  (c) a combination or compound thereof
  (d) acid, or
  (e) explosives
(4) Which violates the elements of the first part of this law.

(D) Public Nuisances (370 PC)
Public Nuisances Defined
A public nuisance is anything which is:
(1) Injurious to health or
(2) Indecent or offensive to the senses or
(3) An obstruction to the free use of property, so as to interfere with the comfortable enjoyment of life or property by
  (a) an entire community or neighborhood, or
  (b) any considerable number of persons, or
(4) Unlawfully obstructs the free passage or use of any navigable lake, river, bay, stream, canal, or basin. or
(5) Unlawfully obstructs the free passage or use of any public park, square, street or highway.

371 PC

The fact that the nuisance affects different people in different ways does not affect this law.

372 PC

Committing or maintaining a public nuisance, or failing, upon court order, to remove it, is a misdemeanor.

(E) Maintaining or Permitting Public Nuisance After Notice (373a PC)
(1) Each person who, upon receiving a reasonable notice in writing from:
  (a) a health officer or
  (b) a district attorney or
  (c) city attorney or
  (d) other prosecuting attorney

(2) To correct the public nuisance
(3) And fails to do so
(4) Is guilty of a misdemeanor for each day the public nuisance continues thereafter.

Litterbug Laws

(A) Dumping Refuse on Public or Private Roads or Property (374.3 PC)
(1) Dumping or causing to be dumped
(2) In or upon any public or private property
(3) By a person, firm or corporation
(4) Is an infraction.

__Definition:__

To litter: to discard, drop or scatter small quantities of waste matter ordinarily carried on or about the person in any place other than a proper waste container, or to allow same to escape from a container (waste matter: beverage containers, packaging, wrappers, waste paper, newspaper, magazines).

Chapter VII Case Citations

Study Questions for Chapter VII

(1) Under the laws on bribery, peace officers are not mentioned. They come under the law that covers ____ officers.

(2) If the property offered in a bribe does not have an established value, there is no crime of bribery. T or F

(3) Officer Hank sells Sam Sleezy a sticker to put on the rear of his car window. It says "Police Friends Assn." Officer Hank insinuates that Sam will get fewer tickets with this sticker. Officer Hank is guilty of a misdemeanor. T or F

(4) In the crime of perjury, it must be shown that the person who committed the perjury did so with intent to cause harm to another. T or F

(5) Franny Farkle has been legally sworn in as a witness in a murder trial. When questioned by the defense attorney about her age, she replies that she is 39 years old when it is obvious to the members of the jury that she is closer to 49. Because she lied out of vanity, and it was not a material matter, this is not perjury. T or F

(6) If Arnold Aardvark stated in court under oath that he could not remember a particular situation, when it could be shown that he did remember it, he could be charged with perjury. T or F

(7) An opinion can never be the subject of a criminal charge of perjury. T or F

(8) To come under the law on perjury, a signed affidavit must pass out of the possession of the person that signed it. T or F

(9) Perjury can be proved by the sole testimony of one witness. T or F

(10) When a person gets another to commit perjury, it is called ______________ of perjury.

(11) In the offense "compounding a crime," the term "compounding" most closely means

(A) ____adding to   (B) ____concealing

(C) ____committing   (D) ___refusing to prevent

(12) In the offense of "compounding a crime," the person compounding the crime must actually receive something of value in order for the crime to be completed. T or F

(13) A District Attorney who refuses to prosecute a person in exchange for a campaign donation, would be guilty of subornation of perjury. T or F

(14) A case of "compounding a crime" may be legally compromised if it is a misdemeanor. T or F

(15) Legally, "compromising a crime" is a bar to further prosecution. T or F

(16) A crime cannot be compromised when the victim is a peace officer performing his duties. T or F

(17) Riotous acts can be compromised if they are misdemeanors. T or F

(18) Officer Wagwump takes a report from Annie Akinankle, who stated that her ex-boyfriend told her in front of 18 witnesses that he was going to kill her. He just bought a gun from a friend of hers. Another friend told her that her ex-boyfriend was now looking for her. Officer Wagwump can take no legal action at this time. T or F

(19) When someone threatens another, and the victim goes before a judge with this information, the judge may issue a warrant of arrest for the person making the threats. T or F

(20) Persons who go before a judge with the complaint that another person has threatened them must make the statement in writing and sign it under oath. T or F

(21) If Clyde Crashcup threatens to smash Betty Bump's new stereo set she can have a judge make Clyde put up a bond to insure that he will not carry out his threats. T or F

(22) A "peace bond" is issued by a judge. If a judge makes Clyde put up a "peace bond," it is good for ________________ months.

(23) The Penal Code section for "failure to provide for children" is ________________ PC.

(24) If the courts assign total custody of a child to its mother, the father is no longer required to provide for the support of that child. T or F

(25) A mother of a small child must legally provide the basic necessities of life, if the father is unable to provide them, and she is able to. T or F

(26) An unborn child in the mother's womb is considered to be an existing person as far as 270 PC is concerned. T or F

(27) If a husband consents in writing to allow his wife to have a baby through artificial insemination, he is considered to be the legal father of that child. T or F

(28) An individual, who has sufficient ability, is responsible to provide food, shelter, clothing and medical care for his/her wife or husband, unless his/her misconduct has justified abandonment. T or F

(29) If a parent is without means of support, every adult child who has the ability must provide for that parent. T or F

(30) The Penal Code section for contributing to the delinquency of a minor is ________ PC.

(31) Contributing to the delinquency of a minor refers to those persons under the age of ____.

(32) Contributing to the delinquency of a minor refers to those persons who cause a minor person to come under the sections 300, 601, and 602 W & I Code. T or F

(33) A child who is without the necessities of life can be a ward of the court under section 300 of the W & I Code. T or F

(34) A habitual truant can be made a ward of the court under section 601 W & I. T or F

(35) A police officer cannot transport or confine any child under the age of __________ with adults who have been charged with criminal acts without an official being present.

(36) Percy Pester has six children. He gets mad at his 5-year-old girl and abandons her in the center strip of a major freeway at night. This is a misdemeanor. T or F

(37) The term "habitually drunk" as used in 273g, generally means ____________ times.

(38) The key as to whether gambling comes under the classification of a lottery is:

(A) ____Skill is involved in determining the winner

(B) ____There is more than one winner

(C) ____The winner is determined by chance

(D) ____It is run by a large organization

(39) To be a lottery, the persons participating must have actually paid something of value for their chance to win. T or F

(40) Pitching pennies is an example of a lottery. T or F

(41) Sammy Sharp sets up a sales company which people can join for a price. Each person who joins gets a percentage of the money paid by each new person that they recruit, and a small portion of the money paid by any members that the new recruits recruit. It is like a pyramid with the people at the top receiving more money as the base of the pyramid grows. This operation is legal in California. T or F

(42) What is the name commonly used for the operation in question 41? ____________

____

(43) A percentage or banking game is one where:

(A) ____Only a certain percentage of the players participate at one time.

(B) ____The house or person banking the game gets a percentage of each pot.

(C) ____Everyone bets against the bank for an increased percentage.

(D) ____Each player loses only a percentage of the bet.

(44) "Snake Eyes" Sam and his friends are playing dice on the porch of a local cannery. Officer Sharp spots them and quietly moves in on them. Before they realize that he is there, he has observed enough to testify in court that they were playing dice, but saw nothing that would indicate that someone was "running" the game for a "take." Officer Sharp arrests the players for section 330 PC. This is false arrest. T or F

(45) The crime of bookmaking applies only to those who make a business or occupation of bookmaking and not those who commit just one act. T or F

(46) A person who claims to have inside information on a horse race and offers this information in exchange for a percentage of the winnings is called a ____________

(47) Illegal dumping (374.3) applies only to public property. T or F

(48) To be classed as a public nuisance, something that is offensive must offend the whole community where the nuisance exists. T or F

(49) A person who maintains a public nuisance is only guilty after receiving reasonable notice in writing from a required official. T or F

(50) A person who is guilty of maintaining a public nuisance is guilty of a separate offense each day that the nuisance continues. T or F

(51) As a joke, Morty Snerd traps a wild skunk and drops it through the window of the house next door. He has violated 375 PC. T or F

(52) Morty gets such a kick out of his "skunk" joke that he tries it again, but this time he drops one through the window of a local dance hall. This violates 375 PC. T or F

(53) Homer Hashtag is a chemistry major. He makes a "stink bomb" and tells friends that he made it to throw into the Falcon Restaurant because they refused to serve him liquor. He has violated section 375 PC. T or F

(54) In "Offenses Committed by Telephone," 653m PC, the perpetrator must say something to the victim. Heavy breathing into the telephone or silence do not fulfill the elements of the crime. T or F

(55) In 653m PC, the jurisdiction of the cases is only in the court district where the call was received. T or F

CHAPTER VIII

CIVIL DISORDER AND CRIMES AGAINST PUBLIC PEACE

Crimes Against Peace

(A) Disturbance of Religious Meetings (302 PC) (Misdemeanor)
(1) Who willfully disturbs or disquiets
(2) Any assemblage met for religious worship
(3) By:
 (a) profane language or
 (b) rude or indecent behavior or
 (c) unnecessary noise
(4) Either
 (a) in the place where the meeting is held or
 (b) near enough to disturb the order and solemnity of the meeting.

(B) Disturbance of Public Meetings (Not Religious or Political) (403 PC) (Misd.)
(1) Every person, who, without authority of law
(2) Willfully disturbs or breaks up any assembly or meeting not unlawful in its character
(3) Other than
 (a) religious meetings (302 PC)
 (b) meetings listed in 18340 Elections Code.

(C) Unlawful Assembly (407 PC)
(1) Two or more persons
(2) Assemble together
(3) To do either
 (a) an unlawful act
 (b) a lawful act in a violent, boisterous or tumultuous manner.
(4) Such assembly is an unlawful assembly.

(D) Rout (Attempted Riot) (406 PC)
(1) Two or more persons
(2) Assembled and acting together
(3) Make an attempt at or advance toward an act of riot.
(4) Such assembly is a rout.

(E) Riot (404 PC)
(1) Two or more persons acting together
(2) Without authority of law
(3) Using or threatening to use any force or violence or disturbance of the peace
(4) When accompanied by the immediate power of execution

(5) Is a riot.
 * This law also applies to any place of confinement such as a jail, prison, industrial farm, jail farm, or road camp.

(F) Urging Riot, or Burning or Destroying of Property (404.6 PC)

(1) Every person who, with intent to cause:
  (a) a riot
  (b) acts of force
  (c) acts of violence
  (d) property burning or destroying.
(2) Does an act urging these offenses or
(3) Engages in conduct encouraging these offenses or
(4) Urges others to commit these offenses
(5) At a time and place and under circumstances
(6) Which produce a clear, present and immediate danger of these acts being committed.

Exception:

Lawful activities of labor organizations.

Elements:

By the adding of certain elements, unlawful assembly can become rout, and rout can become riot. (See chart below)

(G) Damage to Public Property, Jail or Prison (4600 PC)

Any person willfully and intentionally damaging any jail, prison or public property is guilty of a felony if the value of the damage is over $950.

Note:

Straight vandalism requires $400 damage with prior conviction, or over $10,000 damage to be a felony. (594 PC)

(H) Police Authority to Close Area During Calamity (409.5 PC)

(1) When a menace to public health or safety is created by a calamity, including but not limited to flood, storm, fire, earthquake, explosion, accident or other disaster, officers of the California Highway Patrol, police department or sheriff's office, peace officers (park rangers) from the Department of Forestry and Fire Protection, Department of Parks and Recreation, or Department of Fish and Game (830.3) full-time publicly employed lifeguards and Marine Safety Officers may close the area where the menace exists for the duration thereof by means of ropes, markers or guards to any and all persons not authorized by such officers to enter or remain within the closed area. If such a calamity creates an immediate menace to public health, the local health officer may close the area where the menace exists pursuant to the conditions set forth above.
(2) Officers of the California Highway Patrol, police departments or sheriff's office, peace officers (park rangers) from the Department of Forestry and Fire Protection, Department of Parks and Recreation, or Department of Fish and Game (830.3 PC) full-time publicly employed lifeguards and Marine Safety Officers may close the immediate area surrounding any emergency field command post or any other command post activated for the purpose of abating any calamity enumerated in this section or any riot or other civil disturbance to any and all unauthorized persons pursuant to the conditions set forth in this section whether or not such field command post or other

(1) Two or more persons
(2) Assemble together to do:
  (a) An unlawful act, or
  (b) A lawful act in a violent boisterous manner.

Unlawful Assembly

(3) Make an attempt or advance toward a riotous act

Rout

(4) Threaten to use, or use any:
  (a) Force without authority of law, or
  (b) Violence, or
  (c) Disturb the public peace
(5) Accompanied by immediate power of execution

Riot

Fig. VIII–1 Relationship between Unlawful Assembly, Rout and Riot.

command post is located near to the actual calamity or riot or other civil disturbance.

(3) Willfully remaining in a closed area after receiving notice to leave is a misdemeanor.

(4) Nothing in this section shall prevent duly authorized members of the news media from entering closed areas.

(I) Police Authority to Close Area of Avalanche (409.6 PC)

(1) Whenever a menace to the public health or safety is created by an avalanche, a public officer may close the area.

(2) In conducting safety operations at the scene of an avalanche, a command post may be established and declared off limits to all unauthorized persons.

(3) Persons who enter or remain after being notified, are guilty of a misdemeanor. Members of the news media are excepted.

(J) Punishment for Rout and Unlawful Assembly (408 PC)

Every person who participates in a rout or unlawful assembly is guilty of a misdemeanor.

(K) Remaining Present at Place of Rout, etc. After Warning Given (409 PC)

Unauthorized persons remaining present at the place of a riot, rout, or unlawful assembly, are guilty of a misdemeanor.

(L) Refusal to Disperse Upon Lawful Command at Unlawful Assembly (416 PC)

If two or more persons assemble for the purpose of an unlawful act, and do not disperse on being commanded to do so by a public officer, each person is guilty of a misdemeanor.

(M) Lines of Authority in Medical Emergencies (1798.6 H & S)

Authority for patient healthcare management in an emergency shall be vested in that licensed or certified healthcare professionals, which may include any paramedics or other pre-hospital emergency personnel at the scene of an emergency, who are most medically qualified specific to rendering emergency medical care. If no licensed or certified healthcare professional is available, the authority shall be vested in the most appropriate medically qualified representative of public safety agencies, who may have responded to the scene.

<u>Instructions to Members of Routs and Unlawful Assemblies</u>

Although 408 PC makes it a misdemeanor to participate in a rout or an unlawful assembly, it is the policy of police agencies, based on the wording of Penal Code sections 409, 416, and 726, to give such participants fair and ample warning to disperse before legal action is taken.

(N) Magistrates and Officers to Command Rioters to Disperse (726 PC)

Where any number of persons, whether armed or not, are unlawfully or riotously assembled, the sheriff of the county and his deputies, the officials governing the town or city, or any of them, must go among the persons assembled, or as near to them as possible, and command them, in the name of the people of the State, immediately to disperse.

(O) To Arrest Rioters If They Do Not Disperse (727 PC)

If the persons assembled do not immediately disperse, such magistrates and officers must arrest them, and to that end may command the aid of all persons present or within the county.

<u>Order of Dispersal</u>

An order of dispersal may be worded as follows: "I am Lieutenant Smith of the Eastridge Police Department, a peace officer of the State of California. I hereby declare this gathering to be an unlawful assembly and, in the name of the people of the State of California, command you to disperse immediately."

It is best to have a higher ranking official give the order. He or she should repeat the order several times to make sure it is heard. The best method of transmitting the message is by use of a portable "bull-horn." Most police cars now have external loudspeakers attached to their microphones, so an officer can make the command from within the safety of the police car. If the crowd is angry, and has come prepared for violence, officers standing in the open can be pelted with a variety of missiles.

(P) Looting (463 PC) (Wobbler)

(1) Anyone who, during either
  (a) a state of emergency,
  (b) a local emergency, or
  (c) under an evacuation order
(2) When the cause is an earthquake, flood, fire, riot, or a natural or man-made disaster
(3) Commits:
  (a) second degree burglary (even if the building has been damaged by the disaster), or
  (b) grand theft, or
  (c) petty theft
(4) In any county affected by the emergency
(5) Is guilty of the crime of looting.

Conditions of Probation:

Misdemeanor: If given probation, minimum 90 days in county jail.

Felony: Minimum 180 days if probation is given. Exceptions must be justified in writing by judge.

Definitions:

State of Emergency:

Conditions which, due to their magnitude, are or are likely to be beyond the control of the services, personnel, equipment and facilities of any single county, city, or city and county, requiring the combined forces of mutual aid regions to combat.

Local Emergency:

The same as a "State of Emergency" except that it is declared by the local governing body pursuant to section 8630 of the Government Code.

Duration of Emergency:

The emergency shall last from the time of the proclamation until seven days thereafter.

Exceptions:

This law does not cover burglary, grand theft, or petty theft involving consensual entry into a commercial structure with the intent to commit:

(a) forgery (470 PC)
(b) issuing fictitious notes (476 PC)
(c) checks with insufficient funds (476a PC)
(d) use of false credit card (484f PC), or
(e) illegal use of credit card (484g PC).

(Q) Disturbing the Peace (415 PC)

The following shall be punished:

(1) Any person who unlawfully fights in a public place or challenges another person in a public place to fight, or
(2) Any person who maliciously and willfully disturbs another person by loud and unreasonable noise, or
(3) Anyone who uses offensive words in a public place which are inherently likely to provoke an immediate violent reaction.

(R) Vehicle Sound Systems (27007 CVC)

(1) Operating, or permitting the operation of, a sound amplification system from a vehicle
(2) Which can be heard outside the vehicle from 50 or more feet
(3) When the vehicle is operated on a highway.

Exceptions:

  (a) requesting assistance
  (b) legally advertising
  (c) warning of hazards
  (d) emergency vehicles
  (e) in parade with permit
  (f) political announcements
  (g) public utility or communication vehicles.

Note: Local authorities can prohibit (b) (e) & (f).

(S) Willful or Malicious Obstruction of Street or Sidewalk (647(c) PC) (Misdemeanor)

Every person who willfully and maliciously obstructs the free movement of any person on or in any street, sidewalk, or other public place, or any place open to the public. This section is a "catchall" and has been used in many ways. One recent use has been to arrest prostitutes stopping persons on the street and soliciting them. Generally, in cases of this sort, the person solicited does not want to get involved and will not cooperate. By using 647(c) only the stopping need be proved.

(T) Willful Obstruction of Land (420.1 PC)

(1) Anyone who willfully and knowingly
(2) Prevents, hinders, or obstructs any person having the legal right to do so
(3) From entering, passing over, or leaving land.

This section does not apply to anyone engaged in lawful labor union activities, or engaged in activities protected by the United States or California Constitution.

(U) Unlawful Entry (603 PC) (Misdemeanor)

(1) Every person other than a peace officer engaged in the performance of duties as such,
(2) Who forcibly and without the consent of the owner, representative of the owner, lessee or representative of the lessee thereof,

(3) Enters a house, cabin or other building occupied or constructed for occupation by humans,
(4) And who damages, injures, or destroys any property of value in, around or pertaining to such house, cabin or other building.

Disturbances at Colleges and Schools

(A) Offenses Committed in Buildings/Grounds of Community Colleges, Universities, or State Universities (415.5 PC) (Misdemeanor)

(1) Unlawfully fighting within any building or upon the grounds of any community college, university, or state university, or challenging another within any such building or upon such grounds to fight.
(2) Maliciously and willfully disturbing another person within any such building or upon such grounds by loud and unreasonable noise.
(3) Using offensive words within any such building or upon such grounds which are inherently likely to produce a violent reaction.

This is the same as 415 PC except instead of "public place," the term "college or university" is used.

Definition:

As used in this section, "state university," "university," "community college" and "school" have the same meaning. (Also the same in 626 PC)

Punishment:

(1) **1st Offense:** Up to $400.00 and/or up to 90 days in county jail.
(2) **2nd Offense:** Min. 10 days county jail, up to six months and/or up to $1,000 fine. No parole or probation until 10 days imprisonment.
(3) **3rd Offense:** 90 days to six months county jail, $1,000. No parole or probation until 90 days imprisonment.

(B) Willfully Obstructing a Student's or Teacher's Access to Classes (602.10 PC)

(1) Every person who uses physical force,
(2) With the intent of preventing attendance or instruction at classes
(3) And willfully obstructs or attempts to obstruct any teacher or student from attending classes,
(4) At any UC, CSU, or community college,
(5) Is guilty of a misdemeanor.

Threat of Injury to Prevent Performance of Duties (71 PC)

(1) Every person who by direct communication,
(2) Threatens to inflict an unlawful injury upon another's person or property,
(3) With the intent to cause
    (a) any officer or employee of an educational institution, or
    (b) any public officer or employee
(4) To refrain from doing any act in the performance of their duty
(5) When it reasonably appears to the recipient that such threat could be carried out,
(6) Is guilty of a wobbler. (2nd offense is a felony)

Definitions:

School: any school (K–12); also any public right-of-way situated immediately adjacent to school property or any other place if a teacher and one or more students are required to be there in connection with assigned school activities (example: a field trip).

Directly Communicated: means a direct communication with the victim by any means.

(C) Willfully and Knowingly Entering Upon Campus of State College or University After Suspension or Dismissal (626.2 PC)

(1) Every student or employee of a community college, state university, the University of California or a school,
(2) Who, after a hearing, has been suspended or dismissed for disrupting the orderly operation of the campus or facility, and
(3) Who has been notified by certified or registered mail, that they have been denied access to the campus or facility, and
(4) Who, without express written permission from the Chief Administrator,
(5) Enters such property,
(6) Is guilty of a misdemeanor. (2nd offense = min. 10 days) (3rd + offense = min. 90 days)

Knowledge shall be presumed if notice has been given as prescribed in this section. The presumption established by this section is a presumption affecting the burden of proof.

(D) Withdrawal of Consent to Remain on Campus (626.4 PC)

Section A:

(1) The Chief Administrative Officer or agent of a community college, state university, university, or a school campus or facility,
(2) May notify a person that consent to remain on the property has been withdrawn (up to 14 days)
(3) Whenever there is reasonable cause to believe that such person has willfully disrupted the orderly operation of the campus or facility.

Section B:

(1) Within 24 hours of withdrawal of consent
(2) The Chief Administrative Officer, or agent thereof, must review and confirm the decision
(3) Or withdrawal of consent becomes invalid.
Note: Any arrest based upon probable cause made under this section shall be valid.

Section C:

(1) The person who was banned from campus may submit a written request for a hearing,
(2) Within the 14-day period.
(3) A hearing will then be granted within 7 days,
(4) And a notice will be immediately mailed, stating the time, place and date of the hearing.

Section D:

(1) When a person has been notified by the proper authority that consent to remain on campus has been withdrawn,
(2) And who willfully and knowingly enters or remains on such property during the period that consent has been withdrawn,
(3) Is guilty of a misdemeanor.

Exception:

Such a person can enter the campus or facility for the sole purpose of either applying for an appeal, or attending the hearing.

Punishment:

Second offense: minimum of 10 days in jail.
Third offense: minimum of 90 days in jail.

(E) Persons Other Than Students and Employees Who Interfere With Peaceful Conduct on Campus (626.6 PC)

(1) Any person who is not a student or employee of a community college, state university, the University of California, or a school,
(2) And is not, by reason of employment, required to be on campus,
(3) And it reasonably appears to the Chief Administrative Officer, or agent, that such person
  (a) is committing any act likely to interfere with peaceful conduct of activities on the property, or
  (b) has entered for the purpose of committing such an act.
(4) The Chief Administrative Officer or agent may direct that person to leave the property.
(5) If that person returns within seven days after being directed to leave, it is a misdemeanor.

Punishment:

Second offense: minimum of 10 days in jail.
Third offense: minimum of 90 days in jail.

(F) Entry of School Property by Person Not on Lawful Business; Disruption; Refusal or Re-entry After Request to Leave (626.8 PC)

Section A:

(1) Anyone entering upon
  (a) school property, or
  (b) an adjacent street or sidewalk,
(2) Whose presence or acts interfere with the peaceful conduct of school activities,
(3) And who
  (a) remains there, or
  (b) re-enters within 7 days,
(4) After being asked to leave by the Chief Administrative Officer or agent thereof,
(5) Is guilty of a misdemeanor.

Section B: If the same person establishes a "continued pattern of unauthorized entry," even after the seven days, that person is guilty of a misdemeanor.

Punishment:

(1) 1st offense—$500 and/or six months in county jail.
(2) Prior conviction—any offense in chapter or 415.5 PC. Min. 10 days–six months and/or $500. No probation or parole until after 10 days.
(3) Two or more prior convictions as listed in (2) minimum 90 days–six months, and/or $500. No probation or parole until after 90 days.

Lawful Business:

Means a reason for being present upon school property which is not otherwise prohibited by statute, ordinance or regulation.

Sex Offenders on School Grounds (626.81 PC)

290 PC registrants who come onto any school ground (K-12) or adjacent sidewalks or streets, unless they are a parent or guardian of a child attending the school or is a student there, or has written permission of the chief administrator, is guilty of a misdemeanor. If he is asked to leave on two prior occasions (even if he leaves), he has established a "continued pattern of unauthorized entry," and will be guilty of another misdemeanor.

(G) Trespassing at Schools (627 & 627.1-11 PC)

No outsider shall enter or remain on school grounds (including those suspended) from one hour before classes begin to one hour after the last class ends when signs are posted (627.6 PC) without first requesting from principal or designee, permission to register. Those posing imminent danger to others at the school can be refused registration and must leave. (1st offense is an infraction)

(H) Gun-Free School Zone Act of 1995 (626.9 PC)

(1) It is unlawful for anyone to possess a firearm
(2) When they know or should reasonably know that they are in
  (a) a school zone, or
  (b) the grounds of a college or university, including marked off-campus buildings and housing (when firearm is loaded). At universities and colleges prominent signs will be posted declaring property a "Gun-Free Zone."

Punishment:
(1) Possession of firearm. (Def. 16520 PC) — 2, 3 or 5 years
(2) Discharge of firearm with reckless disregard for the safety of others. — 3, 5 or 7 years.

Exceptions:
(1) Person is on private property, a residence or a business.
(2) Firearm is in a locked container (25610 PC).
(3) Firearm is locked in trunk of vehicle.
(4) Person has permission from school or college authorities equivalent to superintendent.
(5) Possession is at a shooting range on the grounds or campus.
(6) Possessor is a security guard or retired police officer (25850 PC).
(7) Person reasonably believes that his or her life or safety is in great danger based on a current, non-mutual, restraining order.
(8) A person holding a valid license to carry a firearm, who is carrying that firearm within a distance of 1,000 feet from the grounds.
(9) This section does not apply to appointed peace officers authorized to carry a firearm.
(10) This section does not apply to activities of a program involving shooting as a sports activity (i.e. skeet shooting)
(11) This section does not apply to a state certified hunter education program if the firearms are not loaded and if participants possess no ammunition.

Definitions:
School Zone: On the school grounds or within 1,000 feet from the grounds of a public or private school (K through 12)
Loaded: For purposes of this section, an unexpended cartridge or shell is attached in any manner to the firearm or clip or magazine of that weapon.

(I) Possession of Ammunition on School Grounds (30310 PC)

No person shall carry ammunition or reloaded ammo onto school grounds.

Exceptions:
(1) Sworn law enforcement officers on duty.
(2) Ammunition is in a locked container.
(3) Person summoned to assist a police officer in an arrest or to assist in preserving the peace.
(4) Armored vehicle guard(s) engaged in their duties.
(5) Honorably retired police officers.
(6) California or U.S. military forces performing their duties.

(J) Possess/Brandish Firearm Where Children Gather (626.95 PC)
(1) Exhibiting a deadly weapon in a threatening manner
(2) In a playground or youth center with minors present
(3) During its hours of operation
(4) Or at any time minors are using the facility.

Definitions:
Playground: Park or recreation area with playground equipment or areas designed for athletic activities.
Youth Center: Public or private facility that hosts recreational or social activities for minors.

(K) Possession of a Non-Firearm Weapon on Grounds of a Public or Private School or College (Wobbler) (626.10 PC)

It is illegal to bring or possess any of the following weapons upon the grounds or within any public or private school, university or community college:

(1) Dirk or dagger
(2) Knife with
  (a) blade longer than 2 ½ inches or
  (b) a folding blade that locks into place
(3) Razor with an unguarded blade
(4) Taser or a stun gun
(5) Ice pick
(6) BB or pellet gun
(7) Spot marker gun
(8) Razor blades and box cutters (are prohibited in school grounds K-12).

This law applies to possession, not just the carrying of the weapons concealed. Any certificated or classified employee of the school may seize these weapons on school property based on probable cause that the person illegally possesses the weapon.

Exceptions:

(1) Peace officers (830 PC) (incl. out-of-state)
(2) State peace officers on official duty
(3) Federal peace officers on official duty
(4) Members of the military on official duty
(5) Persons bringing weapon on school property at the direction of a school employee for a class activity
(6) Persons carrying weapons for a lawful purpose within the scope of their employment

Coverage:

This covers kindergarten through university.

Criminal Gangs and Terrorism

Street Terrorism Enforcement and Prevention Act (186.20 PC)

(A) Legislative Intent (186.21 PC)

All persons in this state have the right to be secure and protected from fear, intimidation and physical harm caused by the activities of violent groups and individuals. Criminal street gangs in California have increased in numbers and have been responsible for such a large number of deaths that some legal action must be taken to control the problem.

(B) Active Participation in Criminal Street Gang Activity (186.22 PC) (186.26 PC)

Section A:

(1) Soliciting or recruiting another
(2) To actively participate in a street gang
(3) With the intent that the person solicited or recruited would participate in a pattern of criminal street gang activity
(4) or with the intent that the person solicited or recruited would promote felonious conduct by the gang members.

Section B:

(1) Threatening another with physical violence
(2) On two or more occasions within a 30-day period
(3) With the intent to coerce or solicit a person to actively participate in a criminal street gang.

Section C:

(1) Using physical violence
(2) To coerce or solicit another
(3) To actively participate in a criminal street gang.
(4) Or to prevent the person from leaving the gang.

Section D:

(1) If the person recruited or solicited
(2) Is a minor
(3) Three years are added to the sentence.

Definitions:

Credible Threat (186.22(a) PC)

A threat made with the intent, and apparent ability to carry out the threat, and cause the victim to reasonably fear for his or her safety or the safety of a third person.

Threat of Violence (186.22(b) PC)

A threat to commit a violent felony as defined in 667.5(c) PC.

Criminal Street Gang (186.34 PC)

(1) Any ongoing organization, association or group of three or more persons,
(2) Whether formal or informal
(3) Having as one of its primary activities, the commission of one or more of the criminal acts listed in 186.22(e) PC (see below).
(4) Having a common name or common identifying sign, symbol, or name
(5) And whose members individually or collectively engage in, or have engaged in a "Pattern of Definable Criminal Activity."

Pattern of Criminal Gang Activity (186.22(e) PC)

(1) Commission, attempted commission or solicitation of two or more of the following offenses, including sustained juvenile petitions by two or more persons:

(a) 245 PC — Assault With a Deadly Weapon
(b) 211 PC — Robbery
(c) 187 – 192 PC — Unlawful Homicide
(d) Narcotic offenses (11054-11058 H & S)
(e) 246 PC — Shooting at dwelling etc.
(f) 12034 PC — Discharging firearm from vehicle
(g) 450 PC — Arson
(h) 136.1 PC — Witness intimidation
(i) 487 PC — Grand Theft (when exceeding $10,000)
(j) Grand Theft of vehicle, trailer or vessel.
(k) 459 PC — Burglary
(l) 261 PC — Rape
(m) 463 PC — Looting
(n) 186.10 PC — Money Laundering
(o) 207 PC — Kidnapping
(p) 203 PC — Mayhem
(q) 205 PC — Aggravated Mayhem
(r) 206 PC — Torture
(s) 518 & 520 PC — Felony Extortion
(t) 594 PC — Felony Vandalism
(u) 215 PC — Carjacking
(v) 12072 PC — Illegal sale, delivery, or transfer of firearms
(w) 12101(a) PC—Possession of a pistol, revolver, or other firearm capable of being concealed upon the person.

<u>Buildings Used by Criminal Gangs (186.22a PC)</u>

(1) Every building or place,
(2) Used by "Criminal Street Gang" members
(3) For the purpose of committing offenses listed in 186.22(e)PC, or
(4) Any offense involving dangerous or deadly weapons,or
(5) Burglary or rape, or
(6) Anywhere such criminal conduct takes place
(7) Is a nuisance which shall be enjoined, abated and prevented, and for which damages may be recovered. (This means the D.A. can close the place down and sue the gang for costs.)

<u>Exception:</u>

This chapter shall not apply to unions or to employees engaged in concerted activities for their own mutual end and protection. (186.23 PC)

(C) Inducing Another to Participate in Criminal Street Gangs (186.26 PC)

<u>Section A:</u>

(1) Any person who solicits or recruits another
(2) To actively participate
(3) In a criminal street gang
(4) With the intent that the person solicited participate in a pattern of criminal street gang activity as defined in Section 186.22 PC
(5) Is guilty of a felony. (16 months, 2 or 3 years)

<u>Section B:</u>

(1) Any person who does the above by threats of violence on two or more separate occasions
(2) Within a 30-day period
(3) Is guilty of a felony. (2, 3 or 4 years)

<u>Section D:</u>

If the person solicited is a minor, an additional term of three years shall be imposed.

(D) Criminal Street Gang – Registration Required (186.30 PC)

Any person who has been convicted of a crime involving illegal street gang activity shall register with the chief of police in the city in which he or she resides, or the sheriff of the county, if he or she resides in an unincorporated area. This shall be done within 10 days of release from custody or within 10 days of his or her arrival into their city or county residence, whichever is first.

(E) Sale of Vehicles Involved in Firearm Assaults (246.1 PC)

(1) A vehicle may be forfeited if used in the following crimes and the defendant is found guilty:
    (a) murder, manslaughter (or attempts)
    (b) assault with a deadly weapon
    (c) unlawful brandishing or discharge of a firearm
(2) And it is at or from an occupied vehicle,
(3) And it involves a firearm, OR
(4) A criminal street gang member (186.22(f) PC) unlawfully possesses a firearm while in vehicle.

<u>Exceptions:</u>

(1) When the vehicle has been stolen.
(2) When the vehicle belongs to another.

(F) Conspiracy Toward Terrorism (527.7 CCP)

It is unlawful for a group to meet and advocate an unlawful act of violence, and then take a substantial action toward that goal, when it is likely to produce serious bodily injury or death.

(G) Terrorizing (11413 PC) (Felony)

(1) A person who explodes or attempts to explode
(2) Any destructive device, or explosive
(3) Or commits arson
(4) For the purpose of terrorizing another, or

(5) In reckless disregard of terrorizing another in
   (a) a health or medical care facility
   (b) any church or place of religious worship
   (c) the buildings, offices, meeting sites or lecture or film showing locations of organizations for or against abortions
   (d) any bookstore or library
   (e) any courthouse
   (f) the home of a judicial officer (judge, justice, commissioner, or referee)
   (g) a facility regularly occupied by County Probation Department employees
   (h) any private property targeted because of race, color, religion, ancestry, national origin, disability, gender, or sexual orientation of the owner
   (i) any public or private school K–12.

(See also Terrorism Through Symbols, 11411 PC, on page 127.)

(H) Control of Terrorist's Telephone (PUC 7907 repealed)

A supervising law enforcement official may no longer order a telephone company to cut, reroute, or divert telephone lines in an emergency involving a hostage or a barricaded person resisting apprehension by threats of force. This was to allow the supervisor to contact the suspect as well as prevent him from telephoning unauthorized persons. (Misd.)

This action currently requires a judicial officer to issue an order and assure the action does not suppress constitutionally protected speech. Obviously, this would likely use too much time in a hostage situation.

Study Questions for Chapter VIII

(1) To be guilty of "Disturbing Religious Meetings," the perpetrator must be present at the place of the meeting. T or F

(2) In order to have a riot there must be ________________ persons.

(3) A large group of union members who are on strike assemble in front of their plant. They make a huge slingshot and threaten to break the windows on the front of the building. Because they are members of a legal union, they have not violated the law. T or F

(4) Rout is really "attempted riot" T or F

(5) When two or more persons assemble to do an unlawful act, it is called ____________

(6) Under 409.5 PC, the only calamities for which an area can be closed are floods, storms, fires, earthquakes, explosions and accidents. T or F

(7) If the police set up a command post near a riot or calamity, they can forbid unauthorized persons from coming in the immediate area. T or F

(8) 409.5 PC lists a classification of persons exempt from this section. It is ___________

(9) A person has not violated the law on unlawful assembly unless some peace officer first declares to the crowd that the gathering is an unlawful assembly and he commands them to disperse in the name of the State. T or F

(10) Officers who command unlawful assemblies to disperse, do so in the name of the people of the State of California. This, however, is not a legal requirement. T or F

(11) The Penal Code section for Disturbing the Peace is ________________ PC.

(12) In order for the law on Disturbing the Peace to be violated, the peace of two or more persons must be disturbed. T or F

(13) The elements of 415.5 PC are the same as 415 PC only at a college or university. T or F

(14) Forcibly preventing a student from attending classes at a community college is a misdemeanor. T or F

(15) Willy Wild, a leader in the SDS, threatens Casper Milktoast, a community college instructor, with bodily harm if he goes to class during a student strike. This is a felony. T or F

(16) Unlawful Entry 603 PC, requires that the entry be forcible, and that some damage be done to the property. T or F

(17) A person convicted two or more times for 415.5 PC or one of the 626 PC sections cannot by law receive probation. T or F

(18) Willy Wild states that he never received the letter notifying him of the suspension. Burden of proof is upon him since the presumption in law is that he received it. T or F

(19) Willy Wild, a leader of a protest organization, is arrested for "Entering a Community College Campus After Suspension" (626.2 PC). To obtain a conviction for this offense, all but one of the following must have taken place:

(A) ____He was arrested for violating campus regulations.

(B) ____He was suspended for disrupting the orderly operation of campus.

(C) ____He was notified of the suspension by registered mail.

(D) ____He was suspended after a hearing.

(20) Barbara Blather, another member of Willy's protest organization, disturbs the orderly operation of the Community College campus, and is told by the Dean of Students to leave. If the Dean does not file a _____________ written report on the situation to the Administrative Head of the college within _________ hours, the Dean's order is no longer in effect.

(21) The maximum time that a person can be ordered to leave a Community College campus is ________ days according to 626.4 PC.

(22) If a person who has been ordered to leave a campus, wants to file for a hearing, the Chief Administrative Officer must grant one within _______ days of a written request.

(23) Section 626.8 PC uses the term "school." This term includes adult school. T or F

(24) Kevin Klamor, a non-student member of an activist group, comes on campus to disrupt the peaceful conduct of the campus by demanding that students start a strike, and that teachers not go to class. The Chief Administrative Officer of the college or his designated officer can ask Kevin to leave the campus and if he returns within________ hours, it becomes a misdemeanor according to 626.6 PC.

(25) Harry Hinder, a non-student activist, comes on campus without permission of the college authorities. While giving a speech, he starts waving an unloaded gun over his head. He is guilty of a felony. T or F

CHAPTER IX

CRIMES AGAINST THE ADMINISTRATION OF JUSTICE AND EMERGENCY SERVICES

Crimes Against Officers

There are two Penal Code sections dealing with resistance of officers in the performance of their duties. 69 PC can be a felony, and 148 PC is a misdemeanor. The major difference between the two is that 69 PC involves the use of force or violence, and can be classed as a felony if the amount of force is significant.

(A) Resisting Executive Officers (69 PC)
(1) Every person who attempts by any means of threats or violence
(2) To deter or prevent an executive officer
(3) From performing any duty required by law, OR
(1) Who knowingly resists by use of force or violence
(2) Such executive officer in the performance of his or her duties. (Wobbler)

(B) Resisting or Obstructing Public Officers (148 PC)
(1) Every person who willfully resists, delays, or obstructs,
(2) Any public officer or peace officer or Emergency Medical Technician
(3) In discharging or attempting to discharge an official duty.

(C) Disrupting Police Radio Transmission (148(a)(2) PC)
(1) Every person who knowingly and maliciously interrupts, disrupts, impedes or interferes with
(2) A police radio transmission
(3) Is guilty of a misdemeanor.

(D) Attempting to Take an Officer's Weapon While Resisting (148 (b, c & d) PC)
(1) Any person who, while resisting arrest,
(2) Does any of the following:
    (a) Removes any weapon, other than a firearm, from the person or immediate presence of a peace officer. (Wobbler) OR
    (b) Removes or attempts to remove a firearm from the person or immediate presence of a peace officer. (An attempt is a wobbler and the removal is a felony.)

(E) Disarming an Officer (Exception) (148(f) PC)

(1) This section shall not apply
(2) If the public officer, peace officer or EMT
(3) Is disarmed while engaged in a criminal act.

Specific Intent, How Proved

Specific intent to take an officer's weapon can be proved by:

(1) Defendant unfastened officer's holster strap.
(2) Firearm partially removed from the holster.
(3) The firearm safety released by the defendant.
(4) An independent witness corroborates a statement by the defendant that he or she intended to take the weapon, AND the defendant actually touched the weapon.
(5) An independent witness corroborates that the defendant had his/her hand on the firearm and tried to take it from the officer who was holding it.
(6) The defendant's fingerprint was found on the firearm or holster.
(7) Scientific physical evidence shows that the defendant did in fact touch the weapon.
(8) In the course of a struggle, the firearm fell and the defendant tried to pick it up.

(F) Punishment for Violating 148 PC and Causing Death or Serious Bodily Injury (148.10 PC)

If a violation of 148 PC is the proximate cause of an officer's death or "serious bodily injury," the resistance becomes a "wobbler." (Maximum 4 years for the 148 PC.) However, the following facts must be found in court:

(1) The officer's actions were reasonable based on circumstances.
(2) The detention and arrest was lawful.
(3) There was reasonable cause to detain.
(4) The suspect knew or reasonably should have known that the victim was a peace officer engaged in the performance of his or her duties.

Exceptions:

This section shall not apply to the following:

(1) Labor picketing
(2) Demonstrations
(3) Disturbing the peace.

Multiple Convictions:

A person cannot be charged with multiple subsections of 148 PC against the same officer. It can however apply to more than one officer at the same time.

Definitions:

Serious Bodily Injury: The same as defined in 243 PC (see page 94).

Proximate Cause: The probable and natural outcome of an act is the legal result of that initial act.

Example:

Snerdley Snudbugger hits Officer Homer Hornswoggle and knocks him into the street where he is hit and killed by a passing car. The natural outcome of knocking a person into oncoming traffic would likely be an injury. Snerdley is guilty of the officer's death even if he had no intent for the officer to die.

(G) Interception of Police Radio Messages (636.5 PC)

(1) Unlawfully intercepting by radio scanner or other means
(2) Any police radio communication
(3) And using that information to:
    (a) assist in a criminal offense, or
    (b) avoid arrest, trial or conviction, or
    (c) assist another to escape justice.

(H) Impersonating Officers

There are two sections in the Penal Code dealing with the impersonation of officers. They are both misdemeanors, but 146a PC involves either an illegal arrest, intimidation or search. 538d PC involves the use of some badge or device as a means of impersonating.

Impersonating Public Officers (146a PC)

(1) Falsely representing oneself to be a public officer, investigator, inspector, deputy or clerk in any state department,
(2) AND in such assumed character,
    (a) arresting or threatening arrest
    (b) detaining or threatening to detain
    (c) intimidating any person
    (d) searching
        (i) any person
        (ii) property of any person
        (iii) any building, or
    (e) obtaining any money, property, or thing of value.

Impersonation of Peace Officers (538d PC)

Section 1:

(1) Any person other than an authorized peace officer
(2) Who willfully wears, exhibits or uses any authorized badge, insignia, emblem, uniform, or identification of a peace officer
(3) With the intent of fraudulently impersonating a peace officer
(4) Or fraudulently inducing such belief.

Section 2:

(1) Any person who willfully wears, exhibits, or uses, makes sells loans, gives or transfers to another,
(2) Any badge, insignia, device or identification of a peace officer
(3) Which either
    (a) falsely purports to be police identification or
    (b) would reasonably deceive one into believing that it is authorized police identification or insignia.

(I) Giving a Police Officer a False Name Upon Arrest (148.9 PC) (Misdemeanor)

A person who is arrested, and gives the arresting officer false identification or a false name, OR does the same during lawful detention, with the intent of evading proper court processes, or preventing the officer from properly identifying him.

(J) Disclosure of Address or Phone Number of Peace Officer or Family (146e PC)

(1) Every person who maliciously and with intent to:
    (a) obstruct justice
    (b) the due administration of law
    (c) with the intent or threat to inflict imminent physical harm in retaliation for carrying out the law
(2) Publishes, disseminates or discloses
(3) The residence address or phone number
    (a) of any peace officer
    (b) dispatcher
    (c) employee of city PD
    (d) county SO employee
    (e) public safety official
    (f) the relative of the above who resides with them
(5) Without authority of the employing agency,
(6) Is guilty of a misdemeanor; or if harm results, a felony.

This statute was put into effect after a Los Angeles "underground" newspaper obtained and printed the addresses and phone numbers of all narcotic agents in that area. The officers and their families received considerable harassment. In this case, a civil action was initiated against the paper in the form of a class action suit, and the court awarded the officers a considerable sum of money.

This illustrates the fact that police officers are also citizens and are entitled to their rights the same as everyone else.

(K) Advocacy of the Killing of Peace Officers (151 PC)

(1) Advocating the willful and unlawful killing or injuring of a peace officer
(2) With the intent to actually cause that act
(3) When such advocacy is likely to cause such action.

Punishment:

Misdemeanor: When officer is not killed or injured.

Felony: When officer is either killed or injured.

Definition:

Advocacy: The direct incitement of others to cause the imminent willful and unlawful killing or injuring of a peace officer, and not the mere abstract teaching of a doctrine.

(L) Impeding Police Officers, Firefighters or Other Officials at the Scene of an Emergency (402 PC) (Misd.)

(1) Every person who
    (a) goes to, or
    (b) stops at the scene of an emergency,
(2) For the purpose of viewing the scene, or emergency personnel (including operating a drone to view the scene),
(3) During the time it is necessary for emergency vehicles to be either at, or moving to and from the scene.
(4) Unless it is part of such person's employment to be there,

(5) And thereby impedes police officers, firefighters or other emergency personnel.

For the purposes of this section, an emergency includes, but is not limited to, a fire, an explosion, an airplane crash, a flood, windstorm damage, a railroad accident, a traffic accident, a power plant accident, or toxic chemical or biological spill.

False Bomb, Emergency and Criminal Reports

(A) False Bomb Reports (148.1 PC) (Wobbler)

(1) Any person who reports to any:
- (a) law enforcement or fire personnel, or
- (b) news media employees (e.g. newspaper, radio, TV), or
- (c) public communications employees (e.g. telephone co.), or
- (d) public transportation employees (e.g. air, bus, train), or
- (e) occupants of a building, or
- (f) district attorney or deputy district attorney, OR

(2) Who maliciously reports to ANY person, (148.l(b) PC)
(3) That an explosive device has or will be placed
(4) In any public or private place,
(5) Knowing that such report is false.

(B) Sending Facsimile Bombs (148.1(d) PC) (Wobbler)

(1) Maliciously possessing, giving, mailing, sending, causing to be sent, or placing
(2) Any false or facsimile bomb
(3) With the intent to cause another to fear for his, her, or another's personal safety.

(C) False Report of an "Emergency" (148.3 PC)

(1) Anyone reporting to a government agency, commission or board,
(2) That an "emergency" exists,
(3) Knowing that such report is false.

Punishment:
- (a) Felony: Great bodily injury or death.
- (b) Misd.: No great bodily injury or death.

Any individual convicted of violating this section, and the report resulted in an emergency response, is liable to the public agency that responded for reasonable costs.

Definition:

"Emergency" as used in this section means any condition which results in, or which could result in, the response of a public official in an authorized emergency vehicle, or any condition which jeopardizes or could jeopardize public safety and results in, or could result in, the evacuation of any area, building, structure, vehicle or of any other place which any individual may enter.

(D) False Reporting of a Criminal Offense (148.5 PC)

(1) Every person who reports to any law enforcement officer, district attorney, or deputy D.A.,
(2) That a felony or misdemeanor has been committed,
(3) Or a firearm has been lost or stolen,
(4) Knowing that such report is false,
(5) Is guilty of a misdemeanor.

This section does not apply to reports made by persons required by statute to report suspected child abuse, dependent adult abuse, or elder abuse.

(E) False Reports by Peace Officers (1181.1 PC) (Wobbler)

(1) Every peace officer who files a report with the officer's employing agency,
(2) Of any crime or investigation of a crime,
(3) When he or she knowingly and intentionally makes a false statement,
(4) Regarding any material matter in the report,
(5) Even if the statement is not
- (a) certified (sworn) or
- (b) expressly reported as true.

Exceptions:

Statements which the officer attributes in the report to another person are exempt.

(F) Falsely Reporting Fires (148.4 PC) (Misdemeanor)

(1) Any person who willfully and maliciously,
- (a) tampers with, molests, injures or breaks any fire protection equipment or any fire alarm apparatus, or
- (b) sends or transmits by any means whatever a false alarm of fire.

(2) Any person who willfully and maliciously commits any of the above acts and any person suffers great bodily injury or death as a result of those acts is guilty of a felony.

(G) Falsely Filing a Claim Against a Peace Officer (148.6 PC)
(1) It is a misdemeanor to file a civil claim against a peace officer
(2) For an action that occurred while on duty
(3) Knowing the claim or lien to be false
(4) With the intent to harass or dissuade an officer from carrying out his or her official duties.

(H) False 911 Calls With Intent to Annoy or Harass Another (653x PC) (Misdemeanor)
(1) Any person who telephones the 911 emergency line,
(2) With intent to annoy or harass another person.
Definition:
"Intent to annoy or harass" an intent to annoy or harass is established by proof of repeated calls that are unreasonable under the circumstances.

Escape and Rescue

The two major sections in the Penal Code on escape will be covered in this chapter.

(A) Escape or Attempt to Escape from State Prison, etc. (4530 PC) (All are felonies)
(1) Every prisoner
- (a) confined in a state prison or correctional facility,
- (b) who by force or violence,
- (c) escapes or attempts to escape; OR:

(2) Every prisoner
- (a) committed to a state prison,
- (b) who by force or violence,
- (c) escapes or attempts to escape,
- (d) while being conveyed from one correctional facility to another,
- (e) while under the custody of prison officials or employees; OR:

(3) Every prisoner
- (a) who escapes or attempts to escape,
- (b) while on "work release" program; OR:

(4) Every prisoner
- (a) who, while on either a "work release" or an "education release" program,
- (b) fails to return to the correctional facility by the arranged time

(5) Is guilty of escape.

(B) Escape From County or City Jail or Officer Custody (4532 PC) (Felony)
<u>Section 1:</u>
(1) Every person who is confined to a city or county correctional facility
(2) As a (an)
- (a) inebriate (under W & I Code 5654, 5656 or 5677), or
- (b) criminal offense prisoner, or
- (c) in the lawful custody of an officer or person of authority, or
- (d) a "work furlough" or "education furlough" prisoner, or
- (e) is being transported to or from a correctional facility,

(3) And who escapes or attempts to escape from that facility or the custody of an officer or person of authority; OR:
(4) Any prisoner
- (a) who is away from a correctional facility while on either work or educational furlough, or home detention (1203.016 PC)
- (b) and who fails to return to that facility or home upon the arranged time,

(5) Is guilty of escape.
<u>Section 2:</u>
(1) Every prisoner who
- (a) is arrested and booked for a felony, or
- (b) is charged with a felony, or
- (c) has been convicted of a felony,

(2) And is
- (a) confined to a county or city correctional facility, or
- (b) under the lawful custody of any officer

(4) And who escapes or attempts to escape from
- (a) the facility, or
- (b) the lawful custody of an officer,

(5) Is guilty of escape.

The topic of escape has been confusing for peace officers due to the wording of the law and the lack of higher court decisions. In 1992, a new law took effect that resolved the problem of which section to use if a person who was just arrested were to escape.

(C) Escape From a Peace Officer (836.6 PC) (Misdemeanor)
(1) It is unlawful to escape the custody of a peace officer

(2) When either:
   (a) a judge remands the person to police custody, or
   (b) when a person has been lawfully arrested by a peace officer and knows or should reasonably know he or she has been arrested.

Punishment When Injury Occurs:

If the escape involves violence AND causes an officer serious bodily injury, it is a Wobbler.

(D) Fleeing Officers and Causing Hazards to Person or Property (2800.2 CVC)

Existing law states that punishment is increased when a person flees the police in a vehicle and while doing so drives with a "willful or wanton disregard for the safety of persons or property." This amendment defines what the "willful disregard for safety" is.

(1) While fleeing or attempting to elude a pursuing police officer
(2) Either three or more violations occur that are assigned a traffic violation point count (12810 CVC), or
(3) Damage to property occurs.

(E) Rescue (4550 PC) (Felony)

(1) Rescuing, attempting to rescue, or aiding any other person in the rescue of,
(2) Any prisoner from a prison, prison road camp, jail, county road camp, or
(3) From a peace officer or other person having lawful custody of the prisoner.

(F) Lynching (405a PC) (Felony)

(1) Person who participates in the taking, by means of a riot, of another person
(2) From the lawful custody of any peace officer
(3) Is a lynching.

Because of the movie and television versions of "lynching," it is sometimes difficult for police officers and students to understand that hanging a person is not part of the elements of lynching. The small word "riot" is important in that it adds extra elements to the offense. The elements are:

(1) The taking of a prisoner from the lawful custody of a peace officer,
(2) By two or more persons, acting together without authority of law,
(3) By threat or use of:
   (a) force
   (b) violence
   (c) disturbing the peace.
(4) When accompanied by the immediate power of execution.

Study Questions for Chapter IX

(1) There are two sections in the Penal Code dealing with "Resisting Officers." One is a felony. It is a felony if ____

(2) In 69 PC, a peace officer is called an ________________________________ officer.

(3) Percy Pester is unemployed. He goes into a bar and sees Betty Binkle sitting alone at the bar. He goes over to her and starts a conversation, and to impress her, he tells her that he is a detective with the local police department. He is guilty of a misdemeanor. T or F

(4) When Percy sees that Betty believes him, he tells her that he has information that she has been selling narcotics, and that he has been watching her carefully. She denies this very emphatically. Percy tells her to come with him into the back room so that he can make a search, and prove his theory. In the back room, Percy makes a very thorough search of Betty's person and then tells her that she can go. Percy is now guilty of 146a PC. T or F

(5) Herbert Honebone has a deep need for recognition. He goes to a uniform shop and orders a police uniform and an "extra" badge. He tells the clerk that he was just hired by the local department. He picks up the uniform and badge in a few days, then goes to several churches on Sunday and helps people across the street, stopping traffic for them. After four weeks of this, various pastors write letters of commendation to the Chief, and Herbert's little act is discovered. Because he did nothing harmful, Herbert is not guilty of 538d PC. T or F

(6) Disclosing a peace officer's phone number can be a misdemeanor. T or F

(7) At a riot, Mervin Messup makes a speech and advocates that members of the crowd "kill them some pigs." This is a misdemeanor. When does it become a felony? ______

____

(8) It is a felony to make a false bomb report. T or F

(9) Kitty Krump makes a simulated bomb out of a clock, and as a joke, sends it to her ex boyfriend. Which of the following is true?

(A) ____Since it contains no explosive, no law is violated.

(B) ____It is a felony.

(C) ____It is a crime only if she calls someone and tells them that it is a bomb.

(D) ____It is a misdemeanor.

(10) Flossie Furd calls the police and tells them of a false emergency. She is guilty of a misdemeanor. Under what conditions would she be guilty of a felony? ____________

____

(11) Annie Farkle tells her sister Franny that she was raped when she was not. Franny calls the police and reports it. Which of the following is true.

(A) ____Annie is guilty of falsely reporting a crime.

(B) ____Franny is guilty of falsely reporting a crime.

(C) ____Neither of them are guilty of falsely reporting a crime.

(D) ____Both of them are guilty of falsely reporting a crime.

(12) To be guilty of 402 PC, a person must not only be present at the scene of a disaster, but must also impede emergency personnel. T or F

(13) Sending a false fire alarm applies only to pulling a fire alarm box. T or F

(14) When does 148.4 PC "False Fire Alarms" become a felony? ____________________

____

(15) Arnold Aardvark is serving a sentence in a county jail. He is also on a "Work Furlough" program in which he goes to work each day and returns to jail each night. One night he fails to return to jail. This is classed as an escape according to 4532 PC. T or F

(16) Officer Sharp notes that there is a felony warrant issued for Huston Hardrock. Later that night he spots Huston and arrests him. On the way to jail, another car goes through a stop sign and hits Sharp's police car. In the confusion, Huston slips away unnoticed. He is guilty of escape. T or F

(17) Later, Officer Sharp responds to a silent burglar alarm and catches Bernie Bergle inside a jewelry store. He arrests him for burglary. On the way to jail, Bernie jumps out of the car and hides in a creek. Bernie is guilty of escape. T or F

(18) The taking by means of a riot of any person from the lawful custody of any peace officer is called ____

(19) An important element of lynching is that the prisoner be taken away and hanged. T or F

(20) The difference between Rescue and Lynching is that in Rescue, there need be only ___ ____ and the taking need not be by means of ____

CHAPTER X

BURGLARY AND ARSON

Burglary (459 PC)

(A) The Elements of Burglary

The three basic elements of burglary are:

(1) The entry
(2) Of a building OR one of the following:
   (a) tent
   (b) vessel (7 PC) (9840 CVC) (21 H & N)
   (c) floating home (18075.55 H & S)
   (d) railroad car
   (e) locked or sealed cargo container
   (f) trailer coach (635 CVC)
   (g) house car (362 CVC)
   (h) Inhabited camper (243 CVC)
   (i) locked vehicle (670 CVC)
   (j) aircraft (21012 PUC)
   (k) mine, or any underground portion
(3) With the intent to:
   (a) commit a theft, or
   (b) commit a felony.

Definitions:

(1) Vessel (21 H & N Code): The word vessel includes ships of all kinds, steamboats, canal boats, barges, and every structure adapted to be navigated from place to place for the transportation of merchandise or persons.
(2) Trailer Coach (635 CVC): a vehicle, other than a motor vehicle, designed for human habitation or human occupancy for industrial, professional commercial purposes, for carrying persons and property on its own structure, and for being drawn by a motor vehicle.
(3) Vehicle (670 CVC): a device by which any person or property may be propelled, moved, or drawn upon a highway, excepting a device moved by human power or used exclusively upon stationary rails or tracks.
(4) Aircraft (21012 Public Utility Code): includes any contrivance used or designed for flying except a parachute or other contrivance used primarily for safety.
(5) House Car (362 CVC): a motor vehicle originally designed, or permanently altered, and equipped for human habitation, or to which a camper has been permanently attached.
(6) Camper (243 CVC): a structure designed to be mounted upon a motor vehicle and to provide facilities for human habitation.

(B) Meaning of the Elements of Corpus Delicti

(1) Entry: There are two types of entry:
   (a) actual
   (b) constructive

Unlike in other states and the military, a forced entry is not required in California, any entry is sufficient. (People *v.* Ferns, 27 Cal. App. 285). The perpetrator could even be invited in.

(a) Actual Entry: To complete the element of entry, any part of the body may enter. For example, reaching in through a window and taking a purse would be an entry even though the whole body did not enter. (People *v.* Pettinger, 94 Cal. App. 297)

(b) Constructive Entry: No part of the body made entry, but entry was made by some contrivance under the control of the defendant. For example: a trained monkey or a fishing pole placed into an open window to retrieve valuables inside. (People *v.* Allison, 200 Cal. 404)

(2) Of a building (or other item in the code)

The legal definition of a building is a structure with walls on all sides and covered by a roof. (People *v.* Stickman, 34 Cal. 242) This definition is important, for it does not specify a number of walls. Therefore it can include a round house, or an octagonal house. It can also include a cave that has a wall constructed at its entrance. (People *v.* Buyle, 22 Cal. App. 2d 143) Although it must have walls on all sides, one wall can be substituted with a door, as in a garage. The door need not be closed, but it must be in working order. (People *v.* Picaroni, 131 Cal. App. 2s 612)

The building need not be intended for human habitation. A chicken house can be a building for the purposes of burglary. (Brooks *v.* Sessagisimo, 139 Cal. App. 679) An old-style telephone booth can also be a building because it has walls on all sides and a roof, and a door functions as one wall. (People *v.* Miller, 95 Cal. App. 2s 631)

For a vehicle to be the subject of burglary, the doors must be locked. If the doors and trunk are locked, and a tire is taken from the locked trunk, it is burglary. (People *v.* Toomes, 148 Cal. App. 2d 465) However, if a sealed semi-trailer is attached to a cab, breaking into the semi-trailer would be burglary even if the cab is not locked. (People *v.* Massie, 241, Advanced Cal. App. 1023) An old passenger bus that has been put up on blocks and is used as an office can also be the subject of burglary. (People *v.* McLaughlin, 156 Cal. App. 291)

(3) With Intent to Commit Theft or a Felony

No crime need occur once entry is made with specific intent. Entry of a building with intent to commit murder or a felonious assault would be classed as burglary. (People *v.* Schwab, 136 Cal. App. 2d 280)

Proving Intent

Proving intent can be difficult. Good attorneys have books full of excuses for why a person might be in a building apart from being there to commit a felony or theft. There are some California cases in which convictions were sustained with very little circumstantial evidence.

(1) Where a man was found inside a building where he had no permission to be, it was held to be prima facie evidence that he entered with the intent to commit a theft or a felony. (People *v.* Swenson, 28 Cal. App. 2d 636)

(2) A man who ran when hailed by the occupant of a building in which he had no legitimate business was held to be prima facie evidence of intent. (People *v.* Noon, 1 Cal. App. 44)

Despite the cases cited, it is most difficult to obtain a conviction for burglary when there is not some good evidence to show intent. Some cases involving a stronger case of intent are as follows:

(1) A defendant removed his shoes and entered an apartment where he had no legal business, then ran when the owner saw him. It was held that there was sufficient evidence of the specific intent to steal. (People *v.* Franklin, 153 Cal. App. 2d 795)

(2) In one case it was shown in court that the defendant had already made arrangements for the disposal of property that was to be taken in the burglary, before the burglary occurred. (People *v.* Morris, 143 Cal. App. 2d 531)

(3) Where the defendants used a "short change" scheme or trick that involved much practice and skill, it was held that this was proof that they entered the market with the intent to commit theft. (People *v*. Stone, 155 Cal. App. 2d 344)

Shoplifting as Burglary

In the People *v*. Lowen, 109 Cal. 381, it was held that if a person entered a building, and while inside developed the intent to steal, and did then steal something, that it would not be burglary because he did not enter with that intent.

If it can be shown that a person did enter with the specific intent to steal, then it would be burglary. For example, if the defendant entered a store with a booster box (a device with a spring trap door on the bottom in which stolen items may be hidden), the entry of the store with that box would make the person guilty of burglary. (People *v*. De Nava, 119 Cal. App. 2d 82). A special belt made for concealing merchandise would also make one guilty of burglary if one took it into a department store. (People *v*. Coral, 60 Cal. App. 2d 66). The fact that a person had no money when arrested for shoplifting does not necessarily mean that he entered the store to shoplift. He may have been passing time while waiting for the next bus, and formed the intent while inside the store.

If the value of stolen merchandise is $950 or less, then the thief can only be charged with misdemeanor shoplifting (459.5 PC), as of November 2014, unless there have been serious prior convictions.

(C) The Degrees of Burglary (460 PC)

Burglary of the First Degree

Burglary is first degree when it is of an inhabited:

(a) dwelling house
(b) trailer coach (as per CVC)
(c) portion of any other building
(d) vessel designed for habitation or
(e) floating home.

Burglary of the Second Degree

All other burglaries are second degree.

Definition:

Inhabited: When a building is normally used as a dwelling house, it is considered to be inhabited even if no one is there at the time. (People *v*. Allard, 99 Cal. App. 591) The key is whether or not they plan to return. (People *v*. Lewis, 274 Cal. App. 2d 912). Includes places unoccupied due to disaster.

(D) Punishment for Burglary (462 PC)

(1) Except in unusual cases, in the interest of justice,
(2) Probation shall not be granted to those convicted of
    (a) first degree burglary,
    (b) felony burglary of inhabited dwellings (etc.) in daytime.

Exception:

If condition "b" is classed as a misdemeanor, the minimum punishment will be 90 days in jail.

(E) Burglary With Explosives (464 PC)

(1) Entry of a building
(2) With intent to commit a crime
(3) And opens or attempts to open any vault, safe or secure place
(4) By use of acetylene torch, oxygen lance or similar device capable of burning through steel or other solid substance, or
(5) By use of an explosive,
    Is guilty of a felony (3-5-7 years).

(F) Possession of Instrument to Break or Enter (466 PC)

(1) Possession of an instrument or tool (e.g. picklock, key bit)
(2) With intent to break or enter into any building or structure in 459 PC, railroad car, aircraft, vessel, trailer coach or vehicle,
    OR:
(1) Making or altering a key or other instrument
(2) To fit the lock of any place or vehicle above
(3) Without authorized permission,
    OR:
(1) Making, altering or repairing any instrument
(2) Knowing, or believing that it is intended to be used in a crime.

(G) Possession of Instrument or Explosive to Open Coin-Operated Machine (466.3 PC)

(1) Possession of
    (a) an instrument or device
    (b) explosive, or
    (c) drawing or mold of a key or device
(2) Designed to open or break into a coin operated machine,
(3) With intent to commit theft.

(H) Forcible Entry and Detainer (418 PC)
(1) Using force or violence
(2) In entering upon or detaining
(3) Any lands or other possessions of another.

(I) Illegal Possession of Motor Vehicle Master Keys (466.5 PC) (Misd)
(1) Who, intending to use it in an unlawful act,
(2) Possesses
  (a) a motor vehicle master key
  (b) a motor vehicle lock master key
  OR:
(1) Who uses the above on a car lock or ignition
  OR:
(1) Who knowingly manufactures for sale, advertises, offers for sale or sells any of the above.
(2) Except when it is the person's lawful occupation (e.g. locksmith).

(J) Duplication of Vehicle Key (466.6 PC)

Any person making a duplicate vehicle key by means other than from the original (e.g. key code or impression) must obtain the following:
(1) From the person requesting the key:
  (a) name of person
  (b) address
  (c) telephone number (if any)
  (d) date of birth
  (e) driver's license or identification number.
(2) From the vehicle:
  (a) registration or ID number
  (b) license number
  (c) car make, model & color
  (d) VIN number, AND
(3) The key code number (if any)
(4) The requester's signature
(5) The date the key was made.

A copy of the work order with this information must be kept for two years and will be open to inspection by a peace officer.

(K) Illegal Possession of Motor Vehicle Key (466.7 PC)
(1) Who, intending to use it in an unlawful act
(2) Possesses a motor vehicle key
(3) Without consent of the registered or legal owner or possessor.

(L) Illegal Making of Keys (469 PC)
(1) Who knowingly
  (a) makes or attempts to make
  (b) possesses
  (c) uses
(2) Any key to a building owned, operated or controlled by:
  (a) State of California
  (b) State agency, board or commission
  (c) county or city
  (d) public school or community college district,
(3) Without legal authorization.

Arson

Definitions: (450 PC)
(1) Structure: Any building, or commercial or public tent, bridge, tunnel, or power plant.
(2) Forest land: Any brush covered land, cut-over land, forest, grassland, or woods.
(3) Property: Real or personal property other than a structure or forest land.
(4) Inhabited: Currently being used for dwelling purposes whether occupied or not. Does not include the real property on which an inhabited structure or property is located.
(5) Maliciously: Imports a wish to vex, defraud, annoy or injure another person, or an intent to do a wrongful act, established either or by proof or presumption of law.
(6) Recklessly: Being aware of and consciously disregarding a substantial and justifiable risk that an act will cause damage by fire. It involves a gross deviation of proper conduct of a reasonable person.

(A) Elements of Arson (451 PC)
(1) Willfully and maliciously
  (a) sets fire to
  (b) causes to be burned or
  (c) aids, counsels or procures the burning
(2) Of any
  (a) structure
  (b) forest land, or
  (c) property.

Punishment:
(1) Great bodily injury: state prison 5, 7, or 9 yrs.
(2) Inhabited structure or property: 3, 5, or 8 yrs.
(3) Structure or forest land: 2, 4, or 6 yrs.
(4) Property: 16 months, 2, 3 yrs.

Extra Enhancements (punishment) for Arson (451.1, 451.5, 452.1, 454 PC)

The following situations are grounds for increased punishment in arson cases:

(1) Prior convictions of arson.
(2) A firefighter, peace officer or other emergency personnel suffered great bodily injury.
(3) More than one person suffered great bodily injury in one single instance of arson.
(4) The arson caused multiple structures to burn (over 5 structures = even greater punishment).
(5) The arsonist used a device to either accelerate or delay ignition.
(6) The damage is over $8,300,000, including cost of fire-fighting.
(7) Arson occurred during a "State of Insurrection." (143 M & V Code)
(8) Arson occurred during a "State of Emergency." (8625 Govt. Code)

(B) Attempted Arson (455 PC)

(1) Willfully and maliciously attempts to
   (a) set fire to
   (b) burn, or
   (c) aid, counsel or procure any burning
(2) Of any
   (a) structure
   (b) forest land
   (c) property, OR
(3) Commits any preliminary act in furtherance of such attempt.

(C) Unlawfully Causing a Fire (452 PC)

Because it is often difficult to show that a fire was caused as the result of a willful and malicious act, a law has been enacted to cover fires resulting from reckless acts. The only difference between 451 PC and 452 PC is substitution of "recklessness" for "willful and malicious," and the punishment.

Punishment for Unlawfully Causing a Fire:

(1) When great bodily injury results: State prison, 2, 4, 6 years or county jail, Max. 1 year.
(2) Burning of inhabited property: State prison, 2, 3, 4 years
(3) Burning a structure or forest land: State prison, 16 mos., 2, 3 years or county jail, 6 months.
(4) Burning property (not personal) – Misd.

(D) Possession of Flammable or Combustible Material (453 PC) (Wobbler)

(1) Possession of any flammable or combustible
   (a) material
   (b) substance or
   (c) incendiary device
(2) In an arrangement or preparation
(3) With intent to willfully and maliciously use such material etc.,
(4) To set fire to or burn any
   (a) structure
   (b) forest land or
   (c) property.

(E) Possession of Incendiary Device (453(2) PC)

(1) It is a felony to possess, manufacture, give away loan, offer for sale, sell, or transfer,
(2) An incendiary device.

Definitions:

An "incendiary device" is a device that is constructed or designed to start an incendiary fire by remote, delayed, or instant means (not commercial flares). An "incendiary fire" is a fire that is deliberately ignited when a person knows that the fire should not be ignited.

Exceptions:

Peace officers, military and other authorized personnel are exempt from this section when possession involves their duties.

(F) States of Insurrection or Emergency (454 PC)

(1) Violation of sections 451 and 452
(2) During and within an area of:
   (a) a state of insurrection (143 M & V Code), or
   (b) a state of emergency, when proclaimed by the Governor (8625 Gov. Code)
(3) Is punishable by imprisonment in state prison for 3, 5, 7 years.
(4) Violation of 451 PC(a)(b)(c) is punishable by imprisonment in state prison for 5, 7, 9 years.

(G) Fine for Arson (456 PC)

In addition to other penalties, a person convicted of arson can receive extra punishment:

(1) A fine of up to $50,000, or
(2) If the arson was committed for monetary gain, the fine will equal twice the anticipated or actual gross gain.

(H) Psychiatric Examination (457 PC)

Upon conviction for any of the arson sections, the judge may order the defendant to submit to a psychiatric or psychological examination.

(I) Arson Registration (457.1 PC)

(1) Upon conviction of 451, 451.5, or 453 PC,
(2) The judge shall require that the defendant register as an arson offender.

Like sex registrants, arson registrants must register within 14 days when they are to reside in a place for 30 days or more. If they move thereafter, they must re-register within 10 days. Law enforcement agencies must be notified by the Department of Corrections when arsonists are released temporarily from prison to engage in fire-fighting or disaster control activities.

Persons tried as juveniles must register until age 25 after adjudication of the offense. If a convicted arsonist resides on a UC or State University campus, he must also register with the campus Chief of Police.

(J) The Cause of Fires

Since all persons are innocent until proven guilty, a fire is considered accidental until proven to be arson. Because of this, officers should be careful about making statements in a joking manner about a fire probably being arson. It could be a basis for a civil suit by the owner of the building.

Chapter X Case Citations

Study Questions for Chapter X

(1) The Penal Code section for burglary is ________________________________

(2) The entry in burglary must be a forced entry. T or F

(3) In order for the element of entry in burglary to be complete, the whole body must be inside of the building. T or F

(4) Peter Persimmon sends a trained monkey into a building to steal something for him. The type of entry here is called ________________________________ entry.

(5) The legal definition of a building as it applies to burglary is 4 walls and a roof. T or F

(6) A building can still come under the burglary section if a door is substituted for a wall. T or F

(7) In order for the crime of burglary to be committed, any door entered must be closed prior to entry. An open door does not comply with the law. T or F

(8) A chicken house can be a building for purposes of burglary. T or F

(9) An old style telephone booth can be classed as a building under the rules for burglary. T or F

(10) For a vehicle to be the subject of burglary, the doors must be locked. T or F

(11) For an airplane to be the subject of burglary, the doors must be locked. T or F

(12) In order for burglary to occur, some crime must be committed after the entry is made. T or F

(13) Entry of a store with a "booster box" is considered to be burglary. T or F

(14) Arvin Aardvark enters a store and steals something. The fact that he had no money in his pocket is proof of the intent to enter the store to steal. T or F

(15) Percy Pester burglarizes a warehouse at 12 midnight. This is classed as ___________ degree burglary.

(16) Bernie Bergle burglarizes a home during the nighttime, but the occupants are in Europe for two months. He is guilty of ________________________ degree burglary.

(17) Section 464 "Safe Burglary by Explosives" includes acetylene torches and burning bars. T or F

(18) Sam Slurpie works for an accounting company. He wants to do some extra work on a Saturday using the company's machines. He doesn't want the boss to know, so he borrows a key and has a duplicate made. He is now guilty of "Possessing Burglary Tools" 466 PC. T or F

(19) Clyde Crashcup has an uncle in Chicago who works for a company that makes automobile master keys. He writes him that he can send the General Motor's set for $17 a set. Clyde then advertises in a California magazine that he will sell the 72 set of General Motor's keys for $35. This is a violation of section 466.5 PC. T or F

(20) Thadwick Thudy sets fire to a new suit that he just bought. He is guilty of arson. T or F

(21) All fires are by law accidental until proven to be arson. T or F

CHAPTER XI

THEFT AND RELATED OFFENSES

Theft (484 PC)

(A) Definition of Theft:

(1) Feloniously
- (a) stealing
- (b) taking
- (c) carrying
- (d) leading or driving away

the personal property of another, or

(2) Fraudulently appropriating property that has been entrusted to a person appropriating it

(3) By
- (a) false or
- (b) fraudulent representation, or pretense, or

(4) A person defrauds another person of
- (a) money
- (b) labor or
- (c) real or personal property, or

(5) Who causes or procures others to report falsely of his wealth;

(6) And by this obtains credit

(7) And then fraudulently obtains
- (a) money,
- (b) property, or
- (c) labor or service of another.

Value Defined:

(1) The value of property shall be the fair market value.

(2) The value of services shall be the contract price.

(3) If no contract, the going wage shall govern.

(4) In the case of fraud, the value shall be all of that obtained in the course of the fraud.

When Offense Committed

The crime can be considered committed on any date during the particular period of the crime being committed.

Labor Fraud

(1) Hiring any additional employee or employees

(2) Without advising each of them of all labor claims due and unpaid,

(3) And every judgment that the employer has been unable to meet

(4) And then failing to pay the employee

(5) Shall be prima facie evidence of intent to defraud.

Rental or Lease Fraud

(1) When a person rents or leases the personal property of another
(2) Resulting from a written contract
(3) And fails to return the property to its owner within 10 days
(4) After the owner has made written demand by certified or registered mail, for return of the property
(5) Following the expiration of the lease or rental agreement,
(6) Intent to commit theft by fraud is presumed.

OR:

(1) When a person rents or leases the personal property of another
(2) And presents identification that has a false or fictitious:
    (a) name, or
    (b) address
(3) For the purpose of obtaining a lease or rental,
(4) Intent to commit theft by fraud is presumed.

Exception:

Section 10855 of the Vehicle Code is an exception. It states that it is presumed embezzlement of a rented or leased vehicle is not returned within five days after the agreement expires. The presumptions in the above sections affect the burden of producing evidence.

Proper Demand

(1) Within 30 days after the expiration of the lease or rental
(2) The owner shall make written demand for return of property
(3) To the address given at the time of the rental or lease
(4) Or to any other known address
(5) And this shall constitute proper demand according to law.
(6) If the owner fails to make proper demand, the presumption shall not apply.

(B) "Theft" and "Larceny" (490a PC)

When any statute uses the words "larceny," "embezzlement," or "stealing," they will be interpreted as meaning "theft."

(C) Diversion of Money Allotted for Construction (484b PC)

(1) Receiving money for the purpose of obtaining or paying for
    (a) services
    (b) labor
    (c) materials, or
    (d) equipment
(2) And willfully failing to apply such money to such purpose,
(3) And wrongfully diverting the money to a use other than that for which it was received,
(4) Makes one guilty of theft (Wobbler).

(D) Obtaining Funds Through a False Voucher (484c PC)

(1) Any person who submits a false voucher
(2) To obtain construction loan funds
(3) And does not use the funds for that purpose
(4) Is guilty of embezzlement.

(E) The Elements of Theft

There are three main elements of theft. There is sometimes a fourth element, but it is not a legal one, and is assumed in most cases.

(1) The unlawful taking (or asportation),
(2) Of the personal property of another,
(3) With the specific intent of permanently depriving the owner. The sometimes assumed fourth element is
(4) Without the owner's permission.

This element becomes very important later in the discussion of embezzlement and 532 PC. In cases of theft, it is assumed that it is against the owner's will, because consent is a defense to theft. However, since the prosecution is not required to prove this, it is not really an element of the corpus delicti. If the defendant uses it as a defense, the burden of proof rests on him. It must be remembered that, in the crime of fraud, the victim voluntarily gives up the property.

(F) Discussion of the Elements

Asportation

As with robbery, the key to asportation is some movement, and not how far. If, for example, a person were to grasp the handle on a suitcase, and was then arrested, there would be no theft because there was no movement or asportation. If, however, the perpetrator were to lift the suitcase four inches in a vertical direction, there would be movement, and there could be a theft. (People *v.* Davis, 76 Cal. App. 2d 701)

The Personal Property of Another

This does not mean that the victim must own the property himself. It merely means that the property is not owned by the thief. If the victim has rightful possession, the property does not have to belong to him. (People *v.* Hayes, 72 Cal. App. 292)

However, this rule would apply even if the victim had stolen the property himself. The key is that the perpetrator has no legal right to the property. (People *v.* Beach, 62 Cal. App. 2d 803)

In order for the property to be the subject of theft, it must have some legal value. Thus an illegal lottery ticket would be contraband, and would have no legal value. Theft of such an item would not be theft from a legal standpoint. (People *v.* Gonzales, 62 Cal. App. 2d 274)

With the Specific Intent of Permanently Depriving the Owner

Although it is not written in the code, intent must exist in the mind of the perpetrator at the time of the theft. (People *v.* Jersey, 18 Cal. 337)

It is obviously difficult to prove what was in the mind of the perpetrator at the time of the theft. We must rely upon circumstantial evidence. In one case the Appellate Court affirmed a conviction of grand theft auto because the suspect had purchased 16 gallons of gasoline after stealing the car, and this was held to be a significant act toward proving intent to permanently deprive the owner.

Consent

One of the best defenses in a theft case is consent. If the defense can convince one member of the jury that the defendant was given permission to take the property, the trial will at least end in a hung jury. The prosecution does not have to prove lack of consent. (People *v.* Davis, 97 Cal. 194)

(G) Classification of Theft (486 PC)

In California, there are two degrees of theft—grand theft and petty theft. Grand Theft is section 487 and is a felony. Petty Theft is section 488 and is a misdemeanor.

Grand theft is a somewhat complicated classification due to the many considerations or conditions under which a person would be guilty of this felony. The major considerations in determining grand theft are:

(1) What was the value of the item(s) taken?
(2) What was the particular item taken? This can apply two ways:
    (a) certain items can come under grand theft at a reduced value. (e.g. olives)
    (b) there are certain items that come under grand theft despite their value.
(3) Over what period of time? (e.g. small thefts over a period of less than one year)
(4) Was it taken from the person of another?
(5) What was the purpose of the theft? (e.g. stealing animals for the purpose of research)

Classification of Theft Crimes Brought About by Proposition 47

Proposition 47 produced changes in classifications of punishment in theft-related crimes that were previously felonies or wobblers and are now strictly misdemeanors unless committed by ineligible criminals with serious prior convictions. Theft-related crimes that are now misdemeanors effective 11/5/2014 are: forgery of checks of not more than $950 (473(b)); passing NSF checks totaling not more than $950 (476a); grand theft (of any form) not more than $950 (490.2); and receiving stolen property not more than $950 (496(a)).

Grand Theft (487 PC)

(1) When the money, labor or property taken is:
    (a) of a value exceeding nine hundred fifty dollars ($950), or
    (b) of a value exceeding two hundred fifty dollars ($250) wholesale AND the item taken is from the following categories:
        (i) domestic fowl
        (ii) farm crops (e.g., tree fruits, vegetables, olives)
        (iii) aqua-cultural products: (e.g., fish, shellfish, mollusks, kelp, crustaceans and algae)
    (c) the money, labor, or property is taken by a servant, agent, or employee from his principal or employer and the amount aggregates to nine hundred fifty dollars ($950) or more in any consecutive 12-month period, or
(2) When the property is taken from the person of another, or

(3) When the property taken is:
  (a) an automobile
  (b) a firearm.

Shoplifting (459.5 PC)

Shoplifting is a misdemeanor crime as of November 2014, and was a change resulting from Proposition 47. Shoplifting is entering a commercial establishment during business hours with the intent to steal where value does not exceed $950. Anyone charged with shoplifting cannot also be charged with burglary or theft of the same property.

Petty Theft (488 PC)

Theft in other cases is Petty Theft.

Petty Theft as an Infraction (490.1 PC)

(1) When the value of money, labor, real or personal property does not exceed $50, ($49.99 or less) the prosecutor may, in the interest of justice, charge the offense as an infraction.
(2) If the suspect has no prior theft or theft-related convictions,
(3) Maximum punishment will be a fine of $250.

Other Theft Classifications

(A) Theft of Horse, Bovine Animal, Etc. or Animal Carcass (487a PC)

(1) Felonious asportation, or fraudulent appropriation,
(2) Of any horse, mare, gelding, any bovine animal, any caprine animal, mule, jack, jenny, sheep, lamb, hog, sow, boar, gilt, barrow or pig,
(3) Which is the personal property of another OR:
(1) Asportation of the carcass of one of the above farm animals
(2) When one of them has been killed without the consent of the owner,
(3) Is guilty of grand theft.

(The names used in the Penal Code are horse, mare, gelding, any bovine animal, any caprine animal, mule, jack, jenny, sheep, lamb, hog, sow, boar, gilt, barrow or pig. See Appendix A)

(B) Grand Theft of Real Estate (487b PC)

(1) Who converts $250 or more of real estate
(2) Into personal property
(3) By severance from the realty of another
(4) With felonious intent
(5) Is guilty of grand theft.

(C) Petty Theft of Real Estate (487c PC)

(1) Who commits the above, but under $250,
(2) Is guilty of petty theft.

(D) Grand Theft of Gold Dust, Amalgam, or Quicksilver (487d PC)

(1) Every person who feloniously steals, takes or attempts to
(2) Take from any mining claim, tunnel, sluice, undercurrent, riffle box, or sulfurate machine,
(3) Another's gold dust, amalgam or quicksilver
(4) Is guilty of grand theft.

Amalgam: alloy of silver and another metal

(E) Theft of Dogs for Research or Commercial Use (487g PC)

(1) Every person who feloniously steals or takes an animal belonging to another for purposes of
  (a) sale,
  (b) medical research,
  (c) slaughter,
  (d) commercial uses,
(2) Is guilty of grand theft.

Theft of any animal with a value of over $950 is grand theft.

(F) Grand Theft Cargo (487(h) PC)

(1) Every person who steals or takes away cargo of another over $950.
(2) "Cargo" means: goods, wares, or manufactured merchandise that has been loaded into a trailer, rail car or cargo container awaiting in transit.

(G) Public Housing Authority Program Fraud (487i PC)

(1) Any person who defrauds a housing program of a public housing authority
(2) Of more than $1,000
(3) Is guilty of grand theft.

(H) Theft of Copper Materials (487j PC)

(1) Every person who steals, takes or carries away copper materials belonging to another
(2) Including copper wire, copper cable, copper tubing or copper piping
(3) Which are of value over $950
(4) Is guilty of grand theft.

(I) Theft of Tractors, All-Terrain Vehicles, or Other Agricultural Equipment (487k PC)

(1) A person who steals, takes, or carries away tractors, all-terrain vehicles or other agricultural equipment used in production of food for public consumption
(2) Which are of value over $950
(3) Is guilty of grand theft.

(J) Use of a Code Grabbing Device (466.9 PC)

(1) Every person possessing or using a "Code Grabbing Device,"
(2) With intent to use it to commit an unlawful act,
(3) Is guilty of a misdemeanor.

Definition:

Code Grabbing Device: a device which can receive and record the coded signal of a transmitter of a motor vehicle security alarm system and play back the signal to disarm it.

(K) Theft of Retail Merchandise and Library Materials; Detention (490.5 PC)

490.5 PC, commonly referred to as "shopkeeper's privilege," says that shopkeepers, store owners, merchants, or library facility operators may detain a customer if they have probable cause that the person is guilty of shoplifting (per Penal Code 459.5).

Under the law, a store owner (or store staff) can detain a suspect only for a reasonable time and the detention must be used solely for the purpose of investigating the suspected shoplifting offense.

A shopkeeper may use reasonable, non-deadly force to detain a suspect in order to protect themselves, and to prevent escape or loss of merchandise.

A shopkeeper must be careful to detain a suspect only as allowable under 490.5 PC to avoid being charged with False Imprisonment (236 PC).

The Fraudulent Obtaining of Utilities

This is to prevent persons from making adjustments in public utilities pipes and wires, and in that way defrauding the utilities companies by obtaining gas, water and electricity without paying for them. Intent to defraud is not the only element; injuring the pipes or changing the wiring can also make a person guilty of this offense.

(A) Fraudulent Means of Obtaining Telephone Service (Briefed) (502.7 PC)

(1) Using another's telephone number or credit card number.
(2) Charging the call to a nonexistent or terminated phone number, or a revoked or canceled credit card number.
(3) Using a prearranged scheme or strategy (e.g., you call your home and ask for Harrison Von Potsribble to signal that you have arrived safely. Your spouse tells the operator that Harrison is not home and avoids the charge.)
(4) Tampering with the phone or using some mechanical or electronic device.
(5) Using any other means, such as:
  (a) conspiracy to defraud,
  (b) fraudulent use of false, stolen, or altered identification,
  (c) selling a phone card or code number knowing that it is to be used to defraud,
  (d) using an electronic bulletin board system to promote fraud.

A second offense is now a felony.

(B) Injuries to Gas Service (Briefed) (498 PC)

This covers the adjusting of pipes that bring in illuminating or fuel gas and by doing this bypassing the meter for measuring and registering the quantity of gas passing through. (Misd.)

(C) Injuring Telegraph, Telephone, Cable Television or Other Electric Line (591 PC)

(1) Unlawfully and maliciously, taking down, removing, injuring, cutting or obstructing
(2) Any line for telegraph, telephone or cable television, or any other line used to conduct electricity, or
(3) Any part or apparatus connected with such lines, including a backup deep cycle battery or other power supply, or
(4) Making an illegal connection with a line that conducts electricity
(5) Is a "wobbler."

(D) Cable Television or Information Service Provider, Illegal Connection (Briefed) (593d PC)

(1) Making an illegal connection or interception
(2) By any means
(3) With the intent of using any program or other service carried by a multi-channel video or information service provider.

(E) Interference With Electric Lines (593 PC)

(1) Who unlawfully and maliciously takes down, removes, cuts, interferes with, injures or obstructs
(2) Any electrical line erected or maintained by proper authority, or
(3) Any part or apparatus connected with such line
(4) For the purpose of transmitting electricity to produce light, heat or power,
(5) Is guilty of a "wobbler."

(F) Vandalism to Gas or Hazardous Liquid Main, Pipeline or Equipment (593c PC)

(1) Who willfully and maliciously breaks, digs up, removes, obstructs, injures, interferes with, shuts off or obstructs
(2) Any
  (a) gas pipe or main, or
  (b) hazardous liquid pipeline, or
  (c) any apparatus connected with such lines
(3) Whose purpose is the conveying or distributing gas or hazardous liquid
(4) To be used for light, heat, or <u>any other purpose,</u>
(5) Is guilty of a felony.

(G) Theft of Water (Briefed) (592 PC)

Theft of water intended for business purposes. If any damage is done to the water system, it is also vandalism. If value is over $950, or two prior convictions for this offense, it is a felony.

(H) Breaking or Obstructing Water Pipes (624 PC)

(1) Who willfully breaks, digs up, obstructs, or injures any pipe or main or connection for conducting water
(2) Or any parts, appendages or works erected to supply water
(3) Is guilty of a misdemeanor.

Other Thefts

(A) Thefts Involving Trade Secrets (499c PC)

This section deals with the now prevalent offense of stealing trade secrets by those who are either members of a competing firm, or by members of a firm that is developing new products. It involves the copying and stealing of any trade secret. It also makes illegal the offering of any type of bribe or compensation to induce someone to steal or copy trade secrets. ("Wobbler")

(B) Taking Bicycle etc. Temporarily ("Joy Riding") (499b PC)

(1) The unlawful taking
(2) Without permission of the owner
(3) Any bicycle, motorboat, or vessel
(4) For temporary use.

Theft of automobiles and motorcycles is now prosecuted only under 10851 CVC. (The CVC does not have the requirement that the theft be for the purpose of permanently depriving the owner.)

(C) Punishment for 499b PC With Prior Auto Theft Convictions (499 PC) (Wobbler)

<u>Section A:</u>

(1) Any person who, having been convicted of
  (a) 10851 CVC auto theft
  (b) 487 PC auto theft, or
  (c) 487 PC grand theft vessel,
(2) And having served time for that offense,
(3) Is later convicted of 499b PC. (Joy Riding)

<u>Section B:</u>

(1) Any person who has been convicted of two or more offenses against 487 PC
(2) Involving a vehicle or vessel
(3) And who has served time at least once for one of these offenses
(4) And who is convicted of 499b PC.

<u>Section C:</u>

(1) Three or more prior 499b, or
(2) Two prior 499b and a 487h. (A felony)

(D) Prior Felony Theft Conviction Involving Vehicle, Trailer, Construction Equipment or Vessel Known to be Stolen (666.5 PC)

(1) A person convicted of a felony violation under
  (a) 10851 CVC or
  (b) 487(h) PC
  (c) 496d

(2) Who has a prior conviction for one or more of those offenses
(3) Whether or not the person served time for it
(4) Can be charged with a felony. (2, 3, or 4 years)

(E) Theft of Aircraft (Felony) (499d PC)
(1) Taking or operating an aircraft—
(2) Not one's own—
(3) Without the consent of the owner,
(4) With intent to take it permanently or temporarily.

*Note the difference between theft of aircraft, and grand theft auto. (Element #4)

(F) Unauthorized Use of Locomotives (587.1 PC)
(1) Who maliciously and without authorization, moves or causes to be moved
(2) Any locomotive
(3) Is guilty of a misdemeanor, or
(4) When moving the locomotive causes substantial likelihood of injury or death to a person
(5) The crime is a wobbler.

(G) Theft of Plant Material (384a PC)
(1900 Fish & Game Code)
(80001 Food & Agricultural Code)
California Desert Native Plants Act

Outlaws the taking, purchasing, or transporting of certain trees, shrubs or boughs and native desert plant material
   (a) that is growing upon state or county highway rights-of-way or
   (b) growing on public land or land that is not his or hers without a written permit from the owner.

A person shall not knowingly sell, offer or expose for sale, or transport for sale plant material that is cut or removed in violation of this subdivision.

Most of the plants mentioned are varieties of cactus.

Exception:
   (1) Persons employed by the state or county engaged in work required to maintain the road or highway.
   (2) Persons engaged in the necessary cutting of plant material to maintain electric power lines or telephone lines.
   (3) Scientific or educational purposes under permit issued by the Food & Agriculture Division.

(H) Theft of Plants, Transportation Permits (384b, c, d, i PC)

Makes it theft to take or remove certain desert plants without a special permit. Makes certain U.S. Department of Interior personnel peace officers for the purposes of enforcing this section. It requires private growers of the desert plants to have a validated transportation tag in order to transport those plants.

(I) Defrauding Proprietors of Hotels, Motels, etc. (537 PC) (Misdemeanor)
(1) The obtaining of
   (a) food
   (b) accommodations
   (c) credit
   (d) fuel
   (e) services
(2) From any motel, hotel, restaurant, marina or marine facility
(3) Without paying for same
(4) With the intent to defraud the proprietor, or
(5) Removal of any baggage without paying for food or accommodations.

Proof
(1) Evidence that the defendant left without paying shall be *prima facie* evidence that there was the intent to defraud.
(2) Removing baggage either surreptitiously or by force, menace or threat is prima facie evidence of intent to defraud.

Punishment:

If the amount defrauded is over $950, it is a wobbler.

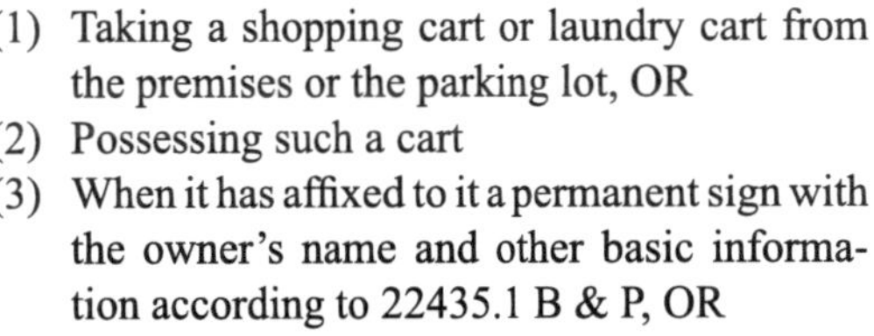

(J) Theft of Shopping Carts (22435.2 Business & Professions Code)
(1) Taking a shopping cart or laundry cart from the premises or the parking lot, OR
(2) Possessing such a cart
(3) When it has affixed to it a permanent sign with the owner's name and other basic information according to 22435.1 B & P, OR
(4) Possession of such cart
(5) When the identification or serial number has been removed.

Some might look upon this as a duplication of the laws on theft, but this law is much easier to prove in court. No specific intent need be proven. It also contains a presumption of guilt which means that the defendant can rebut the charges in court, but that the burden of proof rests with him.

(K) Illegal Transfer Recorded Sounds (653h PC)

(1) Who knowingly and willfully transfers
(2) Any sounds recorded on a phonograph record, disc, tape, film or other device for recording sound
(3) With the intent to sell, or cause to be used for profit through public performance
(4) Without consent of the owner, or
(5) Sells same knowing that the sounds have been transferred without consent of the owner.

As used in this section, "person" means any individual partnership, corporation or association. "Owner" means the person who owns the "master" recording. This law shall have no effect on civil suits by owners.

(L) Illegal Recording of Live Performances (653(u) PC)

Who without the consent of the owner of the sounds of a live performance records the same, with intent to sell for commercial advantage or financial gain, is guilty of a misdemeanor.

(M) Failing to Return School Property (48904(b) Ed. Code)

(1) Student fails to return loaned school property
(2) After the school has made proper demand
(3) School can hold grades, diplomas and transcripts until property is returned or paid for.

(N) Pawn Brokers (21647 B & P)

(1) Peace officers with probable cause to believe
(2) Property in pawnbroker's possession is stolen
(3) May place a hold on the property for up to 90 days.

(O) Pawn Broker Reports to State (21625-29 B & P)

This law pre-empts local ordinances and requires secondhand dealers to report tangible personal property taken in pledge on state mandated forms, and to hold the property 30 days after the report is submitted.

What Is Not Tangible Property (21627 B & P)

"Tangible personal property" does not include coins, monetized bullion, or commercial grade ingots of gold, silver, or precious metals.

"Commercial grade ingots" means .999 fine gold, silver, platinum, or .925 fine, sterling bars or medallions if they contain the refiners mark with their assay fineness.

(P) Fraudulent Use of Telecommunications (538.5 PC)

Improperly obtaining information by scheme through wire, radio or TV communications any confidential or restricted information, or any signals or pictures, without permission (wobbler).

(Q) Computer-Related Crimes (502 PC)

(1) Intentionally
  (a) gaining access or causing access to be gained,
  (b) causing a computer contaminant such as a virus or worm to infect another's computer, or
  (c) knowingly and without permission using an internet domain and causing damage
(2) To any computer system or network
(3) For the purpose of:
  (a) devising or executing any scheme or artifice to defraud or extort, or
  (b) obtaining money, property or services with false or fraudulent intent, representations or promises, or
  (c) to maliciously access, alter, delete, damage or destroy any computer system, network, program or data.

Punishment:

Punishable as a "wobbler."

(R) Restrictions on Probation For Theft of Over $100,000 (1203.045 PC)

(1) Except in special cases where the interest of justice would be served, (the judge must explain in writing)
(2) When the amount of theft is over $100,000
(3) There will be no probation granted.
(4) The fact that the theft was over $100,000 must be listed in the accusatory pleading.

Offenses Involving Fraud

(A) Theft by False Pretenses

Every person who knowingly and designedly, by any false or fraudulent representation or pretense, defrauds any other person of money, labor, or property, whether real or personal, or who causes or procures others to report falsely of his wealth or mercantile character, and by thus imposing upon any person obtains credit, and thereby fraudulently gets possession of money or property or obtains the labor or service of another. This section is a duplicate of part of 484 PC, and since that section is more recent, it supersedes.

In the crime of theft by false pretenses, the perpetrator obtains control of the money or property by the use of a false representation. The owner gives up complete title and possession to the perpetrator as a result of his being taken in by the fraud. The characteristics of false pretense are such that they resemble a normal legitimate transaction, but there was a clear misrepresentation of that which was sold to the point where the buyer or victim would not have made the purchase if it were not for the falsehood.

Examples would be buying a business when the previous owner lied about the number of customers that he had; (People *v*. Helminger, 69 Cal. App. 139) or being told that an apartment house was occupied by permanent tenants; (People *v*. Reid, 72 Cal. App. 611) or selling barrels of whiskey that contained colored water.

Puffing

American law has long embraced the Roman concept of *"Caveat Emptor"* (Let the buyer beware). There does seem to be a present move away from this concept in consumer protection laws. Our present case law, however, gives businesses the benefit of the doubt when it comes to "puffing," or building up the product that a person is selling. Many times advertising comes close to fraud, but because of this legal concept, little is done to prosecute those who have committed the fraud. Federal legislation does seem to be moving in this direction. The wording is very important in cases of this nature, and often a trial amounts to the word of one person against the other regarding what was said to perpetrate the false pretenses. If the item sold is obviously a fraudulent item, and there have been many complaints about the defendant, it will help considerably in the prosecution.

(B) Theft by Trick or Device (487 or 488 PC)

This type of theft is often referred to as a "confidence game" or "Bunco." The difference between theft by trick or device and false pretenses is that in theft by trick or device, the owner of the money or property never intends for that money or property to pass to the defendant. The money is given to the defendant for a temporary purpose. The defendant intends to feloniously steal the money or property from the first and obtains the money or property through some type of scheme.

Most "bunco" or "confidence" operations work on the greed of the victim. The scheme involves the victim putting up a certain amount of money on a temporary basis that will result in his or her receiving a large amount of money in return. It should be remembered that in false pretenses, the victim permanently gives up the money. In theft by trick or device, the victim never actually intends to give up the title of the money.

Corroboration

In a crime of false pretenses corroboration is necessary. In a crime of theft by trick or device, corroboration is not necessary. (People *v*. Reinschreiber, 141 Cal. App. 2d 688) A dishonest card game comes under the classification of theft by trick or device. (People *v*. Solano, 48 Cal. App. 2d 126)

(C) Winning at a Game by Fraudulent Means (332 PC)

(1) Any person using any game, device, sleight of hand or pretension to fortune telling, or any means whatever, or
(2) While betting on sides or hands of such play
(3) And fraudulently obtains another's
 (a) property or
 (b) money
(4) Is guilty of theft.

(D) Mock Auctions (535 PC) (Wobbler)

(1) Obtaining money or property or a signature
(2) From another
(3) By means of any false or fraudulent sale of property,
(4) By auction or mock auction.

Embezzlement and Receiving

(A) Embezzlement (503 PC)

Embezzlement is the fraudulent appropriation of property by a person to whom it has been entrusted. A distinct act of taking is not necessary to constitute embezzlement. The five elements of embezzlement are:

(1) A fiduciary relationship between the defendant and the victim.
(2) The property that was embezzled came into the defendant's possession as property belonging to the victim.
(3) The property was received by the defendant during the course of employment or other such relationship.
(4) The defendant appropriated the property for:
   (a) his or her own use, or
   (b) some use for which it was not intended,
(5) With the intent to deprive the owner of that property.

If a person becomes a principal to embezzlement, these elements do not have to apply. For example:

Ronnella Rimp is a cashier in a movie theater. She receives money for tickets that she gives to patrons. The money belongs to the owner of the theater. Her friend, Priscilla Primrose, by prearrangement, comes to the ticket booth and pays for a ticket with a dollar bill. Ronnella, with intent to defraud, gives her change for a twenty.

If we look at the elements, we can readily see that Ronnella would certainly fit all the elements. Priscilla, however would not as she neither works there, nor receives money from the theater as part of her job. However, since she aided and abetted the act of embezzlement on Ronnella's part, she would be a principal to the crime, and would be just as guilty.

Punishment for embezzlement is the same as for theft (514 PC).

Fiduciary Relationship

A fiduciary relationship is one in which a person receives money or goods belonging to another, usually through employment or a special trust relationship. An example would be a warehouse worker or a bank clerk.

(B) Receiving Stolen Property (496 PC)

Receiving or concealing goods obtained through theft or extortion. Every person who buys or receives any property which has been stolen or which has been obtained in any manner constituting theft or extortion, knowing the property to be so stolen or obtained, or who conceals, sells, withholds or aids in concealing or withholding any such property from the owner, knowing the property to be so stolen or obtained, is guilty of a wobbler. A person who stole the property may be charged with receiving stolen property (496 PC), but not both theft and 496 PC.

In the crime of "attempted" Receiving Stolen Property, the property need not have been stolen; the defendant only needs to believe it was stolen. (People *v.* Moss, 55 Cal. App. 3d 179) If the value is $950 or less, it is a misdemeanor unless the defendant has prior convictions listed in Section 667 PC that require sexual offender registration (290 PC).

Duty to Inquire (Subsection (b))

(1) Any person whose principal business is dealing in merchandise and personal property
(2) Who fails to make a reasonable inquiry as to the seller's right of ownership
(3) When it is reasonable to do so
(4) Is guilty of a misdemeanor.

Elements of Receiving Stolen Property

(1) The property received was obtained by theft or extortion.
(2) The defendant bought, received, concealed or withheld it.
(3) The defendant knew it was stolen or extorted.

While it must be shown that the property was stolen or extorted, the thief's identity is not an element. (People *v.* Ribolsi, 89 Cal. 496)

Proving defendant had knowledge of the theft
Mere possession of stolen property is not sufficient to justify a conviction. (People *v.* Fierro, 140 Cal. App. 490) It requires corroboration, even if slight. (People *v.* McFarland, 58 Cal. 2d 748)

Corroboration

Examples of overt acts that would corroborate a charge of receiving are:

(1) Selling the item under a different name.
(2) False or conflicting statements as to how the person came into possession.

(3) Selling the item for a price considerably below its value.
(4) Inability to name or find the person from whom he claims he bought it.
(5) Alteration of stolen item to cover up identity.
(6) Evidence of him or her being told it was stolen.
(7) The person selling the property has the reputation in the community of being a thief.

Civil Damages

If the receiver loses or damages the stolen property, he or she may be liable to pay the owner three times its value.

Receiving Stolen Vehicles & Vessels (496d PC)

(1) Every person who buys, receives, conceals, sells, or withholds (or aids in such an act) any
(2) Motor vehicle (415 CVC), trailer (630 CVC), special motorized construction equipment (565 CVC), or motorized vessel (21 H & N)
(3) That has been stolen or extorted
(4) Knowing that the property was stolen
(5) Is guilty of a wobbler. (16 mos., 2 or 3 years)

Access Card Violations

Definitions (484d PC):

As used here and in sections 484e to 484j, inclusive:

"Access card" means any card, plate, code, account number, or other means of account access that can be used, alone or in conjunction with another access card, to obtain money, goods, services, or any other thing of value, or that can be used to initiate a transfer of funds, other than a transfer originated solely by a paper instrument.

"Cardholder" means any person to whom an access card is issued or any person who has agreed with the card issuer to pay obligations arising from the issuance of an access card to another person.

"Expired Access Card" means an access card which shows on its face it has elapsed.

"Card issuer" means any person who issues an access card or the agent of such person with respect to such card.

"Retailer" means every person who is authorized by an issuer to furnish money, goods, services or anything else of value upon presentation of an access card by a cardholder.

"Incomplete Access Card" An access card is incomplete if part of the matter (other than the signature of the cardholder) which an issuer requires to appear on the access card before it can be used by a cardholder has not been stamped, embossed, imprinted, or written on it.

"Revoked Access Card" means an access card which is no longer authorized for use by the issuer, such authorization having been suspended or terminated and written notice thereof having been given to the cardholder.

(A) Prohibited Possession of an Access Card (484e PC)

(1) Who acquires an access card from another without the cardholder's or issuer's consent or who, with knowledge that it was so acquired, acquires the access card, with intent to use it or to sell or transfer it to a person other than the issuer or the cardholder is guilty of petty theft.
(2) Who acquires an access card known to have been lost, mislaid, or delivered under a mistake of identity or address of cardholder, and who retains possession with intent to use it or to sell or transfer it to a person other than the issuer or the cardholder is guilty of petty theft.
(3) Who sells, transfers, conveys or receives an access card with the intent to defraud is guilty of grand theft.
(4) Every person other than the issuer who, in any consecutive 12-month period, acquires access cards issued in the names of four or more persons which he has reason to know were taken or retained under circumstances which constitute a violation of subdivisions (1) or (2) of this section is guilty of grand theft.
(5) Every person who acquires access card account information for a card validly issued to another person, without the cardholder's or issuer's consent with the intent to use it fraudulently is guilty of grand theft.

(B) Altering Access Card or Signing Name of Another With Intent to Defraud (484f PC)

(1) Who, with intent to defraud, makes, alters, or embosses a card purporting to be an access card or utters such a card or attempts to use a counterfeit access card is guilty of forgery.

(2) A person other than the cardholder or person authorized by him who, with intent to defraud, signs the name of another or of a fictitious person to an access card, sales slip, sales draft, or instrument for the payment of money which evidences an access card transaction, is guilty of forgery.

(C) Fraudulent Use of Access Card to Obtain Money, Goods or Services (484g PC)

(1) Every person who, with intent to defraud, uses for the purpose of obtaining money, goods, services or anything else of value,
  (a) an access card or access card information obtained or retained in violation of Section 484e or 484f, or
  (b) an access card which he knows is forged, expired, revoked or altered;
  OR

(2) Who obtains money, goods, services or anything of value,
  (a) by representing without the consent of the cardholder that he is the cardholder, OR
  (b) by representing that he is the holder of an access card, and such card has not in fact been issued,

(3) Is guilty of theft.

If the value obtained exceeds $950 in any consecutive six-month period, then it shall constitute grand theft.

(D) Retailed With Intent to Defraud by Furnishing Goods, Services or Money or Forged, Expired or Revoked Access Cards (484h PC)

Every retailer who, with intent to defraud:

(1) Furnishes money, goods, services or anything of value upon presentation of an access card obtained or retained in violation of Section 484e or an access card which he knows is forged, expired or revoked, and who receives any payment therefore, is guilty of theft. If the payment exceeds $950 in any consecutive six-month period, then it shall constitute grand theft.

(2) Presents for payment a sales slip or card transaction and receives payment for this action and fails to furnish money, goods, services or anything else of value which he represents in writing to the issuer that he has furnished, and who receives any payment therefore, is guilty of theft. If the difference between the value of all money, goods, services and anything else of value actually furnished and the payment or payments received by the retailer therefor upon such representation exceeds $950 in any consecutive six-month period, then the same shall constitute grand theft.

(E) Access Cards; Counterfeiting (484i PC)

(1) Every person who possesses an incomplete access card, with intent to complete it without the consent of the issuer is guilty of a misdemeanor.

(2) Every person who, with intent to defraud, alters, varies, changes, or modifies access card account information on any part of an access card, including information encoded in a magnetic stripe or other medium not directly readable by the human eye, or who authorizes or consents to alteration, variance, change, or modification of access card account information by another, in a manner that causes transactions initiated by that card to be billed to a person other than the cardholder to whom the access card was issued, is guilty of forgery.

(3) Designing, making or trafficking in incomplete card marking equipment is guilty of a wobbler.

(F) Publication of Number or Code of an Existing or Nonexistent Access Card (484j PC)

(1) Any person who publishes
  (a) the number or code of an existing, canceled, revoked, expired or non-existent access card, or
  (b) the numbering or coding for access cards, personal identification numbers, computer passwords, access codes, debit card numbers, or bank account numbers,

(2) With the intent that it be used or with knowledge or reason to believe that it will be used to avoid the payment of any lawful charge,

(3) Is guilty of a misdemeanor.

As used in this section, "publishes" means the communication of information to any one or more persons, either orally, in person or by telephone, radio, television or on a computer network or computer bulletin board, or in writing of any kind, including without limitation a letter or memorandum, circular or handbill, newspaper, magazine article, or book.

(G) Illegally Obtaining Personal Identifying Information (Identity Theft) (530.5 PC)

(1) Who willfully obtains personal identifying information or medical information
(2) Of another person without authorization of that person
(3) And uses that information and name to obtain credit, goods, or services
(4) Without consent of that person
(5) Is guilty of a misdemeanor.

Laws Designed For the Control of Theft

(A) Purchase of Wire by Junk Dealers (496a PC)

(1) Any dealer, employee or representative of a dealer in junk, metals, or second hand materials
(2) Who buys or receives any wire, cable or metals
(3) Which he should reasonably know belong to a utility company or government agency
(4) Without using proper caution in identifying the seller and his right to sell the material
(5) Is guilty of receiving stolen property.
(6) Buyers under this section shall obtain a minimum of the following identification:
    (a) full name
    (b) signature
    (c) address
    (d) driver's license number
    (e) vehicle license number of seller
    (f) license number of delivery vehicle.

(B) Purchase or Sale of Articles From Which Identification Marks Have Been Removed (537e PC)

(1) Who, knowingly buys, sells, receives, disposes of, conceals, or has in his possession
(2) Any mechanical or electrical device, appliance, contrivance, material, piece, apparatus, or equipment
(3) From which the manufacturer's name plate, serial number, ID number or electronic serial number, or any other distinguishing number or identification mark
(4) Has been removed, defaced, covered, altered, or destroyed.

__Examples:__

Radio, piano, phonograph, sewing machine, comptometer, bicycle, safe, vacuum watch case, vehicle or vessel (or component).

__Punishment:__

Up to $950–6 Mo. Jail. Over $950–1 Yr. Jail. If it is an integrated computer chip or panel, it is a wobbler if value is $950 or more.

(C) A Pawnbroker Can Accept Nothing From a Minor (21207 Fin. Code) (Misd.)

(1) No pawnbroker shall receive anything in pledge
(2) From any person under the age of 18.

(D) Identification on Appliances (22411 B & P)

(1) No manufacturer shall sell any appliance
(2) In the state of California
(3) Without having a permanently marked, unique serial number on the appliance.

(E) Petty Theft With Similar Prior (666 PC)

(1) Every person who is convicted of
    (a) petty theft or grand theft,
    (b) burglary,
    (c) robbery,
    (d) receiving stolen property (496 PC) felony,
    (e) car jacking,
    (f) auto theft (10851 CVC)
    (g) property theft, embezzlement, identity theft of an elder or dependent adult (368 PC),
    (h) violent or serious felony specified in 667(e) PC (habitual criminals defined),
    (i) or is required to register per the Sex Offender Registration Act,
(2) And has served at least one day in jail or prison
(3) And who is later convicted of petty theft
(4) Is guilty of a "Wobbler."

(F) Receiving Money or Property in a False Character (530 PC)

(1) Every person who falsely impersonates another,
(2) And in such assumed character, receives money or property,
(3) Knowing that it is intended for the individual who was impersonated,
(4) With intent to deprive the intended owner of the money or property.
(5) Is guilty of theft.

(G) Theft by False Representation (484.1 PC)

(1) Any person who knowingly gives false information or verification
(2) About another's
   (a) true identity
   (b) ownership in property or
   (c) authority to sell property
(3) In order to receive money or valuables from pawnbroker or second hand dealer
(4) And that money or property is actually received
(5) Is guilty of theft. (Over $950 is a felony.)

(H) Use of Unqualified Statements in Charitable Solicitations (532d PC)

(1) Soliciting, attempting to solicit, or receiving
(2) Money or property of any kind
(3) For charitable, religious or eleemosynary (charitable) purposes
(4) And making an unqualified statement about the organization such as the purpose of the organization or use of the money
(5) When such statement is knowingly or negligently false.
(6) For proof, the statement must either
   (a) be in writing or
   (b) be witnessed by one person.
(7) Cities and counties may regulate such solicitations.

Important Items Dealing With Theft in General

(A) Value

(1) Value shall be determined in U.S. currency. (687 PC)
(2) Value of property shall be the reasonable and fair market value. (484 PC)
(3) Value of services, if no contract, is the reasonable and going wage. (484 PC)
(4) Value of notes is amount still owed. (492 PC)
(5) Value of tickets is the value at which they are usually sold. (493 PC)
(6) Antiques at fair market value by expert testimony. (People *v*. Mitchell, 80 Cal. App. 252)
(7) Owner's estimate is admissible as opinion. (Kirstein *v*. Bekins Co., 27 Cal. App. 587)
(8) Value at place taken. (People *v*. Ciani, 104 Cal. App. 596)
(9) Value at time taken. (People *v*. Ciani, Supra)
(10) Value taken, not that received by defendant. (People *v*. Tenant, 32 Cal. App. 2d 1)

(B) Number of Offenses as Affecting Value

The number of offenses is important as far as value is concerned. If, for example, a person took three amounts of $200 from three persons, it could amount to either three charges of petty theft, or one charge of grand theft.

(1) The property of several persons taken at the same place and time is but one theft. (People *v*. Sichofsky, 58 Cal. App. 257)
(2) Property taken from different persons at different places would amount to separate thefts. (Sichofsky, Supra)
(3) Property taken from different persons by the same trick and device will be classed as separate thefts. (Sichofsky, Supra)
(4) Property that is taken from the persons of different individuals at the same time would be separate thefts. (Sichofsky, Supra)
(5) Where the thief is taking so much property, that he has to make several trips, it amounts to several takings, but is classed as just one theft. (People *v*. Dillian, 1 Cal. App. 2d 224) This concept is based on the fact that the intent is to take all the property and involves one general impulse. (People *v*. Bailey, 55 Cal. 2d 514)

(C) Possession

When a piece of property is said to be in a person's possession, it is under his "dominion and control," or he knowingly carries it on his person, or it is in his "immediate presence." The property can also be immediately accessible and exclusive to him. Two persons can share possession.

(D) Bringing Stolen Items Into State (497 PC)

Every person who, in another state or country, steals or embezzles the property of another, or receives such property knowing it to have been stolen or embezzled, and brings the same into this state, may be convicted and punished in the same manner as if such larceny, or embezzlement, or receiving, had been committed in this state.

(E) Thefts Not Normally Thought of as Theft

The following examples of theft are often not thought of as theft by the average person. The key in each situation is that those involved have knowingly received something that does not belong to them, and that the original owner did not voluntarily or knowingly give up the right to this property.

(1) Property that is delivered by mistake
(2) Receiving too much change in a store or bank
(3) Ordering a certain number of items, and having more delivered
(4) Found property

There is a federal law dealing with items intentionally sent through the mail in the hope that the recipient will pay for them which states that the recipient has no responsibility for the item and need not return it. This does not include contracts where a person agrees to buy so many books or records.

Procedures For Finders of Lost Property

Found Property

Unfortunately, we have all been raised on the saying "Finders keepers, losers weepers." Many people will recite it as though it were the Eleventh Commandment. It has no basis in law. The key to finding property is to make some reasonable effort to find the owner—this removes the element of criminal intent. If the owner of the property were to find you with it, he could recover the property civilly, but there could be no criminal prosecution.

The California Civil Code contains several sections that set forth the proper procedures in dealing with found property. They are as follows:

(A) Duty of Finder (2080 Civil Code)

Any person who finds a thing lost is not bound to take charge of it, but if he does so, he is thence forward a depository for the owner, with the rights and obligations of a depository for hire. Any person who finds and takes possession of any money, goods, things of action, or other personal property, or saves any domestic animal from drowning or starvation shall, within a reasonable time, inform the owner, if known, and make restitution without compensation, except a reasonable charge for saving and taking care of the property. Any person who takes possession of a live domestic animal shall provide for humane treatment of the animal.

(B) Unknown Owner (2080.1 Civil Code)

(1) If the owner is unknown or has not claimed the property, the person saving or finding the property shall, if such property is worth $100 or more, within a reasonable time, turn the property over to the police department of the city, if found therein, or the sheriff's department if found outside the city limits, and make an affidavit stating when and where the affiant found or saved the property, particularly describing it. If the property was saved, the affiant shall state:
   (a) from what and how it was saved.
   (b) whether the owner of the property is known to him.
   (c) that no part of the property has been secreted, withheld, or disposed of.
(2) The police department or the sheriff's department shall notify the owner, if his identity is reasonably ascertainable, that it is in possession of the property and where it may be claimed. The police department or sheriff's department may require payment by the owner of a reasonable charge to defray costs of storage and care of the property.

(C) Claiming Ownership of Property (2080.2 Civil Code)

If the owner appears within 90 days and proves ownership, and pays all reasonable charges, the department shall give him his property.

(D) Lost and Unclaimed Property, Locating Owner (2080.3 Civil Code)

(1) If found property has a value of $250 or more
(2) And owner does not claim it within 90 days
(3) The police agency shall advertise at least once in the newspaper.
(4) If after seven days following the publication, no owner appears
(5) The finder shall gain possession, after paying newspaper costs.
(6) If the finder is an employee of a public agency and the property was found through the course of their job, the property will be sold at a public auction.

(E) Lost and Unclaimed Property, Disposal of (2080.4 Civil Code)

(1) Unclaimed property in the possession of a police agency
(2) Shall be held for a period of at least three months.
(3) If not claimed, shall be sold at public auction
(4) When a notice has been put in the newspaper five days before auction.

(F) Theft of Lost Property (485 PC)

Who finds lost property under circumstances which give him knowledge of or means of inquiry as to the true owner, and who appropriates such property to his own use, or to the use of another, without first making a reasonable and just effort to find the owner and restore the property to him, is guilty of theft.

(G) Disposal of Stolen Property

Several sections determine what a peace officer will do with stolen and embezzled property when it has been taken in as evidence.

1407 PC:

The peace officer must take custody of the property awaiting the judge's order on what to do with it.

1408 PC:

On hearing all evidence, the judge may order the property returned to the proper owner, or the state. Expenses may be charged.

(H) Stolen or Embezzled Property (1411 PC)

(1) A peace officer submitting stolen or embezzled property into storage
(2) Shall, when ownership is known,
(3) Notify the owner of its location and how it can be obtained.
(4) If there is no response by the owner after three months, or
(5) In any case, six months after conviction of person who stole it, or
(6) In a case where there is no conviction, then six months after its seizure,
(7) It may be sold at public auction by:
 (a) the police,
 (b) the court,
(8) Pursuant to section 2080.4 of the Civil Code.

If a peace officer has probable cause to believe that property in the possession of a licensed pawnbroker or second hand dealer has been lost, stolen or embezzled, the peace officer may place the property on hold for 90 days (21647 B & P).

 (a) If the pawnbroker or second hand dealer refuses to consent to a statutory hold, the property shall be seized, with or without a warrant, subject to Section 1411 as described above.

1412 PC:

The officer taking the property must give duplicate receipts, one each to the defendant and property clerk.

1413 PC:

A book must be kept listing all stolen and embezzled property. The property clerk must attach a number to each article and record that number in the log book. If the owner has been notified that his property is in custody, and he does not respond by picking up the property within 15 days of the time of notification, the property may be disposed of.

Chapter XI Case Citations

Study Questions for Chapter XI

(1) A person's labor can be the subject of theft. T or F

(2) Millie Munch, who has very poor credit, gets her friends to falsely report on her credit so that she can get a TV set that she could not otherwise obtain. When she obtains the set, she is guilty of theft. T or F

(3) Sam Sharpie owes several employees wages, and some have quit. He then hires two new employees, and does not tell them that he owes others back wages. When he fails to pay the new employees, it becomes a *prima facie* case of theft. T or F

(4) Ronella Rimp rents a TV for 30 days. After the rental time is up, she fails to return the TV. The owner makes a written demand for the return of the property. In ________ days it is "presumptive evidence" that she intends to defraud the owner of his property.

(5) In the above case, the owner must make a written demand on the person renting the property to return it. This demand is made by____________or _______________ mail.

(6) Buster Badbetter wants to rent a trailer. He has lost his driver's license, so he borrows Harry Hashbrown's license and uses it and Harry's name to rent the trailer. Under section 484 PC, this is presumptive evidence of intent to defraud. T or F

(7) Asportation is an element of theft T or F

(8) One element of theft in the Penal Code is that the taking is against the owner's will. T or F

(9) Consent is a defense in the crime of theft. T or F

(10) Sam Slipshod steals an illegal lottery ticket. This would be a case of theft. T or F

(11) In California, the theft of $950 cash from a beach blanket while the owner was in swimming, would be classed as:

(A) ____ grand theft. (B) ____ theft by trick or device.

(C) ____ petty theft. (D) ____ robbery.

(12) Marvin Middlewiff steals $252 worth of ducks from a farm. He is guilty of a felony. T or F

(13) Sam Slurp reaches into Arvin Aardvark's pocket and steals a nickel. He is guilty of___

____

(14) Claud Klunk steals a car worth $20. He is guilty of ____________________________

(15) A person who steals a $25 dog and sells it to a lab for research is guilty of a felony. T or F

(16) Stealing a $5 gun is classed as Grand Theft. T or F

(17) Theft of $1 worth of quicksilver from a mine is a misdemeanor. T or F

(18) Amalgam is:

(A) ____ powdered cement. (B) ____ a silver alloy.
(C) ____ an explosive. (D) ____ a tool.

(19) A dealer of used metals and junk, who buys a roll of copper wire just like that used by the telephone company must obtain all of the following information from the seller except one:

(A) ____ license number of vehicle. (B) ____ driver's license.
(C) ____ telephone number. (D) ____ seller's signature.

(20) Any person knowingly possessing an electrical or mechanical piece of equipment with any of the identification removed is guilty of a misdemeanor. T or F

(21) Andy Gump finds a tape recorder on a park bench. He keeps it and makes no effort to find the owner. He is guilty of theft. T or F

(22) Henry Honebone buys tickets for a three-day cruise from a "scalper" because the tickets were all sold out. He paid $500 for the tickets which normally sold for $300. If these tickets were stolen from Henry, the value for the police report would be $ __________

(23) The value in theft is the value at the time and place taken. T or F

(24) Henry Hackbidder went to a steam bath in a private club and took $200 from each of the wallets in three pairs of trousers that were hanging on a rack in the locker room. Henry is guilty of just one theft. T or F

(25) Dippy Dunkinheim goes to a wedding and picks the pockets of three persons. He obtains $100 from each person. He is guilty of just one theft. T or F

(26) Harvey Hooligan steals 10 items from a house where the owners are on vacation. The items are so large that Harvey has to make five trips.The several takings are legally classed as one offense. T or F

(27) Two persons can technically be in possession of a single article. T or F

(28) Possession can mean all but one of the following:

(A) ____ under his dominion and control. (B) ____on the person.
(C) ____ in his immediate presence. (D) ___legal ownership.

(29) If a person steals a TV set in Nevada and brings it to San Jose, California, he can be tried for theft in San Jose just as if he stole the TV in San Jose. T or F

(30) Terrance Toadtoes visits his cousin in Oregon. While there, his cousin learns that Terrance doesn't have a plasma TV set at his home in San Francisco. His cousin, who is a pretty good burglar, steals one for him. Terrance accepts the TV, knowing that it was stolen and brings it back to San Francisco. Terrance can be tried in San Francisco just as if he has stolen the set there. T or F

(31) A principal to embezzlement must commit all of the four elements required for the crime in order to be a principal. He cannot just aid in one of the elements. T or F

(32) Kitty Krump orders three sets of curtains from Macy's. When they are delivered, she finds that they delivered four sets by mistake. She feels that it is their tough luck and says nothing. Kitty is technically guilty of theft. T or F

(33) Which of the following persons would have a "Fiduciary Relationship" necessary for the crime of embezzlement?

(A) ____ a file clerk. (B) ____ a cashier.

(C) ____ a telephone clerk. (D) ____ a janitor.

(34) The most difficult part to prove in a crime of "Receiving Stolen Property" is:

(A) ____ that the property was stolen.

(B) ____ that the person receiving it knew that it was stolen.

(C) ____ that the person receiving the property tried to sell it.

(D) ____ that the person receiving the property tried to conceal it.

(35) Receiving stolen property (496 PC) also includes property that has been extorted. T or F

(36) Sam Shyster owns a pawn shop. An inebriate comes into the shop and sells a set of sterling silver tableware. Sam gives him $5 for the set. He doesn't ask for any identification. Sam is presumed by law to have bought the silverware knowing that it was stolen. T or F

(37) In the above case, the burden of proof is upon Sam to prove that he did not know that it was stolen. T or F

(38) Someone steals a gold serving tray from Clyde Crashcup. The value is $100. The thief sells the tray to a "fence" for $5. The "fence" is arrested and convicted, but the tray is accidentally destroyed. Clyde can sue him civilly for how many times the value of the tray?

(A) ____ 2X (B) ____ 4X

(C) ____ 3X (D) ____ 5X

(39) In convicting a person of "Receiving Stolen Property," the identity of the thief must be shown in the trial. T or F

(40) Mervin Messup buys some stolen property and alters the property so that it cannot be identified. This is *prima facie* evidence that he knew that it was stolen. T or F

(41) There must be corroboration for a conviction for "False Pretenses." T or F

(42) The key to "Theft by False Pretenses" as opposed to a "Bunco" or "Theft by Trick or Device" is that in "Theft by False Pretenses," the victim intends that the money permanently go to the perpetrator. T or F

(43) The Roman concept of "Caveat Emptor" means:

(A) ____ the laws of the Emperor prevail. (B) ____ legal ties are binding.

(C) ____ let the buyer beware. (D) ____ all sales are final.

(44) The term "Puffing" associated with business fraud means:

(A) ____ cheating. (B) ____ over-pricing.
(C) ____ building up the product. (D) ____ duplicating.

(45) All but one of the following are associated with each other. Which one is not?

(A) ____ Bunco. (B) ____ Confidence Games.
(C) ____ Theft by trick or device. (D) ____ Charlie horse.

(46) In a crime of "Theft by Trick or Device" corroboration is not necessary. T or F

(47) A dishonest dice game comes under the classification of "Theft by Trick or Device. T or F

(48) Henrietta Hucknoodle buys a "gold brick" that turns out to be gold plated lead. This is an example of "Theft by Trick or Device." T or F

(49) A person is guilty of Grand Theft if he acquires access cards in the names of ________ persons or more, within any consecutive ________________________ month period.

(50) Making a phony access card with intent to defraud is classed as forgery. T or F

(51) Using an access card to defraud is Grand Theft if the amount defrauded accumulates to over $950 in any consecutive ________________________________ month period.

(52) Freddie Froghair illegally possesses a machine that embosses access cards. He plans to use it to make phony credit cards, but hasn't used it yet. He is guilty of a felony even though he has not yet used the machine. T or F

(53) "Trade secrets" can be the object of theft. T or F

(54) In the "Taking of an Aircraft" (499d PC), there must be the intent to permanently deprive the owner of the aircraft, as there is in Grand Theft Auto. T or F

(55) Terry Tiddlywink flies to Chicago and wants to let his wife know that he has arrived safely. He calls long distance, person to person for Arvin Aardvark. His wife answers the phone and states that Arvin is away, but will be back tonight. This was a pre-arranged plan to let Mrs. Tiddlywink know that her husband arrived safely in Chicago. Terry is guilty of theft. T or F

(56) To convict a person for making a false oral statement about charitable solicitation, there must be two witnesses, or one witness and corroboration. T or F

(57) In section 532d PC, the term "Eleemosynary" is used. It means:

(A) ____ for charity. (B) ____ religious.
(C) ____ begging. (D) ____ soliciting.

(58) Section 537 PC, "Defrauding Proprietors," pertains to the defrauding of food or _____
____

(59) Peter Persimmon buys a new CD for $10, and re-records it on a blank CD. He then sells the re-recorded CD to a friend for $5. This is a misdemeanor. T or F

(60) To be charged with "Petty Theft with a Prior," the suspect must have actually served some time on the first convicted offense. T or F

(61) Stolen property that is to be used as evidence in a trial must, according to 1407 PC, be given to the custody of:

(A) ____the peace officer. (B) ____ the court clerk.

(C) ____the judge. (D) ____ the legal owner.

(62) Stolen property that is not claimed in __________ months by the owner, can be sold at auction. (1411 PC) or in any case _______________months after a conviction in court.

(63) If found property has a value of $ ________ or more and the owner is unknown, it shall be turned over to the proper police agency.

(64) A person finding property may charge the owner reasonable fees for saving and taking care of the property. T or F

(65) If found property is turned over to a police department, and the owner is not known, or does not appear within 90 days for the property, the department shall publish a notice in a newspaper at least how many times? _________ This applies only to property of a value of over $___________________.

(66) If the above notice is published in a newspaper, and no one appears to claim the property, the person finding the property shall gain title to it _________ days after the notice first appeared. (2080.3 Civil Code)

(67) The police department can charge the owner of lost property reasonable fees for handling and advertising. T or F

(68) When a peace officer finds lost property while on duty, and it is not claimed, the property:

(A) ____ is given to the officer. (B) ____ is sold at public auction.

(C) ____ is kept six months then delivered to the officer. (D) ____ is destroyed.

CHAPTER XII

FORGERY AND CHECKS

Forgery (470 PC)

(A) Forgery of Wills, Conveyances, etc.
Every person who, with the intent to defraud,

(a) Knowing that he or she has no authority to do so, signs the name of another person or of a fictitious person to any of the items listed in subdivision (d), or

(b) Counterfeits or forges the seal or handwriting of another, or

(c) Alters corrupts, or falsifies any record of any will, codicil, conveyance, or other instrument, the record of which is by law evidence, or any record of any judgment of a court or the return of any officer to any process of any court, or

(d) Falsely makes, alters, forges, or counterfeits, utters, publishes, passes or attempts or offers to pass, as true and genuine, any of the following items, knowing the same to be false, altered, forged, or counterfeited: any check, bond, bank bill, or note, cashier's check, traveler's check, money order, post note, draft, any controller's warrant for the payment of money at the treasury, county order or warrant, or request for the payment of money, receipt for money or goods, bill of exchange, promissory note, order, or any assignment of any bond, writing obligatory, or other contract for money or other property, contract, due bill for payment of money or property, receipt for money or property, passage ticket, lottery ticket or share purporting to be issued under the California State Lottery Act of 1984, trading stamp, power of attorney, certificate of ownership or other document evidencing ownership of a vehicle or undocumented vessel, or any certificate of any share, right, or interest in the stock of any corporation or association, or the delivery of goods or chattels of any kind, or for the delivery of any instrument of writing, or acquittance, release or discharge of any debt, account, suit, action, demand, or any other thing, real or personal, or any transfer or assurance of money, certificate of shares of stock, goods, chattels, or other property whatever, or any letter of attorney, or other power to receive money, or to receive or transfer certificates of shares of stock or annuities, or to let, lease, dispose of, alien, or convey any goods, chattels, lands, or tenements, or other estate, real or personal; or falsifies the acknowledgment of any notary public, or any notary public who issues an acknowledgment knowing it to be false; or any matter described in subdivision (b),

(e) Is guilty of forgery.

Definitions:

(1) **Instrument:** A legal document that has either value or power of executing some action, or affecting the rights of some person or agency. Examples: A birth certificate, escrow instructions, a prescription for narcotics, divorce papers, a will, an order for the delivery of goods.

(2) **Utter:** To utter (or publish) a forged instrument would be to assert or declare either directly or indirectly that the instrument was genuine. To utter a forgery would be to present it as being the real article.

(3) **Codicil:** An addition or supplement to a will. It adds to, or in some way, changes it.

(4) **Conveyance:** A transfer of title (e.g,. a transfer of the title to a piece of land or property.)

Forgery actually involves six different offenses. A simple breakdown of the elements of each offense is as follows:

Offense A:

(1) Every person who with intent to defraud
(2) Signs the name of another person, real or fictitious
(3) Without authority to do so;

Offense B:

(1) Who with intent to defraud, falsely
    (a) makes,
    (b) alters,
    (c) forges, or
    (d) counterfeits
(2) Any document or instrument dealing with:
    (a) legal powers,
    (b) property, or
    (c) money;

Offense C:

(1) Who with intent to defraud, either
    (a) counterfeits, or
    (b) forges either the
        (i) seal of another, or
        (ii) handwriting of another.

Offense D:

(1) Who with intent to defraud
(2) Either
    (a) utters, or
    (b) publishes
(3) Any falsely
    (a) altered instrument, or
    (b) counterfeited instrument
(4) Dealing with
    (a) legal powers, or
    (b) property, or
    (c) money
(5) Knowing the same to be
    (a) false,
    (b) altered,
    (c) forged, or
    (d) counterfeited
(6) With the intent to
    (a) prejudice any person,
    (b) damage any person, or
    (c) defraud any person.

Offense E:

(1) Who with intent to defraud
(2) Either
    (a) alters,
    (b) corrupts, or
    (c) falsifies
(3) Any
    (a) will,
    (b) codicil,
    (c) conveyance, or
    (d) other instrument.

Offense F:

(1) Who with intent to defraud
(2) Attempts to do any of the above.

Case Law on Forgery

The statute on forgery is quite long and repetitious. Basically there are two types of action:

(1) The fraudulent making of an instrument, or
(2) The uttering of a forged or altered instrument as being genuine knowing that it is false.

Forgery can be proved by circumstantial evidence. (People *v*. Sheeley, 151 Ca. App. 2d 611)

Once the document is forged, it does not have to be passed in order for the law to be violated. (People *v*. West, 34 Cal. App. 2d 55) The major test in forgery is whether the instrument is of apparent legal acceptance, and which, if genuine, would or could affect the personal or property rights of some other person. (People *v*. Somsky, 46 Cal. App. 377)

It is still forgery if the document is only partially altered (People *v*. Brotheron, 47 Cal. 388)

The major element in forgery is the intent to defraud. However, it is not essential for a conviction that someone actually be defrauded or suffer loss. (People *v*. Garin, 174 Cal. App. 2d 654)

Since the intent to defraud is a major element in forgery, if a person is given authority to sign the name of another, no forgery has legally been committed. (People *v*. Whiteman, 114 Cal. 338)

It is also forgery to obtain the legitimate signature of another by means of some type of fraud. (People *v*. Nesseth, 127 Cal. App. 2d 712) For example, if a personal secretary brought in a large number of papers for her boss to sign and slipped in an extra one that was an authorization for her to buy a gold necklace, even though the signature was her boss's, it would be classed as forgery because it was obtained by fraud.

Since forgery requires that the forger sign the name of another or of a fictitious person, if he was to sign his own true name, it would technically not be forgery. (People v. Rushing, 130 Cal. 449)

Since the words "intent to deceive" have been added to the statute, it has made the law much broader in that there now need be no intent to cause another to suffer a monetary loss. The intent to deceive another will suffice. Theft is not an element of this offense. If the offense does result in someone losing money, the offense does not merge. It then becomes two separate offenses.

(B) Falsification, Alteration of Driver's License, Identification (470a PC)

(1) Altering, forging, duplicating, falsifying in any manner
(2) Any
  (a) driver's license, or
  (b) identification card issued by a government agency
(3) With the intent that such document be used to commit forgery.

(C) False Government Documents (112 or 113 PC)

(1) Manufacturing or selling,
(2) Any false document that is normally issued by the United States, state or local government,
(3) With the intent to conceal the true citizenship or alien status of another. (e.g., Green Card)

(D) Simulated Governmental Identification Cards (22430 Bus. & Prof. Code)

(1) Any person manufacturing or selling
(2) Identification cards that resemble those issued by DMV
(3) Must print in permanent ink, diagonally across the face
(4) The words "NOT A GOVERNMENT DOCUMENT."

This law was passed due to the widespread sale of identification cards (mostly in flea markets) that were similar to those issued by the DMV.

(E) Making, Passing or Uttering Fictitious Bills, etc. (476 PC)

(1) Any person who makes, passes or publishes
(2) With intent to defraud any person, or
(3) Has in his possession with intent to defraud
(4) Any fictitious bill, note, check or written instrument for payment of money or property
(5) From a bank, corporation or individual
(6) Whether or not such does, in fact, exist
(7) And knowing that the instrument is fictitious,
(8) As described in 186.9 PC,
(9) Is guilty of forgery.

(F) Manufacture or Sale of False Certificate of Birth or Baptism (529a PC)

(1) Every person who
  (a) manufactures
  (b) produces
  (c) sells,
  (d) offers, or
  (e) transfers
(2) To another person
(3) Any document purporting to be either:
  (a) a certificate of birth
  (b) baptism certificate
(4) Knowing it to be false or counterfeit.
OR:
(1) Every person who
  (a) offers,
  (b) displays, or
  (c) possesses
(2) Any false or counterfeit birth or baptismal certificate, or

(3) Any genuine certificate of someone living or deceased
(4) With the intent to falsely identify himself with that document
(5) Is guilty of a misdemeanor.

(G) Falsely Obtaining Documents of ID (529.7 PC)

(1) Obtaining or assisting another to obtain
(2) any official document issued by DMV
(3) knowing the person obtaining the document
(4) is not entitled to the document.

(H) Issuing Checks With Intent to Defraud (476a PC)

(1) Any person who for himself or as the agent or representative of another or as an officer of a corporation, willfully, with intent to defraud, makes, draws, utters or delivers any check, draft or order upon any bank or depository, person, firm or corporation for the payment of money, knowing at the time of such making, drawing, uttering or delivering that the maker, drawer or corporation has insufficient funds in, or credit with said bank, depository, person, firm, or corporation, for the payment of such check, draft or order, and all other checks upon such funds then outstanding, in full upon its presentation, although no express representation is made with reference thereto.
(2) <u>**Punishment**</u>
    (a) when the total amount of all checks for which the defendant is charged does not exceed $950, it is a misdemeanor.
    (b) <u>Exceptions:</u> when the defendant has three or more violations of Sections 470, 475, 476 PC, has habitual criminal penalty enhancements (667 PC) or is a sex offender registrant (290 PC).
(3) <u>**Proof of Presentation, Nonpayment and Protest**</u> A notice sent to the issuer of an in-sufficiency of funds will be proof of presentation, nonpayment and protest.
(4) <u>**Credit**</u> An arrangement or understanding with a bank, depository or person for payment of such check draft or order.

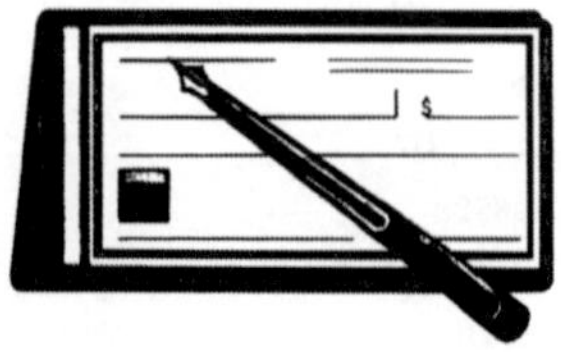

(I) Elements of 476a PC

The six basic elements to the crime of issuing a check with the intent to defraud are:

(1) The intent to defraud *
(2) The making, drawing, uttering or delivering
(3) Of a check, draft or order for payment of money
(4) Upon a bank or person,
(5) When there is a lack of sufficient funds or credit in the account at the time the check was written,*
(6) And the defendant knew of such lack of funds.

*These are the most important elements for conviction.

This is one of the most difficult crimes in the code to prosecute because it is almost impossible to have a jury of 12 adults not one of whom had ever in their life accidentally had a check "bounce." Some of the most common excuses are:

(1) I didn't know my wife also wrote a check for so much money.
(2) I guess I'm not very good at math.
(3) I was promised a check in plenty of time to deposit it and cover the check that "bounced."

The major element in this offense is intent. Proving intent is a difficult task unless the defendant is a professional check "kyter" (check passer) who has passed a great number of bad checks.

Another problem is that merchants do not want to prosecute. When they get a small bad check, they call the police department, wanting them to "hassle" the check writer into making it good. They are fearful of criminal prosecution because the check writer will then never pay up on the check. Many bad check writers will call the victim and tell him that he will make it good when he "gets back on his feet," but if he is sent to jail, the merchant will never get his money. Even when the merchant wants to prosecute, proving criminal intent in court is most difficult.

The difference between felony and misdemeanor check offenses is whether the amount of the check is over $950, or he has been previously convicted of theft, forgery or bad check charges.

(J) Proof of Identity (476a(d))

Clerks often receive many checks on a daily basis. Much time usually passes between the issuing of the check and the identification of the suspect in court. The result is often a problem in the clerk identifying the suspect after so much time has passed. Because of this, the legislature passed this law to make such identification easier.

(1) Under the following conditions identification of a person being charged with passing bad checks will be *prima facie*.

(2) When the following information is obtained at the time the check is passed:
  - (a) name
  - (b) residence
  - (c) mailing address
  - (d) either
    - (i) valid driver's license number, or
    - (ii) DMV identification card number
  - (e) home or work phone number or
  - (f) place of employment.

(3) The receiver of the check
  - (a) witnesses the signature and
  - (b) initials the check.

(K) Problems in Prosecuting Bad Check Cases

If one of the elements is missing, it is sometimes impossible to prosecute a bad check charge, even when some type of fraud has taken place. If the check is not in perfect order, it can become a promissory note and be strictly a civil matter.

(L) Post Dated Checks

If the writer of the check tells the merchant that tomorrow is payday and that he might not have quite enough in the bank to cover the purchase right now, but if it is all right with the merchant, he will post date the check for two days from that date, and by then he will have plenty of money in the bank. If the merchant accepts the check, that check is no more than a promissory note and the writer of the check could not be charged with 476a PC. The fact that he told the merchant that he didn't have enough money in the bank would remove the element of intent. If he did not mention it to the clerk, and the clerk did not check, it would be a violation of 476a PC.

(M) Lack of Sufficient Funds at the Time of the Writing

Element 5 states that there is a lack of sufficient funds in the bank at the time the check is written. Kevin Kyter puts $200 in the bank and then goes to a merchant and buys a $100 suit after the merchant checks with the bank to make sure that he has money. Kevin then goes to the bank and withdraws his $200 (or puts a stop on the check) on the grounds that he didn't like the suit.

When the check comes back marked "insufficient funds," or "Account closed," the merchant is out some money. If he calls the police, they could only charge Kevin with fraud, if they could prove it in court. If one of the elements is missing (as No. 5 would be in this case) there would be no offense of 476a PC.

(N) Two Party Checks

It is almost impossible to obtain a conviction on a bad two party check because the intent to defraud is so difficult to prove.

Arvin Aardvark comes into a store and tells the owner that he just sold a piece of furniture and that the guy gave him a check for it. He shows a lot of identification. The merchant cashes it for him. A few days later he calls Arvin and tells him that the check bounced. Arvin tells him that he is shocked, but not to worry about it, he will make it good. Arvin never comes in.

The merchant calls the police department. They tell him that they will not handle two party checks because they can never obtain a conviction. A two party check is only as good as the reputation and ethics of the person cashing it.

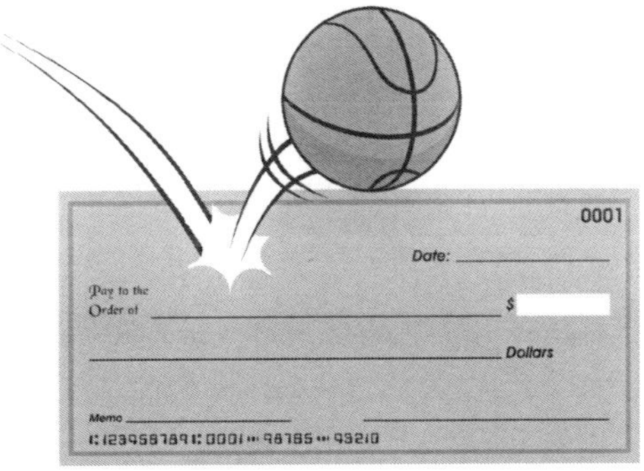

Chapter XII Case Citations

Study Questions for Chapter XII

(1) The Penal Code section for forgery is ________________ PC.

(2) The crime of forgery also includes counterfeiting. T or F

(3) The crime of forgery also includes the passing or attempt to pass altered or counterfeit instruments. T or F

(4) In a conviction for forgery, it must be shown that someone was in fact defrauded or suffered some loss. T or F

(5) Ken Kiter forges a check and takes it to a grocery store. The manager knows the person whose name Ken forged. Before Ken can pass it, the manager stops him. Ken then runs off with the check. He is guilty of forgery. T or F

(6) Forgery can only be proved through direct evidence and not by circumstantial evidence. T or F

(7) To "utter" means:

(A) ___to speak or say something (B) ____to forge

(C) ____to present as genuine (D) ___to give to another

(8) Herbert Hickup goes away on a business trip. He is away during payday, and his wife, Helen, needs the money from his paycheck to cover household expenses. He told her to pick up the check and sign his name on it so that she can cash it. On payday she picks up the check, signs her husband's name on it and cashes it. She is guilty of forgery. T or F

(9) Millie Munchworth works for Arvin Aardvark as an administrative assistant. Each morning she brings a stack of typed papers for him to sign. One morning she secretly includes a piece of paper that authorizes her to take $250 from the company account. Since the signature is really Arvin's, there is no legal case or forgery. T or F

(10) Sam Slipshod finds a blank check for a construction company. He signs his own name to it and cashes it. He is technically guilty of forgery. T or F

(11) The crime of "Issuing Checks with Intent to Defraud" is found under Section ____ PC.

(12) Passing bad checks is a felony when the amount of all the checks the defendant is charged with passing is over $________________.

(13) A person is also guilty of a felony if he is charged with passing bad checks, and if he has a prior conviction for ____

(14) The major element, and the most difficult to prove in the charge of "Passing Bad Checks" is____

(15) The term used for a person who is a professional passer of bad checks is:

(A) ___paper man (B) ___shill

(C) ___kyter (D) ___bounder

(16) Buster Badbetter buys two fifths of whiskey at the local liquor store. He writes a check and tells the clerk that since tomorrow is payday, and he is probably a little low on funds in his account, he will "post date" the check for two days from now, and in that way make sure that there is enough money in the bank. The clerk accepts the check, and two days later it bounces. Buster is guilty of passing bad checks. T or F

(17) Buster Badbetter goes into a grocery store and buys $30 worth of groceries. He writes a check. Unknown to the clerk, Buster "post dates" the check, and the clerk is so busy that he doesn't notice it. Two days later the check bounces. Buster is guilty of passing bad checks. T or F

(18) Kitty Kiter opens a bank account with $200. She then goes to a dress shop and buys a coat for $100. She pays for it with a $100 check. The owner calls the bank and is told by them that she has $200 in the account. She then immediately goes to the bank and withdraws the $200. The check that she wrote bounces on the grounds of "Insufficient Funds." Kitty is guilty of "Issuing Checks with Intent to Defraud." T or F

(19) "Two Party" or "Two Signature" checks are worthless because it is almost impossible to prove____

(20) Sherman Slipshod runs a local downtown clothing store. Homer Hashbrown comes in and wants to buy a $100 suit, but does not have enough money. Sherman takes $20 down and has Homer sign a "counter check" for the other $80, even though Homer does not have a bank account. He tells Homer that if he doesn't pay him the other $80 by the end of the month, he will have Homer arrested for "Issuing Bad Checks." Homer could be legally guilty and charged with 476a PC. T or F

CHAPTER XIII

MISCELLANEOUS OFFENSES

Crimes of Vandalism

(A) Crimes on Transit Vehicles (742.16 W & I)

(1) When a juvenile commits vandalism on a public transportation vehicle (640 PC)

(2) The judge must order the juvenile to wash, paint or repair the damage, pay full restitution (either by the juvenile or his or her parents), or perform "Specified Community Service."

(3) If the judge fails to do this, he must state in writing why.

(B) Crimes on Transit Vehicle or in Transit Facilities (640 PC)

It is an infraction for any person, while riding on a public transit vehicle, or in a public transit facility, to do any of the following:

(1) Evade the paying of fares.

(2) Defraud system through misuse of transfers.

(3) Play any sound equipment (e.g. smartphone music apps) in an audible manner (so others can hear it). Earphones OK

(4) Smoke, drink or eat in prohibited areas.

(5) Spit on floor of facility or vehicle.

(6) Disturb others by boisterous/unruly behavior.

(7) Unauthorized writing, spraying, scratching, affixing, of graffiti, regardless of content, on or in systems facilities or vehicles.
<u>Punishment:</u> $250 fine or 48 hours of public service (within 30 days). Parents can be assigned to supervise work.

(8) Carrying an explosive, acid, flammable liquid, or toxic, or hazardous material.

(9) Urinating or defecating on transit vehicles or property.

(10) Skateboarding, roller skating, bicycle riding, or roller blading.

(11) Unauthorized use of discount tickets.

(12) Willfully blocking the free movement of others on transit vehicle or property.

(13) Willfully tampering with, removing, displacing, injuring or destroying any part of a transit vehicle or facility.

(14) Sale or peddling of goods, merchandise, property or services unless written consent granted by a duly authorized representative.

(C) Vandalism (Wobbler) (594 PC)

(1) Who does one of the following:
  (a) defaces with graffiti or other inscribed material; or
  (b) damages; or
  (c) destroys
(2) Real or personal property not his or her own
(3) Is guilty of vandalism.

Punishment:

(1) If value is less than $400 (Misdemeanor 1 year and/or up to $1,000)
(2) If value is between $400 and $10,000 (Misdemeanor 1 year and/or up to $10,000)
(3) If value is $10,000 or more (Wobbler 1 year and/or up to $50,000)

Vandalism (Aerosol Containers) (594.1 PC)

(1) It is illegal to sell, give or furnish any aerosol container (over 6 ounces)
(2) To persons under 18.

Exceptions:

(a) When minor presents seemingly valid identification; or
(b) Parents and legal guardians may purchase said containers on minor's behalf
(c) When furnished for school-related activities and instruction, under supervision and within project site (instructors shall maintain inventory).

Possession of Graffiti Instruments (594.2 PC) Misdemeanor

Possession of a masonry or glass drill bit, a carbide drill bit, a glass cutter, a grinding stone, an awl, a chisel, a carbide scribe, an aerosol paint container, a felt tip marker, or any other marking substance, with the intent to commit vandalism or graffiti.

Definitions:

Felt Tip Marker: Any broad-tipped marker pen with a tip exceeding three-eighths of one inch in width, or any similar implement containing an ink that is not water soluble.

Marking Substance: Any substance or implement that could be used to draw, spray, paint, etch or mark.

Vandalism to Place of Worship (594.3 PC)

(a) Vandalism to
  (1) church
  (2) synagogue or
  (3) a building owned and occupied by a religious educational institution.
(b) If the vandalism is to one of the above places, and it was committed by reason of race, color, religion, or national origin, and its purpose was to intimidate and deter members from freely exercising their religious beliefs, it becomes a felony.

Graffiti on Government Vehicle (640.5 PC) or Real Property (640.6 PC)

Punishment is increased for prior offenses.

Graffiti Within 100 Feet of a Highway (640.7 PC)

Graffiti or vandalism on or within 100 feet of:

(a) a highway, or
(b) its appurtenances, including, but not limited to, guardrails, signs, signals, snow poles and similar facilities, excluding street signs. (6 months and/or $1,000 – 2nd offense: 1 year)

Defacing or Damaging Structures With Butyric Acid (594.4 PC)

(1) Injecting or throwing on any structure used for commercial or dwelling purposes
(2) Butyric acid or similar noxious or caustic chemical or substance.

The fine increases ($1,000 to $50,000) based on value of damage done.

Defacing Property (Misd.) (594.5 PC)

(1) Any person who without the owner's consent
(2) Willfully defaces, by paint or any other liquid
(3) The property of another

Nothing in this section prevents local jurisdictions from passing ordinances controlling sale of aerosol paint containers. A court may require, as a condition of probation, that a person guilty of this violation wash, paint, or repair the defaced property or otherwise make restitution to the owner.

(742.16 W & I): Requires a juvenile to restore damage if given probation.

(594.3 PC): Vandalism of place of worship. (felony)

Displaying Weapon at One Cleaning Graffiti (417 PC)

Every person who displays a weapon against a person who is cleaning up graffiti or vandalism is guilty of a misdemeanor (3 months to one year).

(1) If a jurisdiction has adopted a "Graffiti Abatement Program"
(2) The court MAY, upon conviction, in addition to other punishment

(a) Order the defendant, and parents or guardians (when applicable) to keep a specified property graffiti-free
(b) For a set period of time (time is increased based on prior convictions).
(c) The court may also require the defendant to undergo counseling.

Liability Limits for Vandalism (1714.1 Civil Code)

The liability of parents for damage committed by their children is limited to $25,000. (Property or injury, per child, per act). If damage is to school property, limit is $10,000 (Ed. Code 48904).

Vandalism of Archaeological Caves (Misdemeanor) (623 PC)

Section A:
(1) Prohibits disturbing or altering of archaeological evidence
(2) Of prior occupation in a natural cave.

Section B:
(1) Prohibits vandalism to cave
(2) Removal/harm to animal or plant life inside
(3) Setting fire inside such cave, or
(4) Vandalism of lock, gate or door to such cave.

Vandalism of Cemetery or Funeral Home (594.35 PC) (Wobbler)

Any vandalism of a cemetery or funeral home is seen as a very serious offense. It can be a felony. If the vandalism is an alleged hate crime, it will be filed as a felony.

Desecration of Peace Officer Memorial (621 PC) (Wobbler)

(1) Desecration or vandalism of any memorial
(2) For Peace Officers, Firefighters or Veterans. (1318 M & V)

Crimes Involving Trespassing

(A) Trespassing After Threats of Serious Bodily Injury (601 PC)

(1) Who makes a credible threat to cause serious bodily injury to another (as defined in 417.6(a) PC, "serious bodily injury" means a serious impairment of physical condition such as loss of consciousness; concussion; bone fracture; injury to an organ; a wound requiring extensive suturing; and serious disfigurement),
(2) With intent to cause reasonable fear in either the victim or an immediate family member
(3) And who, within 30 days of the threat,
(4) Without lawful purpose,
(5) Enters either the:
  (a) residence of the threatened person (or property next to the residence), or
  (b) the workplace of that person,
(6) And locates or attempts to locate that person
(7) With the intent to execute the threat,
(8) Is guilty of a wobbler.

Exceptions:
(1) The residence or workplace is also that of the person making the threats, or
(2) The person making the threats is involved in labor union activities carried out on the property and permitted by CALRA or NLRA rules.

(B) Trespassing (in general) (602 PC) (Upon lands enumerated by other acts)

This section enumerates many acts besides simple trespass. Since most of these acts are also violations of other Penal Code sections, we will simply list the general categories and the most important subsections for peace officers to know.

Acts Listed:
(1) Vandalism
(2) Digging
(3) Theft
(4) Building fires
(5) Driving vehicles
(6) Discharging firearms
(7) Interfering with lawful business
(8) Cutting down trees etc.,
(9) Destroying signs etc.,
(10) Carrying things away
(11) Damaging road signs.

(C) Important subsections:

(1) Trespassing on Commercial Shellfish farms
  (a) Taking shellfish, damaging crops.
  (b) Moving boundary signs or markers.

(2) Damaging Fences or Gates
  (a) Willfully damaging or tearing down fences
  (b) Or leaving open any gate
  (c) Or damaging "no hunting" signs
  (d) On property belonging to another
  (e) Without written permission.

(3) Building Fires on Posted Property
  (a) Building a fire on private property
  (b) When posted with trespass signs which are placed no greater than one mile along the boundary
  (c) Without written permission.

(4) Trespass for Purpose of Obstructing or Interfering with Lawful Business

This subsection was upheld by the high court in People *v.* Brown, 236 Cal. App. 2d Supp. 915. In People *v.* Poe, 236 C.A. 2d 928 the court held that even subterfuge violated this law where the defendant remained at a bank counter for 30 minutes in an effort to hold up business (although his excuse was that he was counting change).

(5) Trespassing on Posted Property

(a) Trespassing on land that is either cultivated or fenced
(b) Or trespassing on land not cultivated or fenced,
(c) But is posted with at least three signs per mile
(d) AND
(e) Refuses to leave when requested by owner or
(f) While hunting destroys "no hunting" signs or
(g) Removes or tampers with gate locks or
(h) Discharges a firearm.

(6) Trespassing in Structures

(a) Entering and occupying
(b) Real property or structure of any kind (buildings)
(c) Without lawful consent.

(7) Trespass with Vehicle

(a) Driving a vehicle on the property of another
(b) When it is known that it is not open to the public
(c) Without legal consent.
Exception: A process server who is carrying out duties.

(8) Refusing or Failing to Leave Property

Refusing or failing to leave property belonging to or lawfully occupied by another, and not open to the general public, upon being asked to leave by:

(a) A peace officer at the request of:
(i) the owner
(ii) his agent, or
(iii) the person in lawful possession, or
(b) The owner, his agent or person in lawful possession.

Note: Section B does not apply to labor unions who are acting under the rules of the CALRA.

Public Housing Definition:

Land, real property or structures owned and operated by any housing authority for tenants (34213.5 H & S) constitutes property not open to the public, and is subject to the law on trespassing. (Purpose of this law is to help control the sale of narcotics in public housing projects)

Exceptions:

(1) Those engaged in constitutionally protected activities.
(2) Those on the premises with permission of a resident or the management AND who are not loitering or suspected of violating the law.

(9) Refusing to Leave Public Buildings

(a) Refusing or failing to leave a public building of a public agency,
(b) During those hours of the day or night when the building is regularly closed to the public,
(c) Upon being requested to do so by a regularly employed:
(i) guard, or
(ii) watchman, or
(iii) custodian of the public agency,
(d) If the surrounding circumstances would indicate to a reasonable individual that such person has no apparent lawful business to pursue.

These laws were passed by the legislature as a special subsection of 602 after the infamous city hall and college "sit-ins" by students and militants during the so-called "militant" or "protest" era. They were contested on the grounds that they violated the defendant's rights under the first amendment.

In the case in point, students and militants remained in public buildings after closing hours to make a protest of their grievances. The high court, in Parrish *v.* Municipal Court, 258 Cal App. 2d 497, ruled that this law was not unreasonable nor did it violate first amendment rights.

(10) Refusing to Leave Hotels and Motels

(a) Refusing to leave hotel or motel
(b) When rooms are not paid for.

(11) On Private Property after Violent Felony (Streleski-Stanford Law)

(a) A person convicted of a violent felony
(b) Committed at a private location,
(c) And the person in control of the property requests that the perpetrator not return there,
(d) And the perpetrator has received notification of this ban by a peace officer,
(e) He or she would be guilty of trespassing.

(12) Airport Passenger Vessel Terminal, Public Transit Facility, or Operations Area Trespassing

(a) Unauthorized person who knowingly enters
(b) Any airport operations area, passenger vessel terminal, or public transit facility
(c) When that area has been posted with notices restricting access to authorized persons only
(d) And when the signs are posted not more than 150 feet apart along the exterior boundary.

Punishment:

Although basically an infraction, it becomes a misdemeanor when the subject refuses to leave when requested by a peace officer.

Definitions:

Airport Operations Area: That used by aircraft for landing, taking off, surface maneuvering, loading and unloading, refueling, parking or maintenance, where aircraft support vehicles and facilities exist, and which is not for public use, or public vehicular traffic.

Authorized Personnel: Those having a valid airport ID card issued by the airport operator, or those being escorted for legitimate purposes by a person with such an ID card.

Airport: Any facility whose function is to support commercial aviation.

(13) Refusing To Leave Women's Shelter

Refusing to leave a battered women's shelter after being requested to leave by the managing authority.

(14) Intentionally Avoiding Screening Process When Entering a Sterile Area of an Airport Terminal

(15) Entering or Remaining in a Neo-Natal Unit Without Lawful Business to Pursue There

(D) Trespassing (602.5 PC) (Misdemeanor)

(1) Every person other than a public officer or employee
(2) Acting within the course and scope of his or her employment
(3) In performance of a duty imposed by law
(4) Who enters or remains in any noncommercial dwelling house, apartment or other such place
(5) Without consent of the owner, his agent, or person in lawful possession of the property.

The important words in this section, "or other such place," broaden the application considerably. This is used as a general trespassing section in most cities when officers have to deal with persons trespassing on private residences. (Covered on page 226.)

(E) Trespassing in Order to Illegally Rent Dwelling (602.9 PC)

(1) Any person who, without the owner's or agent's consent
(2) Claims ownership or takes possession of a residential dwelling, or causes another to enter or remain in that dwelling
(3) For the purpose of renting that dwelling
(4) Is guilty of a misdemeanor.

(F) Returning to Lands Taken by Legal Proceedings (419 PC)

(1) Every person who, after being removed by legal process from any lands
(2) Or having left such land pursuant to a lawful action against them,
(3) And later unlawfully returns to settle, reside, or take possession of such lands,
(4) Is guilty of a misdemeanor.

(G) Loitering at Fairground (602.6 PC)

(1) Every person who remains on any state, county, district or fruit fair building or grounds,
(2) When such property is not open to the general public,
(3) After having been directed by a peace officer, or fair manager to leave the property,
(4) When the order is issued after determination that the person has no apparent lawful or legitimate purpose for being there,
(5) And the person fails to identify him or herself,
(6) And account for his or her presence,
(7) Is guilty of a misdemeanor.

(H) Trespassing on BART (Selling or Soliciting) (602.7 PC) (Infraction)

(1) Any person who enters or remains on BART trains or property
(2) And sells or solicits goods or services
(3) Without permission of Board or representatives.

(I) Trespassing on Posted Property (602.8 PC) (Infraction)

Section A:

(1) Who, without written permission of the landowner or agent,

(2) Willfully enters any land belonging to another that is:
  (a) under cultivation or
  (b) enclosed by fences.

Section B:
(1) Who enters uncultivated or unenclosed land,
(2) Where signs forbidding trespassing are displayed not less than three per mile on exterior boundaries and at all roads and trails entering the lands. Continued offenses against same owner will result in increased punishment.

Exceptions:
(1) Lawful labor activity.
(2) When activities are protected by Constitution.
(3) When in the service of a lawful process.
(4) Lawful process of land surveying.

(J) Trespassing Signs on Industrial Property (553 PC)
(1) Trespassing signs on industrial property must be a minimum of one square foot in area.
(2) Lettering must be at least two inches high.
(3) The wording on the sign must be either:
  (a) trespassing-loitering forbidden by law, or
  (b) a description of use of the property, followed by the words "No Trespassing."
(4) Posting does not need to follow legal descriptions of the property and can cover just that area to be restricted.

(K) Tampering With Aircraft (625b PC) (Misd.)
(1) Any person who injures or tampers with any aircraft, or any parts or contents inside, or
(2) Removes any part without consent, or
(3) With intent to commit injury or vandalism handles any control or equipment
(4) While it is at rest and unattended, or
(5) Who illegally sets an aircraft in motion.

Damage that makes the aircraft unsafe for flight is a "Wobbler."

Invasion of Privacy

(A) Legislative Intent (630 PC)

This chapter's intent is to protect the right to privacy of the people of this state. The Legislature recognizes that law enforcement agencies have a legitimate need to employ modern listening devices and techniques in the investigation of criminal conduct and the apprehension of lawbreakers. Therefore, it is not the intent of this chapter to place greater restraints on the use of listening devices and techniques by law enforcement agencies than existed prior to its effective date.

(B) Intentional and Unauthorized Eavesdropping (631 PC) (Felony)

Illegal Wiretaps
(1) Who, by means of any machine, instrument or contrivance or by any other means
(2) Intentionally "taps" or makes an unauthorized connection by any means,
(3) With any
  (a) telegraph or telephone wire or
  (b) line, cable or instrument of any internal telephonic communications system, OR:
(1) Who, without consent of all parties to the communication, or in any unauthorized manner,
(2) Reads, attempts to read or to learn the contents or meaning of any communication in transit over a wire, line or cable,
(3) When sent or received anywhere in this state. OR
(4) Who uses or communicates any information obtained from such an act.

Exceptions (631(b) PC):
(1) Public utility companies as part of their business duties, or
(2) Any telephonic communications system that is legally used exclusively within this state, or a local jurisdiction, or
(3) A correctional facility.

Communications as Evidence (631(c) PC):

Evidence obtained in violation of this section shall not be admissible in any judicial, administrative, legislative, or other proceedings (The rules of evidence do not normally apply to administrative proceedings).

(C) Unauthorized Use of Recording Devices (632 PC) (Wobbler)

Illegal "Bugging"

(1) Who, intentionally and without consent of all parties to any confidential communication,
(2) By means of any electronic amplifying or recording device,
(3) Eavesdrops upon or records such communications
(4) Unless the communication was over a radio.

Exceptions:

The exceptions are the same as in 631 PC, except the use of hearing aids and similar devices by hearing impaired persons is a listed exception.

Definitions:

(1) Person: An individual, business association, partnership or other legal entity or agent of any government department.
(2) Confidential Communication: Communication carried on in circumstances reasonably indicating that any party to such communication desires it to be confined to such parties.

(D) Legal Police Use of Wiretaps (633 PC)

Nothing in 631, 632, 632.5, 632.6, or 632.7 PC shall be construed as prohibiting law enforcement personnel and prosecutors, acting within the scope of their authority, from overhearing or recording any communications which would have been legal prior to the enactment of this law (Jan 1968). Nor does it affect admissibility of evidence obtained in this manner.

(E) Recording for Purpose of Obtaining Evidence in Crimes (633.5 PC)

(1) A private person may record a confidential conversation
(2) When the purpose is to obtain evidence of:
  (a) extortion
  (b) kidnapping
  (c) bribery
  (d) obscene phone calls
  (e) felonies involving violence
  (f) human trafficking and
  (g) domestic violence (with judge's order).

Admissibility of evidence shall not be affected.

(F) Manufacture, Sale and Transportation of Eavesdropping Devices (635 PC) (Wobbler)

(1) It is illegal to manufacture, assemble, sell, offer for sale, advertise, possess, transport, import or furnish to another,
(2) Any device primarily designed or intended for eavesdropping on another's communications.

Exceptions:

(1) Public communications companies in the normal course of their business.
(2) Law enforcement agencies in the course of their duties.
(3) Subscribers to a communication service when such a device is furnished by the utility company to enhance reception.

(G) Eavesdropping on a Person in Custody (636 PC) (Felony)

(1) Every person, who, without permission of all parties to a conversation,
(2) Eavesdrops or records by any means,
(3) A conversation of a person in custody and
  (a) anyone on the property of a law enforcement agency, or where there is a reasonable expectation of privacy, or
  (b) a person's attorney, religious advisor, or licensed physician.

Exception:

Public utility employees as part of their job.

(H) Unauthorized Opening of Sealed Messages and Fraudulent Representation as an Addressee (637.1 PC) (Wobbler)

Section A:

(1) Any person not connected with a telephone or telegraph company
(2) Who, without authority, or the consent of the person receiving the message,
(3) Willfully opens any sealed envelope containing a telegraphic or telephonic message,
(4) Addressed to another person,
(5) For the purpose of learning the contents of such message.

Section B:

(1) Who fraudulently represents self to be the person to whom the message is addressed,
(2) And receives such message,
(3) With the intent to use, destroy, or prevent the intended person from receiving the message.

(I) Liability for Violation (637.2 PC)

(1) Any person who has been injured by a violation of this chapter may bring an action against

the person who committed the violation for the greater of the following amounts:
(a) five thousand dollars ($5,000).
(b) three times the amount of actual damages, if any, sustained by the plaintiff.

(2) Any person may, in accordance with the provisions of Chapter 3, (commencing with Section 525) of Title 7 of Part 2 of the Code of Civil Procedure, bring an action to enjoin and restrain any violation of this chapter, and may in the same action seek damages as provided by subdivision 1.
(3) It is not a necessary prerequisite to an action pursuant to this section that the plaintiff has suffered or been threatened with actual damages.

(J) Invasion of Privacy by Use of Voice Prints or Voice Stress Analyzers (637.3 PC)

(1) It is illegal to use a "Psychological Stress Evaluator" or similar system
(2) To determine the truth of another's statements
(3) Without written permission given in advance.
(4) This section shall not apply to peace officers carrying out official duties.
(5) A victim of this section may bring action against the violator for
(a) actual damages or
(b) $1,000, whichever is greater.

Disorderly Conduct

(A) Acts Defined As Disorderly Conduct (647 PC)

An individual who commits any of the following acts is guilty of disorderly conduct.

(a) Engaging in or soliciting lewd or dissolute conduct in any public place or in any place open to the public or exposed to public view.
(b) (1) Soliciting, agreeing to engage in, or engaging in any act of prostitution when the person receives compensation, money or anything of value from another person (targets the seller)
(2) Soliciting, agreeing to engage in, or engaging in any act of prostitution with an adult when the person provides compensation (targets the buyer of adult sex)
(3) Soliciting, agreeing to engage in, or engaging in any act of prostitution with a child when the person provides compensation (targets the buyer of child sex)
(4) Acceptance of an offer or solicitation to engage in an act of prostitution must involve an agreement to engage, and to commit an act to further the commission of the act of prostitution (i.e. drive to the hotel the prostitute or undercover officer suggested).
(5) This subdivision does not apply to a child under 18 years of age who is alleged to have engaged in prostitution. The minor would be taken into temporary custody rather than be criminally prosecuted.

(c) Who accosts other persons in any public place for the purpose of begging or soliciting arms.
(d) Loitering in or about any toilet open to the public for the purpose of engaging in or soliciting any lewd or lascivious or any unlawful act.
(e) Who lodges in a building, structure, vehicle, or place, public or private, without the permission of the owner.
(f) Who is found in a public place under the influence of an intoxicating liquor, drug, controlled substance, toluene, or any combination of the above, and is in such a condition that he or she is unable to exercise care for his or her safety, or the safety of others. Or, while under the influence, interferes with or obstructs, or prevents the free use of any street, sidewalk or other public way.
(g) If a person has violated subdivision (f) of this section, a peace officer, if reasonably able to do so, shall place the person, or cause him or her to be placed, in civil protective custody. Such person shall be taken to a facility, designated pursuant to Section 5170 of the Welfare and Institutions Code, for the 72-hour treatment and evaluation of inebriates. Peace officers may place a person in civil protective custody with that kind and degree of force which would be lawful were they affecting an arrest for a misdemeanor without a warrant. No person who has been placed in civil protective custody shall thereafter be subject to any criminal prosecution or juvenile court proceeding based on the facts giving rise to such placement.

This subdivision shall not apply to the following persons:

(1) A person who is under the influence of any drug, or under the combined influence of alcohol and any drug.

(2) A person who, a peace officer has probable cause to believe, has committed any felony, or who has committed any misdemeanor in addition to subdivision (f) of this section.

(3) A person who, a peace officer in good faith believes, will attempt escape or will be unreasonably difficult for medical personnel to control.

(h) Who loiters, prowls, or wanders upon the private property of another, at any time, without visible or lawful business with the owner or occupant thereof.

(i) Who, while loitering, prowling, or wandering upon the private property of another, at any time, peeks in the door or window of any inhabited building or structure located thereon, without visible or lawful business with the owner or occupant thereof.

(j) (1) Invading Another's Privacy By Looking Into a Hole/Opening
Looking through a hole or opening, into, or otherwise viewing, by means of any instrumentality, including but not limited to: a periscope, telescope, binoculars, camera, camcorder, motion picture camera, mobile phone, or unmanned aircraft, the interior of a bathroom, changing room or tanning booth, or the interior of any other area in which the occupant has a reasonable expectation of privacy, with the intent to invade the privacy of a person or persons inside.
Exception: A room for counting currency or negotiable instruments.

(j) (2) Use of Hidden Camera to Secretly Record for Sexual Purposes (647(j)(2) PC)
Using a concealed camera (video or photographic) to secretly videotape, film, photograph or record by electronic means another identifiable person, under or through the clothing of the perpetrator, for the purpose of viewing the body or undergarments of the victim, without their consent or knowledge, with the intent to arouse, appeal to, or gratify the lust, passions, or sexual desires of the perpetrator, and invade the privacy of that person when the victim has a reasonable expectation of privacy.

(j) (3) Viewing Into a Bathroom, Changing Room, Etc.
This subdivision is similar to (j)(2) but involves viewing into a bedroom, bathroom, changing room, or interior of any other area in which that other person has a reasonable expectation of privacy, with intent to invade that privacy.

(j) (4) Any person who intentionally distributes the image of another identifiable person's intimate body part, or the image of the person depicted engaged in any sexual act, with the intent to cause serious emotional distress.

(k) A court may suspend, for not more than 30 days, the privilege of the person to operate a motor vehicle for any violation of subdivision (b) (Solicitation) that was committed within 1,000 feet of a private residence and with the use of a vehicle.

Although officers receive more calls regarding section 415 of the Penal Code, they make more arrests under section 647. They often have little choice. For example, if officers find an inebriate passed out in the street, they must either arrest the suspect or take him into "protective custody."

(B) Breakdown of the Elements and Discussion of the Subsections

(a) Soliciting or Engaging in Dissolute Conduct

(1) Any person who solicits anyone to engage in lewd or dissolute conduct, or
(2) Engages in lewd or dissolute conduct
(3) In any public place (e.g. public park, library)
(4) Any place open to the public (e.g. dept. store)
(5) Any place exposed to public view.

Since the punishment is the same for soliciting and actually engaging in the lewd act, and since it is best to arrest before the act is committed, this section is used mostly for soliciting. The "engages" part is very broad and can be used in many ways, for example, a case of molesting of a person who is over 18. (288 PC covers the molesting of a person under the age of 14, and 647.6 PC covers the molesting of a person under the age of 18.

In California, acts of soliciting require corroboration. This is to protect citizens from being arrested due to misunderstandings, and from violations of their First Amendment rights. The corroboration required can be very slight. An undercover agent is carrying a small recording device on his person, and his partner is recording the conversation in a nearby police car. If the statement is clear on the recording, it is enough corroboration.

In other cases, the undercover officer would have to ask the suspect questions about his sex habits or taste for fetishes, so that there would be no doubt that the suspect did solicit the undercover agent to commit a lewd and dissolute act.

The legislature did not intend that engaging in lewd or dissolute acts as a part of legitimate theatrical performances would come under this law. (Barrows *v.* Municipal Court, 1 Cal. 3d 821). However, this does not prevent an arrest under this section for bottomless dancing in a bar. (People *v.* Newton, 9 CA 3d Supp. 24).

An important key to this section is where the solicitation took place, not where the act solicited took place. (People *v.* Dudley, 250 CA 2d 955) A closed room in a massage parlor is a "place open to the public" according to this section. (Steinke, In re., 2 CA 3d 569).Whether or not the act was lewd or dissolute is a "question of fact" for the jury to determine. (Dixon *v.* Municipal Court, 267 CA 2d 789).

This subsection does not violate the First Amendment guarantee of freedom of speech. (Silva *v.* Municipal Court, 40 CA 3d 733). Nor is an act of oral copulation a means of "oral expression" protected under the First Amendment. (People *v.* Drolet, 30 CA 3d 207). This section is covered under 290 PC, and any person convicted of this offense must register as a sexual criminal.

Definitions:

"Lewd" and "dissolute" mean "obscene." The term "obscene" means sexual conduct which is grossly repugnant, and patently offensive to generally accepted notions of what is appropriate and decent according to contemporary community standards. It ordinarily includes conduct that is disgusting, repulsive, filthy, foul, abominable or loathsome. (Silva *v.* Municipal Court, supra)

(b) Soliciting or Engaging in Prostitution

(1) Any person who solicits an act of prostitution
(2) Or engages in an act of prostitution anywhere.

When Crime of Soliciting is Complete

(1) Soliciting is completed when there is an agreement to engage in an act of prostitution
(2) And the prostitute has the intent to engage in that act
(3) And the prostitute accepts an offer to so engage in that act,
(4) Regardless of whether the "John" had that intent (this protects the undercover officer who converses with the prostitute);
(5) And there is an overt act to further the commission of the act beyond the agreement (it can be very slight, such as going to her room); (asking her what strange things her customers ask for);
(6) And the soliciting and overt act occurs in this state.

Definition:

Prostitution includes the performance of ANY lewd act between persons for money or other considerations. This act covers more than prostitution as we might commonly think of it. It covers any act that is lewd. It also covers persons of any sex. It does not, however, cover acts with animals by prostitutes who are hired to perform at parties since the term "between persons" is used. Such an act would be a violation of Bestiality, (286.5 PC)

When vice officers equipped an undercover agent with a recording device (bug) and heard the suspect solicit the agent, the soliciting was legally done within their "presence" (836 PC – any of the five senses) and they were justified in entry, search and arrest. (People *v.* Lewis, 214 CA 2d 799).

Similarly, the courts upheld the right of officers to enter an apartment house that was known to be used by prostitutes when they observed two known prostitutes enter the building with two men after midnight. They had reasonable cause to believe that a misdemeanor was being committed in their presence (836 PC) and their search did not violate the Fourth Amendment of the U.S. Constitution. (People *v.* Seals, 263 CA 2d 1002).

Loitering for the Purpose of Engaging in Prostitution (653.22 PC)

(a) It is unlawful for any person to loiter in any public place with the intent to commit prostitution. This intent is evidenced by acting in a manner and under circumstances which openly demonstrate the purpose of inducing, enticing, or soliciting prostitution, or procuring another to commit prostitution.

Definitions:

Commit Prostitution: To engage in sexual conduct for money or other consideration. This excludes stage performances, plays or other forms of entertainment.

Public Place: Any area open to the public, or an alley, plaza, park, driveway, or parking lot, or an automobile, whether moving or not, or a building open to the general public. The doorways and entrances to a building or dwelling, or the grounds enclosing a building or dwelling.

Loiter: To delay or linger without lawful purpose for being on the property, and for the purpose of committing a crime as opportunity may be discovered.

(b) Among the circumstances that may be considered in determining whether a person loiters with the intent to commit prostitution are that the person:
   (1) repeatedly beckons to, stops, engages in conversations with, or attempts to stop or engage in conversations with passersby, indicative of soliciting for prostitution;
   (2) repeatedly stops or attempts to stop motor vehicles by hailing the drivers, waving arms, or making any other bodily gestures, or engages or attempts to engage the drivers or passengers of the motor vehicles in conversation indicative of soliciting for prostitution;
   (3) has been convicted of violating this section, 647(a) or 647(b) PC, or any other offense relating to or involving prostitution, within five years of the arrest under this section;
   (4) circles an area in a motor vehicle and repeatedly beckons to, contacts, or attempts to contact or stop pedestrians or other motorists, indicative of soliciting for prostitution;
   (5) has engaged, within six months prior to arrest under this section, in any behavior described in this subdivision, with the exception of paragraph (3), or in any other behavior indicative of prostitution.

(c) The list of circumstances set forth in subdivision (b) is not exclusive. They should, however, be considered particularly salient if they occur in an area known for prostitution activity. Any other relevant circumstances may be considered in determining whether a person has the requisite intent. Moreover, no one circumstance or combination of circumstances is in itself determinative of intent. Intent must be determined based on an evaluation of the particular circumstance of each case.

Directing, Supervising, Recruiting Prostitutes or Collecting Proceeds from Them (653.23 PC)

(a) It is unlawful for any person to do either of the following:
   (1) Direct, supervise, recruit, or otherwise aid another person in the commission of a violation of 647(b) (prostitution) or 653.22(a) (loitering for prostitution).
   (2) Collect or receive all or part of the proceeds earned from an act or acts of prostitution committed by another person in violation of 647(b).

(b) Among the circumstances that may be considered in determining whether a person is in violation of subdivision (a) are that the person does any of the following:
   (1) repeatedly speaks or communicates with another person who is acting in violation of 653.22(a) PC;
   (2) repeatedly or continuously monitors or watches another person who is acting in violation of 653.22(a) PC;
   (3) repeatedly engages or attempts to engage in conversation with pedestrians or motorists to solicit, arrange, or facilitate an act of prostitution between such persons and another person who is acting in violation of 653.22(a) PC;
   (4) repeatedly stops or attempts to stop pedestrians or motorists to solicit, arrange, or facilitate an act of prostitution between such persons and another person who is acting in violation of 653.22(a) PC;
   (5) circles an area in a motor vehicle and repeatedly beckons to, contacts, or attempts to contact or stop pedestrians or other motorists to solicit, arrange, or facilitate an act of prostitution between such persons and another person who is acting in violation of 653.22(a) PC;
   (6) receives or appears to receive money from another person who is acting in violation of 653.22(a) PC;
   (7) engages in any of the behavior described in paragraphs (1) through (6), inclusive, in regard to or on behalf of two or more persons who are in violation of 653.22(a) PC;
   (8) has been convicted of violating this section, 266h, 266i, 653.22(a), 647(a), or 647(b) PC, or any other offense relating to or involving prostitution within five years of the arrest under this section.

(9) has engaged, within six months prior to arrest under subdivision (a) in any behavior described in this subdivision, with the exception of paragraph (8), or in any other behavior indicative of prostitution.

(c) The list of circumstances set forth in subdivision (b) is not exclusive. they should, however, be considered particularly salient if they occur in an area known for prostitution activity. Any other relevant circumstances may be considered. Moreover, no one circumstance or combination of circumstances is in itself determinative. A violation of subdivision (a) shall be determined based on an evaluation of the particular circumstances of each case.

(d) Nothing in this section shall preclude the prosecution of a suspect for a violation of 266h or 266i PC or for any other offense, or for a violation of this section in conjunction with a violation of 266h or 266i PC or any other offense.

Special Punishment for Prostitution Convictions

(1) If defendant has a prior conviction for 647(b) PC, and the accusatory pleading charges it, the defendant shall receive:
   (a) a minimum of 45 days in county jail and
   (b) no probation during that 45 days, and
   (c) no suspension of sentence during the first 45 days.
(2) If defendant has two or more prior convictions for 647(b) PC and the accusatory pleading charges it, the defendant shall receive:
   (a) a minimum of 90 days in county jail, and
   (b) no probation during that 90 days, and
   (c) no suspension of sentence during the first 90 days.

If the complaint lists the act as one of soliciting, it should be remembered that such an offense requires some corroboration.

(c) Accosting Other Persons in Public While Panhandling

A person who accosts other persons in any public place, or in any place open to the public, for the purpose of begging or soliciting alms is guilty of disorderly conduct. This subsection originally defined begging in public as a crime, but was found unconstitutional in 1992 on the grounds that it violated First Amendment rights to freedom of speech. If the offense occurs on private property, trespassing (602.5) could be used rather than begging with accosting actions.

(d) Loitering About Public Toilet for Purpose of Soliciting

(1) Any person who loiters
(2) About or in any toilet open to the public
(3) For the purpose of
   (a) engaging in, or
   (b) soliciting any
      (i) lewd act, or
      (ii) lascivious act, or
      (iii) unlawful act.

This section is a specific intent crime, and arresting officers must be prepared to present their justification for the arrest in court. One of the exceptions regarding the presentation in court of the defendant's prior record is to prove specific intent. If the defendant has been arrested before for 647(a) "Soliciting Lewd Acts," it would be good evidence to use in proving his intent in loitering about a public toilet. In most cases the suspect will leave when questioned by patrol officers, and the problem will be solved without an arrest. If the suspect is observed accosting men who are passing by, it would be grounds to ask the suspect for identification. If a check with Records and Identification shows that the suspect is a 290 PC registrant, this could also be used to show intent.

(e) Illegal Lodging

(1) Any person who lodges
(2) In any
   (a) building,
   (b) structure,
   (c) place, or
   (d) vehicle
(3) Whether public or private

(4) Without the permission of the
  (a) owner,
  (b) person in possession of property, or
  (c) person in control of the property.

Definition:
Lodges: (Webster) Lives in a place for a time.

This section was enacted primarily to control the problem of homeless persons and "inebriates" sleeping in abandoned or unoccupied houses.

Loitering Upon the Streets and Refusing to Identify Self (657(e) Amended)

In Kolendar *v.* Lawson, LED 2d 903, the U.S. Supreme Court declared that Section 647, Subdivision (e) of the California Penal Code, requiring persons to provide credible and reliable identification to police officers, was unconstitutionally vague on its face. Edward Lawson was detained or arrested on 15 occasions on the basis of 647(e) PC. Rather than appealing the case criminally, he initiated a civil action seeking a declaratory judgment that the statute was unconstitutional. The Supreme Court felt it vested complete discretion in the hands of the police to determine whether or not the suspect satisfied the requirements of the statute. They felt that it promoted arbitrary enforcement of the law. Officers must now search for probable cause to arrest if they wish to know the identity of the suspect and he refuses to volunteer that information. (This applies to public streets, not cases involving private property.)

(f) Being Under the Influence of Intoxicating Liquor or Drugs in Public

(1) Any person who is found
(2) In a public place
(3) Under the influence of:
  (a) an intoxicating liquor
  (b) any drugs or hydrocarbons
  (c) toluene (model glue) (see 381 PC)
  (d) any combination of the above,
(4) And is unable to exercise care for his or her safety or the safety of others,
(5) Or because his or her condition:
  (a) interferes with
  (b) obstructs or
  (c) prevents the free use of any street or sidewalk or other public way.

The word "safety" is not unconstitutionally vague, even though it is opinion evidence. (Joseph G. In re, 7 CA 3d 695)

Selling Glue Containing Toluene (380 PC)

(1) Illegal to sell any glue to minors (under 18)
(2) When it contains toluene
(3) Unless it is a type, approved by the state, that cannot be sniffed.

Possession of Toluene With Intent to Become Intoxicated (381 PC)

Any person possessing toluene with intent to become intoxicated is guilty of a misdemeanor.

Possession of Nitrous Oxide With Intent to Inhale (381b PC)

(1) Any person who possesses Nitrous Oxide
(2) Other than a licensed dentist, physician or surgeon
(3) With intent to ingest or inhale for purposes of intoxication.

In Powell *v.* Texas, 392 United States 514, the U.S. Supreme Court was presented with the argument that alcoholism was a "status" offense and really a sickness rather than a crime. The high court upheld Powell's conviction. This case did, however, have a great effect on state law regarding the treatment and handling of inebriates or recidivist drunk arrests. States like California have enacted laws designed to treat the chronic drunk less as a criminal and more as a sick person. Prosecuting an alcoholic under this section is a punishment of an "act" and not a "status." It is not a violation of the Eighth Amendment (Cruel and Unusual Punishment). (Spinks, In re., 253 CA 2d 748)

Public Place

Persons who are intoxicated in a "place exposed to public view" do not violate this section, since other subsections of 647 PC specifically list this condition when required. A city ordinance cannot make intoxication in a private place illegal. The state has pre-empted the laws on intoxication. (Koehne, In re, 59 Cal. 2d 646).

A barbershop is a public place within the meaning of this section (Zorn, In re, 59 C 2d 650). An intoxicated person in an automobile that is parked on a public street is in a public place. (People *v.* Belanger 243 CA 2d 654).

The front area outside of a person's home is a public place if a stranger would be able to walk through the outside area to the door without challenge. (People *v*. Olson, 18 CA 3d 592).

Searching for Drugs and Suspicion of Drug Influence

A search of the person of one suspected of public intoxication from drugs was valid when the suspect appeared to be intoxicated, yet had no odor of alcohol on his breath. (People *v*. Medina, 15 CA 3d 845).

When the suspect had very slurred speech, and her eyes had little reaction to the officer's flashlight, and responses to the officers' questions were incoherent, the Appellate Court upheld the officers' reasonable belief that the suspect was under the influence of drugs. (People *v*. Kemick, 17 CA 3d 419). Again, an officer's reasonable cause to suspect drug influence was upheld when the suspect's speech was thick, and she had difficulty enunciating, her head swayed back and forth, her eyes would not focus, and the officer smelled no alcohol on her breath. This was further substantiated by a companion's statement that she was "stoned." (People *v*. Blatt, 23 CA 3d 148).

Suspicion of Intoxication by Alcohol

Suspicion of public intoxication was upheld based on observation of the suspect walking with an unstable gait, the inability to walk a short distance without making stops, having an alcoholic breath, bloodshot eyes and slurred speech. (People *v*. Steeples, 22 CA 3d 993). The suspect's testimony of his own intoxication can be used to corroborate observations of the apparent state of intoxication. (People *v*. Jones, 19 CA 3d 437).

General Search of Arrested "Drunk in Public" Suspects in Field

When an officer was about to place a 647(f) suspect into a police van for transportation to jail, and the van contained other prisoners, the courts held that the van was an extension of the detention facility, and that the officer had the right and duty to search the suspect in order to insulate the other arrestees from any contraband or weapons. (People *v*. Maher, 41 CA 3d 152).

In the field search of a suspect under 647(f) PC for contraband, it must be shown that the suspect was ACTUALLY going to be arrested and incarcerated. (People *v*. Longwill, 13 C 3d 943).

Driving While Intoxicated (DWI)

These laws are found in the Vehicle Code Felony Drunk Driving (23153 CVC), Misdemeanor Drunk Driving (23152 CVC) and Juvenile with blood alcohol of 0.05% or greater (23140 CVC).

Operating a Vessel While Under the Influence (655 Harbor & Navigation Code)

No person shall operate any recreational vessel or manipulate any water skis, aquaplane, or similar device if the person has an alcohol concentration of 0.08 percent or more in his or her blood (commercial vessels are .04 percent).

(g) Civil Protective Custody of Intoxicated Persons

Elements and Discussion:

(1) When a person has violated 647(f),
(2) A peace officer, if reasonably able to do so,
(3) Shall see that the suspect is placed in civil protective custody
(4) At a detoxification center, (if available),
(5) For 72-hour treatment and evaluation.
(6) No criminal prosecution shall result unless:
  (a) suspect is under the influence of drugs or combination of alcohol & drugs.
  (b) the peace officer has probable cause to believe that the suspect has committed a crime in addition to 647(f).
  (c) the peace officer, in good faith, believes the suspect will attempt to escape.
  (d) the peace officer, in good faith, believes the suspect will be unreasonably difficult for medical persons to control.

When the law provides that a person will be provided special treatment as an inebriate by civil confinement rather than jail, it is not a violation of the Fourteenth Amendment (Equal Protection Under The Law), when some counties do not have the proper facilities, since the code states "where appropriate facilities are available." (People *v*. Superior Court, 29 CA 3d 397).

Definition:

Inebriated: A habitually intoxicated person.

(h) Prowling on Private Property

(1) Any person who
  (a) loiters
  (b) prowls, or
  (c) wanders
(2) Upon the private property of another
(3) Any time of the day or night
(4) Without visible or lawful business

(a) with the owner of the property, or
(b) the occupant of the property.

When a suspect was found in a parked vehicle on a private university campus which he did not attend, and where he knew no one attending, and there was reasonable cause to believe he had committed some criminal offense, an arrest for 647(h) was upheld. (People *v.* Wilkins, 27 CA 3d 763).

When a suspect hid between buildings upon seeing a uniformed police officer in a marked police car, ran as the officer approached, and was unable to supply verifiable facts as to his whereabouts immediately before, when a prowling had occurred nearby, the courts upheld an arrest for 647(h). (People *v.* Superior Court, 15 CA 3d 146).

Often, the person was arrested just for trespassing, but later the offense was viewed as sexual in nature. Even today, with the separation, officers should use the regular trespassing section rather than 647(i) unless there is considerable evidence that the suspect was prowling.

(i) Peeking in a Door or Window of an Inhabited Building

(1) Any person who
(2) Any time of the day or night
(3) While:
  (a) loitering,
  (b) prowling, or
  (c) wandering on private property of another
(4) Peeks in a
  (a) door or
  (b) window
(5) Of any inhabited
  (a) building or
  (b) structure located on that property
(6) Without visible business with owner/occupant.

Definition:

Inhabited: Where someone normally resides, even if they are not there at the time.

(j) Peeping Into Bathrooms/Changing Rooms

(1) With the intent to invade someone's privacy
(2) Either
  (a) looks into, or
  (b) views by any means of an instrument (telescope, camera, etc.)
(3) The interior of any room or area
(4) In which the occupant(s) have a reasonable expectation of privacy.
(5) Any matter obtained in violation of 647 subdivision (j) that is in possession of any city, county, state official or agency, is subject to forfeiture. (647.8 PC)

Additional Punishment

(1) If the defendant committed the act within 1,000 feet of a private residence
(2) And used a vehicle to assist in the act
(3) And has a prior conviction for this section
(4) In addition to any other punishment, shall have his driving privilege suspended for up to 30 days. (13201.5 CVC)

Other Laws That Deal With Prostitution

(A) Red Light Abatement Laws

(1) Every place or building used for
  (a) illegal gambling
  (b) lewdness
  (c) assignation
  (d) prostitution
  (e) narcotics sale
  (f) human trafficking
(2) Or where these things occur
(3) Or a building or place used as a bathhouse whose primary activity encourages or permits conduct that can transmit AIDS
(4) Is a nuisance which shall be
  (a) enjoined
  (b) abated and
  (c) prevented

Bathhouse: A business which, as its primary purpose, provides facilities for a spa, whirlpool, communal bath, sauna, steam bath, mineral bath, mud bath or swimming.

(B) Injunctions (11227 PC)

A judge can issue a temporary writ of injunction to prevent the condition from continuing.

(C) Taking a Person for the Purpose of Prostitution (266a PC) (Felony)

Each person who within the state takes any person against his or her will and without his or her consent, or with his or her consent procured by fraudulent inducement or misrepresentation, for the purpose of prostitution.

(D) Taking a Person by Force, Duress, etc. to Live in Illicit Relation (266b PC) (Felony)

Any person who takes any other person unlawfully, against his or her will, and by force, menace, or duress, compels him or her to live with such person, or any other person, in an illicit relation, without his or her consent.

(E) Placing a Person in Custody for Purpose of Cohabitation (266d PC) (Felony)

Any person who receives any money or other valuable thing for or on account of placing in custody any other person for the purpose of causing that person to cohabit with another to whom that person is not married.

(F) Purchasing Person for the Purpose of Prostitution (266e PC) (Felony)

Every person who purchases or pays any money or other valuable thing, for any person, for the purpose of prostitution (647(b)), or for immoral purposes with any person, with or without that person's consent.

(G) Selling a Person for Immoral Purposes (266f PC) (Felony)

Every person who sells any person or receives money or other valuable thing for or on account of his placing that person in custody for immoral purposes, with or without that person's consent.

(H) Placing One's Wife in a House of Prostitution (266g PC) (Felony)

(1) Any man who, by any means, places or leaves his wife in a house of prostitution, or
(2) Consents or permits her to remain in such house.
* A wife may testify against her husband under this section.

(I) Soliciting or Deriving Support from a Prostitute (Pimping) (266h PC) (Felony)

(1) Anyone who, knowing another is a prostitute,
(2) Derives any support or maintenance from his or her earnings or future earnings
(3) Or solicits or receives compensation for soliciting for him or her.
*Also see section 647(b) PC, pages 222-223.

Punishment: If the prostitute is under the age of 16, the punishment is increased from 3, 4 or 6 years to 3, 6 or 8 years.

(J) Procuring Persons (Pandering) (266i PC)

(1) Procuring another person by
  (a) promises
  (b) threats or
  (c) any scheme
(2) To
  (a) work in,
  (b) remain in, or
  (c) enter
(3) A place of prostitution (or where prostitution is encouraged)
(4) For the purpose of prostitution.
OR:
(1) Who receives, or agrees to receive
(2) Anything of value
(3) For procuring another person
(4) For prostitution
(5) Is guilty of pandering, a felony. (Punishment is greater if victim is under the age of 14.)

Although most people use the term "pimp" and "panderer" interchangeably, it should be noted that sections 266h and 266i make a distinction. A pimp derives support from prostitution; a panderer procures individuals to become prostitutes.

Punishment:

If the person solicited is under the age of 16, the punishment is increased from 3, 6 or 8 years.

(K) Massage Parlors Control (51032 Gov. Code)

(1) A licensing authority may deny a license for a massage parlor
(2) When operator/owner has been convicted of:
  (a) Prostitution, or
  (b) Related sex offenses, or
  (c) A narcotics offense
(3) In either this state or another.

Other General Offenses

(A) Body Piercing (652 PC)

(1) Performing or offering to perform body piercing
(2) On a person under the age of 18
(3) Unless it is
  (a) in the presence of a parent or legal guardian, or
  (b) as directed by a notarized writing by such parent or guardian.

(B) Tattooing a Minor (653 PC) (Misd.)

Every person who tattoos or offers to tattoo a person under the age of 18 years.

(C) Installation of Two-Way Mirrors (653n PC) (Misd.)

Any person who installs or maintains any two-way mirror permitting observation of any rest room, toilet, bathroom, washroom, shower, locker room, fitting room, motel room, or hotel room.

Exceptions:

This law shall not apply to jails, penal, medical, mental or educational institutions, or to police agencies.

(D) Responsibility of Law Enforcement Agencies Toward Victims of Violent Crimes (Government Code 13962)

It shall be the duty of every local law enforcement agency to inform crime victims of the provisions of this chapter, of the existence of victim centers, and to provide application forms to victims who desire to seek compensation pursuant to this chapter. The **California Victim Compensation Board** shall provide application forms and all other documents that local law enforcement agencies and victim centers may require to comply with this section. The board shall conduct outreach to local law enforcement agencies about their duties under this section. The Attorney General shall set standards to be followed by local law enforcement agencies for this purpose and may require them to file a description of the procedures adopted by each agency to comply.

For years the State of California has had available funds for the purpose of reimbursing innocent victims of violent crimes. Because less than 1% of those victims actually applied for such aid, the legislature decided to make law enforcement agencies legally responsible for notifying the victims of such crimes.

(E) Assistance Centers for Victims and Witnesses (13835 PC)

Public or private agencies are to set up "Victim and Witness Centers." They will assist victims in obtaining compensation from the state under existing law, conduct follow-up on victims, provide encouragement and moral support to witnesses to crimes so that they will be encouraged to show up in court and provide needed testimony.

(F) Domestic Violence Project Centers (18290 W & I)

Provides for a statewide network of experimental Domestic Violence Project Centers to assist victims of domestic violence, providing 24-hour shelter, legal assistance, family, marriage and job counseling.

(G) Selling Tobacco to Minors (and Minor Possession of Tobacco) (308 PC)

Subsection (a):

(1) Every person or business which knowingly sells or gives any tobacco product
(2) To a person under the age of 18
(3) Is guilty of a misdemeanor.

Subsection (b):

(1) Every person under the age of 18
(2) Who possesses any tobacco, cigarette or cigarette papers, or instrument for smoking tobacco
(3) Shall be punished by a fine of $75 or 30 hours community service.

(H) Loitering About School or Public Playgrounds (653b PC)

Who loiters about any school or public place at or near which children attend or normally congregate or remains there after being asked to leave by a school official or peace officer, is a vagrant.

As used here, "loiter" means to delay, to linger, or to idle about any such school or public place without lawful purpose. (This is to control child molesters who may loiter around schools. It was declared unconstitutional until the "rider" was attached that explained the legislative intent and allowed those with lawful purpose to be exempt.)

(I) Loitering About "Off-Sale" Premises With Open Containers (647e PC)

(1) Any city or county may, by local ordinance
(2) Without violating the state's pre-emption on alcohol laws
(3) Provide the following regulation of open containers:
    (a) It is illegal to possess any open
        (i) bottle
        (ii) can or
        (iii) other receptacle

(b) That contains an alcoholic beverage
(c) While on
 (i) the premises of a retail package off-sale store,
 (ii) a posted parking lot of that store, or
 (iii) an adjacent public sidewalk
(d) When such premises is "posted" with clearly visible notices that the ordinance has been adopted and is in effect.
(e) This shall not apply to a private residential parking lot which is immediately adjacent to the posted premises.

(J) Restriction on Metallic Balloons (653.1 PC)

(1) No person or group shall release, outdoors, balloons made of electrically conductive material
(2) And filled with a gas lighter than air
(3) As part of a public or civic event, promotional activity or product advertisement.

Exceptions:

(1) Manned hot air balloons.
(2) Government or scientific research projects.

(K) Transfer of Drug Paraphernalia (11014.5 & 11364.7 H & S)

It is illegal to deliver, furnish, possess with intent to deliver or transfer drug paraphernalia when one should know reasonably that it is to be used in connection with illegal drugs or narcotics.

(L) Displaying of Drug Paraphernalia (11364.5 H & S)

(1) It is illegal for a place of business to display drug paraphernalia
(2) Unless maintained in a separate room or enclosure
(3) From which persons under 18, unaccompanied by parents, are excluded. This is a civil offense and punishment is revocation of license.

(M) Interfering With CB Broadcast (653t PC)

(1) Interfering with a "CB" broadcast
(2) That is an emergency in nature
(3) Is a "wobbler."

(N) Intercepting Cellular Radio Communications (632.5 PC)

(1) Who, with malicious intent and without consent of all parties to communications,
(2) Intercepts a cellular radio telephone communication.

Exceptions: Utility companies and law enforcement personnel when it was legal before this law. This includes any person who is recording to obtain evidence in a criminal action (admissible in court).

Cellular Radio Telephone: A wireless telephone authorized by the FCC to operate in a reserved frequency band width.

(O) Interception of Cordless Telephone Communications (632.6 PC)

Same as 632.5 PC except that it applies to cordless phones rather than cellular radio phones.

(P) Resale of Tickets at Excess Prices (346 PC)

(1) Who, without permission of the owner or operator of the property where the entertainment is being held
(2) Sells an admission ticket on the grounds or property where the event is being held
(3) At a price over that printed or endorsed on the ticket
(4) When the ticket was obtained for the purpose of resale
(5) Is guilty of a misdemeanor.

This offense is often referred to as "Scalping." If it is offered at a person's place of employment, there is no violation. If it is sold in front of the event at a discount, there is no violation.

(Q) Abandoned Refrigerators, Deep Freeze Lockers, etc. (402b PC) (Misd.)

Section A:

(1) Any person who discards, abandons or leaves
(2) A refrigerator, icebox or deep freeze locker
(3) Having a capacity of one and one half cubic feet or more
(4) In any place accessible to children
(5) And which has not had the door, hinges or latch removed.

Section B:

(1) Any owner, lessee or manager
(2) Who knowingly permits such appliances to remain on premises under his control
(3) Without having door or hinges and latch mechanism removed.

Section C:

(1) Guilt of a violation of this section shall not in itself render one guilty of manslaughter, battery, or other crime
(2) If a person suffers death or injury
(3) From entrapment in one of the above appliances.

Section D:
Does not apply to a vendor or seller of appliances
(1) Who keeps or stores them for sale purposes
(2) If the vendor takes reasonable precautions to secure the door
(3) So as to prevent entrance by children small enough to enter it.

(R) Requirements for Latches on Refrigerator Doors (Misd.) (402c PC)
(1) Any person who sells
(2) A new refrigerator, icebox, or deep freezer
(3) Having a capacity of 2 cubic feet or more
(4) Not equipped with a lock that can be opened from the inside
(5) By exerting 15 pounds of force against the latch edge of the closed door.

(S) Legal Requirements of Rooming Managers to Report Fires (13006.5 H & S) (Misd.)
(1) Persons in charge of hotels, motels, or rooming houses
(2) Who fail to report any fire
(3) That occurs in any place under their care and control.

(T) False Telegraph or Telephone Messages (474 PC) (Wobbler)
(1) Every person who knowingly and willfully sends by telegraph or telephone
(2) To any person
(3) A false or forged message
(4) Purporting to be from a telegraph or telephone office, or
(5) Any other person knowingly and willfully delivering such message.

(U) Using Another Person's Name in Writing to a Newspaper (Misd.) (538a PC)
(1) Every person who signs any letter addressed to a newspaper
(2) With the name of a person other than himself
(3) And sends such letter to the newspaper
(4) Or causes it to be sent
(5) With the intent of misleading the newspaper into believing that it was sent by the person whose name is on the letter.

(V) Fighting Animals, Dogs (597.5 PC)
Section A:
(1) Owning, possessing or keeping any dog
(2) With the intent that the dog will engage in an exhibition of fighting with another dog.
Section B:
(1) Causing one dog to fight another
(2) For the purpose of amusement or gain.
Section C:
(1) Permitting any violation of this law to occur
(2) On a premises under his charge or control.
Section D:
(1) Anyone who is knowingly present at a location
(2) Where preparations are being made for a dog fight, or dogs are actually fighting.

Punishment:
All sections classed as felonies. Also allows the seizure of dogs and paraphernalia.

(W) Fighting Cocks
(310 PC): Minor under 16 attending a cockfight; Allowing a minor under 16 to attend a cockfight.
(597b PC): Promoting cockfights or other animal fights.
(597c PC): Training fighting cocks or other animals for exhibitions.
(597d PC): Allows peace officers to enter place of cockfights without a warrant.
(597i PC): Manufacture, sale or possession of equipment for fighting birds.
(597j PC): Ownership or possession of fighting cock with intent that it be used for fighting.

(X) Some Other Codes Where Important Laws May Be Located
The State of California has over 30 different codes. Some containing laws important to Peace officers are:

Agricultural Code:
Laws pertaining to the theft of certain plants.
Business & Professions Code:
Alcoholic beverage control laws, licensing laws, laws on prescription drugs.
Education Code:
Laws on criminal acts when committed on school property.
Fish & Game Code:
Hunting and fishing laws.
Government Code:
Laws controlling police departments and officer rights.

Harbor & Navigation Code:
Traffic laws for boats and vessels on lakes and in harbors.
Health & Safety Code:
Laws on narcotics and controlled substances; duties of the coroner, and dead bodies.
Military & Veterans Code:
Laws on the illegal wearing of military uniforms, military awards and badges; laws dealing with U.S. and state flags.
Vehicle Code:
Traffic laws.
Welfare & Institutions Code:
Laws on juvenile control and detention, and laws dealing with the mentally ill or emotionally disturbed.

(XI) Weapons of Mass Destruction (11418 PC)
(1) Any person who, without lawful authority
(2) Possesses develops, acquires (etc.)
(3) Any weapon of mass destruction
(4) Is guilty of a felony (4, 8, 12 years),
or
    (1) Any person who uses a weapon of mass destruction
    (2) Against another person
    (3) That may cause widespread illness, damage or injury to humans
    (4) Is guilty of a felony (life).
    (5) If injury is to water or food supply (3, 4 or 6 years).
    (6) If injury is against animals, crops or seed (4, 8 or 12 years).
    (7) If injury is to a public natural resource e.g. lake, park, beach (3, 4 or 6 years).
    (8) Creating new pathogens for use as a weapon of mass destruction (4, 8 or 12 years).
    (9) Nothing in this section shall prevent a greater punishment under other laws. (e.g. first degree murder)

(XII) Facsimile Weapons of Mass Destruction (11418.1 PC)
(1) Any person who gives, mails, sends or causes to be sent
(2) Any false or facsimile weapon of mass destruction
(3) With the intent to cause fear
(4) And it does in fact cause fear. (Wobbler)

(XIII) Definition of Weapons of Mass Destruction (11417 PC)
Weapons of mass destruction include:
(1) Chemical warfare agent
(2) Biological warfare agents
(3) Nuclear agents
(4) Radiological agents
(5) Industrial agents used as a weapon
(6) List of examples in 11417(2) PC.

Chapter XIII Case Citations

Study Questions for Chapter XIII

(1) "Sam the Scalp" buys several tickets to a Broadway musical debut to be held in San Francisco. Three days before the show, he goes to several bars in San Jose and offers the tickets at twice what he paid for them. He is guilty of 346 PC. T or F

(2) Fred Farkle buys a new refrigerator because his old one stopped working. The old one had a capacity of one and a half cubic feet. Fred dumped it in a vacant lot without removing the door. A neighbor saw him do it and reported it to the police, along with Fred's license number and description. If you investigated this case and found the report to be true, you could obtain a complaint for 402b PC from the D.A. T or F

(3) Arnold Aardvark owns an appliance store. He imported a new 2 cubic foot freezer and put it on sale. Kitty Krump bought one and took it home. Her husband, who is a scientist, tested the door on the freezer and found that it took 15 pounds of pressure to open the door from the inside. This is a violation of 402b PC. T or F

(4) Betsey Bloominheimer got mad at Clyde Crashcup and scratched the paint on his new car. She is guilty of the crime called ____________________________________

(5) Mervin Messup is mad at Franny Farkle so he sends her a telegram, supposedly from a relative back east, stating that her mother has died. Mervin is guilty of a wobbler. T or F

(6) Herbert Honebone sends a letter to the editor of a local newspaper and signs the letter with the name Cecil Coffinstopper. Herb is guilty of a misdemeanor. T or F

(7) Trespassing, 602.5 PC, covers only non-commercial dwelling houses. T or F

(8) Under 630 PC, the legislature stated that their purpose was to place greater restraint on the use of listening devices by law enforcement agencies. T or F

(9) Wiretapping, as listed under 631(b) PC, does not apply to a state or local correctional facility. T or F

(10) The only time wiretapping evidence is admissible in court under 631(c) PC is when it is to be used to prosecute a case involving the wiretapping. T or F

(11) It is all right to tape record a legislative, executive, judicial or administrative proceeding that is open to the public. T or F

(12) Sections 632 and 633 do not restrict the eavesdropping activities of law enforcement personnel that were permissible before these laws were enacted. T or F

(13) Huston Hardrock phones Casper Milktoast and threatens him with a felony involving "violence against the person." Casper records the conversation. Under 633.5 PC, he is allowed to do this and can even use it as evidence in court. T or F

(14) Trespassing for the purpose of eavesdropping or recording conversations is a felony. T or F

(15) It is a felony to manufacture or sell eavesdropping devices, except to _____________

(16) It is a felony to eavesdrop on the conversation of persons in physical custody of a peace officer and their attorneys. This also includes their ________________________ or ________________________.

(17) Herbert Honebone's mother, Harriet Honebone, signs for a telegram that is addressed to her son. Because she is curious about the contents, she opens it and reads it. She did this without her son's permission. She is guilty of a felony. T or F

(18) Under 647(a) PC, to be guilty, a person must actually engage in some form of lewd act. T or F

(19) Under 647(b) PC, to be guilty of prostitution, a woman must actually engage in a lewd act in return for money, and not just agree to perform such an act. T or F

(20) A woman who takes $50 to perform a sex act with a donkey at a private party is not only guilty of bestiality, but of prostitution as well. T or F

(21) A pimp, as listed in 266h PC, can be described as a person who:

(A) ____procures women for a house of prostitution.

(B) ____has intercourse with a prostitute

(C) ____derives support from a prostitute.

(D) ____lives in a house of prostitution.

(22) A panderer, as listed in 266i PC, can be described as a person who:

(A) ____procures women for a house of prostitution.

(B) ____has intercourse with a prostitute

(C) ____derives support from a prostitute.

(D) ____lives in a house of prostitution.

(23) Willy Willful goes into a private apartment building and "panhandles" for money. He is guilty of____

(24) Section 647(f) PC is referred to as "Drunk in Public." However, it also includes being under the influence of drugs. T or F

(25) An inebriate is:

(A) ____a sex offender (B) ____an intoxicated person

(C) ____a mentally ill person (D) ____none of these

(26) A person who is arrested by a peace officer for being "Drunk in Public" only shall be placed in civil protective custody if at all possible. T or F

(27) Persons who are arrested for drunk charges shall be taken to a facility for the treatment and evaluation of inebriates. They can be kept there for a maximum of _______ hours.

(28) Facilities for the treatment and evaluation of inebriates are described in Section 5170 of the____________________and ________________ code.

(29) Name three conditions under which an intoxicated person shall not be taken to a facility for treatment and evaluation of inebriates:

(a) ____

(b) ____

(c) ____

(30) The Trespassing section of 647 PC requires that the trespassing be done when? ______
____

(31) The Penal Code section for Disorderly Conduct is ____________ PC.

(32) "Box Car Bernie" doesn't have a place to sleep, and it is a cold night. He sneaks into the public library before it closes and hides out. When the library closes, he goes to sleep on a couch. This is not a violation of 647(e) because the building is not a private building. T or F

(33) Persons convicted of prostitution with prior convictions for the same offense must serve jail time and cannot be given probation or parole until at least __________ days have been served.

(34) It is illegal to tattoo any person under the age of ____________.

(35) Larry Lacksey works in a gas station. He installs a two-way mirror between the women's rest room and the storeroom. In order for the law to be violated, he must be observed looking at someone through the mirror. T or F

(36) The major narcotic laws are found in the ____________ and ____________ Code.

(37) The Juvenile Control Laws are found in the ____________ and __________ Code.

(38) The Alcoholic Beverage Control Laws are found in the ________ and _______ Code.

CHAPTER XIV

CONTROL OF DEADLY WEAPONS

The Deadly Weapons Control Law

The Deadly Weapons Control Law was originally passed as the Deadly Weapons Control Act in 1923. It is part of the California Penal Code starting with section 16000, where many code numbers were changed effective January 2012, as part of the Deadly Weapons Recodification Act of 2010.

There is often some confusion about weapons laws and the Second Amendment of the U.S. Constitution. The Second Amendment reads:

A well-regulated militia being necessary to the security of a free State, the right of the people to keep and bear arms shall not be infringed.

There has long been a controversy over the meaning of the Second Amendment of the U.S. Constitution. One viewpoint is that it gives each citizen the right to own and bear arms. The other side feels that the amendment gives the people that right collectively. That it allows each state to maintain an armed militia (or National Guard) in United States *v.* Miller, 307 United States 174, the Supreme Court supported the latter decision by ruling that a sawed off shotgun had no reasonable relation to the preservation of a well-regulated militia and that the possession of such a weapon was not within the meaning of that Amendment.

In Farmer *v.* Higgins, the 11th Federal District Court of Appeals ruled that the Second Amendment did not give individuals the right to possess guns banned by the government.

In 2001, the 5th Federal District Court of Appeals, which covers Louisiana, Texas and Mississippi, took an opposing view when it stated that the Second Amendment right applied to individuals.

In the latter part of 2002 the 9th Federal District Court of Appeals (covering nine western states, including California) ruled in the opposite direction by stating that the right is collective and not individual.

When two courts disagree on a case it is resolved by taking it to the next highest court. In this case it would be the U.S. Supreme Court, the "Court of Last Resort."

In the meantime officers in California should follow the 9th District ruling. John Marshall, fourth Chief Justice of the U.S. Supreme Court, often referred to as the "Father of U.S. Constitutional Law," was once asked what the Constitution meant. His answer was "it means whatever the Supreme Court says it means."

Code Sections Used in This Chapter

In this chapter, only code sections that are applicable to peace officers working on patrol duty have been selected. Administrative or dealer sections have been omitted where possible.

Definitions of Words and Phrases

In order that students may gain a deeper understanding of this chapter, definitions of words and phrases used will first be given.

Air Gauge Knife:
An air gauge that has concealed within it a pointed metal shaft which is exposed by a gravity lock or mechanical action, designed for stabbing.

Belt Buckle Knife:
A knife which has been made an internal part of a belt buckle, and has a length of at least $2^1/_2$".

Ballistic Knife:
A knife-like blade projected by any means.

Billy:
A policeman's club or baton. From the 15th century word "billet" meaning a thick piece of wood. In the 18th century, the term "billy" was used for a wooden stick that was part of the British textile industry. In 1795, it became a slang term for a short iron crowbar used by burglars.

Blackjack:
A club of woven leather containing lead shot in the end and a spring in the handle. Usually black.

Caliber:
A measurement for weapons and ammunition. It is the diameter in 100ths of an inch. .50 caliber would be half an inch in diameter.

Camouflaging Firearm Container:
A container that allows the firing of an enclosed firearm by external controls while the firearm is in the container.

Cane Gun:
A firearm mounted or enclosed in a stick, staff, rod, crutch or such device, designed to be or capable of being used as an aid in walking, if firearm may be fired while mounted or enclosed therein.

Cane Sword:
A cane, swagger stick, stick, staff, rod, pole, umbrella or similar device, having within it a concealed blade that may be used as a sword or stiletto.

Dirk or Dagger:
A knife or other instrument, with or without a hand guard, capable of ready use as a stabbing weapon that may inflict great bodily injury or death.

Felon:
A person convicted of a felony regardless of whether he served a term of imprisonment or was granted probation.

Fire Bomb:
Any breakable container which contains a flammable liquid with a flash point of 150° F or less and has a wick or similar device capable of being ignited, other than a device which is commercially manufactured primarily for the purpose of illumination.

Fixed Ammunition:
A bullet in which the projectile is attached to the cartridge and has its own primer and propellant.

Flechette Dart:
A dart capable of being fired from a firearm, measuring approximately one inch in length, with tail fins which take up $^5/_{16}$" of the body.

Leaded Cane:
Any rod, pole or similar device unnaturally weighted with lead.

Lipstick Case Knife:
A knife enclosed within and made an integral part of a lipstick case.

Machine Gun:
Any weapon which shoots or is designed to shoot, automatically, more than one shot without manual reloading, by a single function of the trigger. Also includes any frame or receiver which can only be used with such weapon. (Or BATF defined machine gun)

Metal Knuckles:
Any device made wholly or partially of metal, worn for purposes of offense or defense, in or on the hand, and which protects the wearer's hand while striking a blow, or increases the force of impact from the blow or injury to the individual receiving the blow. The metal contained in the device may help support the hand or fist, provide a shield to protect it, or consist of projections or studs to contact the person receiving the blow.

Multiburst Trigger Activator:

A device designed or re-designed to be attached to a semiautomatic firearm which allows the firearm to discharge two or more shots in a burst by activating the device.

Nunchaku ("Chucks"):

An instrument consisting of two or more sticks, clubs, bars or rods to be used as handles, connected by a rope, cord, wire or chain, in the design of a weapon used in connection with the practice of a system of self-defense such as karate.

Pistol, Revolver or Firearm Capable of Being Concealed (16530 PC)

(A) Basic Definition: Any device
  (1) designed to be used as a weapon
  (2) from which a projectile is expelled by force of an explosion or other form of combustion
  (3) and whose barrel is less than 16 inches in length.

(B) Any device
  (1) with a barrel of 16 inches or more
  (2) designed to be interchanged with a barrel less than 16 inches in length.

(C) Nothing shall prevent a pistol, revolver or firearm capable of being concealed upon the person from also being classed as a short-barreled rifle or shotgun.

For the purposes of this law, the term "firearm," "major component" and "security Exemplar" have the same meaning as those terms defined in section 922 Title 18 United States Code.

Razor:

Also called a "straight razor" or a "barber's razor" sharpened with a leather strap. The blade folds out of the handle. Exceedingly sharp.

Rifle:

A weapon that is designed or re-designed to be fired from the shoulder. The projectile is fired through the energy of an explosive in a fixed cartridge. It will fire only one bullet through a rifled bore for each single pull of the trigger.

Sandbag:

Any cloth container filled with sand. The most common is a man's sock filled with sand. It is used as a club for committing robbery.

Sandclub:

Similar to a large blackjack. It is made of leather and filled with sand. It can easily knock a person out without causing a break or laceration in the scalp.

Short Barreled Rifle ("Sawed-Off Rifle"):

(1) An original or modified rifle having a barrel length of less than 16," or
(2) An overall length of less than 26," or
(3) Any device that can be assembled to fit the description when under control of one person.

Short Barreled Shotgun ("Sawed-Off Shotgun"):

(1) An original or modified firearm designed to fire a fixed shotgun shell
(2) Having a barrel length of less than 18," or
(3) With an overall length of less than 26," or
(4) Any device that can be assembled to fit the description when under control of one person.

Shotgun:

A long-barreled gun having a smooth bore with a length greater than 18" or an overall length greater than 26," which uses shotgun shells containing either single or numerous projectiles.

Shobi-Zue:

A staff, crutch, stick, rod or pole concealing a knife blade within it which may be exposed by a flip of the wrist or mechanical action.

Shuriken (Star):

An instrument without handles consisting of a metal plate with three or more radiating points and one or more sharp edges in the shape of a polygon, trefoil, cross, star, diamond or other geometric shape, designed to be used as a throwing weapon.

Silencer:

Any device attached to a firearm to reduce the noise of that firearm. (17210 PC)

Slungshot:

A small mass of metal or stone fixed on a flexible handle, strap or the like.

Tear Gas:

Any liquid, gaseous, or solid substance intended to produce temporary physical discomfort or permanent injury through being vaporized or otherwise dispersed in the air, but does not apply to, and shall not include any substance registered as an economic poison (12751 Agricultural Code), provided that such substance is not intended to produce discomfort or injury to human beings.

Unconventional Firearm:

A firearm that does not have a rifle bore. A barrel of less than 18" or an overall weapon length of less than 26."

Undetectable Firearm:

Either of the following:

(1) When by removal of grips, stocks and magazines, it is not detectable as the "security exemplar" by walk-through metal detectors calibrated and operated to detect the "security exemplar."

(2) When subjected to inspection by the type of X-ray machines commonly used at airports, does not generate an image that accurately depicts the shape of the component. Barium sulfate or other compounds may be used in the fabrication of the component.

Undetectable Knife (Misd.) (20810 PC):

(1) Who commercially manufactures or imports into this state

(2) Any undetectable knife.

Definition: Any knife or other instrument, with or without a hand guard, that is capable of ready use as a stabbing weapon and that may inflict great bodily injury or death, manufactured to be used as a weapon, and which is not detectable by a metal detector set at standard calibration.

Wallet Gun:

Any firearm mounted or enclosed in a case resembling a wallet, designed to or capable of being carried in a pocket or purse, if such firearm may be fired while mounted or enclosed in such case.

Writing Pen Knife:

A writing pen having concealed in it a pointed metallic shaft to be used as a stabbing instrument. The knife is exposed by removing the cap, and is extended by a gravity lock or mechanical action.

Zip Gun:

Non-commercially made weapon that fires a projectile by the force of explosion or combustion from a barrel taped or wired to a handle or frame.

Exceptions to Law (22215 PC)

Nothing in this chapter prohibits police officers, special police officers, peace officers, or law enforcement officers from carrying a wooden club, baton or any equipment authorized for the enforcement of law or ordinance in any city or county.

Briefing of Laws

In this chapter, an effort will be made to brief the elements of various weapons laws. In order to clarify a statute, many laws will use a considerable number of different words to describe the same or similar act. For example, a law might state that it is illegal to manufacture, import, keep for sale, expose for sale or to give, lend or possess certain weapons. In order to provide a briefing of such laws, this book will use the word "possess" since any person doing any of the other acts will also possess the weapon.

Underlining of Key Words and Phrases

Key words and phrases in the various laws in this chapter will be underlined. These will help students to more easily grasp the substance of each law and understand its vital elements.

Deadly Weapons Control Law Sections

(A) Possession of "Short Barreled Shotgun or Rifle" (33210 PC)

It is illegal to manufacture or possess a "short barreled shotgun" or a "short barreled rifle" in the state of California.

(B) Possession of Club or Baton by Security Guard (22295 PC)

Uniformed, regularly employed security guards for any lawful business may possess wooden clubs or batons when:

(1) They are on duty.

(2) They have satisfactorily completed a POST course in their use.

(C) Unlawful Possession and Concealment of Weapons (16590 PC)

(1) It is illegal to possess any of the following:

- Air gauge knife
- Ballistic knife
- Belt buckle knife
- Billy
- Blackjack or sap
- Bullet containing explosives
- Cane gun
- Cane sword
- Camouflaged firearm or container
- Disguised firearm
- Flechette dart
- Large capacity magazine (accepts more than 10 rounds)
- Leaded cane
- Lipstick case knife

- Metal knuckles
- Metal replica hand grenade
- Military practice hand grenade
- Multiburst trigger activator
- Nunchaku
- S & P
- Sandbag or sandclub
- Shobi-zue
- Short barreled shotgun (rifle)
- Shuriken
- Slungshot
- Unconventional pistol
- Undetectable firearm
- Wallet gun
- Writing pen knife
- Zip gun.

(2) It is illegal to carry concealed on the person any of the following:
  (a) explosives other than fixed ammunition.
  (b) a dirk or dagger (Unless openly carried in a sheath from the waist).

Exceptions:

(1) Possession of a nunchaku on the premises of a licensed school that teaches self defense.
(2) Peace officers and military personnel may possess short barreled guns when on duty and when authorized by their agency.
(3) Those holding permits issued by the Dept. of Justice may possess short barreled guns.
(4) Large capacity magazines do not include 22 caliber ammunition-feeding devices.
(5) Shotgun tracer ammunition.
(6) Antique firearms manufactured before 1899.

A taser or similar electrical charge weapon does not come under the heading of an "unrecognizable firearm" as listed under section 24510 PC. It is, however, restricted by the regulations of the Treasury Department. (Registration)

(D) Advertising Illegal Weapons (17505 PC)

(1) Advertising in any publication or on any billboard
(2) Any of the weapons listed in sections 16590, 32625, 30600, 18740, 30315, 30320, 20110 or 33410, or armor-penetrating ammunition
(3) Is a misdemeanor.

(E) Persons Forbidden to Possess Firearms (29800 PC and 29805 PC)

(1) Felons (also see 22610 PC – restriction on possession of stun guns).
(2) Any person convicted of a violent offense listed in 29900 or 29905.
(3) Persons convicted of offenses under 23515(a), (b) or (d) PC (Assault with a firearm, shooting at an inhabited dwelling, exhibiting a firearm in the presence of a peace officer). Juveniles who are certified to adult court (707 W & I) and convicted of these same offenses are subject to this restriction.
(4) 273.5 PC inflicting injury on a spouse or significant other.
(5) Two or more convictions of 417 (a)(2) drawing a firearm in the presence of another.
(6) Any person who is subject to a temporary restraining or protective order (6218 FC) pursuant to 527.6, 527.8 or 528.85 CCP.
(7) When possession is a restriction of probation.
(8) Any person who is mentally unstable or is a danger to himself/herself because of a mental illness (decided by a court and includes those who are mentally incompetent to stand trial or found not guilty by reason of insanity).
(9) Persons addicted to a narcotic drug.

The following violations are generally a 10-year firearm possession ban:

(10) Persons convicted of misdemeanor violations (or have an outstanding warrant for: 71, 76, 136.1, 136.5, 140, 148d, 148.5(f), 171(b), (c) or (d), 186.28, 240, 241, 242, 243, 243.4, 243.5, 244.5, 245, 245.5, 246.3, 247, 273.5, 273.6, 417, 417.6, 422, 422.6, 626.9, 646.9, 830.95, 17500, 17510, 25100, 25135, 25200, 25300, 25800, 30315, 32625, 26100(b) or (d), 27510 of the Penal Code and 8100, 8101, 8103 W & I, and 871.5 or 1001.5 W & I (firearms related), theft of property if property taken is a firearm (490.2 PC), and various violations of 27590, involving sales and transfers of firearms.

These misdemeanors are mainly crimes involving threats, violence, deadly weapons and firearms.

Any person who has an outstanding warrant for a felony or any of the above-listed offenses is forbidden to possess a firearm.

Since peace officers need the right to possess firearms, they may petition the court only once for relief from the prohibition. Officers shall show, by a preponderance of evidence, that they will use firearms in a safe and lawful manner. Petitioners may not have any felony convictions and the court may order that they participate in counseling.

<u>Exceptions to 29800 PC:</u>

(1) The person found the firearm.
(2) The person took the firearm from another who was committing a crime against him or her.
(3) The person possessed the firearm no longer than was necessary to deliver it to a law enforcement agency under the following conditions:
 (a) the person gave the law enforcement agency prior notice of the transportation
 (b) the transportation was in accordance with 29850 PC.
(4) The defendant has the burden of proving, by a preponderance of evidence, that he or she comes within this exemption.

<u>Minors and Weapons Capable of Being Concealed (29610 PC)</u>

A minor (under 18) shall not possess a pistol, revolver, or other firearm capable of being concealed upon the person, or live ammunition except:

(1) When accompanied by a parent or legal guardian AND is engaged in (or in transit to or from) one of the legitimate activities listed in 29615(a) PC.
(2) When accompanied by a responsible adult (21 years) AND has written permission from a parent or legal guardian AND is engaged in one of the listed legal activities.
(3) When the minor is alone, AND is at least 16 years of age AND has written permission from either a parent or a legal guardian, AND is engaged in one of the listed legal activities.

(F) Commission of Street-Gang Crime While Armed (12021.5 PC)

<u>Section A:</u>

(1) Any person who, during the commission or attempted commission of any street-gang crime (described in 186.22 (a) & (b)),
(2) Carries a loaded or unloaded firearm (on person or in vehicle),
(3) Shall receive an additional one, two or three years in state prison.

<u>Section B:</u>

(1) Doing the above acts while carrying any of the following attachments:
 (a) detachable shotgun magazine
 (b) detachable pistol magazine
 (c) detachable magazine
 (d) belt feeding device
(2) An additional sentence of 2, 3, or 4 years.

(G) Committing a Felony While Armed — Added Sentence (12022 & 12022.5 PC)

If a person is armed with a firearm, a machine gun or an assault weapon, dangerous weapon, or is an accomplice to one who is so armed, during a felony, an enhancement of several years will be added to that person's sentence. If the offense is one of several listed narcotic offenses, the enhancement is increased.

<u>Armor-Piercing Ammunition and Bulletproof Vests (12022.2 PC)</u>

<u>Section A:</u>

(1) Committing or attempting to commit a felony
(2) While armed with a firearm
(3) And has in his or her immediate possession, armor-piercing ammunition for that firearm.

<u>Section B:</u>

(1) Committing or attempting to commit a violent offense (as described in 29905 PC)
(2) While wearing a bullet-proof vest.

(H) Firing From a Vehicle Causing Great Bodily Injury or Death (12022.55 PC)

(1) Any person who, with intent to inflict great bodily injury or death,
(2) Inflicts great bodily injury or death of a person
(3) As a result of discharging a firearm from a motor vehicle in the commission of a felony or attempted felony,
(4) Shall serve an additional term of 5, 6 or 10 years in state prison.

(I) Armed Criminal Action (25800 PC)

(1) Every person who carries a loaded firearm
(2) With the intent to commit a felony
(3) Is guilty of "Armed Criminal Action."

(J) Loaded Firearm Under 25800 (16840 PC)

(1) For purposes of 25800 PC
(2) A firearm shall be considered loaded

(3) Whenever both the firearm and the unexpended ammunition for that firearm
(4) Are in the immediate possession of the same person.

(K) Carrying a Concealed Weapon CCW (25400 PC)

(1) Carrying concealed
  (a) on one's person, or
  (b) in a vehicle under one's control, or
  (c) within any vehicle in which he or she is an occupant (person caused weapon to be carried concealed)
(2) Any pistol, revolver or firearm capable of being concealed,
(3) Without having a license to carry such firearm.

Punishment:

(1) A misdemeanor unless the person has been previously convicted of:
  (a) a crime against the person
  (b) a crime against property.
(2) A felony-misdemeanor if the prior conviction is for a narcotic or dangerous drug charge.
(3) A felony if the prior conviction is for:
  (a) a felony.
  (b) any crime made punishable by a provision listed in section 16580.
  (c) where the firearm is stolen and the possessor either knew or had reasonable cause to know that it was stolen.
  (d) where the person is an active participant in a criminal street gang (186.22 PC).
  (e) where the person is not in lawful possession of the firearm (25400(b) PC).
  (f) where the person is in a class prohibited from possessing or acquiring a firearm (29800 & 29900 PC; 8100, 8103 W & I).

Concealed, Loaded Firearm, Definition (25400 (6)(A) PC)

Both the pistol, revolver or other firearm capable of being concealed upon the person, and the unexpended ammunition capable of being discharged from the firearm, are either in the immediate possession of the person, or readily accessible to that person, or the pistol or revolver or other firearm capable of being concealed upon the person is loaded as defined in 16840 PC on Page 248.

(L) Firearms Carried in Holsters (25400(b) PC)

Firearms carried openly in belt holsters are not considered concealed.

(M) Special Exception to Carrying a Concealed Weapon (25600 PC)

(1) A violation of 25400 is justifiable when
(2) A person has initiated, and a judge has issued, a restraining order
(3) Against one who has posed a threat to his or her safety
(4) And the complainant has reasonable cause to believe that he or she is in grave danger because of those circumstances.

Exception: When the restraining order is reciprocal (under Division 10 of Section 6200 FC) and there is no factual finding of a threat to life or safety. It is not the intent of the legislature to restrict, limit or narrow the application of 25400 PC. The burden of proof for this exception is on the person carrying such weapon (e.g., 29800 PC).

(N) Where Citizens Can Legally Possess Firearms (25525 PC)

Section 25400 does not prohibit any citizen of the United States, over 18 years of age, from possessing a pistol or revolver or other firearm capable of being concealed, on his or her private property or place of business unless otherwise prohibited.

(O) Transporting Firearms in a Vehicle (25610 PC)

(1) Any person over 18 not prohibited from possessing firearms, (see 29800 & 29900 PC; 8100 & 8103 W & I)
(2) May transport a pistol or revolver or weapon capable of being concealed in a vehicle,
(3) When the firearm is:
  (a) locked in the vehicle trunk, or
  (b) in a locked container in the vehicle, other than the glove compartment, or
  (c) carried to or from the vehicle for a lawful purpose and in a locked container.

Locked Container: A secure container that is fully enclosed and locked by a padlock, key or combination lock or similar locking device. A locked container does not include the utility or glove compartment.

(P) Requirements for Securing Handgun Left in Unattended Vehicle (25140 PC)

(1) A person shall, when leaving a handgun in an unattended vehicle,
(2) Lock the handgun in the vehicle's trunk, or
(3) Lock the handgun in a locked container and place the container out of plain view, or

(4) Lock the handgun in a locked container that is permanently affixed to the vehicle's interior and not in plain view.
(5) Lock the handgun in a locked tool or utility box (permanently affixed to the bed of a pick-up truck).

Locking Handguns in the Trunk of a Car: The trunk must be a secure, separate trunk. The trunk should not be accessible by folding the rear seats to reach the trunk area.

Exception: Peace officer during circumstances requiring immediate aid or action within the course of his or her duties.

(Q) Exception to Law on Carrying Certain Weapons Without a License (29850 PC)

(25505) Transportation of unloaded firearm in locked container.

(25510) Part of a media production (movie, TV show).

(25515) A member of a club that collects or displays weapons, when going to or from meetings, and when in a locked container.

(25520) Going directly to/from a hunter safety class or sporting event that involves firearms.

(25525) Between possessor's residence and business and return.

(25530) Between possessor's residence or business and a gun repair shop.

—From where firearm purchased or received to home or business.

(25535) Going directly to or from a gun show or swap meet.

—A dealer is delivering a firearm for use in a media production.

(25540) Going directly to/from a licensed target range.

(25545) Going to a law enforcement agency to have gun licensed.

—Going to a law enforcement agency to apply for lawful gun transfer.

(25550) Going directly to/from a camping activity when the gun is to be used for personal protection, and the campground or park allows it.

(25555) Transportation of firearm in order to comply with specified provisions.

(25580) Authorized transportation of firearm that is curio or relic.

(25570) Person found or took the firearm from a person commiting a crime against them, and is taking it to a police agency when police have been given prior notice.

(25585) Transportation of a firearm for the purpose of obtaining an identification number or mark assigned for that firearm from the Department of Justice pursuant to 23910 PC.

(29830) Person who is prohibited from owning or possessing a firearm or ammunition, transfers firearm or ammunition to a licensed firearm dealer or ammunition vendor for storage for the duration of the prohibition (dealer must notify the Department of Justice).

Conditions of Transport:

(a) The firearm shall be unloaded.
(b) The firearm shall be kept in a locked container.
(c) Only reasonable deviations from the route are allowed.

(R) Persons Allowed to Carry Concealed Weapons (Briefed) (25605 PC)

—Peace officers.

(25615) Merchants who sell guns (only unloaded).

(25620) Members of the military when on duty.

(25625) Duly authorized military and civil organizations when authorized (i.e. parading and places of meeting).

(25630) Bank guards and messengers when transporting valuables and on duty.

(25635) Members of gun clubs, at range or when going to or coming from range.

(25640) Licensed hunters and fishermen, to, from and during sport.

(25645) Transport of firearms by common carrier in conformance of Federal law.

(25650) Retired Federal officers who hold a permit.

(S) Possession of Loaded Firearms (25850 PC)

(1) It is illegal for any person to carry a loaded firearm
    (a) on his person or
    (b) in a vehicle
(2) While in any public place or street of any:
    (a) incorporated city or
    (b) unincorporated territory when prohibited.
(3) In order to determine whether a firearm is loaded in enforcing this section, peace officers are authorized to examine any firearm carried by anyone on his person or in a vehicle while in any public place or on any public street in an incorporated city or prohibited area of an unincorporated city or prohibited area of an unincorporated territory. Refusing to allow peace officers to inspect firearms pursuant to provisions of this section constitutes probable cause for arrest for violation of this section.

(4) As used here, "prohibited area" means anyplace where it is unlawful to discharge a weapon.

Punishment for 25850 PC

Carrying a loaded firearm in violation of this section is punishable as follows:

(1) Where the person has previously been convicted of any felony, punishable as a felony.
(2) Where the firearm is stolen, punishable as a felony.
(3) Where the person is an active participant in a criminal street gang, punishable as a felony.
(4) Where the person is within a class of persons prohibited from possessing or acquiring a firearm (Chapter 2 section 29800 PC or Chapter 3 section 29900 PC; 8100 or 8103 W & I), punishable as a felony.
(5) Where the person has been convicted of a crime against a person or property, or of a narcotics or dangerous drug violation, punishable by up to one year imprisonment or up to $1,000 fine or both. (Wobbler)
(6) In all cases other than those specified, punishable as a misdemeanor.

Exceptions to 25850 PC

(a) Local, state and federal peace officers; those summoned to assist them; retired peace officers (need special certificate from department) (25900 PC).
(b) Guards or messengers of common carriers, and financial institutions, when on duty, carrying things of value within the state (26030a(i) PC).
(c) Members of the U.S. military, when on duty (26000 PC).
(d) Persons using a target range for practice (26005 PC).
(e) Shooting club members, while hunting on club property (26040 PC).
(f) Patrol Special Police Officers hired by local cities or counties under charter, and assigned certain beats within their jurisdiction. Must be between age 18 and 40 (e.g. City of San Francisco has such a charter appointment).
(g) Those possessing a valid permit (26025(a) PC).
(h) Licensed private investigators and private patrol operators and their patrol officers (26030a(4) PC), when on duty (7500 B & P Code).
(i) Animal control officers, and zookeepers employed by a governmental agency, in the course and scope of employment (26025(b) PC).
(j) Harbor Police Officers, (663.5 Harbors & Navigation Code, 26025(d) PC).
(k) Public agency uniformed security guards or night watch persons in the course and scope of employment (26030a(9) PC).
(l) Uniformed security guards, regularly employed, protecting the property of their employers (26030a(6) PC).
(m) Burglar alarm company employees, while responding to an alarm (26030a(8) PC).
(n) A business person or employee on the business property (26035 PC).
(o) Any person on private property or place of residence (includes temporary residences and campsites) (26055 PC).
(p) Any person, while hunting within an incorporated city, unless prohibited by local ordinance (most cities have such a law) (26040 PC).
(q) Any person who reasonably believes that his or her person or property, or that of another, is in immediate and grave danger and the weapon is necessary to preserve same (26045 PC). **Important definition:** "immediate" means the brief interval before and after a police agency, when reasonably possible, has been notified of the danger and before the arrival of assistance.
(r) Any person when making or attempting to make a lawful arrest.
(s) The same exception as in 25600 PC (those who have initiated a restraining order and are in fear of their safety).

Carrying a Loaded Firearm

Under the following conditions the punishment is increased to felony:

(1) The person carrying the firearm is a felon or has a prior violation of this chapter.
(2) Where the firearm is stolen and the possessor has reasonable cause to know.
(3) Where the possessor is an active participant in a "Criminal Street Gang" (186.22 PC)
(4) Where the possessor is not in "lawful possession" of the firearm.
(5) Where the possessor is prohibited from possession (Chapter 2 [29800 PC or Chapter 3 29900 PC], or 8100-8103 W & I).
(6) Where the possessor has been convicted of a crime against a person or property.
(7) Where the possessor has been convicted of a narcotics or dangerous drug violation.

A misdemeanor violation of this section does not apply to determine federal firearms eligibility under 922(g)(1) Title 18 U.S. Code.

Definition of a Loaded Firearm (16840 PC)

Firearms shall be deemed to be loaded for the purposes of this section when an unexpended cartridge or shell, consisting of a case holding a charge of powder and a bullet or shot, is in, or attached in any manner to, the firearm, including but not limited to: in the firing chamber, magazine, or clip thereof attached to the firearm; a muzzleloader firearm shall be deemed to be loaded when it is capped or primed and has a powder charge and ball or shot in the barrel or cylinder.

(T) Firearms in Vehicles, Driver Responsibility (26100 PC)

Misdemeanor for a driver or owner of a vehicle to knowingly permit another person to bring into the vehicle a loaded firearm in violation of 25850 PC or 2006 Fish & Game Code, or to permit any person to discharge a firearm from the vehicle.

(U) Criminal Storage of Firearm (25100 PC)

Section A: (Wobbler)

(1) Keeping a loaded firearm within any premise under one's control,
(2) And knowing or reasonably knowing that a child or a person prohibited from possessing a firearm/deadly weapon, pursuant to State or Federal law, is likely to gain access,
(3) Without permission of parent or guardian,
(4) And a child or person prohibited does obtain access to the firearm and causes death or great bodily injury to himself, herself, or another person,
(5) Is first degree criminal storage of a firearm.

Section B:

(1) If a child or person prohibited from possession
    (a) carries the firearm to a public place or in violation of 417 PC, or
    (b) causes injury (not great bodily injury),
(2) the adult is guilty of Criminal Storage of a Firearm in the Second Degree. (Misdemeanor)

Section C:

(1) Keeping a loaded firearm under one's control
(2) Knowing or reasonably knowing that a child is likely to gain access to the firearm
(3) is guilty of third degree criminal storage of a firearm.

Exceptions (25105 PC):

(1) Child obtains the firearm through illegal entry.
(2) Firearm is locked with a locking device.
(3) Firearm is in a location which a reasonable person would believe secure.
(4) Firearm is carried on the adult's person or within such close proximity that the possessor would be able to readily retrieve it.
(5) Firearm is equipped with a locking device.
(6) Owner is a peace officer or member of the military; child obtains firearm during or incidental to the performance of the owner's duty.
(7) Child obtains or discharges the firearm in a lawful act of self defense.
(8) Owner has no reasonable expectation based on objective facts and circumstances that a child is likely to be present on the premises.

Conditions of Arrest (25120 PC):

If the adult is the parent of the injured child, and the shooting is accidental, no arrest shall occur until at least seven days after the shooting and not during the time the child remains on life support equipment or is in a medically critical condition.

Definitions:

Locking Device: A device which, when applied to the firearm, renders the firearm inoperable.
Loaded Firearm: See page 245 (16840 PC).
Child: A person under the age of 18.
Great Bodily Injury: Significant or substantial physcal injuries.
Locked Container: See page 245 (16850 PC).

(V) Criminal Storage of Firearms (25200 PC)

Same as 25100 PC, except:

(1) The firearm is a pistol, revolver, or other firearm capable of being concealed upon the person, and
(2) The firearm may be loaded or unloaded.

(W) The Obtaining of a License to Carry a Concealed Weapon (26150, 26155 PC) (Briefed)

(1) Permits are obtained from
    (a) the sheriff of a county, or
    (b) the chief of a municipal department
(2) Upon proof that
    (a) applicant is of good moral character,
    (b) good cause exists for the issuance,
    (c) the applicant is a county resident, and

(d) the applicant has completed a gun training course.

(3) The permit is good for up to two years.

(4) Reasonable restrictions and conditions may be placed on the permit.

CCW licensees can carry throughout the state; however, in counties that issue a CCW license and have less than 200,000 residents, a licensee is only allowed to carry an exposed and loaded firearm capable of being concealed within that same county.

The fact that a weapon is temporarily disassembled is no exception to the requirement of obtaining a permit if the weapon can be easily assembled. (People *v*. Ekstrand, 28 Cal. App. 2d 1) The fact that a gun is in a state of disrepair does not make it an antique, and therefore, allow it to escape requirements for a license to carry it concealed. (People *v*. McCloskey, 76 Cal. App. 227)

(X) Sale or Transfer of Firearms

<u>License Required for the Sale or Transfer of Firearms (26500 PC)</u>

No person shall engage in the business of selling or otherwise transferring, or shall advertise for sale, or offer or expose for sale or transfer any firearm unless licensed pursuant to Article 1 Section 26700 and Article 2 Section 26800 of Chapter 2.

Section 26500 does not apply to sales, lease or transfer under these conditions:

(a) Sale, lease or transfer made by a person who obtains title by the following means:
  (1) Certain sales, leases or transfers (must dispose of the firearm within 60 days of receipt of the firearm (26515 PC)
    (a) bequest of a deceased person
    (b) as the beneficiary of a trust that includes a firearm
    (c) as a surviving spouse
    (d) as decedent's successor as part of probate

(b) Infrequent sales at gun shows or swap meets, but these sales must be brokered by a dealer when transferred (26520 PC)

(c) A person acting pursuant to operation of law or a court order (26505 PC)

(d) A person surrendering a firearm to authorities (18000 PC)

<u>Importation, Transportation or Bringing Firearms Into the State (27585 PC)</u>

Commencing January 1, 2015, a resident of this state shall not import into this state, bring into this state, or transport into this state, any firearm that the person purchased or otherwise obtained on or after January 1, 2015, from outside of this state unless the person first has that firearm delivered to a dealer in this state for delivery to that resident.

Dealers shall require a valid firearm safety certificate for purchases occurring after January 1, 2015 (31615 PC).

(Y) Mail Order Firearms (28465 PC)

(1) No person, unless a licensed dealer,

(2) Shall order a concealable firearm through mail

(3) Unless the dealer obtains a verification approval number from the California Department of Justice (CADO) Bureau of Firearms.

(Z) Tampering With Marks on Firearms (23900 PC) (Felony)

(1) Any person who has knowledge of any change, alteration, removal, or obliteration of:
  (a) name of maker
  (b) model
  (c) manufacturer's number
  (d) DOJ (Dept. of Justice) number or mark
  (e) or other mark of identification

(2) Or has in his or her possession such an altered firearm

(3) Without having first obtained permission from the Department of Justice.

<u>Exceptions (23925 PC):</u>

(1) Member of the military on duty.

(2) Peace officer on duty.

(3) Forensic lab technician (within scope of employment).

(4) A person who meets all of the following criteria:
  (a) the person is not prohibited from possessing firearms or ammunition pursuant to 29800 or 29900 PC or 8100 or 8103 W & I, AND
  (b) the person possesses the firearm no longer than is necessary to deliver the firearm to a law enforcement agency, AND
  (c) the person is transporting the firearm to a law enforcement agency, AND
  (d) the person has given prior notice to the law enforcement agency that he or she is transporting such a firearm, AND

(e) the firearm is transported in a locked container as defined in 16850 PC.

Presumptive Evidence (23920 PC)

Possession of such a weapon is presumptive evidence that the possessor altered it.

Alteration on a Firearm (23915 PC)

Identifying marks may be placed on firearms provided they do not affect existing identification.

(AA) Possession of Machine Guns (32625 PC)

(1) Anyone who sells, offers for sale, manufactures, possesses or knowingly transports any firearm classed as a machine gun,
(2) Except as authorized by this chapter, OR
(3) Anyone who intentionally converts a firearm into a machine-gun,
(4) Is guilty of a felony.

(AB) Unlawful Possession of Silencer (33410 PC) (Felony)

Any person, firm or corporation who within this state possesses any device of the kind commonly known as a silencer for firearms.

Exceptions:

Police officers, military personnel on duty and dealers who sell to them.

(AC) Report of Lost or Theft of Firearm Required (25250 PC)

(1) Commencing July 1, 2017, every person shall report the loss or theft of a firearm he or she owns or possesses
(2) To a local law enforcement agency in the jurisdiction in which the loss or theft occurred
(3) Within 5 days from the time it was known the loss or theft occurred,
(4) And a person shall not be required to report the loss or theft of an antique firearm described in Section 16170(c).
(5) Every person who has reported a firearm lost or stolen shall notify the local law enforcement agency within 5 days if the firearm is subsequently recovered by the person.

Exceptions to 25250 PC (25255 PC):

(1) A peace officer acting in the course of his or her official duties if the loss or theft was reported to their supervisor
(2) A U.S. Marshall, a member of the Armed Forces or National Guard while engaged in his or her official duties
\(3) Licensed firearms dealers who are covered by the regulations in Chapter 44 of Title 18 of the U.S. Code
(4) The loss or theft of firearms lost or stolen prior to July 1, 2017.

Roberti-Roos Assault Weapons Control Act of 1989 and the .50 Caliber BMG Regulation Act of 2004

Illegal Possession of Assault Weapons or .50 BMG Rifles

(A) Unauthorized Manufacture, Sales, etc. of Assault Weapon or .50 BMG Rifle (30600 PC)

Any person who, within this state, manufactures, causes to be manufactured, distributes, transports or imports into this state, keeps or offers for sale, or who gives or lends any assault weapon or .50 BMG rifle, is guilty of a felony (4, 6 or 8 years).

(B) Possession of Unauthorized Assault Weapon (30605 PC)

Any person who, within this state, possesses any assault weapon is guilty of a wobbler. First time offenders may only face a fine of $500 if certain conditions are met.

(C) Possession of an Unauthorized .50 BMG Rifle (30610 PC) — Guilty if a misdemeanor and fine up to $1,000.

30615 PC — Any person who commits another crime while violating this section shall receive an additional one-year sentence.

A gun owner who failed to register their assault weapon or .50 BMG rifle is guilty of an infraction. Category 1, 2 and 3 assault weapons and .50 BMG rifles had registration due dates established which have all passed. Generally, assault weapons and .50 BMG rifles that were legally possessed in the past before California law became stricter were required to be registered with the California DOJ Bureau of Firearms no matter how or where those weapons are being used (30900 PC). In addition to registration, assault weapons or .50 BMG rifles acquired at specified dates in the past require permits in order to use or keep them as outlined in 31000 PC below.

Exceptions to 30600 PC, 30605 PC and 30610 PC:

1. 30625 PC – Sale, purchase by law enforcement agencies
2. 30630 PC – Possession by peace officers for law enforcement purposes
3. 30635 PC – Possession during 90-day period after weapon specified as an assault weapon
4. 30640 PC – Possession of .50 BMG rifle before 1/1/2005.
5. 30645 PC – Manufacture by person who is issued a permit to sell to specified agencies
6. 30650 PC – Sale by person who is issued a permit to sell to specified agencies
7. 30655 PC – Executor or administrator of estate that includes a registered assault weapon or .50 BMG rifle
8. 30660 PC – Loans between persons lawfully permitted to possess with certain conditions met
9. 30665 PC – Nonresident coming into the state to attend a competitive match that uses assault weapons or is practicing at a licensed target range
10. 30670 PC – Importation by registered owner when it complies with conditions of use in 30945 PC
11. 30675 PC – A person who has been issued a permit by the DOJ and complies with conditions of use in 30945 PC
12. 30680 PC – A person who is eligible to possess an assault weapon, lawfully possessed it prior to 1/1/2017 and registered it prior to 7/1/2018.

(D) Legally Owned Assault Weapons – Permits Required (31000 PC)

(1) Any person who lawfully acquired an assault weapon before 6/1/1989 or a .50 BMG rifle before 1/1/2005 and wishes to use it in a manner different than specific in Section 30945 (see page 250) must obtain a permit from the DOJ.

(2) Any person who acquired an assault weapon between 6/1/1989 and 1/1/1990 and wishes to keep it after 1/1/1990 must obtain a permit from the DOJ.

(3) Any person who wishes to acquire an assault weapon after 1/1/1990 or a .50 BMG rifle acquired after 1/1/2005 must first obtain a permit from the DOJ.

(4) Beginning on 1/1/2014, no group entity (i.e. corporation) may be issued a permit to possess an assault weapon or .50 BMG rifle.

(E) Conditions For Those Who Have Legally Registered Assault Weapons or .50 BMG Rifles (30945 PC)

(1) It will be kept at the person's place of residence or business or other property owned by that person, or other property with the owner's permission, or

(2) On premises of a target range if the purpose of that range is to practice shooting at targets, or

(3) On the property of a licensed target range, or

(4) On the property of a licensed shooting club, or

(5) While attending any exhibition, display or educational project about firearms
   (a) which is sponsored by and conducted under the auspices of a nationally or state recognized entity that fosters proficiency in, or promotes education about firearms (e.g. NRA), or
   (b) is approved by a law enforcement agency.

(6) While on publicly owned land, if the possession and use of a firearm is specifically permitted by the managing agency of the land.

(7) While transporting weapon between places it shall be kept in a trunk or locked box (16850 and 25610 PC) — does not include glove compartment.

(8) No person who is legally prevented from owning other types of weapons (e.g. felons, minors, mentally ill) shall own or possess an assault weapon (30950 PC).

(9) Joint registration by family members residing in the same household is permitted (30955 PC).

(10) Weapons may be transported to and from a licensed dealer for servicing or repair.

(F) Transportation by Dealers (31050 PC)

Dealers may transport assault weapons to licensed gunsmiths in their employ, or with whom they have contracts for gun-smithing services.

(G) Assault Weapons That Have Been Declared Illegal (30510 PC)

(a) Rifles:

(1) All AK series, including, but not limited to, the models identified as follows:
   (a) Made in China AK, AKM, AKS, AK47,

AK47S, 56, 56S, 84S, and 86S.
   (b) Norinco 56, 56S, 84S, and 86S.
   (c) Poly Technologies AKS and AK47.
   (d) MAADI AK47 and ARM.
(2) UZI and Galil.
(3) Baretta AR-70.
(4) CETME Sporter.
(5) Colt AR-15 series.
(6) Daewoo K-1, K-2, Max 1, Max 2, AR 100, and ARIIOC.
(7) Fabrique nationale FAL, LAR, FNC, 308 Match, and Sporter.
(8) MAS 223.
(9) HK-91, HK-93, HK-94, HK-PSG-1.
(10) The following MAC types:
   (a) RPB Industries Inc. sM10 and sM11.
   (b) SWD Incorporated MII.
(11) SKS with detachable magazine.
(12) SIG AMT, PE-57, SG 550, SG 551.
(13) Springfield Armory BM59 and SAR-48.
(14) Sterling MK-6.
(15) Steyer AUG.
(16) Valmet M62S, M71S, and M78S.
(17) Armalite AR-180.
(18) Bushmaster Assault Rifle.
(19) Calico M-900.
(20) J & R ENG M-68.
(21) Weaver Arms Nighthawk.

(b) Pistols:

(1) UZI.
(2) Encom MP-9 and MP-45.
(3) The following MAC types:
   (a) RPB Industries Inc. sM10 and sM11.
   (b) SWD Incorporated M-11.
   (c) Advance Armament Inc. M-11.
   (d) Military Armament Corp. Ingram M-11.
(4) Intratec TEC-9.
(5) Sites Spectre.
(6) Sterling MK-7.
(7) Calico M-950.
(8) Bushmaster Pistol.

(c) Shotguns:

(1) Franchi SPAS 12 and LAW 12.
(2) Striker 12.
(3) The Street Sweeper type S/S Inc. SS/12.

(d) Future Firearms:

Any firearm declared by the court to later fit the description of an assault weapon, will come under this section.

(e) Other Assault Weapons (30515 PC):

Notwithstanding 30510 PC, "assault weapon," shall also mean any of the following:

(1) A semiautomatic, centerfire rifle that does not have a fixed magazine, but has any one of the following:
   (a) a pistol grip that protrudes conspicuously beneath the action of the weapon.
   (b) a thumbhole stock.
   (c) a folding or telescopic stock.
   (d) a grenade launcher or flare launcher.
   (e) a flash suppressor.
   (f) a forward pistol grip.
(2) A semiautomatic, centerfire rifle that has a fixed magazine with the capacity to accept more than 10 rounds.
(3) A semiautomatic, centerfire rifle that has an overall length of less than 30 inches.
(4) A semiautomatic pistol that does not have a fixed magazine and any one of the following:
   (a) a threaded barrel, capable of accepting a flash suppressor, forward hand grip, or silencer.
   (b) a second hand grip.
   (c) a shroud that is attached to, or partially or completely encircles, the barrel that allows the bearer to fire the weapon without burning his or her hand, except a slide that encloses the barrel.
   (d) the capacity to accept a detachable magazine at some location outside of the pistol grip.
(5) A semiautomatic pistol with a fixed magazine that has the capacity to accept more than 10 rounds.
(6) A semiautomatic shotgun that has both of the following:
   (a) a folding or telescoping stock.
   (b) a pistol grip that protrudes conspicuously beneath the action of the weapon, thumbhole stock, or vertical hand grip
(7) A semiautomatic shotgun that has the ability to accept a detachable magazine.
(8) Any shotgun with a revolving cylinder.

"Assault weapon" does not include any antique firearm.

Definitions:

The following definitions shall apply under this section:

(1) "Fixed Magazine" means an ammunition feeding device contained in or permanently attached to a firearm so that the device cannot be removed without disassembly of the firearm action.
(2) "Capacity to accept more than 10 rounds" shall mean capable of accommodating more

than 10 rounds, but shall not be construed to include a feeding device that has been permanently altered so that it cannot accommodate more than 10 rounds.
(3) "Antique firearm" means any firearm manufactured prior to January 1, 1899.

This section became operative January 1, 2000.

(H) Addition of New Weapons (30520 PC)

The Attorney General can petition a judge of the superior court in a county with a population of 1 million or more for a hearing in which it will be determined whether or not the new weapon should be added to the list.

(I) Broadcasting Information Regarding Registration of Assault Weapons (31105 PC)

(1) It is illegal for a police officer or dispatcher
(2) To broadcast over police radio that an individual is registered to possess an assault weapon or .50 BMG rifle.

Exceptions:

(1) Individual is or may be engaged in criminal activity.
(2) Police are responding to a crime in which the individual may gain access to the weapon.
(3) The victim or witness at that address may be holding the weapon as a means of self defense.

This section shall not prohibit a peace officer from broadcasting over police radio that an individual has not registered or obtained a permit to possess an assault weapon or .50 BMG rifle.

Transmission of assault weapon or .50 BMG rifle ownership status is permissable using computer systems legally accessible only to peace officers or authorized personnel.

Destructive Devices

(A) Destructive Devices (16460 PC)

Section A – "Destructive Device" Defined:

The term "destructive device," as used in this chapter, shall include any of the following:

(1) Any projectile containing any explosive or incendiary material or any other chemical substance, including, but not limited to, that which is commonly known as tracer or incendiary ammunition, except tracer ammunition manufactured for use in shotguns.
(2) Any bomb, grenade, explosive missile or similar device or any launching device therefore.
(3) Any weapon of a caliber greater than 0.60 inches which fires fixed ammunition, or any ammunition therefore, other than a shotgun or shotgun ammunition, antique rifle or antique cannon.
(4) Any rocket, rocket-propelled projectile, or similar device of a diameter greater than 0.60 inches, or any launching device thereof, and any rocket, rocket-propelled projectile, or similar device containing any explosive or incendiary material or any chemical substance, other than the propellant for such device, except such devices as are designed primarily for emergency or distress signaling purposes.
(5) Any breakable container which contains a flammable liquid with a flash point of 150° Fahrenheit or less and has a wick or similar device capable of being ignited, other than a device which is commercially manufactured primarily for the purpose of illumination.
(6) A sealed device containing CO2 or other chemically reactive substance assembled to cause an explosion by chemical reaction.

Section B – Explosives (16510 PC):

"Explosive," shall mean any explosive defined in Section 12000 H & S Code.

(B) Possession of Destructive Device (18710 PC)

Any person, firm, or corporation who, within this state, possesses any destructive device, other than fixed ammunition of a caliber greater than .60, except as provided by this chapter, is guilty of a public offense and upon conviction shall be punished by imprisonment in the county jail for a term not to exceed one year, or in state prison.

(C) Carrying or Placing A Destructive Device (18725 PC) (Felony)

Who willfully does any of the following:

(1) Carries any explosive or destructive device on any vessel, aircraft, car, or other vehicle that transports passengers for hire.
(2) Places or carries any explosive or destructive device, while on board any such vessel, aircraft, car or other vehicle, in any hand baggage, roll, or other container.
(3) Places any explosive or destructive device in any baggage which is later checked with any common carrier.

(D) Possession of Destructive Device in Specific Areas (18715 PC)

(1) Every person who recklessly or maliciously has in his possession
(2) Any destructive device or any explosive
(3) In, on or near any:
  (a) public street or highway,
  (b) theater, hall, school, college, church, hotel, other public building, or private habitation,
  (c) aircraft, railway passenger train, car, cable road or cable car, vessel engaged in carrying passengers for hire, or
  (d) any other public place ordinarily passed by human beings,
(4) Is guilty of a felony.

(E) Intent To Commit Murder With Destructive Device (18745 PC) (Felony)

Every person who explodes, ignites or attempts to explode or ignite any destructive device or explosive with intent to commit murder.

(F) Willful Use of Destructive Device to Cause Bodily Injury (18750 PC) (Felony)

Every person who willfully and maliciously explodes or ignites any destructive device or any explosive which causes mayhem or great bodily injury to any person.

Penalty: Probation or suspended sentence prohibited (18780 PC).

(G) Weapons of Mass Destruction (11418 PC)

(1) Any person who, without lawful authority, possesses, develops, manufactures, produces, acquires, or retains
(2) Any weapon of mass destruction
(3) Is guilty of a felony.
(4) If used against human beings, the punishment is life.

Definition:

"Weapon of Mass Destruction" includes chemical warfare agents, weaponized biological or biologic warfare agents, nuclear agents, radiological agents, the intentional release of industrial agents as a weapon, or an aircraft, vessel or vehicle which is used as a destructive weapon.

This code section is very long and lists numerous chemical agents as examples that are beyond the scope of normal memory, so they will not be included here. If an officer comes across what appears to be any of the above, he or she should contact the contamination unit of the fire department or the local public health officer and keep a safe distance from the suspected contaminants.

Armor and Ammunition

(A) Minors Possessing Ammunition (30300 PC)

Section A:

(1) Any person who sells ammunition or reloaded ammunition
(2) To a person, knowing him or her to be under 18 years of age

OR:

(1) Sells any ammunition or reloaded ammunition designed for use in a pistol, revolver, or other firearm capable of being concealed
(2) To a person, knowing him or her to be under 21 years of age.

(B) Illegal Possession of Ammunition

(1) It is illegal to possess ammunition or reloaded ammunition
(2) When prohibited by section 29800 or 29900 PC or section 8100 or 8103 W & I from possessing a firearm.

Exceptions:

(1) The person took the ammunition from someone who was committing a crime against him or her.
(2) The person was transporting the ammunition to a law enforcement agency.
(3) The person is prohibited from possessing ammunition solely because of 29800 PC.

Note: The defendant has the burden of proving, by a preponderance of evidence, that he or she is exempt.

(C) Ammunition Vendor Licensing and Sales (30312 PC)

Ammunition vendors as of January 1, 2018 must be licensed by the California DOJ to legally sell ammunition. In addition, all ammunition sales must be a face-to-face transaction with a licensed vendor. Ammunition could technically be sold on the internet, but a California licensed vendor must complete the transaction afterward.

Exceptions: Active sworn peace officers, sworn federal law enforcement officers and target facilities management holding a regulatory license (provided the ammunition is kept on the premises at all times) are exempted from both these requirements. Also exempted are persons who purchase or receive ammunition from an immediate family member.

(D) Transporting Ammunition Into California – Delivery to Licensed Vendor Required (30314 PC)

Beginning January 1, 2018, a resident of California must not bring into the state any ammunition that was purchased or obtained outside of California unless it is first shipped to a licensed ammunition vendor who will then deliver the ammo to the resident.

(E) Armor Penetrating Ammunition

(30315 PC) Possession of armor penetrating ammunition is a misdemeanor.

(30320 PC) Manufacture, importing, selling, or transporting armor penetrating ammunition is a felony.

(30330 PC) Exempts military, police officers, and laboratory personnel.

(16650 PC) Law refers to pistol ammunition, but may be pistol ammo that can be used in some rifles.

(30335 PC) Ammunition with no propellant and primer removed is exempted.

(F) Possession of Body Armor (31360 PC)

Section a:

(1) Any violent felon who purchases, owns, or possesses
(2) Body armor (942(e) CCR (California Code of Regulations)
(3) Is guilty of a felony.

Definition:

Violent Felony — Those offenses listed under 667.5(c) PC.

Section b:

(1) If a person's employment, livelihood, or safety is dependent upon possessing body armor,
(2) They may petition the Sheriff or Chief of Police for an exception to the prohibition.
(3) If granted, the petitioner must carry a certified copy of the exemption.

Tear Gas and Tear Gas Weapons

(A) Tear Gas Defined (17240 PC)

"Tear Gas" as used in this chapter shall apply to and include all liquid, gaseous, or solid substances intended to produce temporary physical discomfort or permanent injury through being vaporized or otherwise dispersed in the air, but does not apply to, and shall not include, any substance registered as an economic poison as provided in Ch. 2 (commencing with Sec. 12751) of Division 7 of the Agricultural Code provided that the substance is not intended to be used to produce discomfort or injury to human beings.

Tear Gas Weapon Defined (17250 PC)

"Tear gas weapon" shall apply to and include:

(1) Any shell, cartridge, or bomb capable of being discharged or exploded, when the discharge or explosion will cause or permit the release or emission of tear gases.
(2) Any revolvers, pistols, fountain pen guns, billies, or other form of device, portable or fixed, intended for the projection or release of tear gas except those regularly manufactured and sold for use with firearm ammunition.

(B) Who May Possess Tear Gas and Tear Gas Weapons (22820 PC) (Briefed)

The following persons are exempt from laws restricting the use of tear gas and tear gas weapons:

(1) Peace officers listed in 830(c), and Youth Authority personnel, when:
 (a) it is used officially in the discharge of their duties,
 (b) the person has completed the required POST course.
(2) Military personnel when authorized in their duties.
(3) Licensed private investigator and patrol operators and their uniformed employees, when:
 (a) it is used for defensive purposes during employment, and
 (b) the person has completed the required POST course.

(C) Possession By Non-Peace Officers (22810 PC)

(1) Non-peace officers may possess tear gas spray.
(2) A 16- or 17-year old, with parent's permission, can now possess such spray.
(3) A minor of 16 years can qualify with a signed affidavit from a parent or guardian. They assume complete civil liability.

Exceptions:

None of the following may possess tear gas spray:

(a) felons
(b) narcotic addicts

(c) minors (other than those specified above)
(d) persons convicted of misuse of tear gas
(e) persons convicted of "assault" crimes.

Rules:

(1) Only aerosol spray (not over $2^{1}/_{2}$ oz.) is permitted.
(2) It can only be used in self defense; any other use of tear gas is a crime.
(3) The spray must have a special warning label.
(4) Printed instructions must be provided at time of sale.

(D) Punishment for Possession of Tear Gas or Tear Gas Weapons (22900 PC) (Misdemeanor)

(1) Knowingly selling, offering for sale, possessing or transporting
(2) within the state of California
(3) Any tear gas or tear gas weapon
(4) Unless permitted by law.

Possession of Firearms by Minors

(A) Sale of BB Devices to a Minor (19910 PC)

(1) The sale to any minor under the age of 18
(2) Of any
    (a) BB or pellet gun
    (b) CO2 pressure gun
    (c) spring-action gun
    (d) spot marker gun
(3) Is a misdemeanor.

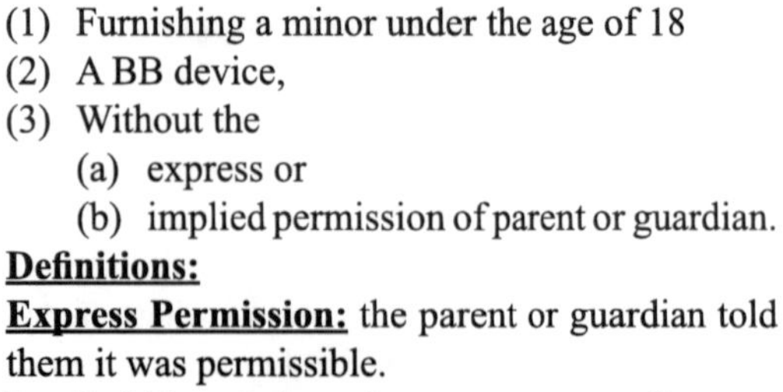

(B) Furnishing BB Device to Minors (19915 PC)

(1) Furnishing a minor under the age of 18
(2) A BB device,
(3) Without the
    (a) express or
    (b) implied permission of parent or guardian.

Definitions:

Express Permission: the parent or guardian told them it was permissible.

Implied Permission: the parent or guardian was aware that the minor had been given the weapon, but did not forbid the minor to have it. (Sometimes called tacit approval).

BB Device: any instrument which expels a metallic projectile, such as a BB or a pellet, through force of air pressure, CO2 pressure or spring action, or any spot marker gun.

(C) Possession of Ammunition (29650 PC)

A minor may not possess ammunition without written permission of a parent or guardian.

(D) Parent Liability for Children's Misuse of Firearms (1714.3 Civil Code)

When a person under the age of 18 injures another by the use of a firearm, the parents shall be civilly liable for up to $30,000 for a single injury, or $60,000 for injury to more than one person, if the parent permitted the minor to have the firearm, or left the firearm in a place accessible to the minor.

(E) Delivering Firearms to Individuals Under 21 (27510 PC)

(1) A gun dealer who supplies, sells, delivers or gives
(2) A firearm to any person who is under 21 years of age
(3) Is guilty of a felony.

Exceptions:

(1) Firearm that is not a handgun or a semiautomatic centerfire rifle to a:
    (a) person 18 years of age or older who holds a current hunting license
    (b) person who is an honorably discharged member of the U.S. Armed Forces, National Guard, Air National Guard, or the active reserve components of the U.S., and provides proper identification.
(2) Firearm that is not a handgun to a person 18 years of age or older who is:
    (a) an active peace officer, active federal officer or reserve peace officer authorized to carry a firearm in the course and scope of employment
    (b) an active member of the U.S. Armed Forces, National Guard, Air National Guard, or the active reserve components of the United States.

Blowguns

Definitions (16270 & 16280 PC)

"Blowgun" means a hollow tube designed and intended to be used as a tube through which a dart is propelled by force of the user's breath.

"Blowgun ammunition" means darts designed and intended for use in a blowgun.

Manufacture, Sale or Possession Prohibited (20010 PC)

Who knowingly manufactures, sells, offers for sale, possesses, or uses blowgun ammunition in this state is guilty of a misdemeanor.

Exceptions:

The following persons are exempt from this law:

(1) Zookeepers
(2) Animal Control officers
(3) Dept. of Fish & Game employees
(4) Humane officers
(5) Veterinary doctors

Deadly Weapons Laws from Other Penal Code Sections

(A) Bringing Weapons Into a Public Building (171b PC) (Wobbler)

(1) Every person who, without legal authority, brings or possesses
(2) In a courtroom or building designated as a courtroom or open public meeting
(3) Any of the following weapons:
  (a) any firearm
  (b) any weapon listed in 17235 PC, or any provision listed in section 16590,
  (c) a switchblade knife
  (d) a fixed blade knife with blade over 4"
  (e) tear gas weapons
  (f) tasers
  (g) stun guns (section 244.5)
  (h) BB, pellet or CO2 guns
  (i) spot marker or paint gun.

Exception:

Taking a lawful weapon to a gun show with a permit.

(B) Restricted Possession of Firearms in Sacramento (171e PC) (Wobbler)

It is illegal to possess a loaded firearm in

(a) the state capitol.
(b) any legislative office.
(c) office of the Governor (or other officer).
(d) legislative committee hearing room.
(e) the grounds of the state capitol between 10th & 15th Streets, and "L" & "N" Streets.

Exceptions:

(a) peace officers.
(b) persons summoned under posse comitatus.
(c) members of military forces on duty.
(d) those with valid permits to carry weapons.

(C) Restricted Possession of Firearms in Official Residences (171d PC) (Wobbler)

It is illegal to possess a loaded firearm in

(a) the Governor's residence, or grounds.
(b) the residence of a member of the legislature or the grounds of that residence.
(c) the residence of a constitutional officer or the grounds of that residence.

Exceptions:

(a) peace officers.
(b) persons summoned under posse comitatus.
(c) members of military forces, on duty.
(d) those with valid permits to carry weapons.
(e) family members or officials living at the residence.
(f) those given permission by officials living at the residence.

For the purpose of enforcing Section 171c or 171d, peace officers are authorized to examine any firearm carried by anyone on his person or in a vehicle while in any place or on the grounds of any place where possession of loaded firearms is prohibited by Section 171c or 171d. Refusing to allow peace officers to inspect firearms pursuant to provisions of this section constitutes probable cause for arrest for violation of Section 171c or 171d.

(D) Loaded Firearm Defined (171e PC)

A firearm shall be deemed loaded for the purposes of Sections 171c and 171d whenever both the firearm and unexpended ammunition capable of being discharged from such firearm are in the immediate possession of the same person.

(E) Switchblade Knives (21510 PC) (Briefed)

(1) Possession of:
  (a) a switchblade knife (snap blade knife)
  (b) a spring blade knife

(c) a gravity knife, or
(d) any similar type of knife (blade over 2")
(2) Released by:
(a) a mechanical device, (button or pressure on handle)
(b) a flip of the wrist,
(c) the weight of the blade
(3) When the blade is two or more inches long.
(4) When in a public place or place open to the public, or in driver/passenger part of car.

In Tijuana, they make a switch blade knife that is just a fraction of an inch under two inches so it complies with California law.

The definition of a switchblade knife now excludes a knife designed to open with one hand utilizing thumb pressure applied solely to the blade of the knife or a thumb stud attached to the blade.

(F) Gun Violence Restraining Order - GVRO (18100 PC)

A court may issue a gun violence restraining order prohibiting a named person from having in his or her custody or control any firearms or ammunition if the person poses a significant danger of causing personal injury to himself, herself, or another.

(G) GVRO Petition by Immediate Family Member, Employer, Coworker, Teacher or Law Enforcement Officer (18150 PC)

The law expands on 09/01/2020 from only law enforcement officers or immediate family members being allowed to petition the court for a GVRO, to also include an employer, coworker who has substantial and regular interactions with the person of concern, or school teacher. This is done "ex parte," which means the action is done without the subject's knowledge. An approved temporary restraining order covers a limited time while a formal hearing can be scheduled.

This law was put into place to prevent gun violence by allowing authorities to intervene when family, employers, teachers, etc., see "red flag" behavior.

Deadly Weapons Sections From Other Codes

(A) Welfare and Institutions Code Sections (Pertaining to Weapon Control)

8100 W & I

(a) A person shall not possess any firearms or deadly weapon if he or she has been admitted to a facility to receive inpatient treatment, and, in the opinion of the attending health professional, is a danger to self or others. Once the person is released from the inpatient facility, they are no longer subject to the prohibition.
(b) A person shall not possess any firearms or other deadly weapons for a period of five years if he or she communicates to a licensed psychotherapist a serious threat of physical violence against a reasonably identifiable victim or victims.

Upon receipt of the attending health professional's report by the local law enforcement agency, the Department of Justice shall notify, by certified mail, a person subject to this subdivision of the following:

(a) That he or she is prohibited from possessing, having custody or control over, receiving, or purchasing any firearm or other deadly weapon for a period of five years commencing from the date that the licensed psychotherapist reports to the local law enforcement agency the identity of the person making the communication.
(b) That he or she may petition a court, as provided in this subdivision, for an order permitting the person to own, possess, control, receive, or purchase a firearm.

8101 W & I

Any person who knowingly furnishes a deadly weapon to any person described in Section 8100 above is guilty of a wobbler. If the weapon furnished is a firearm, it is a felony.

8102 W & I

(1) Whenever the police take firearms or deadly weapons from persons because of their mental condition,
(2) And those persons are later released,
(3) The law enforcement agency will have 30 days in which to initiate a superior court hearing to determine whether the return of such weapons would cause danger to the owner or to another person.
(4) If the department fails to initiate the hearing, weapons shall be returned to their owners.

8103 W & I

(1) Any person found not guilty by reason of insanity
(2) For a serious crime (listed in the code), or
(3) Any act that poses serious threat of bodily injury

(4) Cannot possess any firearm or other deadly weapon.

(B) Possession of Both Drugs and Firearms (11370.1 H & S Code)

(1) Any person in possession of small amounts of cocaine, cocaine-based drugs, heroin, methamphetamine, or phencyclidine,
(2) AND possesses a loaded operable firearm,
(3) Is guilty of a felony. (2, 3 or 4 years)

(C) Possession of Firearm While Under the Influence of Drugs (11550 H & S Code)

(1) Any person under the influence of cocaine, cocaine-based drugs, heroin, methamphetamine or phencyclidine,
(2) While in immediate personal possession of a loaded, operable firearm,
(3) Is guilty of a wobbler. (Second offense: felony — 2, 3 or 4 years.)

(D) Dangerous Fireworks (12702 H & S Code) (Misdemeanor)

(1) Notwithstanding the provisions of 12700 H & S (possession & sale of fireworks illegally).
(2) Selling, giving, delivering "dangerous fireworks" (as described in 12505 et Seq. H & S). <u>Example:</u> firecrackers, cherry bombs
(3) To any person under the age of 18.

For a second offense, there is no probation or suspended sentence. Punishment for illegal possesion or sales of fireworks is greater as the weight of the fireworks increases, i.e. less than 25 lbs, 100 lbs., 5,000 lbs.

(E) Private Patrol Officers, Uniform When Armed (7582.26(i) B & P Code)

No private patrol operator or employee, required by law to be registered as a security guard, shall wear a baton or exposed firearm unless he or she is wearing a legally defined uniform.

(F) Private Patrol Officers, Wearing of Shoulder Patches (7582.27 B & P)

Any private patrol officer or employee authorized to wear a baton or exposed firearm, shall wear a patch that is visible at all times and reads "private security" and the name of the company.

(G) Possession of Loaded Rifle in Vehicle (2006 Fish and Game Code)

It is unlawful to possess a loaded rifle or shotgun in any vehicle or conveyance or its attachments which is standing on or along or is being driven on or along any public highway or other way open to the public. A rifle or shotgun shall be deemed to be loaded for the purposes of this section when there is an unexpended cartridge or shell in the firing chamber but not when the only cartridges or shells are in the magazine.

The provisions of this section shall not apply to peace officers or members of the armed forces of this state or the United States, while on duty or going to or returning from duty.

Chapter XIV Case Citations

Study Questions for Chapter XIV

(1) The Deadly Weapons Control Law is part of the California Penal Code. T or F

(2) What is the amendment of the U.S. Constitution that deals with the "Right of the People to Bear Arms?" ______________________________

(3) The word "Billy" as used in Section 22210 PC originated from the French. T or F

(4) A pocket knife which locks into place when opened can be classified as a "Dagger." T or F

(5) Caliber means diameter in ______________ of an inch.

(6) A fire bomb is a breakable container containing a wick and filled with a flammable liquid with a flash point of:

(A) ____ 50 degrees F (B) ____ 100 degrees F

(C) ____ 150 degrees F (D) ____ 200 degrees F

(7) A machine gun is a gun that shoots, or is designed to shoot, automatically more than one shot with a single pull of the trigger. T or F

(8) A pistol or revolver "capable of being concealed" is one that has a barrel length of less than ______________ inches.

(9) A "sawed-off shotgun" can be a shotgun with a barrel length or less than ______inches.

(10) A "sawed-off shotgun" can also be a rifle with a barrel length of less than______inches.

(11) A "sawed-off shotgun" can also be a rifle or a shotgun with an overall length of less than_________ inches.

(12) A weapon that is described as a "mass of metal or stone, fixed on a flexible handle" is called a ______________________________

(13) It is illegal to possess a "billy club" unless you come under the "Peace Officer" exception. T or F.

(14) It is illegal under 16590 PC to carry concealed on your person any explosive (other than fixed ammunition) or a __________________ or ______________________

(15) An ex-felon cannot possess a pistol "capable of being concealed." T or F

(16) A person under 18 cannot possess a gun "capable of being concealed" unless he has the written permission of his parent or guardian, or is accompanied by one of them, and is actively engaged or in direct transit to participate in a lawful recreational sport. T or F

(17) A person who has been involuntarily committed to a mental institution for over _____ days cannot possess any firearms.

(18) Arvin Aardvark commits a felony while armed with a set of "brass knuckles." He now has an extra minimum sentence of ______________ year(s).

(19) In the above case, the judge may allow the extra sentence to run concurrently with the first sentence. T or F

(20) The term "CCW" means:

(A) ____ California County-Jail Work-Program

(B) ____ Carrying a Concealed Weapon

(C) ____ California Counter-Action Against Weapons

(D) ____ Central Control for Weapons

(21) Percy Pester is stopped by the police for driving a stolen car. Under the seat they find an unloaded pistol with a barrel length of 6". Percy has no license to carry the gun concealed. Percy is guilty of carrying a concealed firearm (25400 PC). T or F

(22) Harry Hotsocks is walking down Market Street in San Francisco. He is wearing a holster with an exposed, but unloaded revolver that has a barrel length of 6 inches. Harry is stopped by a police officer. He has violated one of the laws of the Dangerous Weapons Control Law. T or F

(23) Officer Smith, who works in an incorporated city, asks Homer Honk to assist him in making an arrest. Homer agrees, but runs into his house and gets a loaded revolver. Homer has violated the law. T or F

(24) Officer Smith gets a call regarding an alarm sounding at a laundry, and when he arrives he asked the police radio operator to call the burglary alarm company. Mervin Mushmuscle, an employee of the alarm company responds to shut off the alarm. As he enters the building, Officer Smith notices that Mervin has a loaded 6" revolver in his pocket. Mervin is not a reserve peace officer. Officer Smith can arrest him for carrying a loaded weapon in violation of 25850 PC. T or F

(25) Officer Jones stops Harry Honebone for going through a downtown stoplight. He notices a rifle in the back seat. Officer Jones asks Harry if he can examine the rifle to see if it is loaded. Harry refuses permission. Officer Jones has probable cause to arrest Harry. T or F

(26) Under Section 25850 PC, a firearm is considered loaded if:

(A) ____ the person possessing the gun carries ammunition on his person.

(B) ____ there is ammunition in the glove compartment of the car.

(C) ____ there is an unexpended shell in the clip attached to the gun.

(D) ____ the ammunition is within 10 feet of the gun.

(27) Officer Brown is taking a report from a businessman in his place of business. He notices that there is a gun in the office. He asks the businessman to show him the gun so he can see if it is loaded. If the businessman refuses, it is probable cause to arrest him. T or F

(28) It is against the law to have a loaded gun in your house if you live in an incorporated city. T or F

(29) In the State Capitol, a weapon is considered loaded if the gun and unexpended ammunition are in the immediate possession of the same person. T or F

(30) When a person obtains a carry concealed weapon permit from their own county with a population less than 200,000, that person can carry only a loaded and exposed firearm capable of being concealed in that same county. T or F

(31) A permit to carry a concealed firearm is good for:

(A) ____ six months (B) ____ five years

(C) ____ two years (D) ____ no limit

(32) If a person possesses a gun with the identification altered, and the law presumes that he altered it, he must legally prove that he didn't alter it. T or F

(33) Any weapon or shell over ____________________ caliber in diameter is classed as a "Destructive Device."

(34) It is a felony, carrying a minimum of 5 years in prison, to enter someone's house with a fire-bomb. T or F

(35) Marvin Messup is caught with a "Fire-bomb" in his possession and is convicted of 16460 PC. The judge can give Marvin probation if it is his first offense. T or F

(36) In the above case, if it is Marvin's first offense, the judge can suspend his sentence. T or F

(37) A peace officer may possess tear gas weapons for up to 6 months before he has to take the required POST chemical agent course. T or F

(38) A private patrol officer may use Mace (tear gas) to stop an escaping felon. T or F

(39) Herbert Honebone is 17 years old. He buys a BB gun from a sporting goods store. According to 19910 PC, the clerk who sold him the BB gun is guilty of a misdemeanor. T or F

(40) It is Arvin Aardvark's 17th birthday. His uncle gives him a 22 caliber rifle as a birthday gift. Arvin's parents know his uncle gave him the gun, but they didn't say that he could not have it. His uncle is guilty of 19915 PC. Why? T or F

(41) A switchblade knife is illegal when the blade is over ________________ inches long.

(42) Homer Hashtaghonk has been making and selling blowgun ammunition. When stopped by the police, he had one blowgun dart in his pocket. This is illegal under 16270 PC. T or F

(43) Lester Lump is hunting in his jeep on a friend's private ranch. He is stopped as he is driving over a grassy hill by a game warden. He has a loaded gun in the jeep. This is a violation of the Fish and Game Code. T or F

(44) Later, Lester is stopped on a public highway and he has a shell in the gun's magazine, but not in the chamber. He has violated the Fish & Game Code. T or F

APPENDIX A

Clarification of Animal Definitions

It has been noted that in some cases, the legal definition and the popular definition of the names and terms for animals is not always the same. In Section 487 and 487a of the Penal Code, there is a list of animals the taking of which constitutes grand theft. In order to clarify misconceptions regarding these animals, the following legal definitions are offered. These definitions have been taken from *Black's Law Dictionary,* fourth edition, and *Webster's New International Dictionary,* third edition.

Equine: Latin *"equinus"*–from equus–horse, plus *inus*–akin to. Animals that resemble horses.

Horse: An animal of the genus *Equus*, species *caballus*, and generally used in statutes. The word is used not only on horses strictly called, but also may include colts, mares, foals and fillies. In the strict sense the term is applied only to the male, and only to males four years old. The term includes both stallions and geldings.

Mare: A female horse of breeding age. Younger females are fillies.

Gelding: A horse that has been castrated, and which is thus distinguished from the horse in his natural and unaltered condition.

Mule: A hybrid between the horse and the ass; especially, the offspring of a male ass and a mare.

Jack: The male of various animals especially of the domestic ass or donkey.

Jenny: With names of animals, often used to denote a female; especially a female donkey.

Ovine: Latin *"ovis"*–sheep, plus *inus*–akin to. Being or related to sheep.

Sheep: An animal related to the goat but distinguished by a stockier build, absence of a beard in the male, and horns that when present are more divergent and in older males often coiled into flattened lateral spirals.

Lamb: A sheep, ram or ewe under a year old.

Bovine: Latin *"bos,"* meaning cow or bull. "Cattle" as generally used in the Western States includes only such animals as cows, bulls, and steers.

Caprine: From the Latin *"caprinus."* This is the general term applied to the goat family. The male is called a "billy" and the female a "nanny." Young goats are called "kids."

Swine: Any hoofed mammal of the hog kind. A hog; chiefly used collectively and applied especially to domestic hogs.

Hog: This word may include a sow, and is synonymous with swine.

Sow: The adult female boar, hog, or swine of any age that has farrowed young.

Boar: The uncastrated male of swine, a wild hog.

Gilt: An immature female swine; also a young sow prior to production of her first litter.

Barrow: A male hog castrated before it reaches sexual maturity.

Pig: A young swine of either sex that has not reached sexual maturity. Broadly the term may be applied to a wild or domestic swine.

APPENDIX B

The Public Safety Officer's Bill of Rights

Government Code Sections 3300 – 3311

<u>Political Activity</u>

(1) Except
- (a) as provided by law, or
- (b) when on duty, or
- (c) when in uniform

(2) No public safety officer shall be:
- (a) prohibited from engaging in political activity, or
- (b) required or coerced into engaging in political activity.

<u>Interrogation of Public Safety Officers</u>

(1) When an officer is under investigation for some act that would lead to punitive action,

(2) And is interrogated by a member of his or her employing agency,

(3) The following conditions will apply:
- (a) The interrogation shall be conducted at a reasonable hour unless the seriousness of the offense demands it.
- (b) If off duty, the officer shall receive standard overtime compensation.
- (c) The officer shall not be dismissed from the department for work missed during the interrogation.
- (d) The officer shall be notified prior to the interrogation of:
  - (i) the name
  - (ii) the rank
  - (iii) the command...of:
    - (a) the officer in charge of the interrogation.
    - (b) the interrogating officers.
    - (c) all others present.
- (e) No more than two persons shall interrogate the officer at one time.
- (f) Prior to the interrogation, the officer shall be notified of the nature of the investigation.
- (g) The length of the interrogation shall be reasonable based on the seriousness of the offense.
- (h) The officer being interrogated shall be allowed to attend to his or her own personal physical necessities. (Restroom)
- (i) The officer may choose a representative of his or her own choice to be present during the interrogation, and communications between them is confidential if the matter is non-criminal and involves a department investigation only.
- (j) The officer being interrogated shall not be subjected to:
  - (i) offensive language
  - (ii) threats of punitive action
  - (iii) promises of reward as an inducement to talk.
- (k) An officer being interrogated may be told that refusal to answer questions or submit to interrogation may result in punitive action.
- (l) The officer being interrogated shall not:
  - (i) be subjected to visits by news media
  - (ii) have a home address or photo given to the news media without his or her consent.
- (m) If the interrogation is recorded, the officer may have access to the tape:
  - (i) if further proceedings are planned, or
  - (ii) before further interrogation at a later time.
- (n) The officer being interrogated shall have access to:
  - (i) a transcribed copy of any notes made by a stenographer or
  - (ii) any complaints regarding the matter, or
  - (iii) any investigative reports.

<u>Exception:</u>

Confidential reports in the officer's personnel file.

- (o) Officers being interrogated may bring their own recording devices and record any and all aspects of the interrogation.
- (p) Once it is decided that officers will be charged criminally, they shall immediately be notified of their rights.
- (q) When
  - (i) formal written charges are filed, or
  - (ii) the interrogation focuses on matters that can result in punitive action.
- (r) Officers can have present at all times, if they request, a person of their choice.
- (s) This person shall not be one who is subject to the same investigation.

Exception:

This section shall not apply to an interrogation of an officer or an informal admonishment by his or her superiors or a member of the department during the normal course of duty.

Punitive Action Against Officers

(1) There shall be no duty or location reassignment of an officer that would not normally be given under similar circumstances.
(2) No officer shall be subjected to
 (a) punitive action or
 (b) denial of promotion or
 (c) threats of such action because of the lawful exercise of his rights under this law or of existing department regulations.

Exception:

Section A:
(1) Officers can be charged with insubordination
(2) When the head of their agency orders them to cooperate with another agency involved in a criminal investigation
(3) And they refuse to cooperate.

Section B:
(1) If an agency
 (a) denies an officer promotion, or
 (b) administers punitive action
(2) Based on anything but merit
(3) They must provide the officer with an opportunity for administrative appeal.

Other Rights

Section A:
(1) No officers shall have entered into their
 (a) personnel file or
 (b) similar file
(2) Any adverse comment
(3) Without the officers having first read and signed the document indicating that they are aware of the comment.
(4) Unless the officers refuse to sign it.
(5) The fact that they refused to sign it will be noted on the document.

Section B:
(1) Officers shall have up to 30 days in which to file a written response to any adverse comment entered in their personnel files.
(2) Such comments shall be attached to and accompany the adverse comment.

Polygraph Tests

(1) No officer will be made to take a polygraph test against his or her will.
(2) No disciplinary action of any type shall be taken against an officer who refuses to take a polygraph test.
(3) There shall be no record or notes taken of such refusal.
(4) There shall be no testimony or evidence in a judicial or administrative hearing or trial about such refusal.

Personal Finances and Property

(1) Officers shall not be required to reveal their:
 (a) property
 (b) income
 (c) assets
 (d) sources of income
 (e) debts
 (f) personal & domestic expenditures
(2) Including that of their family and household
(3) Unless such information is
 (a) required under state law,
 (b) obtained through proper legal procedure (court order),
 (c) a conflict of interest in official duties, or
 (d) necessary for employing agency to determine whether officer is suited for a special assignment (such as vice where there might be bribery).

Locker Search

(1) No officer shall have his or her locker, or other storage space searched
(2) Unless:
 (a) in his or her presence
 (b) with his or her consent
 (c) a valid search warrant is used, or
 (d) he or she has been notified that a search will take place.
(3) This shall not apply to lockers not owned by the employing agency.

Local Protective Ordinances

If a public safety agency has in existence a legal procedure which guarantees its officers a minimum of the rights listed in this law, then this law will not apply to that agency.

Mutual Aid

Nothing in this law shall prohibit an agency from assigning any of its personnel to another department under a "Mutual Aid" agreement, nor shall it limit interagency cooperation under a "Mutual Aid" agreement.

Reward for Arrest and Conviction of a Person Who Assaults a Police Officer (1547 PC)

The Governor may offer a reward of not more than $50,000 for information leading to the arrest and conviction of any person who attempts to murder either in the first or second degree, assaults with a deadly weapon, or inflicts serious bodily harm upon a peace officer or firefighter who is acting in the line of duty.

Lawsuits Filed Against Peace Officers

1021.7 CCP: The court can award attorney's fees to officers when suit was without reasonable cause or good faith.

945.3 GC: An officer cannot be sued civilly regarding a criminal case until the case is resolved. It stops blackmail.

Confidentiality of Peace Officer Records (832.5, 832.7 & 832.8 PC)

Under the Rules of Discovery and based on the Pritchess Decision, the defense was able to examine the personnel records of an officer to see if he had been accused of wrongdoing in the past and in that way impeach him in a trial. The new laws correct this problem to some extent.

1043 Evidence Code

(1) An attorney seeking an officer's personnel record pursuant to 832.5 PC
(2) Must file a written motion 10 days before such records are obtained
(3) The agency shall notify the officer of this request
(4) The attorney seeking the request must show good cause for the discovery request.

1045 Evidence Code

(1) The requesting party must show the court that the requested record is:
    (a) relevant and
    (b) material
    in the case being tried
(2) Relevance shall be determined in chambers and not in the courtroom.
(3) If records are obtained, they cannot be duplicated or given to anyone else when it is requested by the officer or agency.
(4) Excluded from the Rule of Discovery are:
    (a) records that are over 5 years old
    (b) conclusions of the officer investigating the complaint
    (c) remote facts of no practical benefit

This prevents the "shotgun" or "fishing expedition" approach often used by defense attorneys.

Confidentiality of Police Personnel Records (832.7 PC)

(1) Peace officer personnel files are confidential
(2) And they shall not be disclosed to anyone
(3) Except by the legal process of discovery (1043 Evidence Code)

Release of Information Regarding an Officer's Disciplinary Investigation (832.7 PC)

(1) When an officer under investigation or his or her attorney (or agent)
(2) Makes a public statement he or she knows to be false concerning the investigation or disciplinary action
(3) And that information is published by an established medium of communication (radio, television, newspaper, etc.)
(4) The officer's agency may release factual information from the officer' personnel file to refute the false statement.

Citizens' Complaints Against Peace Officers (832.5 PC)

(1) Each police agency shall establish a set procedure in writing to investigate citizens' complaints against officers.
(2) These procedures shall be made available to the public.
(3) Complaints and reports against officers shall be kept for at least 5 years.

Frivolous Complaints Against Peace Officers (832.5 PC)

(1) When an officer's department determines that a complaint against that officer is frivolous
(2) That complaint shall not be kept in that officer's General Personnel file.

Records of Deaths Caused by Peace Officers (27498 Gov. Code)

(1) In cases involving death caused by the action of a peace officer
(2) Records of an investigation made by the department
(3) Shall not be turned over to the Coroner's Office by a subpoena duces tecum (1985 CCP)

(4) Without permission of the department. Motor Vehicle Records, Peace Officer's Addresses Confidential (1808.4 CVC)

Although Motor Vehicle Department records are public records, the law allows peace officers, when they so request, to have their home address kept confidential. When the DMV is asked for an officer's address, the address of the department will be given.

Confidential Records of Peace Officer's Address (1808.4 CVC)

(1) Records of a peace officer's address
(2) Kept by the Department of Motor Vehicles
(3) Will be kept confidential
(4) Upon written request to DMV by the officer

Peace Officers Testifying, Confidential Addresses (1328.6 PC)

An officer testifying as a witness need not give his home address, but may give the address of his department instead.

Insurance Practices Against Peace Officers Insurance Code Sections 488.5, 557.5 & 669.5

No insurance company shall increase the insurance rates of a peace officer because of an accident that the officer had while on duty, during the hours of employment.

557.5: A peace officer need not report to his or her insurance company any accident in which he or she was involved, if it occurred in an emergency vehicle while on duty.
669.5: No insurance company shall fail to renew an insurance policy for a peace officer if it is based on an accident that occurred in an emergency vehicle, while on duty, during the hours of regular employment.

13960, 13962, 13964, 13966 Government Code

These laws increase the types of victims whom peace officers must notify of the right of compensation when investigated by the police. It now includes crimes involving automobiles.

Example: drunk driving, hit and run, and cars fleeing crime scenes. The loss must be over $100.00

Peace Officers Excused from Jury Duty (219 CCP)

A peace officer as listed in 836.1 PC and 836.2(a) PC shall be exempt from jury duty because attorneys nearly always exclude them during the examination of prospective jurors.

Topical Index

A

C

D

E

F

G

H

I

J

K

L

M

N

O

P

Q

S

T

U

V

W

Y

Z

Index of Case Citations Referenced in the Text

Index of Terms Defined in the Text

A

B

C

D

E

N

O

P

R

S

T

U

V

W

Y

Z

Index of Codes Referenced in the Text

Harbor & Navigation Code Sections

Health & Safety Code Sections

Insurance Code Sections

Labor Code Sections

Military & Veterans' Code Sections

Penal Code Sections

Public Utilities Code Sections

United States Code Sections

Vehicle Code Sections

Welfare & Institutions Code